782.81
B
Burrows   Burrows, Abram S.

Honest, Abe

© THE BAKER & TAYLOR CO.

Honest, Abe

Honest, Abe

Is There Really No Business Like Show Business?

ABE BURROWS

An Atlantic Monthly Press Book
Little, Brown and Company — Boston–Toronto

FIRST EDITION

A portion of this book has appeared in *The Atlantic*.

"It's All Right with Me" by Cole Porter. Copyright © 1953 by Chappell & Company, Inc. International copyright secured. All rights reserved. Used by permission.

LIBRARY OF CONGRESS CATALOGING IN PUBLICATION DATA

Burrows, Abram S
    Honest, Abe: is there really no business like show business?

"An Atlantic-Monthly Press book."
Includes index.
    1. Burrows, Abram S.   2. Musicians—United States—
Biography.   3. Theatrical producers and directors—
United States—Biography.   I. Title.
ML429.B95A3   782.81'092'4 [B]   79-25358
ISBN 0-316-11771-4

ATLANTIC—LITTLE, BROWN BOOKS
ARE PUBLISHED BY
LITTLE, BROWN AND COMPANY
IN ASSOCIATION WITH
THE ATLANTIC MONTHLY PRESS

MV

Designed by Susan Windheim
*Published simultaneously in Canada
by Little, Brown & Company (Canada) Limited*

PRINTED IN THE UNITED STATES OF AMERICA

For Carin, for everything . . .

These are acknowledgments of many debts. I owe this book to Robert Manning, the Editor-in-Chief of *The Atlantic Monthly*. It took Bob over ten years to talk me into writing it and then he stood over my shoulder while I was grinding it out.

I am also indebted to Upton Brady, my other editor, who stood over my other shoulder.

Another one of my creditors is a remarkable lady, Mrs. Jean Whitnack, the copyeditor. I'll always be grateful for her sharp but brilliant pencil.

And I owe a great deal to my dedicated secretary, Anne Sheldon, for all the help she gave me.

Honest, Abe

Overture

About twenty-five years ago I wrote a song called "Memory Lane." It went like this:

I am strolling down Memory Lane without a single
thing to remember
I am strolling down memory lane without even
a dying ember.
Some folks remember their mothers
And others their girlfriends behind.
But I am strolling down Memory Lane without a goddamn
thing on my mind.

As Damon Runyon would have said, "Any guy who dishes up a ditty like that doesn't figure to be a winner in the Memoirs Game." I never played "Memory Lane" for Damon, but I knew him and that's what he would have said and I would have agreed with him.

I wrote this song while sitting, as usual, at the piano at a party in Hollywood and improvising some songs. I wasn't a songwriter; I was a radio writer doing a weekly comedy show, *Duffy's Tavern*. Every week on millions of radios a phone would ring and Ed Gardner would pick it up and say, "Hello Duffy's

Tavern where the elite meet to eat Archie the Manager speaking Duffy ain't here oh hello Duffy."

In addition to not being a songwriter, I was also not a pianist. Well, not much of a pianist. I played by ear. I had a pretty good ear which was balanced by a pretty lousy voice. However, in spite of my gravelly baritone and my rotten accompaniment, I got asked to a lot of parties and sat at a lot of pianos and sang a lot of my songs. Songs which were meant to satirize (some people called it sabotage) the pop tunes of the day. Pete Martin once wrote a magazine article about my stuff called "Songbuster."

There was my big love-type song called "The Girl with the Three Blue Eyes." There was a torch-type song called "I'm So Miserable Without You That It's Almost Like Having You Around." And one very spirited after-the-war-type song that started out, "How Ya Gonna Keep 'em Down on the Farm After They've Seen the Farm?"

I first sang "Memory Lane" at a party at Frank Loesser's home. Now, Frank *was* a songwriter. This was a long time before he and I worked together on *Guys and Dolls,* but Frank had already come up with some big hits, including "Praise the Lord and Pass the Ammunition." Even though he was a *real* songwriter, he always encouraged me to keep doing my crazy stuff.

It was Frank who saved "Memory Lane" from oblivion because right after I wrote it, I forgot it. Blanked it out completely.

It's true that the party that night was a merry one. It wasn't merry in the way Hollywood parties are merry these days. Nobody was smoking homegrown dreamy cigarettes and nobody was sniffing any sniffable stuff. In those days we stuck to good old Good-For-Your-Health tobacco, nutritious scotch and therapeutic martinis. When I went to sleep that night, I had nevertheless completely forgotten the song.

The next morning Frank woke me with a phone call. Loesser's day used to start out around 5:30 A.M. He would get up and work on his songs for about three hours. Then he would

4

phone a few friends, and after he woke them up he would happily go back to bed. The first thing he said to me that morning was "Hey, Abe, that 'Memory' song was funny." I thought about it for a moment. Then I said carefully, "I don't exactly remember it. I mean I kind of remember the title and I think I know the first line, but I can't remember the rest of it." And he said, "I figured that. But I wrote down your lyrics last night and I typed them out this morning." He sent the song over to me. When I looked at it, I remembered it and I rather liked it.

I thought I had done a satire of all those tired memory-type songs, but now I'm not so sure. First of all, I ad-libbed it. Went through it in rhythm without a pause. Frank later assured me of that. The thing came out just as you see it in print. It must have come from somewhere deep in my gutconscious. As I look at the lyrics now, it could be that what the song really says is that the guy who wrote it would rather not stroll down Memory Lane because he might dig up a lot of forgettable memories.

Howard Lindsay once told me a story about a fellow who goes into a strange restaurant. It's a terrible place, a real dump, but the guy is hungry and it's raining. He figures he'll be safe in ordering a bowl of soup. The waiter brings the soup to him. A few moments later the man is just sitting there, spoon in hand, staring at the soup and looking a bit queasy. The waiter says, "Sir, is there something wrong with the soup?" The man looks up at the waiter sadly and says, "I just wish I hadn't've stirred it."

I guess that's true of memory. But what the hell. A little stirring can't hurt. Besides, as I think of it now, some of my forgettable memories were rather funny.

There was my first adventure in the movie business — or as they would say today, my first involvement in the film industry — in 1945. I had just spent five years on *Duffy's Tavern*. I loved doing it, but after five years I decided to move out and up. In those days going from radio to movies was considered "up." (Today I'm not so sure.)

Paramount Pictures hired me as a writer-producer even though I had never written a movie or produced one. The guy who decided that I "oughta be in pictures" was Joseph Sistrom, then head of production at Paramount. He liked my work and felt that under his wing I would do great things.

It was painful to leave *Duffy's Tavern* and Ed Gardner, a friend and the man who really got me started in radio. I felt very close to him and I'll tell you more about him when I get to my more memorable memories.

So on a Saturday night I said goodbye to *Duffy's Tavern* and the following Monday, early in the morning, I drove to Paramount. The man at the gate looked at me and my Ford suspiciously. Then he found my name on the list, switched to a big smile, and waved me through the gate. I parked my car and walked through the lot to my new office. I was walking on air but it was special air. This was the same air that Bing Crosby, Fred Astaire, Marlene Dietrich and other Greats were breathing.

I went into my new office. I met my new secretary. I was shown my beautiful new desk, my memo pads and my paper clips. I took a quick look into my private bathroom. Very nice, but no shower. Showers were saved for my superiors. Then I hurried to my meeting with Joe Sistrom. My friend. The nice man who was responsible for my being there. I walked into his office, which was magnificent. His desk was about five times the size of mine. But he wasn't sitting at it. There, in this beautiful office, Joe Sistrom was busy taking pictures off the walls, clearing out his desk, and packing papers into two suitcases. I nervously said something like "Hi, Joe." He said, "Hello, Abe," and kept packing his bags. I said, "What's going on, Joe?" He said, "I'm leaving." I gave this a moment's thought, then said, "Leaving?" He said, "Yep. I'm out." I watched him for a moment with a sickly feeling and said, "Out?" And he answered calmly, "Out." And I said, "But Joe, I'm in. You *brought* me in. Who do I talk to if I'm in trouble?" He gave me a long look, sighed, and said, "Nobody. You're really in trouble."

He was right. A new administration was in. I was also in. But I was an "in" who had been hired by an "out." None of the new "ins" paid any attention to me. I attended a few meetings with the new Brass, but nothing came of that. Once I suggested that I would like to make a remake of a certain film. Remakes always interested studios and they asked me what film I wanted to remake. I said, "Going My Way." Nobody thought that was funny because Going My Way had been made a year before. My wisecrack got printed in some of the columns. My ironclad contract rusted out in thirteen weeks. At the end of that depressing period I, too, was an "out." It took me a long time before I decided that this was a funny story.

And what about the time I was a dancer? Not tap, not buck-and-wing, and not classical. I danced the minuet! I was ten years old, and this was my first crack at show business. I almost blew it.

It happened when I was in the sixth grade at elementary school. The teacher told us there was to be a special school assembly in a few weeks, with entertainment, and our contribution was to dance the minuet. She picked six boys and six girls. I was one of the six boys and I was thrilled. When you're ten years old, "thrilled" means you're sick to your stomach. This was a big deal. Parents and relatives were to be invited. (I learned later that they are usually a rotten audience because they are more nervous than the performers.)

We started rehearsing with a piano. The music we danced to was Mozart's Minuet in G. The minuet calls for a lot of bowing and curtsying, but there was a lot of stumbling around at first. The music of the Minuet in G goes *Dum dum dum dum dum dum dee dum. Dum dum dum dum dum deedle deedle dum.* The boys had to bow every time we came to that last *dum.* As we bowed, we kept bumping the girls' heads. I hate to say this but the girls were at fault. They were supposed to just curtsy but they insisted on bowing, too. They finally learned to protect themselves and the minuet began to go pretty smoothly. We all felt very good about it. Then one day our teacher (by the way, I don't remember her name and I'm glad) made an announcement. We were to provide our own costumes. This *dum dee dum* affair was to be performed in costumes that were to recall as

7

much as possible the costumes of the French court in the seventeenth century. I was told to ask my parents to buy or rent a costume for me. This was depressing news because in our home money was something of a problem. At least I thought it was a problem. Whenever my parents discussed money, I was aware that no one was smiling. I never thought of us as poor. I knew we weren't broke, but I also knew we weren't loaded. We ate well, we had a pleasant apartment, and we paid our rent, but I knew my father worked very hard, and when I asked for a nickel I had to explain why I needed it.

When I told my mother what the teacher had said about buying or renting a costume, she listened respectfully. In our home, anything a teacher said was Holy Writ. If the teacher said I needed a costume, my mother agreed that I needed a costume. But she didn't see any sense in paying money for it. She said I was not to worry; she would get me a costume. I worried.

My mother talked the problem over with a neighbor. It turned out that this neighbor had a costume her young son had used recently. She brought it down to our apartment and my mother told me to try it on.

I was very dubious about this costume. It was sort of a clown's outfit, black with gold stars. I knew very little about the French court, but it seemed to me they wouldn't be doing the minuet in what seemed to be a Halloween clown suit. But as far as my mother was concerned, a costume was a costume. Mama was born in Lithuania and she and an American teacher were not on quite the same wavelength. She pooh-poohed my doubts and told me to show this costume to my teacher. Well, in those days when a mother — especially *my* mother — told you to do something, you did it. I did as she told me, but not because I was afraid of her. I loved her and I knew she loved me, and I didn't think she'd ever give me a bum steer.

I took the crazy costume to school. The teacher looked at it with a look that meant "What the hell is that?" And then she held it up in front of the class, and there was great merriment among my classmates.

The rest of that day is now a painful haze in my memory. I remember that it ended with one of the worst things that can happen to a guy in show business. I was to be replaced! Another boy, who had been sort of an understudy, said he was able to get the right kind of costume. And I was out! A famous but cryptic rabbi once said, "The best thing that could happen to a person is not to have been born at all. But unfortunately this happens to very few."

When I was fired from the minuet, I really wished I hadn't been born. But when I went home and broke the news to my parents, I pretended I didn't mind. I took a who-wants-to-do-that-sissy-dance kind of attitude. Even in those days I had learned to hide my misery.

My parents carefully pretended to believe that I didn't mind. They did an unheard-of thing. They blamed the teacher! I tried to feel better. I now know how rotten I felt because I remember how deliriously happy I felt one week later.

The day before the minuet was to go on, the teacher — *that* teacher — called me into her office. She seemed unusually friendly, nervous and maybe desperate. She told me that Arthur, one of the boys in the minuet — the star dancer — was very sick. He wouldn't be able to dance. She asked me if I still remembered the dance steps, and as I nodded, my ten-year-old brain was digesting a thrilling fact. They wanted me back! Back in the minuet. I don't think I've ever since had such a feeling of joyous satisfaction. The teacher said if I would do the dance, Arthur's costume could be altered to fit me.

I guess if it were the same situation today and some producer had given me the same treatment, I would send in my agent to arrange a very tough deal for my services. We'd make the producer beg a little. But in this case I was too anxious to star in the minuet and I eagerly thanked the teacher for giving me a break. The next day they dressed me up, powdered my hair white, and I did the minuet perfectly. Didn't bump anyone's head. My parents were there to see it and they thought I was wonderful. My mother never mentioned that clown costume. Neither did I.

That triumph in the minuet was pleasant but it didn't leave me stagestruck. I wasn't a kid who dreamed of a show-business career. I don't remember ever dreaming about being anything. However, it turned out that my mother did have a dream for me from the moment I was born. She had no desire to be a stage mother. She wanted to be a doctor's mother.

I found this out when I was about twelve years old. My old grandmother got a cinder in her eye; she was in pain and everyone was running around trying to help her. Then I stepped in and removed the cinder. Everyone acted as though I'd performed a miracle. My grandmother, who spoke no English, said something which translates as "He has golden hands." My mother felt that it was a sure sign from God that I was definitely going to be a doctor. Actually, I was able to remove that cinder because I was a Boy Scout and I had learned my great cinder-removing technique in a first-aid class. It seemed to me that the sign from God meant I was to become a Scoutmaster. But I didn't argue with my mother. It was *her* dream. I took a what-the-hell attitude and agreed to become a doctor.

Since most of the doctors I knew at the time were middle-aged, that gave me, I figured, about twenty-five years or more to change my mind if I wanted to do something else. I had no idea what that something else would be.

In interviews I'm frequently asked if I always wanted to be a writer. My answer is that the only reason I started to write is that the Depression was on, I was out of work, and I found out there were many comedians who needed jokes as much as I needed money.

When I started writing comedy, I thought I was no different from a guy who starts working in a store or a bank. It was a way to make a living. Now that I'm old enough to be honest with myself, I must grudgingly admit that I used to do *some* writing when I was a kid; and for no money. In school I was pretty good at what they called compositions. Things like "How I Spent My

Vacation." To me those compositions were just *homework*. Drudgery. But my teachers thought my compositions were pretty good. I think it was because when I wrote them I lied a lot — what a pro would call "adding a bit of color."

I once was actually a ghostwriter. I was thirteen and in my first year of high school. I had a friend named Irving who lived on our block. Irving was in the eighth grade of the elementary school from which I had just been graduated. He had been chosen to be the valedictorian of his graduating class. He was older than I was, but he was an immigrant, and that put him behind the rest of us at school. However, he was bright enough to be the valedictorian even though his English was a bit shaky. He came to me and asked if I would help him out in his valedictory speech. I was flattered and I agreed to write the whole thing for him.

That afternoon I sat down at our dining-room table (I always did my homework at our round dining-room table; even now in our apartment, where I have a study *and* an office, I still gravitate to our dining room which has a lovely round table, and I'm happiest when I'm working there) and I went to work on Irving's speech. I used the brand-new fountain pen I had received for my bar mitzvah and wrote a four-page valedictory address. I don't remember anything from that speech except one line, which sticks in my mind and went something like "and we must thank our teachers because they are truly the men behind the guns."

Irving turned in the speech, his teacher approved it, and he was all set to deliver it on graduation day. When I heard he was actually going to do the speech in public, I was hit with my first author-pangs. At the age of thirteen I began to feel like a Hollywood screenwriter whose work has been taken away from him. I wanted desperately to, at least, hear my work delivered; but I wasn't invited to the graduation doings because I was now a high school freshman.

One afternoon I went to my old school and visited my former teacher in the eighth grade, Miss Herriott. She was then Irving's teacher. She had always been very good to me and I asked her if it would be possible for me, an alumnus of P.S. 23, to attend the graduation exercises. She said that it would be difficult because they were very crowded. I just stood there looking at her with sad eyes. She looked at me quizzically and said, "Abram, why are you so anxious to go?" At that age I didn't know that ghostwriters are not supposed to tell. At the same time I felt somehow guilty about telling, but I finally mumbled, "I wrote Irving's speech and I would like to hear it." She looked at me with an enigmatic smile, patted me on the cheek, and arranged for me to attend the graduation. I later found out that the secret remained between Miss Herriott and me.

When I was a freshman in high school, the class had been assigned to do a piece about Teddy Roosevelt. As usual, that night I goofed off. Fortunately, the next day there was a study period before my English class and I whipped up my Teddy Roosevelt thing very quickly. I put down all the facts I knew about him. I didn't mention his name until the very end, when I wrote the great line "and such a man was Theodore Roosevelt!!" After my teacher read it, she said to me in front of the whole class, "Abram, some day I'll be very happy to follow your career as a writer." I thought she was crazy.

I wrote a lot of compositions in high school, but I still thought of them as homework and goofed off whenever I could. There was another English teacher who was very complimentary about my work. One day our class was told that there would be a citywide competition for high school students. We were to write a composition with the title "Cooperation Is the Basis of Progress." The best composition from each class was to be selected by the teacher. The teacher would keep the composition and the person who wrote it would then go to a central place in the city and write his composition again. This was designed to foil ghostwriters or parental assistance. The composition would then be forwarded to the citywide judges.

Well, the compositions were all turned in to our teacher. And two days later she announced that she had selected my composition as the best one in the class. She said it was very good and I was to go and rewrite it in the citywide competition. I sat there stunned. Not because of her compliments, but because I had not turned one in at all. Something had happened during the week I was supposed to be writing "Cooperation Is the Basis of Progress" — holidays or a wedding or some such distraction — and I just never wrote a word. Our class was a big one and when the papers were being collected, no one noticed that my paper was missing. But when the piece I hadn't written was selected as the best in the class, I was shocked. I thought the unthinkable. The teacher hadn't bothered to read any of the compositions! She knew that my compositions were usually pretty good, so she didn't bother reading any of them and picked mine as the best. It was a confusing compliment for a sixteen-year-old boy. I couldn't confess, for her sake as well as mine. Now I was in trouble.

I didn't sleep well that night. I would have to show up in a class with the other finalists and rewrite an unwritten composition in one hour. I felt scared, guilty and stupid. That title baffled me. "Cooperation Is the Basis of Progress." My only thought on that subject was "Sure it is!" Then I thought maybe I could put together a composition which would deny the truth of the title.

Well, I dragged myself downtown the next morning. There was a big room full of a lot of eager, bright-eyed students. I hated every one of them. I was given some blank paper. I slowly wrote my name and school and went to work on the composition. All I can tell you now is that I scribbled something lousy and I knew it was lousy all the time I was scribbling it. I didn't win the prize.

I once told my wife this strange story and she said it was possible that the teacher *knew* that I hadn't turned in a composition and she did this to punish me and to strengthen my character. I think my wife was being generous to the teacher, although I will admit that secretly I may have had that thought myself. She was very nice to me after that, maybe extra nice. I used to sit in class and study her face and wonder, "Did she know? . . . She couldn't know! . . . She's being so friendly to me!" I was very confused, and as I write this I'm still confused.

The one class I really enjoyed was Latin, the Latin my mother forced me to study in order to become a doctor. I thought it would be boring, but I loved it. I was a good Latin student. I found this out in a peculiar way. My teacher insulted me. I was in my third year of Latin and we were translating Cicero. One day, for homework, we had to translate a long hunk of a speech that Cicero made in the Roman senate, when he was attacking Cataline. It was a feisty, angry speech and I enjoyed translating it. When I turned it in the next morning, I felt rather smug about my good piece of work. The next day the teacher, I think her name was Miss Hiller, called me to her desk; she seemed very disturbed. She held up my paper and said, "I am going to give you an F on this paper." I was startled and said a thing you're not supposed to say to a teacher: "Why?" She said, "I'm disappointed in you. I have read your paper and I'm sure you've been using a trot!" I was baffled. "A trot? What's that?" I said. I had never heard the word. She said in an acid tone, "I suppose *you* would call it a pony." Well, I *had* heard about ponies, literal translations of Latin that some of the kids used. They were obtained in some underground way and they had about the same standing in school that heroin would have today. I was shocked and I know I showed it. Miss Hiller seemed shaken by my hurt and honest outrage.

She never mentioned the subject again; but when she returned my paper to me, it was marked A−. I figure the minus was there to tell me she was keeping her eye on me. But I suddenly felt at home with my Latin.

I took four years of it in high school. Very few Latin students went on to that fourth year. I think most of them fled from the subject after their second year because Caesar's *Commentaries* turned them off. The Latin Department was losing so many students that they (at the suggestion of Miss Hiller!) used me as a shill. I used to talk to the second-year students and beg them to go on with the subject. I told them that Cicero, Virgil and Ovid were exciting and a lot of fun; but I didn't land many customers.

However, I enjoyed talking to these kids and began to have a feeling that maybe I would like to be a Latin teacher. It was the first sign of any sort of real ambition I'd ever had. I started to think about a prize that Cornell University was offering: a four-year scholarship — tuition, room and board free! — to the student who had excelled in four years of high school Latin and would agree to major in Latin or Greek at Cornell. I felt I might have a shot at this beautiful prize, but there was one problem. In my last year of high school Latin — the fourth year — I was a minority. The class consisted of six girls and me. The teacher was the head of the Latin Department, Mrs. Grant. She was a great woman, but since *she* was a woman, the sex odds against me added up to seven to one. At the age of sixteen, when a boy is outnumbered by girls, he tends out of sheer terror to make snide wisecracks. As this was a small class, it was run just like a seminar, and we could all speak up when we wanted to. And I spoke up a lot. I never said anything really awful, but a lot of my speeches started out with the phrase "You girls . . ."

I learned to cool it after a while, but the Latin authors we were translating made things very difficult. Those noble Romans were not very high on equal rights for women. Horace, a romantic poet, was pretty kind to the ladies, but most of the Roman writers were male chauvinist *porcelli.*

When we were translating Virgil's *Aeneid,* I ran into a bit of trouble. If you never took Latin, or quit after Caesar, you might like to know that Aeneas was a Trojan who was driven from his home when the Greeks were beating hell out of Troy. Virgil's work is mainly about his hero's adventures as he tried to make his way back to Troy. It is somewhat like — I hate to say this — the *Odyssey.* There are some picky scholars who say that Virgil swiped the whole thing from Homer. Nonsense. Aeneas was a Trojan and Ulysses was a Greek. So there!

The *Aeneid* was pretty exciting stuff, full of hair-raising ad-

15

ventures — a real thriller. Then Aeneas got into the worst trouble of his life. He made the mistake of stopping off in Carthage and meeting Dido, the queen. She fell madly in love with him and he got stuck on her, too. This passionate stuff took up a lot of pages. The girls in the room thought it was all very beautiful, but I thought that Aeneas was wasting his time. I guess I showed it in my face and in my voice when I was translating the mushy stuff aloud. We finally came to the part where Aeneas at last comes to his senses, decides to leave Dido and go home. She, in despair, throws herself on a funeral pyre. And as I read the account of Dido's death — reciting it very loudly in Virgil's great dactylic hexameter and then translating it into my Brooklyn English — all six girls and Mrs. Grant seemed to look at me with pure hatred in their eyes. I guess they thought I was taking this too lightly. Actually, I did think that Dido was being silly and that Aeneas was right in wanting to go home. When he got there, they made him king of Troy. Had he delayed much more, he would have blown it.

When school was finally over and we were graduated, the big moment came when the Cornell Latin Scholarship was announced. I didn't win it. It was won by one of the girls, a nice girl and a smart one. I tried my best to feel generous and when she walked up to receive the prize, I applauded with everyone else. But if there had been a TV camera on me, I imagine I looked like — and felt like — a loser at the Oscar awards.

I did go on to take two more years of Latin in college, and I'll always be happy I did. It wasn't going to be my profession. I wasn't going to write prescriptions in Latin either, but I enjoyed it, and it helped me pick up a few bucks. I used to tutor some high school kids and help them pass their State Regents exams. My fee was a big dollar an hour. Later, in the fifties, my Latin studies enabled me to become a panelist on a radio and TV program called *We Take Your Word*. My colleagues were Professor Lyman Bryson and John K. M. McCaffery. We used to answer questions about the derivation of English words and phrases, and my good old Latin came in handy. I combined my shaky scholarship with a few jokes. One night just before we went on the air, a note was brought to me saying that my old teacher, Mrs. Grant, was in the audience. When the show started, I looked out and spotted her and smiled. She nodded her head gently and graciously; she was still the teacher I remembered. That night I went lighter on the jokes and spent a little more time flashing my classical scholarship. After the show, I walked into the audience and hugged her. Hugged her? Me hugging Mrs. Grant! She returned my hug and complimented me on the show. She didn't rave; she never did. But she was pleased that I was giving Latin studies just a touch of commercial popularity.

I never saw her again. I've always wondered what she would have said had I told her that I still felt a pang when I thought about that wonderful Cornell Latin Scholarship. As I stumble down Memory Lane, that will always be a small pebble in my shoe.

And I almost forgot about Miss Shapiro! Miss Shapiro ranks very high on my list of forgettables. She was my first — and last — piano teacher.

When I was almost seven years old, my parents bought a piano. It was an old upright and I thought it was magnificent. I always was a musical kid. My folks often told me that at the age of three I sang "It's a long way to Tipperary" at my uncle's wedding, and that I was a big hit. My father always sang songs to me and my kid brother, Selig. (My sister, Shirley, hadn't been born yet.) At the age when other kids were hearing Brahms' Lullaby, I was listening to my dad singing "Who Threw the Overalls in Mrs. Murphy's Chowder?" He was a great vaudeville fan and had a sweet singing voice.

When the new — slightly used — piano arrived, I was fascinated. I automatically gravitated to it and began picking out things like "Eli Eli," "When You Wore a Tulip," "Daisy, Daisy."

My parents were impressed. My mother hadn't yet told me that when I was born, she had decided I was definitely going to be a doctor. Now she evidently wavered when she heard me banging away at the piano. I think she and my father decided that I might become another Paderewski. My mother talked it over with the neighbors and that's how we got Miss Shapiro.

She came to our apartment one day to meet me. My mother very quickly told her that I was already playing the piano a little bit. Miss Shapiro said, "Oh?" And then my mother said, "Abe, show Miss Shapiro what you do." I was reluctant, being an honest kid. But Miss Shapiro said she'd like to hear me. So I slowly went to the piano and picked out a tune. Right in the middle of my concert, Miss Shapiro said, "Stop it! That's terrible!"

Well, I just sat there, with my insides flipping over. The rage of a seven-year-old can be terrible, especially when it's internal. I sat their quietly seething while my mother, who was unaware of how I felt, made a financial deal with Miss Shapiro to come back and teach me. She did come, but I had already turned her off in my mind. I didn't practice between lessons, and finally, after four lessons, we both agreed to call it quits. Exit Miss Shapiro. I didn't touch the piano for about a year. Then I sneaked back to the keyboard and sort of taught myself to sort of play the damn thing.

Later on I had some help from musician friends who were well trained. They taught me chords, progressions, and stuff like that. When I work on TV or in a nightclub, I always use the piano as a comical accompaniment for my songs, and no one objects too much.

Once I was playing the piano and singing my songs at a party at Larry Adler's in Beverly Hills. Artur Rubinstein was there and that made me a bit nervous and, to my ear, my playing sounded pretty frenetic. I kept taking peeks at him while I played, and I was glad to see that at least he didn't seem to be suffering. A little while after I finished, he came over and shocked me by saying, "Abe, I envy you the way you play." I stared at him and mumbled something graceful like "You're kidding!" He said quickly, "No, it's true. I mean it. You are playing the piano with such happiness. Such joy. You love it! Me? I struggle with it!"

He held out those great hands and went on: "I attack that thing with violence." Was it a compliment?

Another pianist reacted strangely to my playing, at a party given by Groucho Marx. I was fooling around at the piano and José Iturbi arrived. Groucho brought him over and said to him, "José, I want you to meet another great pianist, Abe Burrows." I quickly stopped playing. Groucho said, "Keep going, Abe." And Iturbi politely said, "Yes, do, please." So, feeling like an idiot, I kept going in my good old self-taught style (I keep my hands oddly close together when I play). Iturbi watched my hands for about thirty seconds, then said one word, "Impossible," and walked away. I wanted to yell after him, "You didn't have Miss Shapiro!"

Chapter 1

I want to state flatly, unequivocally, and without any apologies, that I am a native New Yorker.

The first time I was in Paris, in 1952, I thought it was absolutely wonderful. Dazzling. But when I told a Parisian friend of mine how glorious his city was, he growled, "It's terrible now. It used to be beautiful, but now it's ruined." Londoners say the same sort of thing about their Big Town. The average New Yorker is no different. A long time ago, on one of my *Duffy's Tavern* radio shows, Archie complained, "People are always saying New York ain't the same no more and my old man always said New York ain't the same no more and my grandfather always said New York ain't the same no more, me personally I think New York never *was* the same no more."

I was born and raised in New York. My father, Louis Burrows, was born and raised in New York. My grandfather, David, came to New York from Russia when he was a young man, and my great-grandfather came to New York with my grandfather. That makes me the product of four generations of pavement.

The family name was originally Borowitz and through the years it gradually was changed to Burrows. My father had four brothers and five sisters. He once told me a story about the time his parents were looking for a new apartment. At that time their family was a bit smaller; they had only nine children. They finally found a place that pleased them.

But before they were allowed to move in, the landlord asked my grandmother if she had children and he was delighted when she answered, "Nine." The landlord was an immigrant too and he thought she said "Nein," which in Yiddish or German means no. When she finally moved in with her nine kids, the landlord was furious but helpless.

My mother's maiden name was Julia Salzberg. She came to America when she was seventeen. My father, who was about twenty then, met my mother soon after she got off the boat. They fell in love, were married within a year, and remained in love for the rest of their lives. When I was a little kid, I got used to seeing them constantly hugging and kissing. I found it very interesting behavior.

I found out that this was a pretty rare thing among the people I knew. In those days most marriages among immigrant families were arranged. Love was not a necessary ingredient. When I used to visit other kids in my neighborhood, I was always puzzled by the fact that their parents seldom talked to each other. Some of them never seemed to *look* at each other. They behaved like strangers.

My home was different. There were some quarrels, but they never lasted very long. Well, there *was* one word that would touch off a big blowup. That was the word *greenhorn*. My father, after all, was born in America — a genuine "Yankee" — and my mother was an immigrant. Well, whenever my father lost his head — it happened rarely — and used the word *greenhorn*, then it was time for us all to batten down the hatches. But they always wound up in a clinch again. It was love all right.

I was born on December 18, 1910, on Second Street and Avenue A in Manhattan. This is now called the East Village, but back then it was called the Lower East Side. The Upper East Side was not only "upper" but "richer."

When I was about two years old, we moved to the Bronx, then considered the "suburbs." This was the beginning of a standard pattern in New York. One is born in Lower Manhattan; one moves to the Bronx; then one moves to the suburbs, which are called Brooklyn; and then one winds up in Upper Manhattan, where I live today. It was the Sacred Cycle of my peer group.

In the Bronx, when I was about two and a half years old, my kid brother, Selig, was born, and a long time after that, we got ourselves a kid sister, Shirley.

In the Bronx we lived on Kelly Street, famous at that time for the fact that the great Russian Jewish writer, Sholem Aleichem, spent his last years there. I remember, vaguely, the big crowds that came to his funeral in 1916. I was only six years old and too young to value him. After all, it took *Fiddler on the Roof*, which was based on his work, to make the whole country appreciate him.

I must confess that to me and my unlettered contemporaries the most glamorous person on Kelly Street was Benny Leonard's mother, the mother of the Jewish Light Heavyweight Champion of the World! We young people would go crazy when Benny came to see her in his beautiful car, a huge, light-blue Cunningham. We'd run after the car waving and shouting, "Hey, Benny! Hey, Benny!" Sometimes he'd wave back at us. Wow!

The Bronx was very peaceful in those days. The crimes we heard about through the newspapers always took place far away in Manhattan or in the Wild West. The police were pretty friendly guys. We were taught that if we were ever in any kind of trouble, a cop would help us out. In those days most kids used to respect cops. Of course we also had a healthy fear of them, but that was because we all felt a little guilty most of the time. It was a vague guilt, based on various crimes, such as telling a lie to your parents or finding a nickel on the street and not telling anyone.

I remember one crime I committed when I was about nine years old. I got up very early that morning with a craving to buy something in the candy store, which was on our block, but I was broke. Then I spotted three empty soda bottles in the kitchen. They were deposit bottles. I could collect two cents for each bottle! I got dressed quickly, hid the three bottles under my jacket, sneaked downstairs and headed for the candy store on the corner to collect the six cents, with which I could buy a candy bar and have a cent left over.

We lived on the third floor, and my mother's bedroom window was her eye on the world. It turned out she was sitting at the window when I came out of the building. My mother and father watched me as I sneaked down the street, hiding my loot like any other criminal. When I arrived at the candy store, it was closed. The lights were out and the doors were locked. I had forgotten that this day just happened to be Yom Kippur! The holiest holiday of the year, and there I was with my three stolen bottles, staring at the locked doors. Every thief needs a fence. My fence was closed that day. What did I do? I panicked. I put the bottles down in front of the store and dashed back home to safety. But this time there was no safety. When I ran up the three flights of stairs and slipped into our apartment, my mother and father were standing there waiting for me.

They looked eight feet tall. To a little kid, parents always look eight feet tall, especially when he's a crooked kid. They stared at me and said nothing. I now realize that they both were repressing wild giggles, but to me they looked like grim Supreme Court justices. Before they had a chance to say a word, I jumped in and confessed everything. But they wouldn't let me get away with a simple confession. My mother told me what six cents meant to our family. How hard my father had to work for six cents. And to top it off, this was happening on Yom Kippur. The holy day of atonement. I learned later that they weren't very pious people, but at this moment they stressed the sanctity of the holy day, and therefore my crime was not only a crime against my parents, but against God himself. That day I really atoned.

I learned that day that I could never get away with anything on my block because of my mother's window. That window was her source of communication when I was out on the street. It was the window from which she broadcast that it was lunchtime or suppertime. (The only people who called the evening meal "dinner" were very rich people who lived far away.)

I found the window very useful, especially in the summer. When I went down on the street in the morning, I used to carry as much of my equipment as possible — my baseball cards in case I was going to do any trading, my marbles, and anything else I needed for my day's work. If we suddenly decided to have a baseball game, I would shout up to my mother, "Mama, throw me down my baseball glove." She would also warn me if there were any cars coming at me on the street, and if any tough kids were showing up.

When I was about fourteen years old, the Bronx was becoming a little less suburban, so we moved to Brooklyn. My parents bought a house. It was a two-family house with a small garden and a big mortgage. This is now known as upward mobility. The idea of a garden was new to me. There's a story they tell about a little city boy walking in the park with his father. The kid points to a bed of beautiful flowers and says, "Hey, Pop, what kind of flowers are those?" And his father answers, "How should I know. What am I, a milliner?"

I loved my garden and I began planting vegetables. My kid brother, Selig, and I had a lot of fights over this garden. He wasn't interested in planting things, only in watering them. I had read that it was wrong to water the garden too much, but Selig wouldn't accept that. He loved the hose and he watered the garden whenever he had a chance. He almost drowned my garden. This didn't discourage me, though I had a lot to learn about gardening. I tried lettuce but the bugs ate it faster than I could grow it. My potatoes were a disaster and so were most of my vegetables. I finally succeeded with tomatoes. At first it was tough because I had to learn the terrible fact that it's almost impossible for an amateur to grow tomatoes from seeds. But then I learned a great new method of tomato gardening.

A couple of blocks from our house, when Brooklyn still had a lot of farms, there was a large piece of farmland and the man who owned it was a professional tomato farmer. This guy had a big field of tomato plants. In the late evening I would sneak over to the tomato farm and swipe a dozen or so small plants from the edge of his big field. I would plant them in *my* garden. I don't know if Luther Burbank started that way, but that is how I learned to grow tomatoes.

When we moved to Brooklyn, I had to change high schools. In the Bronx, I had gone to Morris High School: "There's a song that fills the air Morris *High* school! You can hear it everywhere Morris High School! From the Battery to the park, in the day or in the dark," et cetera, et cetera.

In Brooklyn, I entered New Utrecht, where they sang: "Ten thousand boys, ten thousand girls, united in these high school halls," et cetera, et cetera. Maybe the song wasn't great, but New Utrecht turned out a lot of people who are in show business. Robert Merrill, the opera star; comedians like Phil Foster and Buddy Hackett; Michael Kidd, the choreographer with whom I did *Guys and Dolls* and *Can-Can;* and Cy Feuer, who was coproducer of those shows. Cy was at New Utrecht when I was there. We didn't know each other then, but later on our lives sure came together. I was very happy at New Utrecht. It stayed with me.

When I was graduated, my mother threw a surprise party for me. I'll never forget that party because my mother did a diabolical thing. I was really surprised by the party, but I was even more surprised — and shocked — when I looked around at the guests and I saw that my mother had carefully invited every girl I was going out with at the time. There were four of them: the girl I had just taken to the Senior Prom and three other girls I had been dating. When the four of them arrived at the party, they each figured out what was going on and all four of them stopped talking to me. I never could quite understand my mother's reason for this, but I suspect she was trying to arrange for me to break up with all of them. Which I did.

The next step in my education was City College. In those days it was a tough school and it rated very high scholastically, and for my folks the most important thing was that the tuition was free. My mother still expected me to become a doctor. I was pretty sure I was not going to become a doctor, but I entered CCNY as a reluctant pre-med student. I wasn't very interested in the science courses I was required to take. I enjoyed the English classes and of course I continued with Latin.

There were a couple of good math professors whom I liked, but I was very nervous about trig. The day I took my trigonometry final, I struggled through the exam and then went down to the cafeteria to have some lunch. I wasn't very hungry. I remember eating just half a cantaloupe. As I was eating, my trig professor came into the cafeteria and sat down at my table. He, too, had a half a cantaloupe. And he watched me putting salt on mine. He asked me, "Do you *always* do that?" I confessed that I always did put salt on my cantaloupe. He said, enthusiastically, "So do I! Down home we always do! But I never saw anybody do it up here." He looked at me very fondly. I got very high marks on that exam, and I always have attributed it to the cantaloupe.

However, I was growing less interested in college. This was 1929 and I believed with most people that the country was in a great boom. I didn't know then that our great boom was going to go boom. I wanted to get a job and make some money. Up to this time I had worked only during summer vacation. I worked as an errand boy in various places. My father and my uncles were in the wallpaper and paint business and occasionally I would take summer jobs in their stores. I never liked selling wallpaper. When I had to handle the rough paper, it set my teeth on edge.

I wanted a real job. My father had a friend named Joe Berson, who was a member of the Curb Exchange, later the American Stock Exchange. Originally it was called the Curb Exchange because the brokers actually did their trading on the street. When I told my mother I wanted to leave school and take a job on Wall Street, she didn't take it very kindly. She said to me, "You mustn't stop college. You have to be *something*." To her,

26

working on Wall Street might make me some money, but I wouldn't be *something*.

The NYU School of Finance was in the Wall Street area. I told my mother that if I could get a job on Wall Street, I would go to the School of Finance in the evenings and study accounting. After some thought, my mother bought that. She decided that being an accountant was being *something*. It wasn't as good as being a doctor, but at least it was a profession.

Joe Berson got me a job with a firm named Abrahams, Hoffer. I think that my stretch on Wall Street was almost as exciting as working in the theater. Of course, I didn't know when I joined Wall Street early in 1929, that I was really working on a flop show.

I was hired as a runner. My starting salary was a fat twelve dollars a week. You may remember that in 1929 the dollar was actually worth a hundred cents or twenty nickels or four quarters. Twenty nickels would give me twenty rides on the subway, and four quarters would buy me four good Chinese dinners. So it wasn't a bad salary. Today, Wall Street handles most trades through a foolproof — well, mostly foolproof — computer system. But back in my day any stuff that had to be delivered or picked up was handled by a runner, an errand boy with one difference: a runner really ran. When the stock market was open, Broad Street — the main thoroughfare — was closed to vehicular traffic for a good part of the day; and it became a racetrack. We would pick up stock certificates and deliver them on the dead run. We picked up checks and sprinted to the banks to have them certified before the banks closed. To us it became an exciting game. We threw ourselves into this race against time. We were proud of our speed and we ran our asses off, especially between 2:00 and 2:15 P.M.

Two-fifteen was the crucial time of the day. It was the deadline for delivering stock certificates. If you didn't deliver them by 2:15 on the dot, you were in trouble. Why? Well, I never really understood it in the old days and I'm not sure I can explain it now, but I'll take a deep breath and try.

27

When my brokerage firm sold a customer's stock to the customer of another firm we didn't get paid until we actually delivered the stock certificate to the other firm, and if, God forbid, we didn't deliver it before the deadline of 2:15 my firm wouldn't be paid the money and that would mean we had to borrow Call Money, which was an overnight bank loan at wildly exorbitant interest. On the other hand, the firm I was supposed to deliver the stock to would be happier if the stock wasn't delivered to them on time because that way they avoided having to borrow Call Money to pay my firm, which would then have to . . . It was a brutal game.

At 2:10 every day, the receiving clerks in all the brokerage houses got ready for fast action. They had small receiving windows about two feet high and a foot and a half wide. As the clock got close to 2:15, the receiving clerk would stand at his window ready to slam it down and avoid receiving the stock. Most of the time I would come tearing in and slap the stock down triumphantly just before he slammed his window down, barely missing my hand. But other times I would get to the window half a second late, and the happy, grinning idiot in the cage would slam the window in my face; and there I would be with an undelivered stock certificate. I would creep back to my own company feeling like a football player who had fumbled on the one-yard line.

The same sort of thing happened with checks. When you picked up a check from another broker, you had to get it certified at his bank. I'm not hinting that a broker might give my firm a bum check; the point was that if you had the check certified, it could be used instantly as cash. Three-thirty was the deadline for certifying checks, and the bank tellers played the same game as the receiving clerks in the brokerage firms. They got a big kick out of closing the window in your face if you arrived half a second late.

One thing about my days as a runner I remember with wonder. There we were, a bunch of kids running through the streets carrying stocks, bonds, certified checks, all sorts of valuables; and we were able to do it in absolute safety. Wall Street seemed to be thief-proof, at least as far as the runners were concerned. There may have been peculiar things going on behind the doors of some of the firms, but the streets themselves were safe. I was once told by a policeman that no one with a police record was allowed to set foot on any street below Fulton Street, which was the northern border of the financial district. I can remember only one time when a Wall Street runner was robbed. It happened in the lobby of one of the big buildings. He was hit over the head by someone who got away with a couple of hundred thousand dollars in negotiable bonds.

One of the suspects was Nicky Arnstein, who was once married to Fanny Brice. He had been involved in some strange deals in his time but he denied that he would ever stoop to hitting anyone on the head. To him, crimes of violence were "dirty pool."

Arnstein was a very smooth and attractive man with a great sense of humor. When he heard that he was suspected of this heinous crime, he immediately turned himself in. I read that he did this when there was a police parade going on. That day Arnstein and his lawyer drove uptown at the tail end of the parade, and when he arrived at police headquarters, he gave himself up. He was released very quickly for lack of evidence.

They never caught the guy who robbed the runner. I can't remember another such incident in my time on The Street.

After a few months as a runner, I got myself a new job with a company called Steiner, Rouse and Strook, a member of the New York Stock Exchange, the senior exchange, which was known as the Big Board. They hired me as a board boy. It was a step up for me.

Everybody has seen board boys operating in old movies, kids who looked at the ticker tape and ran around chalking up stock prices on a big blackboard. My firm was a little more modern. We didn't use chalk; we used printed price cards which we slipped into slots under the name of the stock. The time was September of 1929 just before the Crash.

29

It was hell for the customers, but in a peculiar, macabre way it was a wildly exciting time for the clerks, runners and board boys who worked on Wall Street but didn't own a single share of stock. The people who showed the most excitement were the board boys.

You have to picture a typical board room. The one I worked in was in an elegant branch office on Madison Avenue. The customers sat in comfortable chairs and watched the prices being put up by us board boys. We worked on a slightly elevated platform, scurrying back and forth, and calling out news that came from the floor of the exchange. It all had a theatrical feeling. (As a matter of fact, *Variety,* the show-business paper, ran a headline that terrible day — October 29 — when the market went completely to pieces: WALL STREET LAYS AN EGG.)

During that time, because of the volume of business, the ticker tapes were always late in reporting the stock prices; so we had to get the current prices by telephone from the floor of the exchange. The board boys used to call out the falling prices in loud, excited voices. I'm afraid that frequently our excitement sounded joyous. We would call out dreadful things like "Montgomery Ward down twenty points" and I guess we sounded like Mel Allen calling a World Series game.

Occasionally we had a chance to shout out *good* news. We played fair and gave the good news the same excitement as the bad. I remember the time I got to shout "Whitney bids 205 for Steel!" Richard Whitney, a Morgan partner, was on the floor of the exchange trying to stem the falling market by bidding $205 a share for United States Steel, which was then selling below two hundred. The fact that this powerful man was willing to pay $205 showed desperate confidence in the market and it started a modest rally at the time. Very modest.

Another exciting moment came when the stock of Standard Oil of New Jersey was beginning to slide badly. Again, we had a pleasant thing to shout out: "Rockefeller bids fifty dollars a share for *one million shares* of Standard Oil of New Jersey!" The Rockefellers were willing to absorb one million shares at that price to keep the stock from going any lower, and I announced it. I sounded as though I were saying "Babe Ruth hit his sixtieth home run!" Maybe I was acting like a dumb kid, but at least I didn't own any stock.

It was a disastrous time for most stockholders; and some people actually did jump out of windows. But it was — for a while — a very lucrative time for the brokers. And for us kids who worked for the brokers it was a mild bonanza.

The brokerage firms were making a lot of money because of the volume of sales, and they were very generous to us. Some guys were getting an extra salary every third week and we all got big Christmas bonuses. My salary was up to twenty-two dollars a week, and on my first Christmas with the firm I received a princely bonus of one hundred dollars. I came home very proudly and handed it to my parents. There was great excitement in my home. My father said, "A hundred dollars! Abe, you've got a pretty good job." And my mother proudly corrected him. "Job? It's not a job! It is a *position!*"

The crash is called the Crash of '29 but it didn't happen all at once. The market kept going down, and for a while the brokerage business kept going strong. I was promoted to the job of order clerk in the main office on Broad Street. I would sit in the order room with a battery of telephones that connected with our branch offices and I took orders over the phone. That's when I learned to write rapid-fire longhand. When I write now, I still work in longhand. I never learned to type well and I can scribble faster than I can type.

After a while, Wall Street began to feel the Depression. I lost my job in 1932. I went to another firm as a customer's man. A customer's man works in a brokerage office and acts as agent for his own group of customers. Of course, his job is no good if he hasn't any customers. I scratched up a few from friends of the family and people like our neighborhood butcher, who recommended me to a lot of other butchers. It was what you might call a highly specialized clientele, and I got some pretty good business from them. One of my best customers was a wholesale butcher who operated in the big meat center, Washington Market. When I called him on the phone, I had to call Washington Market and — believe it or not — I had to ask for "the Chuck Department, please." I was in a room surrounded by a lot of slick customer's men and I used to get a lot of laughs from them. I tried to whisper that "Chuck Department." I got to be known as the Brisket Specialist.

The market kept going down, and when, in 1933, it hit bottom it just lay there. Roosevelt was now President and the Wall Street people were terrified of him. There were brokers who assured me that FDR was about to start a revolution and overthrow the whole American system. The stock market seemed about to roll over and die. There were periodic small flurries but the volume of sales went lower and lower. People weren't buying stocks and they weren't selling them. I lost my customers. I even lost contact with my chuck-steak man. A customer's man without customers was a useless creature.

I had sweated out a couple of years of accounting in night school at NYU. I hadn't completed the course (I never really was interested) but through some connection I got myself hired by an accounting firm as a junior accountant. Very junior. I was assigned to the job of checking tax returns. The senior accountants would prepare the returns and I would go over them looking for mistakes. I wasn't there to check the honesty or validity of the returns, just the addition, subtraction and frequently the spelling. It was a numbing job. I lasted there for less than a year. I was twenty-three years old and I had no profession and no trade. Milton Berle used to make jokes about his unemployed brother. He said his family was trying to find a job for Frank so at least they could know what kind of work Frank was out of.

Well, I was in that spot, too. What kind of work was I out of? Whatever skills I had learned on Wall Street were of no use on any other street. Certainly not any other street in the real world. I had learned to play the piano by ear, but I couldn't read music so I had no future as a musician. I did seem able to make people laugh, but it never occurred to me that this skill was a way to make a living. It was a ghastly period for me. Even so, I was luckier than most unemployed guys. I had a home in Brooklyn with my family. They were worried about me but they did their best not to show it. I spent every day going into Manhattan to look for work.

Every morning when I was having breakfast, there would be a quarter on the table which my mother had left for me. It would take me through a day of looking for work. She and I never talked about this. Leaving that quarter was embarrassing for us both. A quarter was big money in those days. The subway fare was a nickel; I had fifteen cents to splurge for lunch. Downtown there was a place called Max's Busy Bee. In this splendid eatery a hot dog was a nickel. It was a gorgeous hot dog. In those days nobody knew anything about the danger of additives, but whatever additives Max added to his hot dogs made them delicious. Two hot dogs and a Coke added up to fifteen cents, which left me with a nickel for the fare home. In those days if you lost that nickel, or blew it carelessly on a third hot dog, you had to walk home to Brooklyn, or — and this may come as a shock to kids today — you could always ask a cop for help. My folks had always taught me that if I found myself somewhere with no money to get home, I could go to a policeman and tell him my problem. The cop always came up with a nickel.

I answered all sorts of strange Help Wanted ads. There was one that asked for salesmen to sell a new brand of maple syrup. I held that job for two days. They gave me some samples and sent me out to sell the stuff. I never did sell any syrup, but I took the samples home and they were delicious.

One day I dropped in at my old brokerage firm to see if something was open there; nothing was. However, I got to talk to Milton Cohen, a very successful customer's man who had always been friendly to me. He told me that his brother, Irving, had just started a new company that was selling ladies' knitted goods: knitted dresses, blouses, and stuff like that. He might be able to use me as a salesman. I dashed uptown to see Irving

33

Cohen. He hired me but he told me I'd have to work on commission. He did give me a drawing account of a dollar a day so I didn't need to cadge my mother's quarter anymore. I managed to sell a few things, but it was a tough struggle. I did make some contacts in the garment industry and finally got a job with a woven-label company. They made the labels that were sewn into suits and coats and dresses and furs. I was hired by this firm to sell labels on commission and was given the sensational drawing account of twelve dollars a week. I managed to sell enough labels to take care of my drawing account and I picked up a few bucks extra.

During my great woven-label period, I married Ruth Levinson, my first wife. We were able to manage because Ruth had a job, too. Then something happened that eventually changed my life.

While I was pushing labels, I used to toss around a lot of jokes with my customers. The few customers I had seemed to find my cracks funny. One day I ran into Milton Cohen, who had by then lost his Wall Street clientele and was now in the dress business. That day I was feeling very low. Milton could see I wasn't happy doing what I was doing and he suddenly said something like "Hey, Abe. You're always saying pretty funny things. Why don't you do something about it?" I shrugged and said, "Like what?" He answered, "Writing." I just stared at him and he went on: "Abe, I have a friend who has a son about your age. His name is Frank Galen and he's been writing jokes. A lot of jokes; but he hasn't sold anything yet. Maybe you two ought to get together."

It all sounded wild to me, but Milton insisted on giving me his friend's name and phone number. The next day things were pretty dull in the label business and I thought about Milton's suggestion. I still believed his idea was crazy but . . . what the hell, I might as well get in touch with this Galen. The only thing I had to lose was my twelve-dollar-a-week drawing account.

I called Frank Galen and made a date to come to his office the next day. He gave me the address of a costume jewelry firm, an odd location for a writer. When I went up there, I found out that Frank's father was associated with this firm and had given Frank the use of a small office.

As I walked through a hall toward Frank's office, I could hear the sound of a typewriter. I opened the door and there was Frank doing the typing. He was pretty fast, too. When I saw him typing, and I saw that paper in the typewriter, I had the strangest, most marvelous feeling. If I were putting this scene on the stage today, the kid who was playing me would stop dead in his tracks and the orchestra would play a sharp knife chord. Zing! Then they would go into the "Hallelujah Chorus."

I was in the right place for the first time in my screwed-up life. I saw someone doing something I had always wanted to do but until this moment had never known that I wanted to do it. All this flashed through my excited skull as Frank got up and shook hands with me.

We talked and checked out a lot of stuff we had in common. We had approximately the same sort of education and we had both been beautifully unsuccessful for quite a while, and to top it all, we were both wild baseball nuts and both New York Giants fans. This was a collaboration made in Heaven.

Frank was very honest with me. His father had given him a year to see if he could make it as a writer; he had been at it for six months. He knew the names of all the agents in show business; he knew who was buying funny material, but he hadn't yet sold anything. He felt he needed someone to work with, and I was certain that I needed him. We agreed to become partners.

Of course, there was a slight financial problem. Frank was getting a small allowance from his father, but all I had was my small label clientele. I decided I had better hold on to that for a while. We agreed that at the beginning we'd work for just a few hours every day. When I told my old boss, Irving Cohen, about writing jokes while I was still selling labels, he told me I should have a card printed that read, "Abe Burrows, Gags and Tags."

At the beginning Galen and I concentrated on tailoring jokes

to fit certain radio and vaudeville comics who were always looking for new material. Henny Youngman was a big joke buyer in
those days. He was then on the *Kate Smith Hour* every
week, doing a five-minute spot in which he used up about fifty
jokes a week. Henny's lawyer and agent was Irving Lazar, who
is now known as Swifty Lazar, one of the biggest literary agents
in the country. One of his better-known clients is named Richard Nixon. Swifty paid two dollars a joke. Frank and I eventually sold him a few. (One joke I remember was a panhandler
joke. In those days panhandlers were somehow considered
funny, and there were thousands of jokes about them. In this
particular joke the comic says, "A panhandler came up to me
today and said, 'Could I have ten cents for a cup of coffee?' And
I answered, 'But coffee is only a nickel!' And he said, 'Sir, won't
you join me?' " I think Henny still tells that joke.)

We thought up a lot of panhandler gems. One we sold to
some comic went like this. The comic said, "A panhandler came
up to me and said, 'Could I have four cents for a cup of coffee?'
And I said, 'Coffee costs a nickel.' And he said, 'Who buys re-
tail?' " You can tell from these jokes that we weren't challeng-
ing George Bernard Shaw or Kaufman and Hart, but I think we
worked just as hard as they did.

We finally decided to write a big sketch that some comedian
could use on the radio. There was a well-known mimic in those
days named Sheila Barrett. We didn't know her, but we still
decided that we would tailor a piece to her talent and sell it to
her. The piece was to be a takeoff on one of those Man-in-the-
Street-type radio interviews, and we wrote a piece in which she
would interview various people: a housewife, a Chinese laun-
dryman, a policeman, and stuff like that. She would do all the
parts. It sounds terrible to me now, and it really was kind of
awful, but when we finished, it *was* a piece of material. We
typed it neatly and tried to show it to Sheila Barrett herself.
Frank got hold of her phone number, but when we called she
refused to see us and said she always wrote her own material.

We started thinking of other mimics who might buy our sketch.

The best, and probably the most famous, mimic of that day was a vaudevillian named Eddie Garr. Eddie died in the fifties, but old vaudeville fans still remember him. He did great imitations of people like Jimmy Durante, Al Jolson, Ed Wynn. He not only imitated their voices, but by subtle, quick changes, he even managed to look and move like them.

We decided to get our stuff to Garr, but this time we weren't going to trust the telephone. We had to see Eddie Garr in person and dazzle him with our material. We tried to make contact with him but we had no luck. Then my newfound friend Serendipity nailed things down for us.

One night I was at a small party in Brooklyn. One of the guests was a loud, blustery guy. I don't remember his name, but he was some sort of an agent, a small-time agent who booked people to work in the Catskills on the Borscht Circuit. He was sounding off like a great show-business power. He dropped a lot of names, and I, as a struggling newcomer in show business, was annoyed. Maybe I was just envious, but anyway I felt like putting this guy on the spot. I said, "Do you know Eddie Garr?" And he shot back, "Of course I know Eddie. Good friend of mine." Then I challenged him. I said, "My partner and I have some material that he might like. Could you help us meet Eddie?" And he said, after a moment's hesitation, "Sure thing." Well, I didn't believe the guy, but the next day Frank Galen and I went to see him, and while we were there he actually called Eddie Garr on the phone. It turned out that he did know Eddie, although we could tell he wasn't one of his buddies. He had to say his name a couple of times before Eddie remembered him. However, Eddie finally *did* remember him and after they talked for a moment, Eddie did say he would like to meet us the next morning.

Galen and I rushed back to the office and rewrote the Sheila Barrett script. It wasn't a tough rewrite; wherever the script said

BARRETT, we rewrote it to say GARR. The next morning we went up to see Mr. Garr. It was a big moment for me. Garr was a very good vaudeville performer, but he wasn't a superstar. Nevertheless, when I met him I felt like a young playwright bringing a script to Laurence Olivier. Galen and I were thrilled at just being in the same room with him. He read our script and wonder of wonders he liked it. Then he told us that he had an offer to appear as a guest on a radio show, *The Rudy Vallee Show*. He was looking for new material and he thought maybe our stuff was it. He had an appointment with his agent that afternoon, and he told us he would call us the next morning. That night I couldn't sleep. *The Rudy Vallee Show* was the leading variety show on radio, and if Eddie appeared on that show with our material, Frank and I could begin to call ourselves writers.

The next morning we waited for his call. He said he'd phone us at ten o'clock, and by 10:05 we were already in despair. He called at ten-thirty. Hooray! He told us to meet him that afternoon in the hallowed halls of the William Morris Agency. The agency was then, and still is, one of the most important in show business. Incidentally, that day they became *my* agents and they have been my agents ever since. (They once threw a party for me. When I made a small speech, I said, "The Morris office is to me like family. When I pay them my ten percent, I don't think of it as commission; I think of it as sending money home to mother.")

When Galen and I arrived at the Morris office the next morning, Garr introduced us to a young agent, Sam Weisbord. He seemed very bright and he must have been, because today Sam is president of the agency.

Sam told us that Fleischmann's Yeast, the sponsor, liked our script, and we would be paid $125 for it. A hundred and twenty-five smackers! Sixty-two fifty apiece. I was a professional! I felt enormously rich. This was a couple of weeks before Christmas in 1937 — a great Christmas for me.

Garr went on the air with our script and it worked very well. I remember one particularly dopey joke. Eddie was playing the

Man in the Street and, of course, he played all the people he was interviewing. One of these characters was Chinese and spoke with a broad Chinese accent. The dialogue went like this:

MAN IN THE STREET   How do you do, sir. What's your name?
CHINESE FELLOW   My name Eddie Cantor.
MAN IN THE STREET   Eddie Cantor? That's a strange name for a Chinese person. What's your Chinese name?
CHINESE FELLOW   No Got Son.

Believe it or not, that joke got a big laugh from the studio audience. If you are too young to understand this tremendous joke, I must explain that Eddie Cantor used to do most of his jokes about the fact that he had five daughters and no son. Cantor got a lot of laughs on that subject, and I'm sure he didn't mind our getting that one single laugh.

In the beginning of 1938, Frank and I didn't exactly take the show-business world by storm. We wrote some more material for Garr (for his vaudeville act) and for several other comedians, among them a very good young mimic named Johnny Woods and a smooth comedian named Paul Gerrits. Gerrits had a marvelously twisted sense of humor. For instance, he used this joke: "There was this bum leaning against the building and a cop came up to him and said, 'What are you doing?' And the bum said, 'I'm holding the building up.' And the cop said, 'Don't be a wise guy. Get outa there.' So the bum walked away and the building fell down."

We struggled that year and I still kept selling labels. That extra twelve dollars a week helped. We really didn't seem to be getting anywhere until we met Ed Gardner. Mention of that name should call for another knife chord.

Chapter 2

When I met Ed Gardner, he was producing a radio show for CBS called *This Is New York*. The master of ceremonies was Deems Taylor, the composer and music critic, and Gardner played a mugg named Archie, who heckled Deems and the other guests.

I think Gardner was about thirty-seven then. His real name was Friedrich Poggenburg; his father was German and his mother was Irish. Ed grew up in Astoria, which had many German-Irish families. Ethel Merman's family were neighbors of the Poggenburgs. When Ethel became an entertainer, she changed her name from Zimmerman to Merman. I think that's what gave Ed the idea of a name change. Ethel's mother's maiden name was Gardner, and when Ed went into show business, he swiped that name for himself.

We met him because *This Is New York* wanted Eddie Garr for a guest shot, and Frank and I were told to go over to meet with Ed Gardner and find out what kind of material we should write for Garr's appearance on the show.

We were told to be in Gardner's office at CBS at two-thirty. Gardner didn't show up until about five-thirty. There were at least half a dozen people waiting for him. The phones had been ringing and his staff was growing nervous. Then Gardner walked in, a tall, rangy, good-looking guy, full of energy. He didn't make any apologies. He just walked to his desk, sat down, and said to the room at large, "That was some party last night." Then he pointed at Frank and me and said, "Who are you guys?" We told him we were supposed to write a spot for Eddie Garr. He gave us a long look and then started to talk to his assistant about some other problem. He suddenly switched back to us and asked about what we had been doing, what our experience was. We admitted we were fairly green. We talked a lot and we exchanged a few fairly funny lines, and then he finally said to us, "Look, I haven't got room for Garr on this week's show, but I might be able to use you two guys as writers." Well, we were thrilled, but we felt guilty because we had come there for Eddie Garr, and we said so. Gardner said he'd use Garr later on, but he needed writing help now. He said he would try us out for a week and pay us twenty-five dollars apiece. Well, to us this seemed like a terrific deal and we solemnly accepted his offer. Actually, we would have accepted this tryout for nothing.

We listened as Gardner began talking to the rest of his staff about their show for the coming week. And we were fascinated. This wasn't a matter of loose jokes; this was a whole show. At one point Gardner said something that made me think of an idea that might help, and I opened my mouth and said it. He looked at me, a long long look, and he said, "Tell you what, I'll raise it to thirty bucks a week." When Frank and I left the office, we were almost sick with joy. We had a job at CBS and we had already received our first raise. It was marvelous.

Gardner was a larger-than-life person. I began to see that in the first working session we had on *This Is New York*. The show went on the air on Sundays. The writers worked on the script all day Thursday, all day Friday, *all* of Friday night, and then turned it in on Saturday morning to be mimeographed. Gardner worked with us the whole time. The writing sessions were semiorganized madness. A raft of writers sat in one room. I don't remember them all, but there were some good ones like

Jack Roche and Harry Hermann. It seemed as if everyone was throwing out jokes at the same time. Frank and I were the new kids, so we were rather quiet.

I remember the moment when I won my first Merit Badge. Ed was searching for a line about New York. He wanted something lush and beautiful. One of our guests was Martyn Green, the superb singer of Gilbert and Sullivan songs. We needed a line to follow his number and somehow relate it to the beauties of New York. The song was "John Wellington Wells" from *The Sorcerer*. I've always been a G. and S. fan so I spoke up. I think this was the first time I did speak up. I nervously said, "Ed, you could use a line from Martyn Green's song." Ed stared at me and I went on. "In the song, John Wellington Wells is called a dealer in magic and spells. So why don't you say 'New York, like John Wellington Wells, is a dealer in magic and spells?' " Ed looked at me for a long moment, then he turned to the rest of the group and he said, "This Hebe knows everything." Of course that word "Hebe" was not a reference to the Greek goddess of youth, the daughter of Zeus. Gardner was a guy who had grown up in the firm belief that Jews were smarter than other people. I'm sure he didn't think he was insulting me and I didn't feel insulted. About an hour after this, he took Frank Galen and me aside and told us that he was going to keep us on the show and raise each of us to seventy-five dollars a week! We were off and running.

For the next seven years, until 1945, just about everything I did in radio involved Ed Gardner. He was my friend and my teacher. I still wear the star sapphire ring that Ed gave me when I finally left *Duffy's Tavern* and went out on my own. He remained my friend for the rest of his life, and when I began to work in the theater, Ed told me he felt very proud.

The last time I saw him I was living in New York and he came in from California. He asked me to have lunch with him in the Oak Room at the Plaza. By this time I was going big in the theater and television; and people kept interrupting our lunch by asking me for autographs. Me! He watched with an enigmatic smile. I was embarrassed; Ed was retired by then and nobody came over to ask for *his* autograph. Finally one lady brought over her two kids to meet me and was overly effusive. She told me how wonderful she thought I was on television, and how wonderful my shows were and stuff like that. As she walked away, Gardner looked at me — a long look — and then he quietly said, "How would you like a kick in the ass?" If there ever was a *mot juste,* that was the justest.

He died in the sixties. His wife, Simone, told me that during his last day in the hospital, when they were wheeling him down the hall to try to operate and save his life, he suddenly called out at the top of his voice: "Hey, Abe, throw me an exit line."

There's a saying in the Talmud that there are two things a man must do for himself. God cannot help him in this; it's up to the man. He must find a friend and he must find a teacher. I found many friends and I was lucky enough to find *two* teachers. Ed Gardner and George S. Kaufman. Gardner was my Professor of Freshman Rudimentary Radio, and Kaufman was my Professor of the Science of Turning Comical Sows' Ears into Theatrical Silk Purses.

These two men were very different and yet . . . Well, Kaufman was an elegant, literate man of the theater; Ed was a brilliant primitive. He didn't have Kaufman's education but he had a remarkable literary instinct. He differed from most people in radio comedy because his feelings about comedy writing were influenced by his admiration for stage dialogue. He loved the theater. He had directed some plays in stock and he was for a time married to a well-known actress, Shirley Booth. (Later on, when we did *Duffy's Tavern,* it was Shirley who played that wonderful Miss Duffy.)

At the time we were doing *This Is New York,* Shirley was on the road in a tryout of *The Philadelphia Story* with Katharine Hepburn. It was because of Shirley that Ed spent a lot of his time with people from the legitimate theater.

Ed taught me something about style and (although he would never use the word) grace. His teaching method consisted of certain painfully pithy phrases. When I would come up with a "bad" line, he would say, "That's lousy." Or "That stinks." Or sometimes he would be more polite. He would say, "Hey Burrows, you can do better than that." I remember at one of our early sessions everybody was sitting around trying to find an interesting entrance for some guest star — I think it was Walter Huston. The other writers were coming up with tricky ideas of how to bring him on. I didn't know what they were shooting for and I finally came up with a dazzling suggestion. I said (I really did say it), "Why don't we just say 'Here comes Walter Huston now'?" The other writers all stared at me and Gardner said quietly, "Abe, that's really rotten." And I asked "Why?" And he snapped back, "I don't know why. It's just really really rotten." That may not seem to be much help, but it started me thinking about clichés.

Incidentally, there was something else he introduced me to that had nothing to do with style or grace; it was Benzedrine. The schedule for *This Is New York* was backbreaking. The first time I heard that we would have to stay up all night, I didn't understand how we could do it. I asked Gardner, "What about sleep?" He stared at me as if to say, "Where have you been?" And then he said, "Bennies." To you younger readers, let me say that Benzedrine was the father of Dexedrine and the grandfather of all Uppers. I had never heard of it before. I was told that soldiers used it often and that one little white pill would keep me bright, alert and awake. Boy, did it keep me awake. At the time I didn't know anything about side effects and stuff like that; I only knew I didn't get sleepy that night. When I came home the next morning, I was wide awake and I stayed that way; I wasn't able to sleep for the next two nights. Almost everybody writing for radio was trying Benzedrine in order to meet those hateful deadlines. After a while, most of us learned that it wasn't doing us any good. In terms of writing, it had good and bad effects. It would keep you awake so you could work, but it hurt your editorial judgment. Somebody would come up with a joke and we'd all get hysterical laughing, and the next day the

44

joke looked terrible. We used to refer to that as a "Benzedrine laugh."

Taking Benzedrine was the one suggestion I got from Gardner that I dropped. I'm grateful for the other things he taught me.

Ed was actually the first person who made me feel that what I was doing was writing. Before that I thought of myself as a guy who made up jokes. A gagman. As I worked with him, I slowly and gingerly began to think of myself as a writer.

Writing was an odd profession in my world. My friends were young lawyers, doctors, businessmen, and many were just looking for jobs — any kind of jobs. None of them were writers. That was a peculiar profession, if indeed it was a profession at all. I have since learned that one of the most puzzling creatures for the average man to understand is the writer. Nobody really knows what the writer does. Writers are seen in the movies, sitting at their typewriters, tearing out sheets of paper and crumpling them up and tossing them away, but writing still remains a mystery, an oddball profession.

I was once a guest at a local country club where I was proudly introduced to an elderly businessman, evidently one of the most respected members. As I was taken over to meet him, I was told in a whisper that he was the richest man in the club. The man who introduced me to this fellow immediately told him my credits. "This is Abe Burrows. He is the writer of the Rudy Vallee–John Barrymore show and he works personally with John Barrymore." Things like that. The old gentleman was very friendly and asked me a few things about my work. I tried to answer some of his questions. Finally he said he was due on the golf course but before he left he looked at me with great curiosity, shook his head, and said, "So Abe, that's all you do all day, sit and write?"

I once spoke to a meeting of the old Radio Writers Guild and my opening line was "So that's all you do all day, sit and write?" There was a big laugh. I didn't have to tell the early part of the story. All the writers there knew what I meant.

45

This feeling toward writers is not new. There's a story they tell about Edward Gibbon. He didn't write things like *The Rudy Vallee Show*. But he was a pretty fair writer. His big hit was a book called *The History of the Decline and Fall of the Roman Empire*. He started writing it in 1764 and didn't finish it until 1787. It was in two volumes. When he finished the first volume he was given the honor of presenting the first copy of the book to the duke of Gloucester, the brother of King George III.

When Gibbon finished the second volume, his publisher felt it would be appropriate for Gibbon to present it to the same duke. As the duke accepted the big heavy volume he chuckled and said to Gibbon, "Another damned, thick, square book! Always scribble, scribble, scribble! Eh! Mr. Gibbon?"

When I was doing my own sitting and writing for *This Is New York* I was very proud. I still think of it as an elegant, literate show. Our first master of ceremonies was the critic Gilbert Seldes and he was followed by Deems Taylor. Gardner provided the humor. However, as it comes to all shows, the closing notice came to *This Is New York*. It was a sustaining show, meaning no sponsor. So CBS felt obliged to drop it and Frank Galen and I found ourselves At Liberty.

People in show business are never out of work. They are At Liberty. It doesn't mean you are out of work; it suggests that you are at the moment available. Free to do another show for some lucky producer.

By this time Frank and I knew our way around and we were hired by Colonel Stoopnagle. He was then a famous character on radio who worked with a partner named Budd. Stoopnagle and Budd made a very funny team. Their comedy was far ahead of its time, but they had millions of devoted fans. The team finally broke up and Colonel Stoopnagle went out on his own. Stoopnagle's real name was F. Chase Taylor. Chase, or Stoop as we usually called him, was a lovely big portly gentleman with a beautiful round ruddy face. He looked like a rich banker or a United States senator, but his talent was for slightly mad humor. An example: he lived in Connecticut and one day his wife was standing at the window overlooking the harbor at New London and she saw what looked like a German submarine. "Chase," she said to him, "is that a U-boat?" He took a look and quickly answered, "No, thatsa notta my boat."

Stoopnagle hired Frank and me right after he stopped working with Budd. He was signed to appear on a radio show called *The Magic Key*. The master of ceremonies was Ben Grauer and the show offered what were then wonderful radio marvels. There were conversations between flying airplanes and Ben Grauer on earth. This was early in 1939, and Ben Grauer talking to a pilot ten thousand feet above the ground was regarded with almost the same excited interest later given to the moon shot.

Galen and I wrote a comedy spot each week for Stoopnagle, doing our best to capture his nutty humor. On one show Stoopnagle played a hotel clerk. A customer came up to the desk and asked for a room with a lot of fresh air because "I need lots and lots of fresh air. I'm half Indian." And Stoopnagle said, "What's the other half?" And the man said, "Nothing, I'm just a half Indian."

The last time I heard from him was a letter he wrote me in 1948. He was not well then. He suffered from hypertension, but he still retained his strange sense of humor

Hi, Mister Burrows!
  Just thought of a song title that you may use if you wish — it's such a *scream*, I don't know how you could pass it up — :
  "I'm Looking Over a Three-Leaf Clover That I Overlooked Be-Three."

> Well, goodbye, then,
>   I suppose.
> Best.
> Your shows are su–for goodness' Sakes–perb!
> Sincerely
> "STOOP"

47

Not too long after writing that letter, that delightful man died.

Frank and I worked for Stoop till the end of the summer of 1939 and then Ed Gardner came to us with big news. He had been hired to produce and direct *The Texaco Star Theater,* a big variety show. The show was to originate in Hollywood. And Gardner hired Frank and me to be on the writing staff. Hollywood! That was something. My friends all respectfully kidded me that I would soon be hanging around with Joan Crawford, Jean Harlow, William Powell and Mary Pickford. There was another nice happening: my salary was going to be $150 a week. No more woven labels, no more accounting, no more maple syrup, no more wallpaper. "California, whether you like it or not, here come I."

Gardner had just bought himself a new Packard but he wanted to fly to the Coast. He suggested that Frank and I drive his car out there. I liked that. It would give me a chance to see the country. Frank had done a lot of traveling before; but me, I was a real city boy. When I was a kid I was vague about the rest of the country outside of New York. To me, the Far West meant New Jersey, and beyond that, Indian Country. (A few years later, when I was writing *Duffy's Tavern,* I wrote a piece of dialogue which showed the way a New Yorker thinks about American geography. One of our characters was a guy named Finnegan, Archie's friend and a very dumb character. One day Archie was talking about something happening throughout the forty-eight states. Finnegan said, "Hey, Archie, forty-eight states? Are there really forty-eight states?" And Archie said, "Of course, Finnegan." And Finnegan says, "Gee, forty-eight states. Where are they all?" And Archie said, "Well, there ain't many around New York, but if you go out West the country is full of states.")

We were in a hurry. But we did see some of the country. We saw Old Faithful do her stuff in Yellowstone Park. That geyser was really like a good act on stage, performing on cue. Every hour a ranger would step up and tell people about the geyser. Then he would step away and that geyser would shoot up a stream of water that seemed a mile high. Then she'd subside and rest up for her next show. I wasn't as much impressed by the water she blew into the air as I was by her performance on cue.

We saw the Grand Canyon, and although it was really awesome, I couldn't help remembering an old joke about it. When the writer Harry Leon Wilson first saw it, he marveled at its depth and said something like "This is a marvelous place for getting rid of old razor blades."

We went through miles and miles of beautiful cornfields in the Middle West, and were looking forward to some delicious fresh corn on the cob. But in the restaurants there was no such thing. That beautiful-looking corn was Hog Corn. Not for radio writers. In the Southwest the specialty of the house at roadside restaurants was usually New England Clam Chowder.

When we arrived in Hollywood — at the very moment we entered the town and started up Hollywood Boulevard — our car radio suddenly blared out a Sousa march. We felt like a two-man conquering army. We were there. We stared at the palm trees we had heard about. We later learned that these palm trees were all imported, but when we first saw them, they meant Hollywood. We had heard all the cynical remarks, including Wilson Mizner's famous crack, "Hollywood is Bridgeport with palms." Not to us. It was just beautiful. We loved the place and we happily went to work.

The Texaco Star Theater was my first big-time show. It was a half-hour show starring Ken Murray, the comedian; two singers, Frances Langford and Kenny Baker; a guest star; and our announcer was Jimmy Wallington. This meant, with time out for commercials, about fifteen minutes of actual dialogue. To handle that we had eight writers: Frank Galen and myself, Leo Townsend, Bob Ross, Mac Benoff, Sam Perrin, Keith Fowler and Royal Foster, who also was one of the writers for Edgar Bergen and Charlie McCarthy. Foster was on loan to Ken Murray, who was Bergen's friend. He was a marvelous guy, very funny, but he stuttered. So when we had a conference of all eight writers and Royal had an idea for a good joke, it took him quite a while to get it out. At the beginning, we were all rather tense about his stuttering and we were very polite, but as we all got used to each other, we learned how to handle him. When he bogged down in a heavy stutter, somebody would yell, "Come on, Royal," and immediately he'd speak beautifully.

We used to divide up the writing. Two of us would take Ken's opening monologue and somebody else would write a sketch, and then we would all gather together, eight of us in one room, and "pitch." You sat there, throwing lines out as fast as they came to you, and somebody would write them down. There was a lot of fun but a good deal of tension, much more tension than surrounds today's TV shows. You see, radio shows in those days were done *live*. When Ken Murray walked out on that stage and began telling his opening jokes, if the jokes didn't make that live audience laugh, we were in trouble. There was no laugh track. The show wasn't taped in advance, so it couldn't be edited. Murray was out there naked, and if he died, the writers were in danger of getting killed. I remember one time, Ken was very unhappy with his opening joke. About a minute before the show started, he ran back to the room where the writers were sitting and said he wanted a new joke. He shouted at us like a mule skinner who was about to skin his mules.

It was very hard for us mules to think of something funny when we were tense and we had only forty seconds. Suddenly, I piped up and said, "Ken, we'll come up with something if you'll just quiet down for a second." He stared at me as if I were crazy. He knew that "Quiet down" meant "Shut up!" While he was staring at me, we did come up with a surefire opening joke that did make the audience laugh. I don't remember the joke, but if it was surefire, it had to be a local joke — something about the California weather, or California drivers, or the La Brea tar pits. We writers, if judged by our jokes, were no Noel Cowards.

The show attracted some interesting guest stars, people who were celebrities in 1939 — Mae West, D. W. Griffith, Johnny

Weissmuller. Of course the guest interviews were mostly a series of friendly insults. I remember Ken Murray greeting Benny Goodman with "Hi, Benny. I see you're still cutting your own hair." Great lines like that.

The Texaco show was not as much fun as I thought it would be, but there was one big plus. Ed Gardner lived at the Garden of Allah on Sunset Boulevard. It was an exotic arrangement of small cottages and palm trees surrounding a lovely swimming pool. As I remember it now, it looked like a great picture postcard from the Coast. When I first saw it, I was dazzled; it looked just the way I had dreamed Hollywood would look. I had to spend most of my time there working with Gardner and got to see and meet the denizens. Mind-boggling names to me.

There were F. Scott Fitzgerald, Charles Laughton and Elsa Lanchester and their honeymooning houseguests, a young harmonica whiz, Larry Adler, and his beautiful young English bride, Eileen. There were Marc Connelly and Charlie Butterworth and the respected idol of any comedy writer, Robert Benchley.

Across the street from the Garden of Allah was the Players Club. Benchley liked to go to the Players, but he hated crossing Sunset Boulevard. This part of the boulevard was right at the beginning of what is known as the Sunset Strip, and the cars coming down the Sunset Strip from Beverly Hills turned it into the Indianapolis Speedway. Benchley worked out a plan. He would go by taxi. But you can't call a taxi and tell the driver to go across the street. So Benchley would call for a taxi and when it arrived, he would say "I'd like to go to the Mocambo," a nightclub about a half a mile from the Garden of Allah. At the Mocambo, he would suddenly say to the driver, "Oh, I forgot. I have to meet somebody at the Players Club." The cab would make a U turn and take him right to the Players. And Bob Benchley was safe.

The first time I invited Benchley to my home he asked if he could bring Charlie Butterworth along; I was delighted. After that, they always came together. It was a marvelous combina-

51

tion — Benchley's wit and Butterworth's droll style. They were very much attached to each other, and when Benchley died, Charlie felt lost. Not too long after that, Charlie was killed in an automobile crash. He ran his tiny English car into a lamppost on Sunset Boulevard, on the dangerous part of the road that Benchley always had dreaded crossing. When I read about the terrible accident, I felt that somehow, with Benchley gone, Charlie didn't care anymore about driving carefully.

The Texaco show went off the air in the spring of 1940 and I was out of work again, but this was different from my former unemployment. Now I felt I was a professional — a full-fledged radio writer.

Ed Gardner told me that he was going back to New York to look for some action there. Well, if Ed was going to go back to New York, I was going to take my chances with him. I felt a strong tie to him. I wasn't broke, and I decided that if Ed was temporarily out of work, I would try being out of work with him.

Frank Galen didn't feel the way I did about Gardner. Besides, he was planning to get married and wanted to stay in California. Later on, Frank was very successful writing for Burns and Allen, and later still, he wrote a television show called *Meet Millie,* a big success. A few years after that, he died of a heart attack after a game of tennis. Frank was a very important part of my life.

In New York there was a lull for a while. Then suddenly Gardner was asked to put together a half-hour pilot for a new radio show. Ed was to produce the show and star as Archie, a character he had originated on *This Is New York.* Archie was a New York mugg who constantly talked about a saloon-keeper called Duffy. And, of course, we called the show *Duffy's Tavern.* When the pilot was finished, everyone who listened to the recording thought it was a very funny show, but nobody fought to sponsor it. People were saying it was too New Yorkish, too sophisticated. We heard all the old bromides: "How will it go with the people in Kansas City?" "The rest of the country doesn't care about New York." So for a while we had to put *Duffy's Tavern* on hold.

Now there was a bit of a pinch. My savings were shrinking and so were Gardner's.

Along came Rudy Vallee. Rudy was doing a show for the Sealtest Company. They wanted a new producer and they hired Ed Gardner and Ed hired me. That name, Rudy Vallee, has always been lucky for me. The first time I ever got anything on the air was on *The Rudy Vallee Show.* Now I was going to work with Rudy on his Sealtest program. When Gardner and I joined the Rudy Vallee setup, they already had taken on a lot of other writers, but it finally boiled down to four of us: Norman Panama and Mel Frank (they had been a team for years and were very good), Paul Henning (who later got very rich writing *The Beverly Hillbillies*), and myself. The show had a strange motif. Every week there would be a small musical play about some famous character. For instance, Rudy Vallee would play P. T. Barnum and a guest singer would play Jenny Lind, and we would do a musical fictional love story. Sounds strange, doesn't it? Well, it *was* strange. The show had a fair number of listeners, but it wasn't a world-beater. Sealtest, our sponsor, decided to move it to California to attract more famous guest stars. At that time everyone was saying that the show needed something different to make it a hit nationally. Then Gardner came up with what seemed to be a big but wild idea for this "something" we needed. First of all, he wanted to junk the whole idea of the weekly musical comedy and turn the show into a variety show with John Barrymore as a permanent guest star. Our sponsor didn't think this was such a great idea. Sealtest sold healthful things like milk, cottage cheese, ice cream, and they weren't sure that their customers would be turned on by a fellow who thought milk was a lethal drink. Besides, Barrymore hadn't worked for a while. His personal life was weird, to say the least, and no one really trusted him anymore. But Gardner hung in there, and finally sold the idea to Sealtest. And the show became the smash hit of the year.

53

I was thrilled when I first met Barrymore. I was still new in the business and the idea of meeting the great John Barrymore was like . . . well, like meeting the great John Barrymore.

Things didn't go smoothly right away. Our first rehearsals were a bit shaky. This was John's last flurry, his first crack at national radio and probably his last chance as a performer. He was a sick man. He wasn't drinking the way he used to. He could no longer drink the hard stuff. The doctor had him on a mixture of sweet Italian vermouth and water. The doctor said if he stopped drinking entirely, he would die, so from time to time he would drink down a tall highball glass filled with this noxious mixture. He used to bring it with him in an attaché case. He really didn't want to work, but he had to because of his creditors. He didn't get to see much of the money himself. It was sent to his agents, who paid off part of his debts. The poor man had to drag himself down from Laurel Canyon once a week to do the show. But he was quite marvelous. The audience loved him. On my list of great comedians with whom I have worked, there are two legitimate actors: Charles Laughton and John Barrymore. Both were expert comedians. John had a stylized manner of speaking that sounded Shakespearean, but what he generally was doing was poking fun at himself. The audience loved it and our ratings went higher and higher; but it was a tough job for the rest of us. Each week he would come down from the mountain under duress. Somebody had to get him to the studio on time and when he arrived, he was full of resentment. He used to turn a lot of his resentment on me. I was the head writer of the show and I also was the fellow who worked on the stage during the show and gave cues to the actors and the orchestra. During the show, the actors who weren't in a scene would sit in chairs on stage waiting for their cues. When Barrymore's cue came up and I pointed at him, he would frequently just sit there. Time after time I would have to nudge his elbow to remind him of his cue and he would hiss something like "Don't push me." I once introduced him to my wife and he said to her, "His wife? How do you bear up under it?"

I finally found a way to get along with him. When my father was a kid he used to tell me about getting parts on the New York stage. If they needed kids in a street scene, they would grab a few real kids off the streets and pay them one dollar a night. They were called supers. My father was one of those kids. He once was a super in a play called *Roaring Dick,* starring Maurice Barrymore, John's father. It was about a Tammany politician. My father was in a scene which had this politician feeding a bunch of poor kids. I remembered that story one day when John was very angry with me. When he calmed down, I somehow found a way to mention my father's appearance in *Roaring Dick*. It worked like magic. He said, "Is that so? Your father in *Roaring Dick,* eh? That was a great show!" And suddenly we were friends — temporarily. Two weeks later he was angry with me again and I told him the same story again. I must have repeated the story about ten times during Barrymore's run in the show. He always forgot that I had told it before. He was in that kind of shape.

Whatever John's mood was, when he walked up to the microphone and started to do his lines, he was magnificent. Our only problem was getting him up there. One time he almost didn't make it.

Marlene Dietrich was to be our guest star that night. All of us were excited about having her there, especially John. The day before, we held a meeting to go over the script with our stars. Barrymore arrived early, looking very dapper. His eyes were bright. After all, a beautiful woman was arriving. Dietrich made a late entrance, not very late, just late enough to make sure that we would all be waiting. I expected her to come in dressed to the teeth like a "real" movie star. But when she arrived, she was wearing a simple gray sweater, gray slacks and a black beret, and she looked glorious. She was introduced to all of us. Big excitement and buzzing went on around her. Barrymore kissed her hand in real Barrymore style. Rudy Vallee kissed her hand, too. I wasn't up to kissing stars' hands yet. I just stood there wide-eyed, thinking how beautiful she was. And then, while all the buzzing was going on, she walked over to me and said quietly, "I'm afraid I didn't hear *your* name." And I fell madly in love! It may have been something she often said to people; but that didn't matter to me. As far as I was concerned, it worked.

The next day — the day of the broadcast — a rehearsal was called for two o'clock. Rehearsals in radio were not the same as they are in television or in the theater; nobody had to learn lines. Everyone worked from a script. But we had to run through the show several times to straighten out music cues, and for people to get used to the script. Well, at two o'clock, everybody was there except John Barrymore. We waited for a half hour; then we began calling his home. No answer. Messengers were sent out to try and find him. We were beginning to panic. This was a live show that went on in the East at nine in the evening, which meant we had to broadcast it from California at six. If Barrymore didn't show, there would be no show. We used to have an actor standing by, a young actor named Hans Conried. Hans did a pretty good imitation of Barrymore. He sounded very elegant. We paid Hans fifty dollars a week to stand there and we felt that if anything happened to Barrymore, Hans might be able to keep the network alive. We had some crazy thought that we could introduce him as John Barrymore's cousin or something. Three quarters of an hour before showtime, John walked in.

"Walked" is the wrong word. Two guys helped him in and his doctor followed. John looked terrible — pale and helpless. They stretched him out on the cot in his dressing room and the doctor gave him a shot of glucose. He had been on a bad binge for forty-eight hours. Malnutrition is the standard problem of drinkers; the doctor gave him glucose, then Benzedrine. But John still lay there on the studio cot, lost to the world. Dietrich was starting to panic. This calm beautiful lady had lost her cool. She kept running over to everybody and saying, "What are we going to do? What are we going to do?" I kept reassuring her, although I wasn't very reassured myself. Finally, I walked her into John's dressing room. John lay there and he was really

I was about three. I'm holding my father's watch, which kept me from crying.

My brother, Selig, and I "lopin' along" in the Bronx. I was 6-ish and Selig 3½-ish.

*Brooklyn, 1938. Me and my teen-
age sister, Shirley.*

*Dad and Mama when they visited
me in Hollywood in 1939.*

Carin. When I first met her.

Hollywood, 1939. This sylph-like character is really me. In 1943 I shaved off that mustache. When I did, my three-year-old son, Jimmy, said to me, "Shave it on again."

About 1955. My son, Jimmy, was then a member of the Boys' Chorus of the Metropolitan Opera. His name wasn't on any of the posters, but his sister, Laurie, and I admired him anyway.

James Edwards Burrows. My Son, the Director.

In Beverly Hills. My daughter, Laurie Burrows Grad, her husband, Peter Grad, and my grandson, Nicholas. Nicky is my favorite and only grandchild.

My brother, Selig, threw a bash for me at the Lotus Club on my fiftieth birthday. First row (left to right): My brother-in-law, Paul Alter; Shirley Burrows Alter; Abe Burrows; Carin; Selgi's wife, Gladys; and Selig. Second row; Jimmy and Laurie Burrows; Selig's son Jonathan; Shirley's daughter, Wendy; Selig's son Kenneth; Selig's daughter, Patrica.

With Ed Gardner (Archie) during the Duffy's Tavern *days. Ed wore that apron when we went on the air. It was covered with guest stars' autographs.*

"out." Marlene said again, "What are we going to do? What are we going to do?" And I said, "Hold his hand." Marlene very nervously reached over and took his hand and held it. Then she whispered, "John," and squeezed his hand. He suddenly opened his eyes and he turned slowly and looked at her and said "Hello, darling."

We helped him to his feet and slowly walked him to the stage. I had a tall stool ready at the microphone so he wouldn't have to stand. The doctor said to me, "I'll sit on the side of the stage. If he starts to get shaky, bring him over to me and I'll give him a shot." I'd never had an experience like this: Barrymore working on a stool, and the doctor sitting on the side of the stage, waiting with a needle in his bag. Well, the show started, and wouldn't you know, Barrymore gave a magnificent performance. His voice was weak to start with, but as the show went along it grew stronger. They say the show must go on, and this one did — barely.

After that incident he behaved fairly well. The next time he drank too much was fortunately *after* a show. Gardner had taken him over to Earl Carroll's Vanities, the big nightclub in Hollywood at the time. The headline act was Buster Shaver plus Olive and Ed George, a married couple who were midgets. Olive George, even though she was a midget, was one of the most beautiful women I have ever seen, and when Barrymore was introduced to her that night, he suddenly fell in love with her. He began to talk to her as though he were Romeo and she a tiny Juliet. This was about to lead to a fight with Ed George. Gardner had to drag Barrymore out of there.

One person who wasn't a fan of our show was Ethel Barrymore. I think John was an embarrassment to her and the rest of the family. I remember once we wrote a line in which John was to say something about Ethel. It was a complimentary line, but John came to me looking like a small boy and sheepishly said, "Abe, I hope you won't mind, but I'd rather not mention her. She gets very angry with me." Miss Barrymore actually sent word to our sponsors to "keep my name out of that man's filthy mouth."

A great event happened during the run of the Rudy Vallee–John Barrymore show. My first child was born, a son named James Edward. When I asked Ed Gardner to be his godfather, he was very pleased, but then he found out that in this case a godfather had an extra job. When it came time for Jimmy Burrows' brith — the ritual circumcision — the godfather has to hold the boy. There were ten of us there at the brith, because the ritual calls for a minyan, ten men. Among the ten were my co-workers Mel Frank, Norman Panama, and Paul Henning. And there was the late Mark Robson, a close friend who became a well-known film director.

It turned out that the rabbi was also a matchmaker and he tried to get Mel Frank, who was single, as a customer. Mel shook him off and the rabbi finally got down to the ceremony. When he performed the circumcision, Gardner turned green. But really green. And he staggered and we were afraid he would drop Jim. Ed was in shock for days.

The Rudy Vallee–John Barrymore show was a tremendous success in its day. Our Hooper rating was very high. (The Hooper rating was the predecessor of the Neilsen rating, which television now uses.) Everybody in the industry followed the ratings passionately. If you were number one, the Hoopers were remarkably accurate. If you were down at the bottom, they were a big fraud. It's that way today; everyone knocks the Neilsen ratings, except those who stand number one. I happened to believe in the Hooper ratings in those days because the Vallee–Barrymore show was on top.

Rudy and John worked very well together. They were very different but they made a great combination. John got most of the attention for a while but Rudy was really the backbone of the show. He was very skillful. He was at home on radio and he held everything together.

And of course Vallee still sang like the Vallee who broke

through in the twenties. He was the sensation of his time. His audience was not composed of hysterical bobby-soxers. When Rudy sang, they didn't scream. They sighed.

Chapter 3

In 1941 a sponsor finally got interested in *Duffy's Tavern*. After a few weeks of negotiation the Schick Injector Razor people bought it. The show was Ed Gardner's dream. He and I left the Vallee show and went back to New York. The first *Duffy's Tavern* went on the Columbia Broadcasting System Saturday night, March 1, 1941, with the same cast that had made the pilot program. Archie was played by Gardner; Shirley Booth, Ed's wife, played Miss Duffy; Charlie Cantor played Archie's dumb friend — Clifton Finnegan, we called him; and Eddie Green played Eddie the Waiter. Green was a magnificant comedian. Ed and I had seen him when he played in *The Hot Mikado,* which starred Bill "Bojangles" Robinson. Our orchestra was the John Kirby Quintet. Kirby was a bass player who was married to Maxine Sullivan, and in his group he had musicians who were even then legendary: Charlie Shavers on trumpet; Buster Bailey on clarinet; O'Neil Spencer on drums and Billy Kyle at the piano. (Billy later was our pianist in the orchestra of *Guys and Dolls.*)

We had some really good character actors on the show. There was Teddy Bergman (he later changed his name to Alan Reed) as Clancy the Cop. When Teddy changed his name from Bergman to Reed, Gardner used to kid him by constantly referring to the famous actress "Ingrid *Reed.*" Then we had Millard Mitchell, who later did very well in movies. Millard played Crudface Clifford. This character was by trade a safecracker, and in a scene he once told Archie proudly that the first time he went to jail, he was eleven years old. Archie said, "How can they put you in jail when you're only eleven years old?" And Clifford answered, "Easy! My mother lied about my age."

Shirley Booth was an amazing Miss Duffy. Here was an elegant actress who came from Hartford, Connecticut, doing the best New York accent I have ever heard. If you aren't born in New York, it's very hard to fake this sound. Through the years I auditioned people for *Duffy's Tavern.* They would often step up and say they were New Yorkers, but after two minutes I'd know they were faking it. Shirley Booth really had the right sound. Her ear was perfect. When she played in *The Philadelphia Story,* and *My Sister Eileen,* and even when she played Hazel later on in television, all her accents were absolutely true.

One of the biggest laughs we ever got came when Deems Taylor was our guest star and Archie introduced him to Miss Duffy. He said, "Miss Duffy, this is Deems Taylor." Her response was, "Whose?" Then Archie tried to straighten her out and said, "He ain't nobody's tailor — his first name is Deems." Miss Duffy answered in her wonderful voice, "Oh, how do you do; it's mutual I'm sure."

Shirley had a problem because the show was broadcast on Saturday night and she was then playing in *My Sister Eileen* on Broadway. That day she had a matinee and an evening show. Our show ran till 8:55 and the producers of *My Sister Eileen* used to hold the curtain for her. We'd have a car waiting outside and as soon as she said her last line on the air, she dashed out of the studio into the car and was onstage about ten minutes later.

I remained with *Duffy's Tavern* for five years. Thirty-nine shows a year — that's one hundred and ninety-five shows — one hundred and ninety-five half hours. An average Broadway play runs a little over two hours. So we wrote the equivalent of forty-

61

nine Broadway shows. Of course, part of the shows were commercials, so I'll reduce the number to forty-five Broadway shows. That took a lot of typing and I can only describe it as thrilling, glorious drudgery.

I was the Head Writer. The Head Writer of a radio or television show is a writer and an editor. Of course, when we started out, Ed Gardner was really the editor. As a matter of fact, in most comedy shows, radio or television, the star is usually the editor, because there's a simple law: if the star doesn't like a line, he won't say it. And if he doesn't like a line that some other actor has to say, the star won't allow that person to say that line. After a year or so, when I began to feel my oats, Gardner and I came to an agreement. We used to have a preview with an audience the day before we went on the air. Gardner didn't get to see the script until the night of the preview. After that preview, Gardner, going by the audience reaction and his own taste, would go over the script with us. Sometimes there would be a battle and usually Gardner won it. But as he trusted me more and more, I started to win a few fights.

The first few scripts were written by Parke Levy and myself. Then we were joined by Mac Benoff. We three sweated it out week after week. Our office was a suite in the Hotel Royalton. It was an old hotel, a few steps from the Lambs Club on Forty-fourth Street, and across the street from the Algonquin. The Royalton was known as the Poor Man's Algonquin. It offered a sort of frayed elegance; it had seen better days, but a lot of interesting people stubbornly remained there. George Jean Nathan had a beautiful baroque suite on the floor above us, and Robert Benchley lived in a suite that was — unfortunately for him — right next to ours. Three guys writing a radio comedy show make a lot of noise. We laughed aloud at our own jokes; then twice a week Gardner would join us and there would be a lot of hollering. The noise would go on far into the night.

One day there was a knock on the door. I opened it and it was Benchley. He stood there with two suitcases beside him and I said something like "Good to see you, Mr. Benchley," and he said, "Abe I just want to tell you that you can stop making noise now. I'm leaving." He smiled, picked up his suitcases, and went to California. I stayed in New York making noise. But not for long.

In 1943 everybody decided we ought to move the show to California. By "everybody" I mean the sponsor. Gardner and I were worried about this. The locale of our show was New York. The characters were all pure New York characters, mostly muggs. We felt it would be a little strange to have all these guys talking New Yorkese among the palm trees.

However, in those days the sponsor was the boss. Today in television the commercials are mostly spot announcements. When there's a commercial break on a television show, you get entertained by an antacid spot, a toilet-tissue spot, a new perfume and a cat meowing about cat food. Back in the forties there was usually one sponsor for a whole show.

So we agreed to do the old Horace Greeley "go west" bit. I have always been a bit puzzled by the popularity of that quote. People considered Greeley a very wise man when he kept saying, "Go west, young man." But Greeley himself stayed east. It's something to think about.

Gardner came to like the idea of going to the Coast. He had a yen for what he called the wilds of Hollywood. Besides, the simple fact was that most of the big-name guest stars were out there. However, there was one tough problem: Shirley Booth wouldn't come out with us. She liked doing *Duffy's Tavern,* but her heart was really in the theater. Besides, her marriage to Ed was becoming shaky and it ended soon after while Ed went to Hollywood.

This time I remained on the Coast for a long while. During these years my daughter, Laurie, was born there in the same hospital as her brother, Jim. Laurie is now a writer, married to Peter Grad, and she is the beautiful mother of my only grandchild, Nicky. And Jim is a successful director in television.

This was a very active period for me. Besides my work on *Duffy's Tavern,* I started to write my weird songs. It all really started with Frank Loesser. By then he was most famous for "Praise the Lord and Pass the Ammunition." We became close friends and I started to write those songs to kid Frank. Through Frank I met other songwriters and I would ad-lib my songs to satirize the stuff they were all turning out.

This was the beginning of my "party" period. There were lots of parties where all of us entertained each other. People like Betty Comden and Adolph Green used to come and sing their songs, Frank Loesser would do his stuff, and I did my type-songs. The use of "type" came to me in the early days of the war when I saw a label on a bottle of very poor scotch which read "Scotch-type Whiskey." They weren't shipping scotch from England anymore, so some American companies put together this terrible ersatz drink.

Of course my best-known ersatz opus was "The Girl with the Three Blue Eyes." The important line in that one is "What makes her different?"

I wrote a torch-type song which was called "You Put a Piece of Carbon Paper Under Your Heart and Gave Me Just a Copy of Your Love." I wrote this one night at Ira Gershwin's house. I loved doing my stuff for songwriters. They knew what I was kidding and enjoyed it. Especially when I was kidding *other* songwriters.

I began playing at parties all over town. I became sort of a cut-rate social lion. That "Songbuster" piece that Pete Martin wrote about me appeared after he was invited to a big party that the writer and producer Nunnally Johnson gave for Helen Hayes. Helen had been away from Hollywood for a long time and Nunnally asked her if there were somebody special she wanted to meet at her party. She named two people: Johnny Mercer, who was a *real* songwriter, and me. After us he seemed to have invited everybody else in Hollywood, including Claudette Colbert, Clark Gable, Groucho Marx, Danny Kaye, Bob Benchley, and every other star he could crowd into his home.

I was still just a radio writer as far as my show-business status was concerned. An amateur entertainer and a radio writer. In those days the aristocracy in Hollywood was the movie crowd; radio people didn't rank. (Of course, today the television people and the rock stars seem to be the big wheels in Hollywood.) My songs and my naked eagerness to sing them got me invited everywhere. Sometimes I was invited by people I didn't even know.

One time L. B. Mayer, the head of Metro-Goldwyn-Mayer and the most powerful man in Hollywood, invited me to a party. Nunnally Johnson called me one day and said he'd like me to come to a little party given by him and his friend William Goetz, the producer. Nunnally said, "This isn't going to be a big party, Abe. There are just going to be eight of us." It sounded like fun. Well, Bill Goetz was Mayer's son-in-law and somehow or other L.B. found out about the party and he said, "I've never heard this Burrows fellow, and I'd like to hear him. I'll give a party and let's make it a big one."

Nunnally was a very sensitive man and he called me up very apologetically to tell me that L.B. wanted to give the party. He sounded embarrassed about the whole thing. When L.B. said he wanted something, that was an order. Nunnally and Bill Goetz were about to make a film together at Metro and they couldn't cross the Old Man. So I said I was pleased that Mr. Mayer wanted to hear me and I'd be glad to go.

A week before the party I had my first taste of what kind of party it was going to be. Mr. Mayer's secretary phoned me and said, "Mr. Burrows, this is Mr. Mayer's secretary. I want to confirm your invitation to the party for Saturday night at Mr. Mayer's home." And I said, "Thank you." Then she said, "I am to tell you that the ladies are wearing long dresses, but you may wear a business suit." I couldn't resist a wisecrack answer. I said, "Well, it's going to be tough, but tell Mr. Mayer I'll do my best to dig up a business suit by Saturday." There was a long silence on the other end of the phone and then the poor lady just thanked me. As it happened, she let my wisecrack leak out and the story spread all over town. If it ever got to L.B., I'm sure he would not have been upset; he would have thought that it was a very sound idea for me to try to dig up a business suit.

It turned out to be *some party*. L.B. had invited about two hundred people, and although he had said he was looking forward to hearing me at the piano, he had invited a few other entertainers as sort of insurance. This group of entertainers, who were to play second fiddle to me, consisted of Frank Sinatra, Jimmy Durante and Danny Kaye.

Poor Nunnally was really embarrassed, and so was Bill Goetz. They had no idea that the Old Man would turn what was to have been a small gathering into this tremendous affair, but they swore to me that the real purpose of this evening was for L.B. to hear me at the piano. They kept repeating over and over what Mayer had been saying: "I'm dying to hear this fellow Burrows."

They may have been embarrassed, but I was enjoying myself. It was fascinating to be in the home of the legendary head of MGM. You knew right away who owned the house because the waiters and bartenders all had MGM on their white jackets. It was one of the biggest houses in Bel Air. The walls were covered with beautiful paintings, I thought, but when I looked closer I realized that practically all of them were prints. To L.B. a print was just as good as an original. A couple of the guests made cracks about the prints and about the quality of the liquor, but they did it in hushed tones. This was a royal party given in a royal court and heads could always be chopped off. I remember that when we were having dinner, Marc Connelly was at the same table and said something to me that nearly broke me up. He whispered, "Abe, our host must be a very, very rich man. If you notice, every light in the house is burning."

Finally, after dinner the "entertainment" started. Sinatra was great, Danny Kaye was marvelous, Jimmy Durante was hilarious. Then I went on. A lot of the guests seemed to find my stuff pretty funny. Our host listened to me with what I can only describe as "friendly interest." When it was all over, Bill Goetz walked me over to his father-in-law and said, "Dad, you wanted to hear Abe. How did you like him?" And Mayer said, "Fine, fine. What a great show tonight." I had naively thought of it as a social occasion, but it really was just another show.

A short while after this, Mayer invited me to his house again. We were both at another party, a really big one at a hotel. I was dancing with my wife when suddenly someone slugged me on the shoulder. It was L.B. Mayer, who was dancing with his wife. That hard blow I felt was his way of gently tapping me on the shoulder. I started to say, "How are you, Mr. Mayer," but he cut me off and spoke quickly. "Abe," he said, "I'm glad I ran into you. There's something I want you to do. You are to call my secretary tomorrow morning and tell her you are to be invited to come to my house for New Year's Eve." I started to mumble an answer but he didn't wait to hear me. He'd given me my orders and he danced away with his wife.

It was the sort of invitation Henry the Eighth might have issued. I'm sure Mayer didn't think it was peculiar. But I never called his secretary and never told her that he told me that I was to be invited to his party and I never went to the party. I'm sure he never noticed that I wasn't there.

During my time on the party circuit, there was one party I'll never forget. It was the night I met Charlie Chaplin.

The party was given in the forties by Arthur Kober, a good friend and a very good writer. Arthur was famous for his play *Having a Wonderful Time* and his "Dear Bella" stories in *The New Yorker*. When he called me and invited me to the party, he said he hoped I could make it because Charlie Chaplin was coming. Hope I could make it? I'd have come if I had two broken legs.

I remember my first reaction when I saw him face to face. I was startled by his looks. I had remembered the funny-looking Little Tramp from my childhood; but this man was very, very handsome. Later on, when I told this to my friends and my family, they thought I was exaggerating. The people who have seen

Chaplin in films or in newspaper shots can never imagine what he looked like in person. He was . . . Well, the only word I can think of is *beautiful.*

I had heard many stories about his great ego. He *was* a genius and I'm sure he knew it. When he worked he was a tough disciplinarian. But all I know is that when I started to play some of my songs for him (I didn't need much coaxing), I never had a better or more responsive audience. I could have gone on playing and singing forever (Forever is the name of an occupational disease of all parlor entertainers), but I finally stopped. Chaplin made me repeat my last number. Then he sang it with me. It was a song called "The Rock and the Rose." I called it a botanical-type love song:

> *I looked under a rock*
> *And found a rose*
> *A rose with petals of blue.*
> *I looked under a rock*
> *And found a rose*
> *All sprinkled betwinkled with dew.*
> *Some fellows marry Mohammedans*
> *A Buddhist, a Gentile or a Jew,*
> *But I looked under a rock*
> *And found a rose*
> *And that rose turned out*
> *To be you.*

By this time Charlie was on his feet, moving around the room like a dancer and talking about his music-hall days in England. He began to sing one of the old music-hall songs. He was startled when I began to accompany him. I was brought up on that kind of song because of my father's love for vaudeville. Many English performers came to New York and we owned a lot of their records. One of our favorites was Vesta Victoria, who sang lovely Cockney songs.

Chaplin and I sang her famous number "Waiting at the

Church," a very funny sad song which ended with the would-be bride singing:

> All at once he sent around a note.
>   Here's the very note.
>   This is what he wrote.
> I can't get away to marry you today.
>   My wife won't let me.

And we also sang a lovely short song she used to do. She came on stage pushing a baby carriage and sang:

> It ain't all honey and it ain't all jam
>   Walking around with a three-wheeled pram.
> My old man if I could find 'im
>   A lesson I would give
> Poor old me, I 'aven't got the key
>   And I don't know where I live.

The next time I saw Charlie was a month later on New Year's Eve. It was at my home. A few friends were coming to celebrate and suddenly, the day before, I thought of inviting Chaplin. Of course I was sure he was flooded with invitations to many, more glamorous parties, but I thought, "What the hell, I'll phone him anyway and at least give him a New Year's greeting." Oona Chaplin answered the phone and I nervously mumbled something like "I'm sure you and Charles are busy tomorrow night but if you're not, we'd love to have you here . . ." Before I finished mumbling, she said, "How nice of you to ask us. Let me talk to Charles." After a moment, she came back on the phone and said they had no New Year's plans and would love to come. I was stunned and delighted.

There's a funny thing that happens to the big stars in Hollywood. They often are forced to spend New Year's Eve at home alone. A few of them may do this from choice, but on the other hand, no one thinks of inviting them. People just assume that these beautiful glittering stars must have been invited to a million glittering parties.

I don't believe that Charlie and Oona Chaplin would have been sad and lonely that night had they not been invited out. But we did ask the Chaplins and the Chaplins did come and we had a great party. Charlie turned our home into a happy music hall.

I saw Charlie every once in a while and I always felt these times were great events. He invited us to the first private screening of *Monsieur Verdoux* at his home. It was a marvelous film about the Frenchman who did away with all of his many wives and went to the guillotine unrepentant, having refused a priest's offer of consolation. The story sounds grisly but somehow or other it was hilarious. Louella Parsons, the famed columnist, was at the screening. She and Charlie were old friends and occasionally old enemies. When the picture was over, I heard Louella go over to Charlie and say something like "Charlie, it was funny but what are you going to do about the religious angle?" Charlie, with that charming twinkle in his eye, said, "Louella, when I'm through with the final cut, you'll be happy." I'm sure she didn't believe him, but she smiled because Charlie, when he wanted to be, was irresistible.

The last time I saw Charlie was in Switzerland in 1967. I should say it was the last time I saw him alive, because his films will be around forever and in those films he still lives.

My wife, Carin, and I were in Switzerland as guests of Norman and Earle Krasna. Norman was the author of many hits in the movies and on the Broadway stage — plays such as *Small Miracle, Dear Ruth,* and *Kind Sir.* I had come to Switzerland to work with Norman on a play. (The play never did get on the stage.)

The Krasnas had a beautiful home on the shores of Lake Geneva. Chaplin and Oona lived nearby. One night Krasna invited the Chaplins to his place and we had a delightful reunion. Charlie was then in his late seventies, but he seemed as sharp as ever. He asked me to do some of my old songs, and I was

70

startled when he started singing with me and remembered every one of my lyrics. This was especially surprising because I had been warned that Charlie had become a bit absentminded.

For instance, one night in a restaurant in Montreux he noticed a woman eating a dish of lake perch and he said to Oona, "I'd like to have a dish of that fish." And she said, "You've just had one." He may have been absentminded, but not when he heard music. When he sang, his great wit was still there.

Chaplin's wit was unusual: it was not verbal, it was physical. He wasn't known for dazzling epigrams, and when he sat around and talked, his conversation was interesting but generally serious. When the rest of us were kicking jokes around, he would be a great audience. But then suddenly he would tell a story and stand up to illustrate it, and when he did that, his movements were funnier than any jokes we could think of. Of course, when he was doing a song, his body language was hilarious.

W. C. Fields used to resent Chaplin's physical gifts. He was not too fond of Charlie. Actually, Fields was not too fond of anybody, but Charlie really disturbed him. There's a story told that one time Fields saw a preview of one of Charlie's pictures, and when he came out he said, "That guy is just a goddamned ballet dancer, that's what he is." Charlie did move like a great dancer, a dancer with wit.

And remember those endings in the Chaplin pictures: that lovely long shot of the Little Tramp walking down the road by himself. These days most films don't have anything like those wonderful endings. Actually, they no longer have any endings at all. Even those two magic words "THE END" have been dropped. Now, the only hint that a motion picture has ended is the list of credits rolling on the screen. I know the directors want to get away from the old mandatory fadeout: the chaste kiss between the boy and the girl, the love scene between the cowboy and his horse, and other such forgettables. I believe that a lot of the non-endings happen because the people making the film are stuck for a finish and someone says, "Oh, the hell with it, let's roll the credits." What eventually happens is that when the picture is over, and the lights go on, you can hear the audience whispering, "Is it over?"

I think if a picture doesn't have a satisfactory ending — an ending that resolves the story — there's something basically wrong with the rest of the picture. In the theater there has never been a great play that didn't have a great curtain.

The ending doesn't have to be a "happy ending." Take *Hamlet,* a very sad and bloody tragedy. Just before the end, the stage is strewn with dead bodies. Hamlet is lying there, dead of a sword wound. Laertes, the man who killed him, is also dead. The Queen, Hamlet's mother, is dead. Her husband, the King, is dead. I call that pretty tragic stuff. But suddenly, Hamlet's dear friend Horatio kneels beside Hamlet and speaks:

> *Now cracks a noble heart. Good-night, sweet prince;*
> *And flights of angels sing thee to thy rest!*

As he says this, I always get goose pimples and I think the rest of the audience joins me. Then some soldiers lift up Hamlet's body and carry it off to be honored by the people. Shakespeare has given us a bloody tragedy, but when he sends us out of the theater, we have a feeling of well-being. A kind of release. The Greeks called it catharsis. You feel a helluva lot better.

In Chaplin's films, the endings were frequently sad, but somehow or other they couldn't be called unhappy endings. The Little Tramp was *never* defeated. When Charlie glided down the road twirling that cane, he was a man who was unbeatable. He may have had a few minor setbacks. He may have lost out in a sweet, hopeless love affair, but now that is all behind him. It's as though he had been a person in a dream. And now he is on his way to other dreams.

Charlie was not much interested in analyzing his own work; he seemed to do all his comedy by instinct. It was just natural to him. I once told him that there were some things he did that influenced some of the stuff we did on *Duffy's Tavern.* I was

72

thinking about certain scenes that usually took place in his comedies. The setting was always some public place crowded with people: the ballroom or a grand lobby of a hotel. And the big bearded villain was chasing Charlie all over the place, with the obvious intention of murdering him. Charlie is running for his life. He runs through the crowd. He falls down. He slides down banisters. The heavy keeps chasing him. And while all this is happening no one in the crowd pays any attention. The other people in the film go right on doing what they were doing. Dancing. Shopping. Chatting. Completely oblivious to the wild action going on.

When I raved to Charlie about what a wonderful comic conception this was, he stared at me and said, "Did we do that? I guess we did. I never thought much about it. But it does sound pretty funny."

The crossword puzzles often use the word *oner,* a four-letter word meaning a "unique person." The word used to annoy me but Webster and the Oxford list it and I've decided it's a pretty good description of an extraordinary person. Charlie Chaplin was a oner. There has never been anyone quite like him.

His influence was tremendous. Millions of kids grew up imitating the Little Tramp. Hundreds of mimics do it today, but none of them is nearly as funny as Charlie. The wit is missing.

The word *Chaplinesque* has become a byword, but I think many actors and directors miss the point of the Little Tramp. Their image seems to be that of a loser. They play poor waifs who are sadly abused and badly treated by life. Suffering. But that is not Chaplin. Sure, in his films he was kicked around, but he was not a loser. Somehow or other he took care of those who kicked him by returning their kicks. He actually did *kick* them. Remember that quick little backward kick? I like to call it his backhand kick (Charlie liked that phrase). He did it swiftly and then fled. But when he fled he wasn't running. He was gracefully rolling away on magical skates.

There's a letter I have from Oona, a beautiful woman in every way. It is the answer to the letter I wrote her after Charlie died in 1977, a letter expressing my real sense of loss. Part of her note said, "I'll always remember Charles' 'discovery' of you at Arthur Kober's party — what a happy memory." I was both moved and startled. Charlie "discovering" me?? Actually, I felt that in a strange way *I* had discovered *him*, the real Chaplin.

I met another oner in the forties. He was a strange oner. Charles Laughton — a oner himself — introduced me to this unique person. He was Bertolt Brecht, the director and playwright, who was then a refugee from Germany.

Laughton phoned me one day and said he had a friend, a foreigner, who needed someone to help him with a song for a play. Laughton had heard the songs I sang at parties and thought that my crazy kind of lyrics would fit his friend's work, and I was thrilled with the idea of actually getting *paid* to do a song. Well, it turned out that this friend was Brecht and the play was *Galileo*. Of course, I was interested in meeting Brecht, the legendary playwright who had written *The Threepenny Opera, Mahagonny,* and other famous works. At that time he was trying to get some of his works produced in America. He directed his own shows and he was known as a very strict director. Actors told me it was tough to work with him. He didn't care about motivation or any of that stuff. He hated Stanislavsky and the Method system of acting. He just wanted the actors to do what he told them to do. But Peter Lorre once told me that Brecht was the greatest director he ever worked with.

Laughton certainly thought he was great because Laughton was about to star in a production of *Galileo* that was going to be done in a Hollywood theater. He brought Brecht over to my house for a talk. Brecht was a strange-looking fellow. He wore a cap which he kept on all the time, and he wore a cigar which he kept between his teeth most of the time. He and Laughton explained what they wanted me to do.

In the German version of the play a street singer passes out leaflets about Galileo and sings a song about him. They wanted me to do a new song in English for this character. Brecht wasn't

74

too happy with the German version of the song and said he didn't just want a translation, he wanted something new from me.

I was interested and asked him about the basic content of the song. What was the street singer saying about Galileo? Brecht said, "He's just singing about him." I kept trying to find out what was to be the tone of the song I was going to write. Our conversation went something like this:

ME   Is this fellow praising Galileo?
BRECHT No.
ME   Is he knocking him?
BRECHT No.
ME   Well, Mr. Brecht, how does this fellow feel about Galileo?
BRECHT He feels nothing.
ME   [*Very puzzled*] Well, why does this fellow stand up there and sing the song?
BRECHT Because I want him to.

That was genuine Brecht. As Heinrich Heine might say, "Echt Brecht." I was confused but flattered and interested. It was a chance to do a song for the theater so I took a crack at it. The work was very difficult because of Brecht's restrictions.

Finally, I brought some material to him in his home in Santa Monica. His house was completely unfurnished. We sat on some packing cases. Brecht didn't like what I had written. My lyrics had a slight touch of admiration for Galileo (could I help it if I liked Galileo?) and Brecht did not want that. He admitted that he personally admired Galileo, but he did not want the street singer to feel that way or any way. He repeated what he had told me before: "This street singer should have no feelings at all." He tried to soften things by saying that my lyrics were very funny and clever but not what he wanted.

I went home in confusion. I had a strong feeling that I would never please this man and I was right. I never did finish that song.

Sometime later I went to see *Galileo*. Laughton was wonder-ful, but I was mostly interested in the street singer. He did sing a song, and I think that here and there I detected a couple of words that were mine. But as to the song itself, all I could think was that Brecht had had his way; the song wasn't about anything.

Incidentally, I was never paid a cent for my labor. So as a songwriter I still retained my simon-pure amateur status.

Chapter 4

I finally became co-author of a song that was published: Frank Loesser and I wrote the song for *Duffy's Tavern*. Ed Gardner suggested that on one of the shows Archie should try to become a big-time songwriter. I thought it was a funny idea and talked it over with Loesser, who liked it, too. He and I went to work and came up with a love song which we wrote using Archie's style and syntax. We gave this song the elegant title of "Leave Us Face It." It started off this way:

> *Leave us no longer pretend*
> *That you are merely a friend*
> *For it is wrote in the stars above*
> *Lovelight like in your two eyes*
> *Could win the Pootziler Prize*
> *Leave us face it, we're in love.*

We built a few situations around this song that Archie was supposed to have "wrote," and we cast some guest stars who were willing to risk singing it. The first singer brave enough to sing it was Hildegarde.

After Hildegarde, we had the gall to invite the late Lauritz Melchior to come on the show and sing it. One of the greatest

Wagnerian heldentenors of all time, at the Metropolitan Opera he sang Siegfried, Tannhauser, Lohengrin, and we asked this man to sing "Leave Us Face It." He did sing it and seemed to enjoy doing it. Of course, his own English was not perfect, and I suspect that he didn't know why the lyrics got laughs from the audience. Melchior later told me he liked singing the song because he liked Frank Loesser's melody. Frank had the wit to write some very romantic music to our silly lyrics. That made the song even funnier.

Many people were involved in writing *Duffy's Tavern* through the years. Besides Parke Levy and Mac Benoff, there were other writers who came and went. One was a brilliant young fellow named Bill Manhoff. Years later Bill wrote a big hit for Broadway, *The Owl and the Pussycat.* Alan Jay Lerner, of *My Fair Lady* and *Camelot,* spent a couple of weeks with us. He was a friend of Bill Manhoff's and he sat around with us and started pitching jokes. He was very good, and I wanted him to stay with us but he wasn't going to get himself stuck in a weekly radio show. That was good thinking on Alan's part.

Gardner and I constantly looked for new writers. I had a plan for trying out new writers every week. However, I insisted that I wouldn't do this on "speculation," so I asked Gardner to give me a small budget and to pay a writer fifty dollars for submitting a page or two of comedy material. If we didn't like it, we paid him anyway. If we liked it, he was hired at a pretty good salary. A lot of writers tried out. One of them was Dick Martin. Dick stayed with us for a couple of weeks, but he had other plans for his future and he eventually joined up with Dan Rowan, which led to Rowan and Martin, which led later to *Laugh-In* on television.

One of our real finds was an eighteen-year-old fellow named Larry Gelbart, whose father was a friend of mine. Larry submitted some stuff to us that was wonderful, and we were very happy to have discovered him. He is the fellow responsible for *M*A*S*H* on television. He wrote the book of the hit Broadway musical *A Funny Thing Happened on the Way to the Forum.* His last show on Broadway was another hit, *Sly Fox.*

Something about *Duffy's Tavern* attracted many unusual guests — like Joe E. Brown, "Slapsie" Maxie Rosenbloom, Clifton Fadiman and Jimmy Walker, the ex-mayor of New York. People who wouldn't ordinarily appear on radio shows came because they liked the material they were given to do: stars like James Cagney, Cary Grant, Orson Welles and Tallulah Bankhead. I learned that many serious actors enjoy doing comedy.

(Years later when I was directing a TV variety show for Revlon, the guest star was John Gielgud, the English actor, a man I greatly respected. There was a certain speech I wanted him to say that was seemingly serious, but I wanted him to say it in a way that pointed out the fact that it was comedy. But I couldn't forget that this was Gielgud and I spoke to him in a rather tentative, almost apologetic way. He looked at me for a moment and said, "Abe, you want me to come off the perch, don't you?" I laughed and nodded. He came off the perch beautifully and very comically.)

One of the great actresses who came off the perch for *Duffy's Tavern* was Tallulah Bankhead. Tallulah wasn't just an actress, she was a force. The first time I met her, I found her intimidating. Before the show started, I was left alone with her backstage. I didn't know what to say; I was still a new kid then. Tallulah broke the ice by talking about, of all things, baseball. I was startled to find out that she was a baseball fan. She was American, of course, but she had spent years in England and that colored her speech. Her baseball chatter had some odd phrases, like "Mr. Burrows, I just heard that Camilli knocked a homer." Knocked a homer? Nobody ever says that. But with that voice of hers, Tallulah could say anything.

She was once involved in a radio show with Meredith Willson. Goodman Ace wrote it and there were some fascinating lines in the script. One moment during the show she called out to Meredith Willson in her deep voice, "Mr. Willson," and Meredith answered, "Sir?"

She was not exactly "difficult," but her imperious manner

was sometimes hard to take. Years later I ran into trouble with her at a party that Doubleday gave in honor of Noel Coward. Noel had just published his book *Present Indicative*. He had always liked my crazy songs and asked me to do a couple. As I started for the piano, Tallulah arrived with Joey Bushkin, the famous jazz pianist. She evidently had stopped off for a few drinks on the way to the party and she was, as old-timers used to say, "feeling no pain."

When she came in, Noel gave her a big welcome and said to her, "Tallulah, Abe is about to do some of his songs for us." Tallulah shook her head and said, "Oh no, first I want to hear Joey play." Of course, Joey Bushkin played the piano slightly better than I did, with my fake left hand. As a matter of fact, I think Joey plays better than anybody. I quickly left the piano and said, "Here Joey, take it away." But Noel said sharply, "Abe, you stay right where you are."

Now, this was a tough scene. There were at least a hundred people at that party and they all got tense. I think Joey was as much embarrassed as I was and he said, "Abe, I want to hear you," and Tallulah kept saying, "Joey, I want to hear *you*." Finally, using his sharpest, iciest tones, Noel cut through all the noise and said to me, "Abe, ignore her. She's a bore and she's been a bore for over a quarter of a century."

That caused the loudest hush you ever heard. And in the silence, Noel pointed to me and said, "Abe." And I, with a deep sigh, went to the piano. Tallulah sort of folded up into a chair. I'll never know if she was hurt by Noel's crack, but she was quiet for the rest of the evening. The next time I met her she was warm and friendly, and we got to know each other a little better.

She was very ill for the last couple of years of her life. The last time I spoke to her was in 1968, on the telephone. "Abe," she said in a rather weak voice, "do you know any bookmakers?" Well, I didn't know any bookmakers. I asked why she she needed one. She said, "There is a horse named Abe's Hope running at Belmont today and because of his name, I have to bet on him. And the race is coming on television in a couple of minutes." I was bedridden myself. The flu.

I said, "I can't find you a bookie in time." Meanwhile my wife turned on our television set in the den, and while we all stayed on the line, she and Tallulah watched the race. Suddenly I heard loud shrieks from the ladies. Abe's Hope had won! And there was great joy in the house even though nobody had a bet down. Then suddenly I heard a big groan. The stewards had posted an objection and Abe's Hope was disqualified. Tallulah said to me, "I am sorry, darling." That was the last time I spoke to Tallulah.

One of the biggest moments for me on *Duffy's Tavern* was the time that I actually got to write a monologue for Robert Benchley. When Benchley agreed to be a guest, he startled us by saying he didn't want to do any of his standard material; it was up to us to provide him with something new. I was frightened but excited too. I had begun to tire of the regular weekly routine and the thought of writing a guest spot for Robert Benchley really sparked me. He liked my monologue; when he did it on the air, it went beautifully and it sounded like him.

The Hollywood *Variety* reviewed that show and they said something like "With all the junk we hear on comedy shows, it was a relief to hear Bob Benchley's great humor on *Duffy's Tavern.*" Benchley immediately dashed off a telegram to *Variety*. He told them that he had not written the monologue, that "it was written by Abe Burrows, America's greatest satirist." I knew damned well that I wasn't the greatest anything and I also knew that Benchley was being whimsical; but when I read this wire in *Variety,* I began to think that maybe I could be something besides whatever I was.

Later on, when I started performing professionally. Benchley worried about me. He told me not to let performing interfere with my writing. He said that once he started acting in movies, he stopped writing. The acting was very demanding and it seemed to use up his creativity.

Then, typically, after this confession he quickly told me a story to change the mood. He said that when he started acting, he told his friends he was "throwing away his typewriter." The word spread and finally the New York *Herald Tribune* had a sad editorial about this. The editorial said it was a tragedy that Robert Benchley was throwing away his typewriter. I said that was a helluva tribute and he said, "Nonsense, Burrows. The only response was that the *Tribune* got about two hundred letters from people who needed a typewriter."

In the fall of 1944 another fairly witty fellow agreed to do a guest appearance: Fred Allen. At that time, among the few radio comedians who were thought of as real wits, Fred Allen was the fastest gun in the business.

Fred shocked us by telling us he didn't want to do any of his own stuff on his *Duffy's Tavern* appearance; he would do whatever we wrote for him. That was a scary assignment, writing funny stuff for Fred Allen. It was wanton arrogance. Perhaps the best word is the Jewish *chutzpah*.

All of us who worked on the show were nervous, but I think I suffered most. Not only did I admire Fred as a comedian and as a writer, but I loved him as a friend. I had met him and his wife, Portland, a few years before at a party that Frank Loesser gave. I sang some of my songs for Fred and he was a marvelous audience. He liked them but he wasn't mad about my singing, and he referred to me as the male Sophie Tucker.

He and Portland once talked about me on his radio program. He was doing me the great service of plugging a record album I had made, "The Girl with the Three Blue Eyes." But on the air Fred said, "Portland, this is the new Abe Burrows Jubilee Album." And Portland said, "Abe Burrows? Is he a singer?" And Fred answered, "A singer? Why Abe Burrows is the Sour Cream Sinatra. He writes all his songs on rye bread." Then he said, "One of Abe's best songs is called 'If I Had My Life to Live Over Again, I'd Live It Over a Delicatessen.'" A lot of people have since insisted that it was one of *my* song titles, but it was Fred's.

So when it came time for Fred to come in and read the

Duffy's Tavern script, all of the people who worked on the show were tense, but I out-tensed them all.

Came the moment for our first reading of the script. When Fred and Ed Gardner and the rest of the cast started, I felt not unlike the way I felt years later when *Guys and Dolls* first opened in Philadelphia. Even Gardner was nervous, because Fred was one of his idols, too. As they read on, Fred occasionally chuckled. Professional comedians seldom roar with laughter at jokes they like. The biggest reaction they will give you for a good line is an admiring chuckle. Usually they will just give you a small nod of approval or a little wave of the index finger.

That first reading went very well. And when it was finished, everybody looked at Fred for his reaction. After a moment he tossed the script on the table and quietly said, "Okay." Then he turned to Ed Gardner and said, "Well, Ed, what do we do now? Kick hell out of Abe?" Then he looked at me and he gave me a big grin. I mentally said, "Bingo."

I also felt a bit cocky. Just before Fred saw the script, Ed Gardner was worried. He told me that a few things in it weren't good enough for Fred and would eventually have to be rewritten before we went on the air. However, Fred himself liked everything he read, and when Fred Allen said he liked something, it stayed the way it was. Two days later the show went on the air practically unchanged.

Allen was an unusual man. He and his wife, Portland Hoffa, who was a strong performer on his radio show, lived a simple life. They had a small apartment in the middle of town — Seventh Avenue and Fifty-eighth Street — and one of the rooms was Fred's office. That was where he wrote his weekly radio show. He was known for writing his own material but when it came to doing a half-hour show every week for years and years, he knew he needed help and he had the good taste to pick some good help.

Among the people on his staff was the late Nat Hiken, a comedy genius. Years later Nat created the Bilko television show with Phil Silvers playing the hilarious Sergeant Bilko. There were other fellows working for Fred, including a pretty good writer named Herman Wouk.

In preparing the show, Fred usually did his opening material by himself. Then the others — after conferring with him — would contribute sketches and bits for the rest. Then Fred would sit up all night, by himself, and put the show together.

He loved performing on radio and the radio audience loved him. When TV came along, it didn't treat him well. I think that it was partly the fault of the makeup people. They plastered his face with makeup, removing every one of his interesting wrinkles and craggy spots. They blanked out his face. Fred was an attractive man with a very interesting face that went with his humor. Sure, he had those wrinkles and lines and the bags under his eyes, but I think he was beautiful.

The simplicity of the way he lived didn't mean he was stingy. He was a soft touch for hundreds of guys who were broke. When Fred came out onto the street after his broadcast, several of these fellows would be waiting. Each one would come up to him and say, "Hello, Fred," and Fred would slip the guy a buck. One man used to meet him every Sunday outside Saint Patrick's Cathedral, and every Sunday after Mass Fred would give him a five-dollar bill. One Sunday the man wasn't there and Fred was very upset. He spent the rest of the week checking on the whereabouts of this regular customer. Finally, from the police and some of the panhandlers, he found out the fellow had died. Fred really missed that man.

Before I met Fred, I had heard stories about his being a soft touch and thought they were exaggerations. But one day I came out of the studio before he did, and a guy walked up to me and said, "Hello, Fred." I gave him a dollar. A lot of them didn't know what Fred looked like, but were told that if you go up to a fellow coming out of *that* studio on *that* day and say, "Hello, Fred," you would get a handout. Fred never forgot the days when he was broke. This made him generous to needy people and disapproving of the wasteful.

There was once a bright young writer who ran up against this side of Fred's character. During his first week on Fred's staff this fellow did well and was feeling good about it. When the show he worked on went on the air, it turned out to be very funny. After the show, Fred, as he frequently did, took his staff to dinner at the House of Chan. Fred loved Chinese food and this was one of his favorite places. They all had a very pleasant evening until the fortune cookies came. The bright young writer began opening up all of them. He read the fortunes aloud and discarded the cookies. Everybody laughed except Fred. After the broken cookies piled up in front of the kid, Fred couldn't stand it anymore and he said, "Are you going to waste all that food?" The young fellow laughed and thought Fred was being witty. The rest of the people at the table were quiet; they knew Fred wasn't joking.

Two days later the staff and Fred had their weekly meeting to plan the next show. Our young fortune-cookie waster arrived late. His excuse was pretty weak. He said something like "Oh boy, what a lousy night I had. Played poker until about three in the morning and I dropped a bundle."

The next week that bright young fellow was gone. He really was a good writer and he still is. I wonder if he ever found out what happened to him on *The Fred Allen Show*.

Fred's "feud" with Jack Benny was largely a publicity stunt. Both of them got a lot of press coverage out of it and they also got a lot of material for their shows. They really respected each other. Benny was in awe of Fred's wit. As a matter of fact, Benny was a generous and appreciative audience for *anyone else's* wit. He was a fine performer, a funny comedian and actually a very skillful actor. But he always denied that he himself was a wit or an ad-libber. He never missed praising his writers — people like Bill Morrow, Ed Beloin, Milt Josefsberg and Sam Perrin. There was once a joke about Benny that went around. I don't know where it started but Jack himself used to quote it. He said: "*Ad-lib?* Me? I couldn't *ad-lib* a belch after a Hungarian dinner!" However, witty or not witty, Benny was damned funny. Wherever the dialogue came from, no one else could have done with it what Benny did. He created the character he played, he was a skillful editor, and every one of his writers gave him full credit for whatever went over the air.

For his part, Fred used to admire Jack's work. They were both pros, but so different. Though Benny made a lot of money playing a stingy man, he lived like a man who really did make a lot of money. He and his wife Mary had a big house in Beverly Hills, big cars, and everything that went with being a big star.

Fred lived differently. He always remained in that small apartment in New York, and when he came to Hollywood he used to stay at a place in old Hollywood, the Rossmore Arms on Vine Street. He didn't own or drive a car. He and Portland used to *walk* to my house — about a mile — and always arrived bringing a bottle of scotch. Fred wasn't crazy about California. He actually did say the line which has been quoted many times: "California is all right if you happen to be an orange."

He didn't go to many Hollywood parties. As a matter of fact, he visited very few people. I think the people he saw the most were Jack Haley and his wife Flo, Harry Tugend (a screenwriter and producer who once worked on Fred's radio show), Frank Loesser, and he did come to see me. That was when I was going to all the Hollywood parties, singing my songs and going a little crazy. But I treasured those moments when I relaxed with Fred.

What Fred loved best was his work. And the people who annoyed him the most were those who would hinder him in his work. Number one among those people were the advertising agencies, who would represent the sponsors. The network would have its own censor who looked for dirty words and double meanings. The advertising agency was there to protect the sponsor's product. If your sponsor was selling Royal Gelatin, you couldn't mention the word Jell-O. That was known as a "rival dessert." If you were selling Sal Hepatica, no other laxative existed in the whole world. Fred didn't take these restrictions lightly. The agency was a little afraid of him because his wit, when it was directed at admen, was deadly.

He once told me a story about a certain executive who was head of a big agency: "Abe, I'll tell you why this fellow is good in his job and happy with it. When he went to Yale, he was an All-American quarterback. You know when a quarterback stands behind the line with the linemen stooped over, he is looking at a bunch of assholes. So when he is in a meeting at his agency, he is doing the same thing, and he's happy."

Of course, when Fred told this story it didn't come out as smoothly as that. Fred was a great ad-libber and like all the good ad-lib guys, he used to work a little stall into his speech. It wasn't a stutter, it was a sort of an "ehh ehh ehh." Fred used a very nasal "ehh" while he was thinking. He didn't want a dead spot and he held the floor with that "ehh." And when he was doing that, if you had any sense you wouldn't interrupt him. When Fred was at my home talking to a group of us, I used to nudge friends of mine who started to jump in when he began to go "ehh ehh." Then suddenly he'd get off some great lines, something like "ehh . . . ehh . . . ehh . . . those studio audiences we get are terrible. The network sends people out on the street with free tickets and they find a fellow urinating against a lamppost and they say to him, 'Pardon me, you want to see a radio show?' That's the kind of people we get." Fred would just go on like that, and if you let him roll, it would develop and build until you were in stitches.

He was an avid letter writer. When he typed his letters, he only used lowercase letters. He had a precedent in Don Marquis. Marquis's character, Archy the cockroach, used to write all his letters in lowercase because he wasn't strong enough to punch the shift key. To me Fred's use of the lowercase was a form of modesty. I think he was avoiding the capital I. Anyway, Fred's letters were funny. When my son was born, Fred wrote him a letter telling him what a nut his father was. He did the same thing when my daughter was born. He welcomed her to this world, and then he talked about me. One of the things he told Laurie was, "That bald-headed neurotic hovering over your crib is your father and you might as well face it." At the end of the letter he added a P.S.: "Laurie, as of today, your share of the national debt is $8,766.42."

He wrote a letter to me in 1945 when I finally left *Duffy's Tavern* to go to Paramount. Even though this letter is funny, it shows how serious the man could be:

dear freelance . . .

we read that you had resigned from the duffy's tavern enterprises. i think you have made a smart move. like the infantry frank loesser mentions in his song about roger young, there is no glory in radio. if norman corwin had done the work he has done in radio in any other medium he would have morgenthau's hand in his pocket and a standing in the theatre or in hollywood that would be enviable. the excellent work you have done in radio, apart from the satisfaction you have gotten, the money you have earned and the opportunity you have had to experiment with ideas to perfect your technique, is transient. in pictures, or in the theatre, you can work less, make as much money and acquire a reputation that will mean something. a radio writer can only hope for ulcers or a heart attack in his early forties. with few exceptions radio is a bog of mediocrity where little men with carbon minds wallow in sluice of their own making. for writers with talent and ideas, after it has served its purpose as a training ground, radio is a waster of creative time. good luck to you in new fields of endeavor, mr. b., long may you gambol!

recently a hollywood reporter mentioned that a mr. abe burrows was cutting a social dove-wing out there and that claudette colbert wouldn't think of giving a party without a caterer and this "burroughs." we assume that with this nature spelling you are attending claudette incognito. i hope you have the piano shawl in the act. if you can't get one of those shawls you might get a navajo blanket. an indian blanket with a. burrows sewed on it in birchbark would attract attention before you gained the piano. I am working on a new cellophane sheet of music. this will enable the pianist to look through his music and see how people are reacting to his efforts. many times an entertainer is singing his heart out and behind his music guests are holding their noses or doing acrostics. with the cellophane music sheet the guest will know that the soloist can see him and he will act accordingly. i have another invention you may want later. this is a time stink bomb that explodes in the foyer as guests walk out on the singer. the odor drives the guests back into the room until the artist concludes his program. let me know if you are in the market for any of these parlor devices.

yours until hitler's body is found . . .

F. ALLEN

1 80 west 58th

now that mussolini is dead the devil at last has a straight man.

Of course when Fred wrote that letter, he had no idea that my "smart move" into the movies would turn out to be a very short sprint. I was fated to spend a few more years in radio. Fred was very pleased some years later when I finally escaped to the theater and remained there.

Chapter 5

In the fall of 1945, when I left the movie business, I also left Hollywood and moved back east. I had come up with an idea for a radio show about a couple of retired vaudevillians; I called it *Holiday and Company*. The Philip Morris Company agreed to sponsor the show after they read my first script and they wanted me to put it on in New York.

The performers were Ray Mayer and his wife, Edith, Frances Heflin, and Arnold Stang, a very funny man. As the comical villain, we had Roland Winters, who in the movies was one of the many Charlie Chans. We also had a few guest stars; the best one was Fred Allen. The week Fred came on the show, he gave our rating a big boost; but the show never really caught on and it lasted only thirteen weeks.

I still think it was a very good program and it got excellent reviews, but Philip Morris felt that it was not reaching enough smokers. They canceled us and switched to another show, and I, of course, switched my brand of cigarettes. Incidentally, the new Philip Morris show that replaced mine was not a comedy, but a serious drama called *Crime Doctor*, which I thought was a pretty funny title.

Although *Holiday and Company* was dead, I wasn't. As soon as that show went off the air, I got an urgent phone call from

Hollywood; the Ford Motor Company was about to sponsor a new show starring Dinah Shore. They wanted me to consider becoming the head writer on the show. I didn't have to do much considering; I packed up and left for the Coast. My wife, Ruth, remained in New York; we were separating. It was painful for me to leave my children, although through the years we've remained very close. (Oddly enough, these days Jimmy and Laurie both live in California and I live in New York. But those three thousand miles have shrunk a good deal. With the help of jet planes and the telephone, people who love each other can always manage to be, or at least to feel, near each other.)

When I got back to the Coast, I met with the program executives of *The Dinah Shore Show*. It seemed to be a very promising situation. Dinah's costar was the young comedian Peter Lind Hayes, who was a talented new comic. Dinah, of course, was one of the top singers of the day. Her voice was mellow (as it still is today), and when she sang a song, the words were audible and intelligible. That's something you rarely get when you listen to songs these days. Sometimes I wonder why anyone bothers to write lyrics anymore. They generally are mangled by the singer or drowned out by the orchestra. Our conductor was the late Robert Emmett Dolan. Bobby was a fine musician who felt that the orchestra was there to support the singer, not to bury her.

Carin, who is my present wife, was hired to work on the show as assistant to the producer, and to me. She had been an assistant director on a CBS show in Hollywood and before that she had worked at the local CBS station in Seattle, her hometown.

The sponsor and the advertising agency liked my suggestions for the first program, and I went to work and worked well. But — there's always a "but" — a couple of days before the first show was to go on the air I was hit with some bad news. Selig phoned me from New York and told me that our mother was very ill. I knew she hadn't been well for a while. But now from the way Selig sounded, I got the feeling that her illness was terminal. I rushed back to New York on the night plane. People

91

call the night plane the Red Eye (that describes the way you look when you arrive in New York early in the morning). But it did give me a chance to spend a whole day with my mother and still get back to Hollywood for the show.

My brother had rented an apartment for Mama and Dad at the old Half Moon Hotel in Coney Island; at that time it was a very pleasant place in the fall.

When I saw my mother, I knew why the doctors were so pessimistic about her chances. But although she was obviously very sick, she greeted me with a smile and tried to talk to me in her typical spirited manner, as if nothing were seriously wrong with her. My father behaved the same way. At first I felt that they were putting on an act to make me feel better, but I soon realized that they both absolutely refused to accept the fact that she would never recover.

It was very difficult, but I went along with their act. I spent a couple of strained hours with them and then I had to leave to make a plane back to California. I made my goodbyes as cheerful as possible; but when I got on that plane, I felt very very low. I was depressed about my mother, and depressed about having to think up funny stuff for the radio show. It's tough to write good jokes when you're feeling lousy.

Soon after I returned to Los Angeles, I decided I needed some professional help and I took my head to a psychiatrist. It turned out to be a long process and I did a lot of talking. I talked about my dying mother, I talked about the pain of leaving my children, and I talked about the "Laugh, Clown, Laugh" syndrome that plagues many comedy writers. But I also talked about the good things in my life: my work, which I liked, and Carin, with whom I was very much in love. As I talked, I began to realize that all these different things were mixed up in my skull and were fighting each other.

Of course, now and then I'd let the doctor talk, too. And after a while we began to sort things out. Everything seemed to get clearer to me.

Sam Goldwyn is once supposed to have said, "Any man who

goes to a psychiatrist ought to have his head examined." If Sam were around today, I would enjoy telling him that I did have my head examined and that I will always be grateful for the help the doctor gave me.

I learned that many other comedy writers in Hollywood were seeking psychiatric help. I guess we shared an occupational disease. Although we all had many problems, we were still comedy writers and none of us could resist making jokes about psychiatrists.

Many of these comical brains were being treated by my doctor. One of these fellows was my friend Stanley Prager, an actor and a very creative comedian.

One day Stanley thought up a joke which has since become famous. He said to me, "Hey, Abe, I come to our shrink right after you leave. Why don't we each tell him the same dream! That'll confuse him." We laughed about it, but never actually did it.

However, a few weeks later there was an item in a newspaper column which read, "Abe Burrows and Stanley Prager tried telling their psychiatrist the same dream. First Burrows came in and told him the dream. After Burrows left, Prager came in and told the psychiatrist the same dream. When Stanley finished telling him the dream, the psychiatrist said, 'You know, Stanley, that's the *third* time today I've heard that dream.' "

The story has often been reprinted with the names of many other comics. It's been attributed to Zero Mostel, Jack Gilford, Wally Cox and others. It originated with Stanley and me, but we never found out who the fellow was who thought up that lovely punch line.

The first *Dinah Shore Show* started off very well. Dinah's singing plus Peter's comedy made for a good combination. Peter was a very successful nightclub comedian. When I first saw him, he was appearing with his beautiful wife, Mary Healy, at the Copacabana nightclub in New York. Peter was very funny and a master of mimicry; his most popular routine was his imitation of Joe Frisco.

93

Among show people, Frisco was the most quoted comedian of his time. He was a great wit who stuttered when he worked, and I was always puzzled about that stutter. No one knew whether it was real or a put-on. From time to time I heard him speak without a single stammering sound, but when he was telling jokes he would stutter on the punch line, and it enhanced his comedy timing.

Everyone told Frisco stories. There was one about the time Frisco was offered a job in a café at a salary he didn't think was high enough. He was then living in a small cheap hotel, and the owners of the café kept calling him there, trying to make a deal. Joe wanted a thousand dollars a week and they were offering him five hundred. One day they called Joe and said they'd give him seven hundred and fifty. And Joe said "No, I won't work for that. I'm n-n-n-not that b-b-broke that I have to g-g-g-go to work for less than a th-thousand." And the fellow on the phone said, "Look Joe, why don't you come over to our office and talk about it?" And Frisco said, "Wha-wha-what? And get lo-lo-locked out of my room?"

As a part of Peter Lind Hayes' act at the Copacabana, he did a whole section as a tribute to Joe Frisco. Peter told some of the Frisco stories and got a lot of laughs. When I got back to Hollywood, I ran into Frisco at the Brown Derby. And he said to me, "Abe, did you see the k-k-k-kid at the Copacabana?" (By the "k-k-k-kid" he meant Peter Hayes.) I said, "Yeah, Joe, he was great." And Frisco said with a sad smile, "I hear he's d-d-d-doing a lot of m-m-m-my stuff." And I quickly said, "Joe, he tells a lot of stories about you. But he tells them as a tribute to you. You know Peter loves you, Joe." And Frisco nodded and said, "I know. When you l-l-l-love a guy, you d-d-do his act."

I didn't quote this to Peter for a while. One day I couldn't resist telling him. When I came to that punch line, Peter was convulsed with laughter. No one could ever resist laughing at a Frisco punch line.

After *The Dinah Shore Show,* my next assignment was to take over the Joan Davis radio show. Joan was an amazing lady. For a long time she had been a knockabout comic, playing a low-comedy clown. In films she always played the funny-looking friend of the heroine. So I was startled when I first met her in person; she was a poised and very attractive woman. There's a picture of Joan on my office wall, and people keep saying to me, "Who's that beautiful blonde?"

In those days comediennes were not supposed to be beautiful and poised. Of course, there were women playing elegant comedy on the legitimate stage and in movies — people like Carole Lombard, Irene Dunne and Jean Arthur — but when it came to vaudeville, nightclubs or radio, most of the female comics somehow tended to (or were driven to) turn themselves into broad knockabout clowns. They performed like male comics — but low male comics. Today there are many funny television shows that star women who make you laugh without trying to look ugly and without losing their femininity.

When I saw how attractive Joan was, I started to write material for her that was different from what she had been doing. It turned out to be very successful. John Crosby — who used to be a top radio critic and now is a successful novelist living in London — wrote a review of the show I was writing for Joan, and said, "Abe Burrows has done for Joan Davis what Flo Ziegfeld did for Fanny Brice." I was proud of that mainly because I thought of it as a tribute to Joan. I was very fond of her, and we were very close. She died in the fifties when she was still quite young. She was a fine actress and a good and dear friend.

It was while I was writing Joan's show that I stumbled into the next chapter of my show business life. I say "stumbled" — actually I was pushed. Up to this time I had been clinging to my amateur status as a performer; I only played at parties. I remember Georgie Jessel listening to my songs at a party and saying, "When the hell are you gonna become a professional?"

One day in the studio where we did the Joan Davis show, I finally was deflowered. I became a professional.

The Joan Davis show was broadcast from station KNX, which was the CBS outlet in Los Angeles. The programming chief at

KNX was a young fellow named Ernest Martin. (This was the same Ernest Martin who, with Cy Feuer, later produced my first Broadway show, *Guys and Dolls*.)

Ernie had heard my songs and chatter at parties and he thought I ought to be on the air myself. I grumbled that I was just as happy writing, and didn't plan to be a performer. Ernie insisted that I do an audition before a live audience and make a record he could play for the Big Brass at CBS. I kept saying I wasn't ready; I had never done this sort of thing except at parties. I had no desire to face an audience of strangers. Ernie kept after me and one night when the Joan Davis radio show was having a preview — we always tested the show with a live audience the night before we went on the air — Ernie and Joan tricked me.

At the end of the preview, I was sitting in the control room and I heard Joan talking to the audience. She thanked them for coming, and then I was startled to hear her say, "I have a treat in store for you. The man who writes my show is also an entertainer, and I would like him to do some of his songs for you." I sat there frozen. I watched them shove a piano out in the middle of the stage, I heard Joan shout, "Come out here, Abe," and I had no choice but to straighten my tie and go to the piano. I sang my songs and talked to the audience and frankly — to put it modestly — I was a smash hit.

CBS liked the recording and decided to put me on the air in a show of my own. They gave it the clever title of *The Abe Burrows Show*. It was friendly and relaxed. It consisted of me and an instrumental quartet headed by Milton De Lugg. That really was his name. He was and still is one of the best accordionists in the country.

The director was Carin. She was a big help. She knew my work and she was my most honest critic. (We have now been married for twenty-nine years. Carin has left show business, but she is still close to every project I do.)

As for what I was going to do on the show, I had a simple plan. I was going to talk about anything that would occur to me;

and I'd sing some of my songs and talk about others that I never did write. These had only a first line, which told it all. For instance, on my first show I had one that went "Oh, How We Danced on the Night We Were Wed, I Needed a Wife Like a Hole in the Head." And there was another one that started out, "If You Were the Only Girl in the World and I Were the Only Boy, Okay, But Right Now Let Me Alone." Neither of those songs could ever, or *should* ever, be finished.

My first show took place on Saturday night, July 26, 1947; I opened the show very modestly. I worked this way because I *was* modest, which is a euphemism for scared to death.

The announcer in a stentorian voice said, "The Columbia Broadcasting System and its affiliated stations present — Abe Burrows!" Then Abe Burrows came on — that was me — and said nervously, "Hello, I'm Burrows like he said." (This illiterate sentence remained my opening line as long as the show was on the air.) I went on to say, "I'm a singer — slightly different from the average ordinary singer in that I can't sing. But I'm gonna." After this dazzling start I went on to do my topical-type song. the kind of song guys write immediately after they read about some big event in the newspapers. This topical-type song was a song I wrote right after I read about the capture of the notorious Tokyo Rose:

> *I'll bet you're sorry now, Tokyo Rose,*
> *Sorry for what you done.*
> *I'll bet you're sorry that you went to work*
> *For that old rising sun.*
> *You stuck a knife into the U.S.A.*
> *You forgot what they learned you at U.C.L.A.*
> *I'll bet you're sorry now, Tokyo Rose,*
> *Sorry for what you,*
> *Sorry for what you done.*

Then I did a brave, unprecedented thing. Certainly a radio first. I described my looks. Of course the studio audience could see me in the flesh, but the radio audience had no idea what I looked like. They had seen many radio performers on the movie screen or in person, but I was a stranger to them.

So I bit the bullet and came right out and told them I was bald.

I lost my hair when I was twenty-four years old, which is why I have never minded being bald. I always was. To some guys, baldness is a sign of maturity or a loss of — if you'll pardon the expression — virility. They look in the mirror and begin to crack up. They are all wrong. Since when is lack of hair a sign of old age? Take a look at a baby. Nothing is younger than a baby. And nothing has less hair. As a matter of fact, I think it is the baby's baldness that gives it that youthful appearance.

For years I've dreamed about forming a group called the Society of Bald Eagles. We'd have members like Yul Brynner, Telly Savalas and other such skin-headed greats. I have a slogan for this organization: "Listen, America! We're not bald! You guys are hairy!"

Let's be serious. Scientific. Hair once served a very important purpose. It was protection. Before man evolved into his present messy state he was a wild, unclothed creature with tons of hair covering his body and his head. This hair protected him from the cold, the wind, the rain — all the lousy elements. But as Hart Schaffner & Marx came along and man learned to wear clothes, his need for hair disappeared and the hair went with it. The same sort of thing happened to long toes, which our ancestors used for climbing trees. And the tail. Those early creatures had tails. Today tails are out of style. They are unnecessary.

Now why is it that the guys who wear toupees don't wear fake tails?

As for me, I'm not displeased with the way I look. When I was on the air I told the people, "I have no hair. But to go with that, I have no mustache either. You see? No hair, and no mustache. It's a set." I remember talking about a new invention I'd been working on called STA-BALD. "STA-BALD is a preparation that prevents the growth of unsightly hair on the head."

I told those people who were desperate to have hair that "I've heard of a witch doctor out in the Pacific who does grow hair for people. Actually, what he does is shrink your head to fit the hair you've got."

My show was a casual little show and I enjoyed doing it. But I was a pretty busy fellow. When CBS decided to put me on the air, with my own show, Joan had ambivalent feelings. She was rooting for me to succeed, but I was still the head writer of her show and she didn't want me to abandon her. I was very fond of Joan and grateful to her for helping me to get on the air, and I promised that I would stick with her as long as possible. So I found myself doing two shows a week — writing and acting on my own show, and writing the Joan Davis show.

In August 1947 I got the phone call from my brother that I had been expecting and dreading. My mother had only a day or two to live. I flew to New York and joined my father, Selig and Shirley for a last visit with her. She was under heavy sedation; she looked at us but she couldn't talk to us anymore. She died, and after the funeral I flew back to Los Angeles. Back to my job of being funny.

On the plane I thought about Mama. She would probably have approved of my hurrying back to work. She was pleased with what I was doing. I wasn't the doctor that she had hoped I would be, but at least I was "something."

My mother was one of my favorite critics. I would usually call her after one of my radio shows. "Hello, Mama, did you like the show?" Her answer was always the same. "What could be wrong with it?" That's what I call sound, reliable criticism.

When *Duffy's Tavern* was broadcast from New York, she often sat in the studio audience. One time when Milton Berle was our guest star, Milton's mother happened to be sitting next to my mother. They were strangers to each other. Suddenly Berle was introduced and came onstage to loud applause. His mother then nudged my mother and whispered proudly, "That's my son." My mother's response was very simple. She pointed to the control room where I was sitting and said, "That's *my* son."

Mrs. Berle had no answer for this and Mama felt that she had won a big battle.

My father took Mama's death very hard. I would fly in to New York to visit him from time to time and I could see that he couldn't bear living without her. I remember one night I took him to dinner at the old Toots Shor restaurant, and we were joined by Jimmy Cannon, the talented sportswriter. During dinner my father kept talking to both of us about my mother. There was a moment when he left the table to go to the washroom and Cannon said to me, "Abe, I've been around but I've never seen a guy carry a torch like that."

When Dad came back to the table, he tried to be a bit cheerier; he talked about the old vaudeville days. But before we left he said one more thing about what life was like without my mother. It was a very simple statement of how a man feels when he's lost the wife he loved: "There's nobody to tell you what to do."

One day when I got back from a trip to New York, I found out that my little fifteen-minute show now had a sponsor, Listerine Toothpaste, but I was told that I had to be exclusive with them and give up the Joan Davis show. This time Joan wasn't worried. She was now feeling very secure about her own show; it was a hit and had several good writers. So she kissed me and wished me luck.

The next week I was invited to come to St. Louis to visit the Lambert Pharmaceutical Company, which made Listerine Toothpaste. I was to talk things over with the Brass and meet the toothpaste in person. Ernie Martin, as program chief of the radio station, made the trip with me. On the train, Ernie and I talked about my program and what I was going to do with it, but in addition to that, we talked about something else.

In a relaxed moment, while the train rattled along, Ernie asked me whether I had ever thought about doing something for the legitimate theater. I was startled and told him I thought that for me the theater was Outer Space. Well, he said that the theater was his goal and he told me (he sort of whispered it) that *he* was going to get out of radio fairly soon because he wanted to produce musicals for Broadway. And he wanted to do it with Cy Feuer as his partner. Cy was an excellent musician. He was conducting the Ford Symphony of the Air, and he had been the musical director at Republic Pictures.

Ernie said he thought I *was* ready to write for the theater, and I told him I felt that my funny stuff was okay for radio, but I didn't think people would pay theater prices to hear it. He didn't agree with me; he said I was too modest. I agreed with him and we changed the subject.

I was feeling pretty good. My show had a very loyal following and I had finally won my first trophy — a sponsor. Frank Stanton, then president of CBS, wrote me a letter of congratulation, saying that my little program had the biggest listening audience on CBS for Saturday night.

Abe Lastfogel, who was then president of the William Morris Agency, asked me to come to his office to discuss the deal with Listerine Toothpaste. This was the first time Mr. Lastfogel had invited me into his office and he treated me like a star. I began to feel a little bit like one, until suddenly a *real* star walked into the office. He pushed open the door and walked in without being announced. It was Al Jolson.

This was right after the huge success of *The Jolson Story*. It starred Larry Parks as Al, but when Larry seemed to be singing the songs in the picture, Jolson's voice was dubbed in. This was a big comeback for Al, whose career had slowed down for a while; he was in his sixties at the time. Now a large new audience discovered him. The critics raved and the New York *Times* actually did a piece about him on the editorial page. They welcomed Jolson's rebirth.

The moment I saw him, I stopped thinking of myself as a star. This guy *was* a *star*. He ignored me and started to talk to Lastfogel about some business matter. I stood there waiting to be introduced. Finally, Mr. Lastfogel was able to get a word in and said, "Al, this is Abe Burrows. We're very excited because he just got a sponsor for his radio show." Al turned and gave me a long look. I started saying things like "It's nice to meet you, Mr. Jolson." While I was babbling, he reached in his pocket and pulled out a newspaper clipping and said, "Hey, kid, look what the New York *Times* said about me yesterday." I read the clipping and gave it back to him and said, "That's wonderful." He put the clipping back in his pocket and went on talking to Mr. Lastfogel. I left. That was Jolson.

If he had a big ego and seemed conceited, everyone agreed that he had a right to be that way. Most people called him the greatest entertainer of all time. I know my father thought that, and in our house I grew up listening to every record Jolson ever made. When he was a star on the stage, I was too young to see him. The first time I ever saw him perform was in the original movie version of *The Jazz Singer*. But my father told me I had to see him in person to realize how great he was.

The first time I saw him work in person was when I was asked to perform at a benefit in Hollywood. The other people on the bill were Dinah Shore and Eddie Cantor. We three were sitting at a table waiting to go on, when the master of ceremonies said, "Ladies and gentlemen, we have a surprise guest. We didn't think he could make it but he's here and he has to leave early, so he asked if he could go on first. Here he is. Al Jolson!" The audience went wild.

Al walked on the stage and before starting to perform, he looked down at Eddie, Dinah and me sitting there. He chuckled and said, "You three can all go home." Cantor was furious and whispered to me, "What did we need *him* for?" Jolson started singing. His opening number was "California, Here I Come." That sure needed a lot of energy. You'd think a man in his sixties would start gently and then build up to the big number. Not Jolson. He did the song with the tempo and the vitality of a twenty-year-old. At the end of the song, while the audience was applauding madly, Al stood there trying to catch his breath. Cantor shouted from the floor, "Hey, Al, you want to lie down for a while?" Jolson answered, "Shut up, Cantor." And he went on and on and on. When it came time for the rest of us to enter-tain, we were just an anticlimax.

There were many, many stories about Jolson's monumental ego but they were the kind you tell with a smile. Like the time (about 1920) he appeared at a big benefit at Madison Square Garden. The act he had to follow was a pretty good singer named Enrico Caruso. Caruso gave a tremendous performance and received a wild ovation. Any performer who had to follow this act would have gone home. Not Jolson. As Caruso's ovation slowly died down, Jolson strolled on the stage and said to the audience, "You ain't heard nothing yet." I'm sure that Jolson knew he'd get a laugh when he said that line, but at the same time he kind of felt it was true. And I'm told he did get a bigger hand than Caruso.

The old-timers still sit around and talk about Jolson. About how great he was and how tough he was. He once knocked down Walter Winchell in Madison Square Garden because Win-chell had printed something about Ruby Keeler (then Jolson's wife) and Jolson didn't like it.

George Jessel told me about the time he made Jolson angry. He used something in his act that Jolson felt belonged to him and Jolson said he was "gonna knock Jessel's head off" the next time he saw him. And Jessel really was afraid. He kept avoiding Jolson. But one day he was sitting in the Friars Club when Jol-son walked in and spotted him. Jessel was trapped and terrified. Jolson walked slowly toward him like a gunfighter in a Western movie. Jessel was prepared for a beating. Finally, Jolson came close to Jessel. He looked at him for a moment and then said, "You're too cute to hit." And walked away.

Nobody could ever be really angry with Jessel. I found that out myself. I liked Jessel very much and he did encourage me to become a professional performer. But I remember one time — this was in 1948 — when Jessel was the master of ceremonies of a big bash (the trade papers called it a "Swelegant Shindig") that *Look* magazine held at the Beverly Hills Hotel to celebrate their famous Look Awards. Besides Jessel, the other entertainers were Danny Thomas, Dinah Shore, Eddie Cantor, Tony Martin and — Burrows.

The place was loaded with Hollywood celebrities. Photographers were running around taking pictures. One of the photographers was Hymie Fink, the most famous photographer in Hollywood. He came up to me and said, "Abe, I want to take your picture." I immediately put on a smile and said, "Shoot." He said, "I'd like to have you with Somebody." And then he said, "Stand next to that girl over there." He pointed to an extraordinarily beautiful girl who was about sixteen years old. I posed with her. It was Elizabeth Taylor. That picture never appeared anywhere.

When it came time to do the floor show, my encourager, Jessel, introduced me with a big buildup. I walked out a bit nervously. The Hollywood audience can be a tough one but it's very sharp. I relaxed quickly and after I did my stuff, I received a very good response. (Why must I be so modest? I got an ovation!) The crowd kept applauding and shouting, "More, more." I came back on the floor, acknowledging the applause and not unwilling to do another number, when Jessel quickly whispered in my ear, "Take a bow and tell them you're tired." I took the bow and went off laughing to myself. Jessel encouraged me as an amateur, but when I was a professional he treated me as he would any other pro. The show had to move along. As Jolson said, "Jessel was too cute to hit."

He's still cute and still a great wit. I've been at restaurant tables with wits like Groucho Marx, George Burns, Harry Ruby (a very witty songwriter), and other comedians. They spend hours just telling Jessel stories and repeating his weirdly funny lines. For instance, the way Jessel once described an uncle of his as being "half Jewish and half umbrella." I don't know exactly what that means, but I still laugh at it.

My father, still a rabid vaudeville fan, always liked the fact that I knew people like Jolson and Jessel. He loved show business and he was happy that I was part of it. And, of course, on the nights that I did my radio show, he was my most faithful listener.

One night in April 1948 I did a show devoted almost entirely to him. At the time, he was staying at an inn in Lakewood, New Jersey, and he listened to the program with some friends. That particular night I built my program around Dad and the songs he used to sing to me when I was a kid. Dear old vaudeville songs like "When You Were Sweet Sixteen," and "Me and My Gal." I told the audience how proud I was to be raised on songs like that.

I finished the show and went off the air saying, "Good night, Dad." He died a few minutes later. My brother and sister called me and once more I took that late plane to New York. Dad's friends at the inn told us that he had listened to my show and enjoyed it very much. Then he sat down and died quietly in his chair. The doctor told us his heart just stopped. So it turned out that the last time I spoke to my father I was talking into a microphone about three thousand miles away from him. I'm glad he heard me. And after his funeral I made the same sad trip I made after my mother died — back to California to be funny on the radio.

I was really torn on that trip. I kept thinking about Dad but at the same time I couldn't help thinking about what I was going to do on my next show. I felt guilty and — as often happened — I wondered how someone whose job it is to be funny can do it when he's in pain. Never mind that stuff about "the show must go on." That old saw originally meant that if you didn't put a show on, the customers would get their money back.

I have finally come to believe that people who have comedy minds often use humor as a defense against grief. I have attended wakes. Solemn affairs, but I have heard truly sad people sharing amusing and sometimes hilarious memories of their dead friend.

Edwin O'Connor, in his novel *The Last Hurrah*, wrote a scene that took place at a wake and it turned out to be one of the funniest parts of the book. I loved O'Connor. He was my dearest and closest friend, and when he died, I was shattered.

I was one of the pallbearers at Ed's funeral. The service took place in the Holy Cross Cathedral in Boston. After the service, the pallbearers had to carry the very heavy bronze casket down a long, steep flight of steps. Arthur Schlesinger, Jr., was the pallbearer in front of me, and as we staggered down those scary steps, griefstricken and nervous, I whispered to Arthur, "If O'Connor knew you and I were carrying him, he'd get up and walk." That was not meant to be frivolous; it was just another way of expressing my sadness. O'Connor would have understood.

Everyone shows his grief in different ways. People who write funny, think funny. Howard Lindsay often used that phrase when he tried to help an actor in a comedy scene. He'd say, "Think funny."

Damon Runyon was once standing in front of Lindy's restaurant in New York and somebody came up and told him of the death of one of Damon's friends. Damon's reaction was a sigh and "They're hitting all around us." Damon was deeply sorry that his friend had died, but he saw life as a form of war. Death was the enemy and was shooting at his buddies. People who are in the business of writing comedy always "think funny." No matter what sad things happen to them, they are still able to think funny and it gives them comfort.

I remember George Kaufman's reaction when he read about a friend of his who had just died. He said to me, "Abe, we all finally reach an age when our friends start to die." There's an example of "thinking funny" and yet it's more than just funny. Most of us think of ourselves as immortal.

And so when I went on the air three days after my father died, I realized I was getting a kind of comfort from the laughter of the audience. I know Dad would have gone along with me.

Chapter 6

My program continued doing well — at least the listeners and the critics liked it — but my sponsors were not too happy about the toothpaste sales. In radio the watchword was "love me, love my toothpaste." Or "my deodorant." Or "my powerful but gentle laxative." My listening audience was pretty large and very responsive, but they weren't crazy about the toothpaste. It seems that my fans were being naughty. While they were laughing at my jokes, they were sneering at my toothpaste.

I was in a shaky situation, but I went on doing my best on the air while the sponsor kept trying to figure out why the toothpaste wasn't selling. They finally came to a decision. It *couldn't* be the toothpaste so it had to be me.

This struck me as kind of funny. In the past I had been a bad salesman when it came to selling woven labels, maple syrup, wallpaper, ladies' knitwear and stocks. Now I could add toothpaste to the list.

Came a day in June 1948 when my sponsors and I reached a friendly agreement. They agreed to cancel my program and I agreed to stop using their toothpaste.

I tried to tell myself that this was not really an unfortunate happening. It might even have been a form of success. Look at it this way: After nine years of writing programs for other people, I finally get my own show. And then after one year (think of it, only *one year*) I lose my first sponsor! That's a mark of distinction, of sorts. Usually only real veterans lose their sponsors.

Once again I was At Liberty. It felt good to be free. A CBS executive called from the East and suggested that I come back and discuss the possibility of doing a half-hour show from New York, but I decided to hold off for a while. For years I'd been grinding out radio scripts like Little Link Sausages; now I wanted to try something new. The night spots wanted me in person.

My radio program had been reaching all the big cities. Big cities have big nightclubs, and big hotels with big dining rooms, and in Las Vegas, big casinos — all kinds of places people went to to avoid staying at home.

These offers were flattering but nervous-making. I thought of nightclub patrons as being altogether different from my friendly radio audience. They seemed to me to be tougher — hard-drinking and noisy. The big nightclub stars — Joe E. Lewis, Jimmy Durante, Milton Berle, Dean Martin and Jerry Lewis — were people who grew up in night spots. They knew all the tricks. They weren't afraid of hecklers and raucous audiences and they didn't mind occasionally using blue material. Blue is an elegant word meaning "don't bring your mother."

However, years of radio had conditioned me to keeping my stuff clean. I remember one time I was invited to a Friars Club roast in Hollywood. (A roast is a dinner in honor of some celebrity, during which his friends show their adoration by insulting him.) This particular roast was in honor of Abbott and Costello. I admired them but didn't know them and I wondered why I was invited. I was told that Abbott and Costello were big fans of my radio show and they would like me to come.

I sat on the dais listening to their friends insult them. These insults were generally funny but they were all blue, racy, adult, and mostly just plain filthy. When I finally was called on, I was really embarrassed. I stood up and spoke very apologetically. "I admire Abbott and Costello very much but I don't know them well enough to insult them. Besides, I can't match the jokes that have been told tonight. You see, I only work on radio, and when you're on radio, you can *do* shit but you can't say it." I got a big hand from the audience. That short speech accomplished two things. I had preserved my integrity and they liked the fact that I had presented them with a dirty word.

The nightclub people kept after me, but I was still going through a mental struggle. When I was twelve years old, I was a Boy Scout, and I think that when I perform I am still guided by a touch of Scout's Honor. Then I got an offer that changed my mind. It came from a nightclub in San Francisco. Tommy Harris, who ran a little spot called the House of Harris, sent me a wire which said he'd be "proud" to have me make my first nightclub appearance at his place. I liked the idea of a little spot, and besides, San Francisco appealed to me because of something that had happened a couple of months before this.

It started with a phone call from Herb Caen, the columnist of the San Francisco *Chronicle*. Herb told me that the San Francisco–Oakland Newspaper Guild was putting on a big benefit show in the Civic Auditorium on April 3. The stars were to be Danny Thomas, Janet Blair, Jane Russell, Lili St. Cyr, Connie Boswell and me. Me? I had never performed at any place as big as that (the Civic Auditorium held about twenty-five thousand people). Herb was very insistent and very persuasive. He said I had lots of fans in San Francisco and they all wanted to hear me. Then I suddenly had an out. I realized that April 3 was a Saturday night, my broadcast night. But that didn't bother him at all. He said they would fly us all up from Los Angeles — me, the quartet that accompanied me, and anybody else I wanted — and we could broadcast from the CBS station in San Francisco. "That's how bad we want you." Well, on that Saturday night, there I was doing my show in a strange city with a strange new audience, which, it turned out, was made up of the friendliest people in the world. On the way from the studio to that gigantic Civic Auditorium, I was beginning to feel at home.

When I arrived, the show had already started. Danny Thomas

was onstage and the sound of laughter and applause was deafening. It's impossible to describe the sound of twenty-five thousand people laughing in unison. That roar of laughter sounds like the roar at a bullfight. The whole auditorium was shaking, and so was I.

As I waited in the wings, somebody said to me, "They're great tonight, Abe. You'll kill 'em."

That phrase, "kill 'em," is typical of show-business talk. We speak in violent terms. When a comedian does well and gets a big audience response, he actually says, "I killed the people." "I fractured them." "I murdered them." "I laid them in the aisles." "They died laughing." "I was dynamite." If he doesn't do well, he says, "I died" or "I bombed." People say a funny line "triggers" a laugh. A guest appearance is called a "guest shot." Maybe comedy needs Gun Control.

Even the critics use phrases like "explosive comedy" or "rapid-fire repartee." Or "rapier wit." As I think of it, even that lovely word "hit" is a violent term. And "smash hit" is even stronger. That means we "bowled them over." Maybe it's because the audience, for a split second, is the adversary. The performer is outnumbered and he has to deal with this crowd with the few weapons he has.

When I finally heard Danny Thomas introduce me, I took a deep breath, stopped shaking, walked out onstage and killed the people.

On July 6, 1948, I put on my dinner jacket and opened at the House of Harris in San Francisco. Incidentally, in those days that dinner jacket was protocol. Today, the young comedians come on wearing sweaters, T-shirts, preshrunk jeans. Their clothes are often funnier than their jokes.

I had a good audience that night. A few friends came up from Los Angeles and the rest of the people all seemed to be fans of my radio show. They knew all my songs and they kept me onstage for a long time. Next morning I got pretty good reviews. The one that interested me the most was a review by Ted Friend in *Variety*. The key line was "Abe Burrows looks like a balding accountant but he grabs a lot of laughs." Well, I actually had been a balding accountant and then I became a balding writer and now I was a balding performer. I never became a very slick comedian. Some months later, when I played New York, Doug Watts reviewed me for *The New Yorker*. He evidently enjoyed my work, and he ended his review with something I liked very much: "His prevailing good humor and the feeling that he gives of being terribly embarrassed at having been caught on a stage reminded me strongly of Robert Benchley. That's practically the best thing I can say about any man."

As a performer, I remained an amateur. I got paid as a professional, but mentally I clung to my amateur status. I was a writer performing his own stuff in a sort of friendly, clumsy way. I guess it made me feel safer.

It was in San Francisco that I ran into my first heckler. He was drunk and obviously not enchanted by my performance. Most nightclub comedians use standard insults to put hecklers down. Witty stuff like "Hey mister, your garbage truck is double-parked outside." I took a different track. As this heckler kept making noise while I was singing and kept saying things the equivalent of "Shing 'Melancholy Baby,' " the audience got angry with him and tried to shut him up. I quieted things by saying something which came right from the heart. "Ladies and gentlemen, please don't insult this poor fellow. I'm very sentimental about him. This is my first nightclub appearance and this nice man is my first drunk. I'm gonna have him pressed in a book. A big iron book." The audience laughed and the drunk looked startled. He finally struggled to his feet and walked out. I must confess that I used this same ad-lib about twenty times during the rest of my nightclub tour and each time I "ad-libbed" it, the audience applauded my rapid, "spontaneous" wit.

I played San Francisco for four weeks. The House of Harris became sort of a homey living room where new friends dropped in and we had fun. Tommy Harris was very happy because the place was full every night, and I probably could have stayed on for the rest of my life. But in my fourth week there, I got an offer I wasn't supposed to refuse, although I felt like refusing it. It came from Ciro's in Los Angeles, a big, glamorous nightclub. One of those "where the stars go" places. I hated to leave the cozy atmosphere of the House of Harris but all of my advisers advised that I move toward the "big time." I had no choice. Now I was in the grip of what is called success.

My situation could best be described by a phrase that my wife coined some years later. In the sixties, we were invited to the World's Fair in New York. Visiting a world's fair is a tough chore for anybody, but for me it was even tougher. I was an invited celebrity, so it was really a command performance. When Carin and I arrived, a group of friendly World's Fair officials took us to practically every single exhibit in the place. We had no choice. We were driven for miles and walked for miles and toward the end of the day, when we were staggering with fatigue, Carin said to me, "I feel that we're being dragged around on a red carpet."

My San Francisco reviews and publicity became my red carpet and I was dragged around on it for a long time.

As I was getting ready for opening in Ciro's I suffered a recurrence of stage fright or nightclub fright. But everyone told me the house was going to be full of my friends and they all loved me and it would be a great opening.

Opening night when I was in my dressing room getting into my tuxedo (eventually I got sick of that tuxedo; to me it became a symbol of drudgery, like overalls to a farmhand), telegrams came pouring in from my friends. I was flooded with good wishes. I remember a busboy coming in with a huge beautiful bouquet from Greer Garson. It looked like a bridal bouquet. It might have been appropriate because I felt as though I were being married forever to nightclubs.

When I walked out on the floor, I looked around the room and it was true that my friends had shown up. The place was jammed with practically everyone I knew in Hollywood. They all had heard me at the piano at parties and they were all rooting for me madly. And that was the problem. My friends were more nervous than I was. As I started to do my act, they were rooting for me to get laughs but they were too nervous to laugh themselves.

Danny Kaye and his wife, Sylvia, were sitting at a table about four feet from me. They looked tense, and as I was working, Danny whispered to me and told me to switch to certain numbers of mine that he thought I should do. Danny, a dear friend, was trying to help.

The only good reactions came from the few people who had never caught my act before. After a while everyone sort of relaxed, and I did a few things that were new to my friends and I got through the performance without really dying. But it was close. About the toughest forty minutes I ever lived.

Afterward, my friends left to go to a party that was being given in my honor at the home of my friend Harry Kurnitz. I was to join them later because I had a second show to do that night. I told Carin, who had been a very nervous part of my audience, to go along to the party and I would come right after my late show.

Well, the second show I did at eleven o'clock was a different experience. The place was full of strangers who had not seen me work before, and the response I got was as big as I had become used to in San Francisco.

This same "nervous friends" phenomenon happens in the theater on opening night. The theater is packed with friends of the actors, people who have seen the show out of town, relatives of the author, and backers of the show. And they are frequently a very bad audience because of their personal involvement. Once a friend of mine said to me after a first act, "I saw Walter Kerr laughing his head off." And I answered, "What were you doing while he was laughing?"

After a while I began to enjoy myself at Ciro's. I relaxed. But the audience was never a typically normal audience. A lot of celebrities came, and the people spent as much time staring at the celebrities as they did in listening to me. Following my run at Ciro's, I was booked into a place in Las Vegas, El Rancho

Vegas, but before I went there, I had an exciting experience in Hollywood. I was asked to appear as a guest on Bing Crosby's radio show.

I'll always be happy that I once knew Bing Crosby. I wasn't one of his close friends, but I worked with him many times, and when I was with him, Bing made me *feel* like one of his close friends.

When you're in any branch of show business, people will always ask you questions about various big stars as though you knew them all personally. "What kind of a guy is Cary Grant?" "What is Barbra Streisand *really* like?" "Is Dustin Hoffman shorter than Al Pacino?" But when they ask you, "What kind of man is Bing Crosby?" they ask it in a curious "I-really-want-to-know" manner. There was something about Bing's casual style, his seeming ease and control, that made them realize there was something there besides what they saw on the screen.

He acted casual but behind it all was a sort of steely competence. One time in an interview I was asked, "What kind of man is Bing Crosby?" And I answered that he was warm, enjoyable, amusing, but if he should ever decide to become president of General Motors, he could swing that, too.

I did several guest shots on Bing's show, and one of them took place on the opening of a new series he was doing for a new sponsor, the Philco Dealers. I arrived early at the studio and was startled to see a great big busy-looking banner covering the entire back wall. There, in great big letters of gold on a blue background it said PHILCO DEALERS WELCOME BING CROSBY, et cetera, et cetera. It was huge and eye-catching, but also pretty distracting. I arrived before Bing and spoke to John Scott Trotter, his musical director. He and I stared at the thing and I said, "You think Bing is gonna like that?" John just shrugged and smiled a secret, knowing smile. Then Bing arrived. He crossed the studio toward us, saying hello to people on the show. Then he passed one of the studio pages, and as he went by him he pointed to the banner and said quietly, "Take that down," and kept walking over to John and me. That's all he said. No complaint. No shouting. Just, "Take that down." Within five minutes the banner had gone. He acted just the way he sang. Cool and easy. He was that way with his fans.

I remember once in the fifties he called me and asked me to go see a movie with him on Wilshire Boulevard. I agreed but I was worried. I thought, "What is it going to be like, going to an ordinary movie with Bing Crosby?" I met him in front of the theater and I was amazed by what happened or rather what didn't happen. I thought we'd be mobbed by hundreds of autograph hunters and sightseers. Instead, people stood back and just watched Bing. They were quiet and respectful. If it had been Bob Hope, he'd have been mobbed by loving fans. But not Bing. The people looked at him with love and admiration but they didn't come too close.

One time I was walking with him outside of Paramount Studios and he was telling me a story when a kid came running up waving an autograph book, and before the kid could say anything, Bing said quietly and gently, "You don't want that," and he kept walking and talking with me. The kid wasn't angry; he just stood smiling and watched us walk away.

I once spent five interesting days with Bing on an ocean liner. This was in 1953. Carin and I had flown to London for the opening of the London company of *Guys and Dolls*. The show was a big hit there; we were feeling good and we decided not to rush back to New York on a plane. We booked passage on the beautiful *Liberté* of the French Line. Neither of us had ever sailed the Atlantic before. Carin was raised in Seattle and her voyages were limited to the ferry that crossed Puget Sound. My sailing experience consisted of an occasional voyage on the Staten Island Ferry and once in a while, a long trip on the Hudson River Day Line, to Bear Mountain for picnics.

So when we boarded this great ship we were excited, and a few moments later we became even more more excited when we ran into Crosby. Bing and his son Lindsay — he was fifteen, Bing's youngest — were coming back from a European trip.

Carin and I hurried to finish our chores. Unpacking, noticing that the stateroom was smaller than the photograph we had seen (we loved it anyway), trying to open the portholes (they wouldn't budge), rushing down to the dining room to reserve a table (something you had to do quickly or you'd get stuck with the wrong people for five days and fifteen meals). We arranged to sit with Bing and Lindsay for the whole trip.

Then we just strolled on the deck like people we had seen in the movies. And as we strolled I began to think about the Ship's Gala. Friends in London had told me about the tradition of the Ship's Gala, which is a big party on the last night of the voyage. This one was especially important to the crew because it was held for the benefit of the Sailors' Fund. Any performer who happens to be on the ship is asked to appear in the show. My friends warned me to be prepared.

Many performers feel a need to complain a bit when they are asked to do this. They grumble that they are on the ship for "a rest," or say, "I don't have any accompanist with me," or make some other lame excuse. However, all of us admit that we'd feel terrible if we weren't asked, and one hour after we sailed I started worrying. The Gala was four days off but I was already wondering whether they'd want me to perform. An hour later, the ship's purser, a pleasant young Frenchman, came to me on the deck and asked if I would honor them by being the master of ceremonies. I was relieved and delighted, but I quietly, almost shyly, said, "Well, I guess I can if you want me to." Then the purser said, "I know you're a friend of Mr. Crosby's. Do you suppose he would do something in the show?" He evidently was nervous about approaching Bing directly. I knew that part of his eagerness to have me as the MC was my connection with Bing, but that didn't trouble me. I was eager to be included. I agreed to talk to Bing about it.

That night I casually asked Bing if he would come on the show and sing a couple of songs. He looked at me with a very cool look and said, "No way. I'm on this ship to take it easy." I told him it was for the benefit of the sailors and that I was going to be the MC. He just shook his head. He said to me, "You're like Bob Hope. He'll go anywhere where there's a benefit. I'll come to the Gala but only as a member of the audience." I didn't press him, although I began to feel depressed. I couldn't imagine performing at a show while Bing Crosby is sitting at a table and just watching.

I decided I wouldn't let this spoil our trip. We didn't talk about the Gala again, and we all had a very pleasant time. Crosby was relaxed and charming company. Carin and I and Bing and Lindsay (we called him Linnie) took all our meals together, and what meals they were. It's the last time I remember getting all the caviar I could possibly stuff down. On the *Liberté,* caviar was considered an ordinary part of the menu; all you had to do was ask for it. Of course, if you were a celebrity or a friend of that celebrity, you got a lot more of it.

We shared our table with one other couple. They were from California and Bing knew them slightly. One thing I remember about the man was the unusual tie he wore with his dinner jacket. In those days passengers dressed for dinner every night except the first night out. However, instead of the conventional black bow tie this man wore a long black four-in-hand. He continually stroked it, as though he were very pleased with it and was waiting for some comment. The first time I saw that tie I whispered to Bing, "I never saw anybody wear a four-in-hand with a tux." Bing whispered back to me, "Don't say anything. Don't ask him about that tie because what he'll say is 'Where have you been? This is the new In thing.' " For the rest of the trip we never mentioned the tie and the poor guy just sat there stroking it and waiting for comment.

As we neared the night of the Gala, I began to get more and more nervous. The purser had corralled one more performer besides me. The great Ruth Draper, who was famous for her one-woman show, was on the ship. Miss Draper had agreed to do a few of her fantastic sketches. So the entire show would consist of Ruth Draper and me, with Bing Crosby sitting out front enjoying himself.

The day before the Gala I was walking on the deck thinking

117

and worrying when Linnie Crosby came up to join me. His manner seemed very furtive and he quickly whispered to me, "Abe, I know you've been worried but it's going to be all right. He's just teasing you. He's going to do the show. Don't tell him I told you." And he fled before I could say anything. I'll always be grateful to Linnie for that.

About an hour later Bing came over to me and said, "I decided to do that dumb thing with you. I don't want you making a fool of yourself all alone."

I wasn't going to squeal on Linnie and I put on a very surprised and grateful act. "Hey Bing, that's great. Makes me feel a lot better." He said, "Forget it. Let's get that piano player from the ship's band and we'll rehearse tomorrow afternoon." Now that he was going on, he became completely professional. And he was damned well going to rehearse.

I went to my cabin and wrote a song for us to do together, a parody of "The Sunny Side of the Street." It was based on the fact that for days the ship had sailed in fog. Very little sunshine. The name of the captain of the *Liberté* was Commodore LeVecque, which fortunately rhymed with "deck." That led me to "Please, dear Commodore LeVecque, where's the sunny side of the deck?"

The next day we all met in the lounge. Bing, Carin, Linnie, the purser and the pianist. Bing liked the song I had written, and when we finished singing it together he said, "Burrows, if the ship's foghorn ever busted, we'd always have you."

He ran through the songs he was going to do, including one of my favorites, "When the World Was Young," the lovely song that starts out "Ah, the apple trees . . ." We were all having a good time when a strange thing happened.

Young Linnie was also a pretty good singer. He had just made a hit record in London. The purser suddenly remembered this and he said, "Maybe young Mr. Crosby should sing something at our Gala." Bing said, "Great idea." I saw Linnie grow pale. He was only fifteen and had never performed before a live audience. And I'm sure he wasn't wild about performing with his father watching. He shook his head shyly and said he'd rather not do it. Bing then said something like "Aw c'mon, Linnie, it'll be fun." Lindsay Crosby just shook his head. Bing began to kid him and then started to press him. The boy kept shaking his head. Suddenly the atmosphere began to get tense. Then I opened my mouth and started to say something like "Bing, if Lindsay really doesn't want to, maybe . . ." I stopped talking when Bing said sharply to his son, "Linnie, you're going to do that song. If you don't, you can't come to the Gala and you'll spend the night by yourself in your cabin." He wasn't teasing now. He sounded like a tough military officer. Lindsay responded like a tough private. "Okay, then I *won't* come to the Gala." And he ran out of the lounge. The rest of us were all quiet for a moment. Carin and I looked at each other. She was unhappy about this because she had grown very fond of Lindsay; but we both knew there was nothing we could or should do. Bing looked thoughtful for a moment and then he went on rehearsing.

The next night we performed at the Gala and it went very well. Carin was watching the show from a table in back of the room when she suddenly heard a whispered "Pssst." She turned around and there was Lindsay, crouching behind her chair. He had sneaked in to see part of the show. He hid behind Carin for a while, and then just before the show ended he quickly sneaked out. The next day Bing and Lindsay were strolling the deck together as though the whole thing hadn't happened. Bing loved his sons but he had definite standards of discipline for himself and for the people he loved.

He was someone we all thought would go on forever, and when he died it seemed to shock the whole country. There have been many articles and TV programs about him since he died; his many friends go on the air and talk about him, and true to form they mostly tell funny anecdotes. Bing had died of a heart attack as he finished a golf match, and a friend of his said, "Well, Bing died on a golf course, but not till he finished the eighteenth hole. He would have liked that." I miss him.

Chapter 7

While I was doing my guest shots with Crosby, I kept working in nightclubs. At the end of my first show with him, he told the audience that I was on my way to appear at El Rancho Vegas in Las Vegas and he wished me "lots and lots of luck." Somehow or other the tone of his voice suggested that I would need it. He was right.

Las Vegas is usually a beautiful "Fun-in-the-Sun" resort, but it was January when I got there and we were snowed in. It *does* snow in the desert. There was no golf or swimming or topless sunbathing. The guests had little to do except gamble, which didn't upset the proprietors of the place.

For the performer, nightclubs in Las Vegas are different from most other nightclubs. First of all, you have to keep your act short, really short. The management feels that if the entertainment goes on too long, it deprives the customers of the fun of losing their money in the gambling room.

Then there's a hazard in working there. The management lets performers have chips on credit. They just charge them against your salary, which is why a good many (or many good) performers go home broke. I didn't lose much because my salary wasn't much. (This was before the million-dollar salaries they toss around at Las Vegas today.) The temptation to gamble was always there. At El Rancho Vegas the door that led to the stage was cleverly located in the gambling room. Right next to the door was a large crap table. While a performer was standing there nervously waiting to go on, he found it hard to resist the dice that were rolling under his nose. I certainly couldn't resist it. However, the only time I won any money at that particular crap table, I wasn't there. I had started to roll the dice when I heard the MC introduce me and I had to rush onto the stage. The proprietor of the hotel was standing there and said he would handle my dice for me while I was gone. When I finished my act and came back, he handed me $600 in chips that he had won for me. I didn't hold on to this for very long.

Most performers gamble and most of them lose. The late Chico Marx, Groucho's piano-playing brother, was a legend in Las Vegas. While I was at El Rancho, he was performing at the Flamingo Hotel nearby. Chico was a charming, talented man but an addictive gambler. After only one week at the Flamingo, he was no longer allowed to gamble there because his credit had run out — he had gone through three weeks' salary.

The next night he dropped in at my hotel, El Rancho, and gambled there on credit. He lost a bundle before they found out that he had used up his credit at the Flamingo. As I heard the story later, Chico had to play out his engagement at the Flamingo without getting a cent and then he agreed to settle up with El Rancho by playing two weeks in the fall for practically nothing.

Toward the end of my run, my agent called and told me that my next stop would be Minneapolis. I never expected that. To a New Yorker, Minneapolis is strange territory. But my agent swore that *they* had asked for *me*. I had a lot of fans there because of my radio show.

Groucho Marx once showed me a postcard I had written to him from Las Vegas. I don't remember writing it, but he kept it because he liked it. It said, "From here I go to Minneapolis. I *always* spend my Februarys in Minneapolis."

I went back to Hollywood just before leaving for Minnesota,

and ran into Jimmy Durante. I told him where I was going and he said with alarm, "Mindianapolis?" That's the way he pronounced it. "Don't go there, Abe. The last time I played there I died. Abe, you know that thing I do while I'm singing. I say to the audience, 'If I go down on one knee, Jolson is finished!' Abe, that was always a big laugh, but when I did it in Mindianapolis, I got nothing. In Mindianapolis they never *heard* of Jolson."

I liked Minneapolis very much. I played the Flame Room of the Hotel Radisson (they told me that Peggy Lee had once been a waitress there). It was a lovely place. Yes, the weather *was* cold. When I got off the train, the sun was shining and I said to the cabdriver who took me to the hotel, "What a nice day!" And he answered, "It sure is. The sun is shining and it's only eighteen below."

Having just come from Hollywood, I wasn't dressed for eighteen below. After I checked into the hotel, I went out and bought myself some heavy, long, woolly underwear and a lumberman's cap with big earlaps. I felt nice and cozy for the rest of my stay. And I wasn't bothered by the fact that when I walked around the hotel lobby all bundled up, most of the other men were dressed exactly like New Yorkers on Madison Avenue on a mild day. I stuck to my warm outfit even though I heard some people say I looked like one of the local farmers.

Of course, I took off my earlaps when I got into my dinner jacket and went out on the floor of the Flame Room. There, the audience kept me warm. Besides my dear wife, my beloved family and a few fanatical friends, the most responsive audience I have ever faced was the one in Minneapolis. The people were generous, sharp and knowledgeable. They appreciated my satire, and they made this dyed-in-the-wool, somewhat prejudiced and provincial New Yorker lose his fear of the Middle West.

From there I flew happily to Chicago — to the elegant Mayfair Room of the Hotel Blackstone, a beautiful room with a marvelous audience. I found out later that the owner of the hotel, Mr. Kirkeby, was very surprised that I did so well there. He had told several of his friends that he didn't care for my humor at all,

122

but he was talked into booking me. When he saw that I was a hit, he was pleased but still puzzled.

One of the most pleasant features of the Mayfair Room was the maitre d', the legendary Emile, a Swiss. He was unusually skillful, elegant and very kind. Many friends of mine who grew up in the Chicago area have told me that they knew Emile and had loved him since they were teenagers. A good maitre d' can be a great help to a performer. He often sets the style of the room, keeps the audience orderly and relaxed, and bars the drunks.

Emile liked my material and was very supportive. He would phone me in my room and tell me what kind of an audience I was about to have that night, and he'd alert me when somebody special was expected. One night he sounded excited. Henry Wallace was coming in. And he was bringing some friends. This was in 1948, when Wallace was running for President as an Independent. The Democratic candidate was Harry Truman, who, all the wiseacres predicted, was going to be badly beaten by Republican Thomas Dewey.

I was flattered that Henry Wallace, who didn't seem to be a nightclub fan, was taking time from his shaky campaign to come and hear me. I wondered what kind of reaction a man like him would have. When I came down to the Mayfair Room ready to go on, Emile whispered to me, "He's over there on the side with a party of eight — and they're all drinking milk." Nightclubs don't usually do a milk business. So it was interesting to see this group sitting there swigging milk (I think one of them was downing club soda) while everyone else in the room was happily drinking booze.

When I started my performance I could see Wallace and his friends watching me intently. They seemed to enjoy what I was doing but they weren't falling on the floor with laughter. Later, I was invited to the table to meet Mr. Wallace. Although he was very pleasant and told me that he enjoyed my performance, I had a feeling he was just being polite. He was a very serious man and I imagine that to him comedy was just a form of frivolity.

123

In the fall of 1948 I found myself with only two more dates left in my tour and I wasn't unhappy about that; by this time, even though the audiences were friendly, I was beginning to tire of nightclubs. This may shock the pros, but frankly I only liked performing when I felt like performing. The great night-club stars are great stars because to them performing is the breath of life. They can't wait to get on; it's as though the audience gives them a nightly blood transfusion. I was not a compulsive performer; and I often felt as though I were *giving* blood, not receiving it.

Another thing bothering me was the fact that while I played in nightclubs I didn't write. Not a line. It was the very thing Bob Benchley had warned me against. For the most part, when I went on I stuck to old material that I felt was surefire. The one slightly creative thing I did was occasionally ad-lib a few lines while I was performing. Cole Porter once told me that there was a period in his life — it lasted about two years — when he did nothing but entertain at parties with his songs. During that time, he never wrote a new line.

My last nightclub dates were the Park Plaza in St. Louis and Le Directoire in New York. St. Louis is a basically friendly town (they hate to have you call it "St. Louie" the same way that San Francisco people don't like the word "Frisco"). I enjoyed myself for the most part, even though the room I played in had formerly been a swimming pool and lots of times I felt submerged. I remember one night when a group of geologists from Oklahoma were in the audience. They were in St. Louis for a convention and they were doing a lot of drinking. While I was performing they made a lot of noise. I happened to be talking about my days in good old Brooklyn. They began to shout, "Say something about Oklahoma!" As they kept on with that "Say something about Oklahoma," I finally held up my hand and said in my best Brooklyn accent, "Fellas, I love Oklahoma. I seen the show three times." That puzzled them and shut them up.

Finally, I got to New York. Le Directoire was a new nightclub

124

on West Fifty-eighth Street that had formerly been called Café Society Uptown. It had been taken over by Herbert Jacoby, who also owned the Blue Angel. It had opened just two weeks before I got there. The club's first act was a blockbuster — Kay Thompson and the Williams Brothers. The youngest of those brothers was Andy. Then came a wonderful French singing group, Les Compagnons de Chanson. And now Abe Burrows.

It was an elegant joint which had been decorated by an elegant decorator, William Pahlmann (who later decorated the apartment in which I am writing this stuff on a beautiful dining room table he dug up somewhere).

Naturally, I couldn't resist kidding the posh style of Le Directoire. When I came on, I would say to the audience, "Welcome to The Directoire or rather *The* Le Directoire or rather . . . er . . . er Le The Directoire." I also had a lot of fun with the stage itself, which was a platform that folded up against the back wall like a Murphy bed. When the entertainment started, the stage would come down very slowly. I began to come out a bit early so that I could ad-lib while it was gradually creaking to the floor. This became a permanent part of my act. One time the stage actually got stuck halfway down. I stood there begging it to please come down so I could go to work, and the audience was hysterical. Nothing I could say after could top that. I tried to get the management to arrange for the stage to get stuck every night, but they didn't think much of the idea.

I enjoyed working there. A lot of my New York friends came to see me and I had a very good run, except for one night. Election night. Harry S. Truman versus Thomas E. Dewey. That night during my second show the election returns were coming in. The word spread through the room. I was onstage and I didn't know what was happening, but I suddenly felt that the atmosphere had turned very chilly. For a moment I thought it was my fault, but I soon found out that the fault was Harry Truman's. Le Directoire was a lush, expensive nightclub and most of our customers were Dewey voters. They had arrived in a happy mood, all of them ready to celebrate Tom Dewey's election by a landslide. But through some sort of osmosis the word began to spread throughout the room: Harry Truman is winning! The audience gradually got quieter and quieter. That night I kept my act very short and got off quickly.

Truman's big win was a big loss for the big spenders, and my last two weeks at Le Directoire were a big loss for the management. I finally finished there and went back to California for a long rest. I really needed that rest because suddenly interesting things began to happen. I got lucky.

Life in show business is cyclical (sometimes that should be spelled sicklical). In 1949 and 1950 I rode a pretty good cycle.

Early in 1949 I signed what *Variety* called "an exclusive seven-year, four-way contract with CBS." The "four-way" part of the contract meant I would be a performer, producer, director and writer. Of course, if I flopped, the "seven-year" contract would become a no-year contract.

I joined a new CBS radio panel show called *This Is Broadway*, which later became the hit Sunday-night TV show *This Is Show Business*. I costarred with two fellows named George Kaufman and Clifton Fadiman. And while I was doing this, I started a new weekly radio program of my own, a half-hour show that went on at nine in the evening and was called *Breakfast with Burrows* (*He Gets Up Late*).

I also started a TV show called *The Abe Burrows Almanac*. My radio show turned out not to do too well, and CBS decided to drop it and star me in *Almanac* because I had a pretty good following on *This Is Show Business*.

I also had joined *We Take Your Word*, that TV panel show about the derivations of words.

Then *The Abe Burrows Almanac* was dropped and I was assigned to write and produce a TV show that originated from the Stork Club. The show was cleverly titled *The Stork Club*. It starred Peter Lind Hayes and Mary Healy and the owner of the club, Sherman Billingsley. The director was Yul Brynner. It was a half-hour show, *five* days a week.

And! While I was doing the *Stork Club* show and *This Is Show Business* and *We Take Your Word,* I eventually started to work on the libretto of a musical that was going to be called *Guys and Dolls.*

This crazy schedule makes a fellow think of that old saw "If you want something done well, give it to the busiest guy in the place." As I think of it, that's kind of a dumb saw because if the Busiest-Guy-in-the-Place messes up that extra chore, he usually says, "Why didn't you give that job to somebody else; I've only got two hands."

I found myself enjoying all of this activity. Most of it was a lot of fun, especially *This Is Show Business.* It was the first network panel show on TV and we had an interesting group. George Kaufman and I were the permanent members of the panel, Clifton Fadiman was the moderator, and we invited a woman guest panelist each week.

The producer, the man who dreamed it up and brought us all together, was Irving Mansfield, a bright, friendly and very persuasive guy. He had even persuaded a beautiful girl to marry him. Her name was Jackie Susann. In those days she was known just as "Irving's wife." Later, after she published her first novel, *The Valley of the Dolls,* Irving was happy to be known as "Jacqueline Susann's husband."

This Is Show Business was a tremendous success, even though it was built on a shaky premise. Every Sunday night various performers would appear on the show: singers, dancers, comics, jugglers, acrobats, magicians, animal acts. Some of them were famous and some were justifiably unknown. They all had to bring in so-called problems, which they submitted to our panel of so-called show-business experts. The problems were earthshaking. Things like "Should I study to be a classical virtuoso instead of a jazz pianist?" or "What can I do about stage fright?" or "Should I give up tap dancing and study with Martha Graham?" They would come on the stage, hit us with

127

these problems, and then go into their acts while we, the wise members of the panel, mulled over our answers, which were usually no help whatsoever.

I remember the way Arlene Francis, one of our favorite guest panelists, handled a rather interesting problem. Arlene was a very good legitimate actress, but she also knew how to get a laugh. One night one of our guest entertainers was Joan Diener, a beautiful singer who later starred in *Kismet* and *Man of La Mancha*. Joan had a great figure and that night she wore a low-cut gown that didn't hide much of it. Her problem — which she told to Arlene Francis on the air — was "Should I keep doing musical comedy or should I strive for an operatic career?" Arlene stared at Joan's décolletage for about fifteen seconds and then said, "The way I see it from here, you have *two* problems." It was the biggest laugh we ever got. Kaufman and I kept the laugh going by getting up and pretending to leave the stage in outrage.

I can't imagine how Irving Mansfield ever got Kaufman to do this show. Clifton Fadiman, the distinguished literary critic, took a good deal of persuasion, but at least in radio he had been the well-known moderator of *Information Please*. But George Kaufman?

This was the Kaufman of Kaufman and Hart, of Kaufman and Connelly, of Kaufman and Ferber. In the theater the only "stars" are usually actors. Writers and directors are not often the biggies who are known to the general public. But Kaufman was special. There was something about George that made people write and talk about him. He was widely quoted. His name was synonymous with Theater. People who didn't know him spoke of him with reverence, and the people who knew him well seemed to feel the same reverence. Reverence is a weak word here. They were mostly scared.

I didn't believe George would do *This Is Show Business*. But he did, and he loved doing it. He was also a sensation. I slowly realized that buried inside this brilliant, dignified, respected playwright-director was a good-sized chunk of ham. I confirmed this one Sunday evening when we were backstage at the TV theater waiting to be introduced to the audience. I saw Kaufman slip behind a piece of scenery and ruffle up his hair. He made it look kind of wild and funny. The great GSK was deliberately giving himself a comical look.

Every week I would do the "warm-up." When an audience comes into a radio or television studio, it is generally a bit tense; it is distracted by the cameras, the lights and the other paraphernalia. Someone usually comes on to warm them up so they will relax and laugh at all the jokes, funny or not. This studio-audience laughter somehow seems to make the people watching at home laugh, too. Laughter is generally a shared experience. I remember the many times I used to watch movies in a projection room when I was all by myself. No matter how funny the picture was, I found it difficult to laugh in that empty room. It's almost embarrassing to laugh aloud by yourself. When the people at home hear that studio-audience laugh, they feel free to join it. And if there is one person listening all alone, that laugh is a comforting sound. These days they use laugh tracks for shows that don't even have studio audiences. Some of them overdo this canned laughter and put the laughs in unfunny places; but basically the idea of helping the home audience laugh is not a bad one.

Mostly warm-ups are done by announcers whose warm-up material goes back to the days of Marconi. If a warm-up joke works, you stick to it. These announcers had such goodies as "Folks, we want you all to relax and have a real good time. Don't be afraid to laugh. Relax! All of you gentlemen, sit back and loosen your ties and belts . . . and ladies, do the best you can." That one gets a big yock. Another favorite has the announcer asking in a sincere voice, "Is there someone here from Newark?" If some poor sucker raises his hand and says, "I'm from Newark," the announcer says, "There's a bus leaving in ten minutes." Big laugh.

I didn't do any such jokes. I would get off a few mild funnies and then I would get down to the nitty-gritty. I would say,

129

"Folks, a lot of guys come out in front of the audience and ask you to laugh at the jokes. They get down on their knees and *beg* you nice people to laugh. Well, we don't do that here. We want you to feel free. If you don't feel like laughing, please don't laugh. And don't be troubled by the fact that none of us will ever speak to you again!"

I never changed this warm-up. I did the same routine week after week. Kaufman would sit there on the stage trying his best to look amused, although I know it was painful for him. A small smile on the outside and suffering on the inside. Then one week I had the flu. Who did the warm-up? George S. Kaufman. The producer told me Kaufman had *offered* to do it.

He went out on the stage and told the audience that I was ill but he would try to duplicate what I would have said had I been there. And then he proceeded to do my warm-up word for word. He had been sitting there for all those weeks listening, and the tired lines were burned in his brain.

George and I worked very well together on the panel. Some weeks I would be the Bad Boy and I would give flip answers to the problems, and George would reprove me on the air as though he were a stern father. Other times he would be the Bad Boy. One time he got into trouble in that role. It was Christmas Eve and one of the guests wished George a Merry Christmas. And Kaufman said, "Thank you. I'm happy it's Christmas because that means that next week they finally will stop singing 'Silent Night' over and over on the air." The network received tons of mail condemning this "blasphemy." Kaufman had to apologize. And the public loved him again.

George Kaufman wasn't one of your hail-fellows-well-met. I found that out during World War II. He and I were involved with a committee that was putting on shows for soldiers in camps. I was really excited about being in the same room with him. I was just a young radio writer and he was George S. Kaufman. I actually didn't get to speak to him until after we left the meeting. We happened to be waiting for the elevator together.

130

He said nothing. I finally nervously blurted out something stilted like "It's a great honor to have met you, Mr. Kaufman." He gave me a long look and then he said, "I'm sorry you didn't know me when I was good." I was shocked. George Kaufman was saying that he was all washed up. I later realized that George considered himself washed up any year he didn't have a show on Broadway.

The next week we had to go to Camp Shanks, which was a post of embarkation in upstate New York. Kaufman and I had been asked to help with a show the soldiers were putting on. We were driven there in a station wagon by a sergeant who drove like a hot rodder. George was extremely nervous in automobiles, especially when they were going fast, and this sergeant was hitting eighty. As we raced up the West Side Highway toward the George Washington Bridge, George leaned forward, tapped the sergeant on the shoulder, and said, "Sergeant, don't cross that bridge until we come to it." That was pure Kaufman.

George Kaufman died in 1961 but his name still fascinates people. I have spent hours telling Kaufman stories to some of his biographers. Every year I get letters from college students who are doing term papers or Ph.D. theses which in some way involve him. The letters usually say things like "Dear Mr. Burrows. I am doing my thesis on the Origin, Growth, Development and Sociological Effect of the American Musical Comedy on an Industrial Society. Would you please fill out the enclosed questionnaire and return it as soon as possible."

The questionnaire usually asks about fifteen strange questions. A sampling: "What do you consider the twenty most significant musical comedies?" "What is it that makes them the most significant?" "What meaningful effect, if any, did the work of George S. Kaufman have on them, if any?" "In terms of your own work, when Mr. Kaufman became the director of *Guys and Dolls,* to what extent did he influence your libretto, if at all? Please cite some examples of this influence."

If I were to fill out this questionnaire fully, there would be enough words for the student to type it up and turn it in as his own thesis.

This sort of questionnaire is not limited to show-business people. I have friends in the academic world, scientists who also get long questionnaires from Ph.D. candidates. They have tipped me off to the perfect answer. Just one sentence: "Do your own research."

Lately I have also been receiving letters from professors — people in drama departments of colleges who say they are planning to write a book about George Kaufman and could I be of help. And what was his effect on this or that. My answer to them is simple: "Sorry. I am writing my own book and a lot of it is about Kaufman. I wish you good luck with *your* book."

My relationship with Kaufman became a complicated one. On Sunday nights when we did *This Is Show Business*, we were colleagues. Equals. But when George became the director of *Guys and Dolls*, our relationship changed. He became my teacher. After that, it was kind of a dual relationship. On *This Is Show Business*, we would throw jokes back and forth like two fellow comics, but when we worked on *Guys and Dolls*, he was the tough schoolmaster and I was just a pupil. Actually, I felt like a Kaufman protégé as long as he lived.

I eventually learned that I wasn't alone in this feeling. George was trying out a new play, *The Solid Gold Cadillac*, which he had written with Howard Teichmann. Kaufman had asked Moss Hart to come up and take a look at it; and then he asked me to come along, too. I was flattered but a bit nervous: the pupil was being asked to offer criticism to the teacher.

However, I felt fairly safe with Moss Hart there. He was the man who had collaborated with George on what seemed like a hundred smash hits: *The Man Who Came to Dinner; You Can't Take It with You,* a Pulitzer Prize winner; *George Washington Slept Here;* and more. I was sure that with Hart carrying the ball, I wouldn't get into trouble. On the train, to my surprise, he kept talking about our strategy after we saw the play. Then he went on to say that if we *didn't* like it, and we did have suggestions, he wanted me to give my suggestions first, and then he would join me and that would make things easier. As he talked about our "strategy," I realized that he was just as uneasy about confronting George as I was. Even though Moss had been George's collaborator and pupil for years before he finally made the painful decision to strike out on his own, even though he had written *Lady in the Dark* and other plays and was enormously successful, he still retained the same respect and awe for Kaufman that he had back in 1930, when he was a young, green writer and the great Kaufman had agreed to collaborate with him on his first play, *Once in a Lifetime*.

Five minutes after the curtain went up on *The Solid Gold Cadillac*, Moss and I relaxed. The play was a big hit. Very funny. After the show, we went up to Kaufman's hotel room and met with him and Howard Teichmann. Fortunately, we couldn't find much to criticize. We did feel the play was a bit long, but it was good. The star was Josephine Hull, a lady of great age and great talent; she was magnificent. Moss and I came up with a couple of pretty funny snappers that could be added to her dialogue; but Kaufman said in that weary, unanswerable style of his, "Gentlemen, those are all very good suggestions, but we would have to rewrite Miss Hull's dialogue. She would have to learn a lot of new lines; and this lady is seventy-five years old." That shut us up.

When you work in the theater, you learn that memory is a function of age. I have directed young people and they learn their lines with dazzling speed. I have seen seven- and eight-year-old child-actors learn their parts completely in one day, and after a week of rehearsal they also know everyone else's lines. Often, when an older actor forgets a line, the kids are quick to cue him, which makes the older actor feel embarrassed and murderous — and old.

George was right about leaving Miss Hull's dialogue alone,

and Moss and I told him so. He agreed the play was too long, and he and Teichmann would do some cutting, and "Thanks, Moss and Abe, for coming to Hartford." We told George the show would be a big hit (we were right), and we went back to New York feeling happy and relieved.

Chapter 8

Guys and Dolls opened in New York on November 24, 1950. But back in 1949, when it began, neither Kaufman nor I had anything to do with it.

I knew that Cy Feuer and Ernie Martin were planning to do the show, which was based on a short story from Damon Runyon's book *Guys and Dolls*. Cy and Ernie were living in New York, so we saw each other frequently and they kept me up to date on the show. They told me that Frank Loesser had been composing some great songs for it, but there were problems with the libretto. Cy and Ernie had a definite image in their minds, a picture of what the story should be like. Six or seven writers had tried writing the libretto, and none of them had come up with anything good, or at least anything that Cy and Ernie thought was good.

They asked me if I would like to take a crack at it, but I was all tied up with my radio and television commitments. Besides, I was doing fairly well financially and a Broadway show is always a chancy trip for a writer.

I know that the producers of the show are gambling too — Feuer and Martin had everything they owned riding on *Guys and Dolls* — but many producers have other sources of income. A few own theaters or restaurants or pieces of other shows, and some of them are just born rich. But a writer owns nothing but his head and a typewriter — or a pen. Since I've never learned to type, a pen is my only writing weapon.

A television or movie script takes a week or two to write and you get paid instantly; but when it comes to the theater, you always work on speculation. Writing a Broadway show and getting it staged (*if* you get it on) takes a long time — a year or two years or more. During that period, except for a small advance, you don't make a nickel until the show opens, and very often it doesn't open at all, or if it does open, it can close overnight and you don't even get the nickel.

I'm ashamed now to admit that I was smugly content with what I was doing and in no mood to take a big risk. Of course, it may not have been just money that affected my decision. I probably was afraid of testing myself in the theater. Whatever the reason, I remained up to my ears in television. I was doing those three shows: *This Is Show Business* on Sunday; *We Take Your Word* on Tuesday; and *The Stork Club* five times a week.

One day someone at CBS had decided that it would be a great idea to televise a show live from the Cub Room of the Stork Club. At that time the Stork Club was the most famous dine-and-dance spot in New York. It was a very "in" spot, but inside of this "in" spot was an "inner" spot called the Cub Room. It was a beautiful dining room, closed off from the rest of the club and reserved for celebrities and friends of the owner, Sherman Billingsley. Of course, they allowed in other people — not famous but rich — who could afford to slip the headwaiter a fat tip. The guest's physical appearance was also important. Billingsley used to say he wanted only "classy-looking" customers. It seemed to me that as far as Billingsley was concerned, all rich people were classy-looking.

There is a story about the time George Jessel arrived at the entrance of the Cub Room bringing with him a beautiful and talented lady, Lena Horne. This caused a bit of a stir. Billingsley and his headwaiters weren't very big on racial equality, but Jessel happened to be a regular. The headwaiter was on the spot.

He was trying to figure out what to do, mumbling and fumbling through his reservation book, acting as though there were no tables left. Of course, Jessel knew what was going on and I'm sure Lena did too. After a while, the headwaiter said to Jessel, "Mr. Jessel, who made the reservation?" And Jessel answered, "Abraham Lincoln." A few people heard this and chuckled, and Billingsley across the room finally gave the flustered maitre d' a nod, and Mr. Jessel and Miss Horne walked in and were seated. That night the Cub Room was temporarily integrated.

Some people tell me this story is apocryphal. But it seems to me now that the old Stork Club itself and everything that went on there sounds apocryphal.

All the columnists religiously came to the Cub Room to get quotes from Big Names. Leonard Lyons and Walter Winchell never missed a night. Winchell actually made his base in there. He was the permanent resident of Table Fifty, where he was joined by the Bigger Names.

I used to go to the Cub Room once in a while some years before I started to do *The Stork Club* TV show. My first time was when Fred Allen took me to dinner there. He and Portland ordinarily didn't patronize the glamour spots, but somehow he liked the Cub Room and everyone there admired him. After that dinner I was accepted by the guardians of the Cub Room gate. I wasn't a big tipper so I figure I was allowed in because I was a friend of Fred's and of Leonard Lyons', and especially because Walter Winchell sort of liked me. He had been fond of *Duffy's Tavern* when I worked on it, and he was interested in that radio program I was doing at the time, *Holiday and Company*. Although the show was not a hit, Winchell took to it because it was the story about an ex-vaudevillian who opened a gas station but could never forget vaudeville. Winchell loved that idea. He had started as a vaudeville performer when he was a kid, and from the way he talked about vaudeville I knew that he still missed it. Between the stories my father had told me and my own love for vaudeville, Winchell and I found plenty to talk about.

One night he did something unheard of. He gave me a sheet of memo paper and told me to write out a plug for my show which he would run in his column. I was astounded and wrote out something fairly modest like "Abe Burrows' new radio show about two vaudevillians, 'Holiday and Company,' seems to be a runaway smash. Don't miss it." It was a nice plug but it didn't help.

About this time a great and important moment for me happened at Winchell's table. I met Damon Runyon. This was years before any of us thought of doing Runyon's story as a musical. When I met him, he was in the last couple of years of his life and he surely knew it. He'd had several throat operations and could no longer speak, yet he was cheerful and bright. He used to communicate with little written notes. The first night I met him, he wrote me a note saying that he admired my work on *Duffy's Tavern* and liked the way my New York muggs talked. But when I told him I thought his New York muggs were the greatest, he answered me with another note, saying something like "Abe, my New York dialogue is a fake because I was born and raised in Dade County, Florida." He died before I started on *Guys and Dolls,* but what he said stayed with me when I took on the job of putting his people on the stage. I felt I probably would have had his approval.

When the Big Brass at CBS decided to go ahead with the show from the Stork Club, they built, at great expense, an exact replica of the Cub Room on the second story of the building, directly above the real one.

It was an amazing set. As you looked at it, it was the real Cub Room in every detail — the tables, the linen, the silver, the dishes, the wall decorations, and even the people. Billingsley used to invite Cub Room regulars to come upstairs and sit in the TV Cub Room while the show was going on the air. My wife was one of these guests sometimes. A few of the "customers" were extras. But Sherman always made sure those extras were "classy-looking."

I wasn't involved in *The Stork Club* show when it first started.

I inherited it. It was willed to me by Irving Mansfield, the original producer. Irving had too many other projects to do, and when he left the show I took over as producer and writer. The basic cast remained the same. Sherman Billingsley, Peter Lind Hayes and Mary Healy. The three of them took turns interviewing various Beautiful People.

It was a strange show, but often fun to do. With Yul Brynner as the director, there was a constant flavor of excitement. Most people don't know that Yul was a very skillful television director before he became King of Siam. His assistant director was a stimulating young fellow who later became a successful motion picture director. Sidney Lumet.

Our job had some interesting peaks. Often, before the show, we would have dinner at the Stork Club, and we ate well. Brynner used to order gourmet dishes like *truite au bleu,* which is made by flinging a live trout into boiling water and admiring the way the poor fish curls up.

Yul acted as though he owned the place. I remember once staring at him as he sent back a bottle of Bollinger champagne with an imperial gesture, saying it was flat. Brynner was a very talented director, but his manner was that of an actor. He was exciting to watch even when he was directing. His body moved and his eyes flashed just as they do today on the stage. He had been an actor before he started directing. He was in a play with Mary Martin, *The Lute Song.* He had received excellent reviews but now he was stuck in a control room. Things soon changed. I remember having dinner with him at the Stork Club when he was quiet and much more subdued than I had seen him before. He wanted to tell me something he didn't want me to spread around. He spoke sort of shyly. He said, "Abe, I think Rodgers and Hammerstein want me for *The King and I.* I auditioned for them this morning and I think they liked me." And I said something casual like "Great, Yul. What part are you going to play?" His Tartar face looked puzzled and he said, "The King, of course!"

In his role as the host of the show, Sherman Billingsley had some problems. It's hard to believe that the legendary owner of the Stork Club was rather shy. A good host on a talk show has to be something of an actor, which Sherman was not. He was inhibited in public. When he was interviewing guest stars, he would nervously ask them questions which I had written for him, but he never listened to the answers.

I remember one interview with Beatrice Lillie. Sherman's first question was to ask her what she was doing in New York, and she said, "I just got back from Hollywood, Sherman. I made a film out there and I enjoyed it thoroughly." Then Billingsley asked his next question. "Bea, have you ever done any motion pictures?" Bea, who in private life was Lady Peel and has never been thrown by anything, just sat there and stared at Sherman. And Sherman went right on with his next question.

As soon as the program ended, I gave Sherman a gentle lecture. I told him that whenever he asked a guest a question, he must listen to the answer. Sherman nodded his head and said to me, "I guess that's a good idea, Abe."

The next evening one of our guests was Igor Cassini who, in the press, was Cholly Knickerbocker, the popular society columnist. He was a good subject for an interview. Bright, articulate, and loaded with juicy anecdotes. When the interview started, and Cassini began to talk, Sherman kept staring at him with an intense look in his eyes. As the interview went on, Sherman never took his eyes off Cassini's face — actually he was looking at Cassini's mouth. I could see that this was making Cassini uneasy. Suddenly, in the middle of the interview, Sherman said to Cassini, "Igor, you know why I'm looking at you like this? It's because Abe Burrows told me that I always have to listen very carefully." This speech actually went on the air.

It shook those of us in the control room who were nervously listening, and it certainly seemed to shake Cassini. The interview quickly began to run out of gas. Finally, I gave Brynner our code signal "Send in Red!" Red was a very bright headwaiter with very bright-red hair. Whenever we wanted to end an interview because we were running out of time or, as in this case, when the interview was dying, we would call for a Red Alert and cue Red to come onstage. He would enter the room carrying a small tray with a note on it. The camera would follow Red as he walked over to Billingsley and presented the note. Sherman would then look at the note, and as casually as possible for him, would say something like "I have to go now. I'm wanted on the phone. Thanks for coming here." That was the end of the interview.

Some weeks later I heard from friends that Igor Cassini was very angry with me. I was puzzled, but the next time I ran into him I decided to ask what the trouble was. It seems that Sherman had told him I had arranged to cut the interview short because I didn't like Cassini personally. I finally straightened things out. First, I made him promise that he wouldn't print what I was about to tell him, and then I gave him the real reason. He thought it was very funny, but he kept his word and didn't print it.

Sherman Billingsley was at times a likable and generous man. But he was a strange man. He had learned his business in the speakeasy days of Prohibition. The basic rule then was "Look after yourself because no one else will."

One time he felt that Peter Lind Hayes was getting too much to do on the air. Sherman thought that I was responsible for that, but instead of complaining to me he used another gambit. He talked with Peter and told him, "Peter, I happen to know that Abe is trying to get you off the show." That sounds crazy, but it did make Peter get angry with me, and made me angry with Sherman. And Sherman covered himself with me by sending me two cases of champagne. He figured that would straighten everything out.

When *The Stork Club* finally went off the air (this was a few months after I left it), it was taken off because of a personal decision made by the head of the Columbia Broadcasting System, Mr. William Paley. I am told that he was watching the show at home one evening and on the screen Billingsley was interviewing someone. Paley suddenly stood up, walked over to

141

the television set, and said, "I will not have that man on my network." And he turned off the show with a sharp click.

All this time, while I was doing my panel shows and working and dining at the Stork Club, Feuer and Martin kept working on *Guys and Dolls*. They at last had chosen a librettist, Jo Swerling, who was a well-known screenwriter. He had won an Oscar for a picture called *Man's Castle*. I knew Jo; he was a talented and nice man.

Out in California, Frank Loesser kept writing the songs and Cy and Ernie were very happy about his work. One night when Frank was in New York, Carin and I joined him for dinner at Cy Feuer's home. Ernie Martin was there, too. After dinner Frank played and sang some of the numbers from the show for us; they were enchanting. Frank, in addition to being a composer and lyric writer, was a great performer. Everything he did at the piano sounded marvelous, but as I heard these songs, I felt that they would be effective no matter who sang them.

After Carin and I stopped raving about the songs, Frank played us a brand-new song of his, one that was not intended for *Guys and Dolls*. It was called "Forever," a satirical, amusing but slightly bitter love song. I was crazy about it, and in my enthusiasm I said I thought that it would fit perfectly in *Guys and Dolls*. For some reason (maybe because it was "none of my business") my remark annoyed Ernie Martin and he sharply disagreed with me. We started arguing about it in front of everyone.

It started off as a mild disagreement but it heated up. I was really just teasing Ernie, but it turned out that I was jabbing away at a sore spot. Ernie, it seemed, didn't think of *Guys and Dolls* as a hilarious satirical comedy. But because we usually respected each other's opinions, I believe he was shaken by what I had said. Shaken but also annoyed. Finally, sounding like a judge pronouncing sentence, Ernie said to me, "Abe, if you are a man who thinks that that song is right for *Guys and Dolls,* you could never be the man to write *Guys and Dolls.*" That kind of broke the tension for me. I laughed and said,

142

"Ernie, I never planned to write it and now you're already firing me." Then everybody laughed.

I later realized that Ernie and Cy were very much influenced by the success of *South Pacific,* which was the big hit of that period. *South Pacific* was a wonderful show. It had a basically serious story with some funny lines, and some funny songs. I think that Cy and Ernie thought that *Guys and Dolls* — since it was based on a love story about a beautiful missionary and a wicked gambler — could work on the same serious romantic level as *South Pacific.* When Ernie and I left each other the night of our big debate, I apologized for sticking my nose into the construction of his show and agreed that maybe I would be the wrong man for the project. But, at the end of my apology, I couldn't help adding one wisecrack. I said, "However, Ernie, don't ever close the door." I thought I was only joking when I said this. As a matter of fact, I forgot that I said it until a long time afterward, when Frank Loesser reminded me of it.

Just a few months later, Ernie came to see me and he "opened the door." Jo Swerling had finished a first act which they all thought was well written but not at all what they wanted. Evidently he had based his work on Ernie and Cy's original concept of what the style of the show should be. But now Feuer and Martin began to have second, third and fourth thoughts.

Guys and Dolls was based on a story called "The Idyll of Miss Sarah Brown." The heroine, Miss Sarah, is a lovely young missionary who does her preaching on Broadway. I've been told that the model for Miss Sarah was a real person, a gorgeous former Follies girl who became a missionary and devoted her life to converting the evil sinners and wicked gamblers who inhabited the Broadway theatrical district. Her looks and style drew large, admiring crowds. Walter Winchell once told me that lots of guys fell in love with her, including Winchell himself.

In Runyon's story, Miss Sarah one day meets Sky Masterson — "the highest roller of them all." This wicked, handsome gambler and the lovely Mission Doll eventually fall in love and she cures him of his sinful habits.

To me that seemed to be a sweet story but also kind of funny. Damon Runyon's stories were always funny. They frequently had serious themes, but Runyon liked to make his readers laugh.

In addition to getting the rights to Runyon's story, Feuer and Martin were also permitted to use some of the characters from several other Runyon stories: Harry the Horse, Liverlips Louie, Nathan Detroit, Nicely-Nicely Johnson, Bennie Southstreet, Rusty Charlie and other such wonderful muggs with wonderful names. The basic story, plus the extra ingredients, made me absolutely sure that the show could be and had to be a pretty funny musical.

Feuer and Martin were gutsy enough to risk changing the style of the show, even though they had already raised a good deal of money from their backers on the strength of the fourteen songs Frank Loesser had already finished and Jo Swerling's first act.

After much agonizing, they decided that the show had to be a comedy, which meant there had to be a new libretto. Frank Loesser agreed with them. Cy and Ernie made a settlement with Swerling, and they asked me to do the new script. They didn't ask me in a casual way, as they did originally, but they walked in and ganged up on me.

These two fellows have always been very difficult to say no to. Cy was a fellow student at New Utrecht High School, and Ernie was the man who had pushed me into being a performer. And there was Frank Loesser, one of my oldest and dearest friends. In addition, Ernie and Cy told me that as choreographer they had hired Michael Kidd, who had done the wonderful dances in *Finian's Rainbow*. Even more important, Mike had also had gone to New Utrecht High School. It all seemed to be destiny. Too perfect to turn down.

I now realize that subconsciously my mind had been working on the show ever since I heard those songs that Frank had written. So after a long discussion, I said to Cy and Ernie the words I have always said when I'm going to accept an offer: "Let me think about it."

It wasn't all roses. The three of us had some stormy times. We didn't agree on everything and frequently we didn't agree on anything. But somehow or other things came out right.

I have worked on many shows with other producers. Some were hits; some were not. Ernie and Cy have also worked with other writers and other directors with varying results. But whenever the three of us worked together, we never had a flop. There's something to be said for chemistry.

The same kind of chemistry existed between Frank Loesser and me. The last time I saw Frank was when Carin and I came to visit him at Mount Sinai Hospital. He was obviously fading rapidly. Oddly enough, at this same time in an adjoining wing of the same hospital, my daughter was giving birth to my grandson Nicky. I'll never forget the crazily mixed feelings I had. Great happiness for Laurie and Peter and great grief for Frank and his wife, Jo.

I was in our summer home in Provincetown the day Frank died. Even though I had known there was no hope for him, the phone call that told me the news shocked me. While I sat at my desk feeling lost, the phone rang again. It was the New York *Times*. They asked me to write Frank's obituary for the Sunday *Times* theater section. It was the most painful and difficult assignment I ever had.

I wrote about our long friendship, but mostly I was anxious to describe Frank's work and his contribution to the theater. I started my piece with some words about his monumental talent:

Frank was one of the song men in the musical theater who "did it all." A man with the technique and talent to cover the whole range of what is needed to get a musical show on. Ballads, character things, group songs, comedy numbers, and anything else, including a good overture. There haven't been many men who could "do it all" and, among the few who could, Frank ranks with the greatest.

145

Outside of his musical and lyrical genius, the thing that placed him among the greatest was the tremendous range of his interests. He was intellectually curious, a great reader, a language buff, a skillful painter. He even made fine furniture. He knew something about everything and something from everything always found its way into his work.

It's been many years since I wrote those words. Today, I still think, just as I did then, that Frank Loesser was one of the greatest writers of musical comedy of our time. Maybe of all time.

As a comedy writer, I guess I valued Frank's comedy songs more than anything else he did. I don't think anyone wrote songs that were funnier than Frank's. There have been many clever lyric writers, people whose material is witty and sharp; but Frank's lyrics got laughs, big laughs, the kind of laughs you get with a funny line of dialogue. He frequently had to leave a space in the melody so the audience could laugh without covering the next line of the song. When Vivian Blaine sang "Adelaide's Lament" in *Guys and Dolls,* she was playing a girl who was suffering from psychosomatic sniffles because of her love problems. It was a sort of poignant situation, and yet each time she came to the punch line, "a person can develop a cold," the audience exploded with laughter. Frank was not displeased by that laugh but somewhere deep down he had thought of that moment as a tender one. He never respected his funny stuff as much as he did his love ballads. He was a romantic.

When he heard that I had agreed to write the book, Frank phoned me from California. He sounded delighted.

FRANK   Hey, Abe, I just heard the news. That's great.
ME   [*Modestly*] Thanks, Frank, I hope I can handle it.
FRANK   You'll be great.
ME   Thanks, Frank, I'm going to try to make it as funny as I can.
FRANK   [*A small pause*] Abe . . . not *too* funny.

I was puzzled by this but I answered with a cautious, "I'll do my best, Frankie." I thought Frank might have meant that he

146

didn't want me to go for silly gags. After all, I *had* been a radio writer. It took me a long time to really understand what Frank was thinking when he said "not too funny."

A few years later, in 1956, I was chattering away to Frank about the marvelously funny stuff in his show *The Most Happy Fella*. Songs like "Standing on the Corner Watching All the Girls Go By," "Abbondanza," and "Big 'D.' " He cut me off angrily. "Abe, the hell with that! We both know I can do that kinda stuff. Tell me where I made you cry."

Before I could actually start working with Frank on *Guys and Dolls,* I had to get permission from CBS. They had that four-way contract with me; legally, they owned every word I wrote, good or bad.

The head of programming at the time was the late Hubbell Robinson. Hubbell was a friend of mine and he gave me the go-ahead. I agreed to keep appearing on my panel shows and to keep working on *The Stork Club* show. Sherman Billingsley had heard a rumor that I was going to quit in order to do a Broadway show. And he was very upset. I calmed him down. There was one more roadblock: the money CBS paid me for my exclusive services. To appease the legal department I took a cut in salary. I didn't mind that because by that time I had grown so excited by *Guys and Dolls* that I'd have accepted any deal that allowed me to work on it. Of course, much of that work would have to be done in my spare time.

It was a weird situation. I was under great pressure and so was the play. Sam Levene was signed to play Nathan Detroit, Jo Mielziner had practically finished his plans for the scenery, and Alvin Colt was already designing the costumes. The Forty-sixth Street Theatre was tentatively booked and a good part of the money had been put up by the backers. Now when the word went out that I, who had no theater record, was starting to write a new libretto, some of these backers were feeling a bit shaky.

One of them was Billy Rose, who had invested $10,000 in the show. This was the fabulous Billy Rose who started out as a shorthand whiz, became secretary to Bernard Baruch, then a songwriter with big hits like "I Found a Million-Dollar Baby in a Five and Ten Cent Store," "It Was Only a Paper Moon," and "Without a Song," and then a big impresario with shows like *Jumbo* and the Aquacade, and who, at this time, owned the Ziegfeld Theatre.

Billy and I had been friends for a long time. However, he never let friendship interfere with business, and when he learned that there was to be a new version of the book and that I was writing it, he asked the producers to return his investment. Ernie Martin asked me to phone Billy; maybe, as a friend, I could change his mind. I was a bit reluctant because I didn't like the idea of talking a friend into betting ten grand on me! But I finally agreed to make the call. I told Billy I understood his misgivings, but I felt that I had some good ideas and would come up with a pretty good libretto. He listened to all I had to say, and then he answered, "Kid, you're a good friend of mine and I know you're a great comedy writer, but you've never done a Broadway show. So . . ." He wanted his money back, and Feuer and Martin, with a good deal of pain, returned it.

Strange as it may seem, Billy and I remained good friends for the rest of his life. When *Guys and Dolls* finally opened, Billy was there congratulating us all on our big hit. He and I never mentioned that he was not one of the lucky investors. One night at a dinner party where Billy and Oscar Hammerstein were also guests, Oscar was congratulating me on the fact that *Guys and Dolls* was in its second year and still selling out. He turned to Billy Rose and said, "Hey, Billy, I'm sure you got a big piece of it." And Billy said, "No, Oscar, I didn't put any money into it because I didn't know that Abe was going to write it." I just looked at him with a straight face and nodded. I never teased him or reminded him about that ten grand he took out of the show. As a matter of fact, Billy's investment would have added to the pressure on me when I started working on the script and I sure didn't need any extra pressure.

I was feeling tense enough as it was. I was green and frightened. In a small panic I told Ernie that I needed someone to work with me and we brought in Peter Lyon, a good writer. I worked with Peter for a couple of weeks but it didn't go well. It wasn't Peter's fault; it was just that my TV time schedule was so crazy, my working hours so uneven, and I was so uncertain about what I was doing that I finally decided to start fresh and go it alone. Of course, I wasn't really alone. Frank Loesser was in California, and I used to talk to him by telephone. And Cy and Ernie and I were in constant consultation. I leaned on Feuer very heavily. I would sit with him night after night working on the first draft. I would say that Cy forcibly pulled that first draft out of me. Feuer was a fine musician and that was very important because Frank Loesser's songs were the guideposts for the libretto. It's a rare show that is done this way. Frank Loesser's fourteen songs were all great, and the libretto had to be written so that the story would lead into each of them. Later on, the critics spoke of the show as "integrated." The word *integration* usually means that the composer has written songs that follow the story line gracefully. Well, we accomplished that but we did it in reverse. Most of the scenes I wrote blended into songs that were already written.

After I got rolling on the script, Feuer and Martin came up with a beautiful idea. They wanted George Kaufman to direct the show. They wanted him because he was not only a great director, but a great dramatist. Cy and Ernie felt, correctly, that Abe Burrows needed all the help he could get; and Burrows loudly agreed.

Kaufman wasn't crazy about the idea of doing a musical. At the time, he was relaxing in the south of France (*This Is Show Business* was off the air for the summer). But Feuer and Martin kept after him. Their first move was very cunning. They arranged for Frank to come to New York and play the songs for Max Gordon. Gordon was a friend of Kaufman's and a producer who had produced most of Kaufman's shows. George usually wasn't crazy about other people's judgment, but he did trust Gordon's instincts. Gordon heard Frank's songs and he was mad about them. He cabled George, telling him he should not — repeat "NOT" — pass up this show. Kaufman then cabled Feuer and Martin asking to see what I had written so far. Well, so far I had written only the first three scenes! And they were very rough. But I sent them to George anyway and waited to hear from him. This was the most nerve-racking part of the whole project for me — waiting to hear what Kaufman would say.

At last Kaufman sent a wire to the producers saying he would do the show, but typically he didn't give me a rave. He said he liked the idea of the show and the story, and he thought I was going in the right direction, but that "Abe's stuff isn't as funny as I expected. Abe has the talent to make the material a lot funnier."

That word *funnier* plagued me for a while. As I have mentioned, when I first heard Frank's songs and told Ernie Martin I thought the show probably should be a funny one, he got furious with me. Then he changed his mind and he and Cy decided the show should be a comedy. When I finally agreed to do the show, Frank Loesser told me, "Not *too* funny." Now, here was George Kaufman telling me to be funnier. I found that pretty funny.

It was the first time Kaufman, in the role of my new teacher, rapped me across the knuckles; and of course Kaufman was right. My dialogue was not as funny as I could make it. I was being overly cautious. All this because it was the first time I was writing for Broadway and I was worried about people like Brooks Atkinson, Richard Watts, John Chapman and their scary critical colleagues. Kaufman shook me out of my self-conscious approach. After he read my opening scenes, I had expected him to say something about the play's "construction" and insight into the characters. Instead he hit me with that word *funnier,* and I suddenly remembered that I was a comedy writer and not Ibsen. I felt like the guy we've seen in after-shave commercials who gets frightened and hysterical and his friend slaps him across the face and the guy suddenly relaxes and says, "Thanks, I needed that." Later on I got more such slaps from Kaufman, but this one was the most important.

Chapter 9

I relaxed and began enjoying myself. Damon Runyon's characters were very much like the characters we had on *Duffy's Tavern*. The people on that show were New York muggs, nice muggs, sweet muggs, and like Runyon's muggs they all talked like Ladies and Gentlemen. That's how we treated the characters in *Guys and Dolls*. One of the greatest compliments I ever received after the show opened came from Noel Coward. He said he really enjoyed hearing those lowlifes on the stage being so polite and elegant. He told me they sounded as if he had written their lines himself.

The curtain goes up and the stage is peopled by gamblers, dangerous hoods, tough cops, tough chorus girls — the *crème de la crème* of the underworld — and yet it all seems so fresh and so clean. In the entire script and in all of Loesser's lyrics there is no profanity and there are no prurient jokes — the kind that George Kaufman used to call Single Entendre.

The only time we come close to using a swear word is just before the first-act curtain. Our hero, Sky Masterson, the high-rolling gambler, loses his temper and says to the beautiful missionary, "What the hell kind of a doll *are* you?" That shocks her. And curiously enough it shocks the audience because it is the first time such language has been used in the show and because they've grown to love the Mission Doll.

I've seen the show many times through the years — on Broadway, on the road, in summer stock, in colleges and high schools. Sometimes it's done beautifully and sometimes it's shaky, but I'm always pleased that it retains its unusual style.

While the writing was going on, the producers were looking for actors. Only one actor had been definitely set for the show: Sam Levene. He was signed to play the part of Nathan Detroit, a character who was the "sole owner and proprietor of the oldest established permanent floating crap game in New York." Sam was a great actor, but he had never done a musical. Nobody connected with the show had yet heard him sing. One night, right after I started the writing, I was sitting in a restaurant with Sam. It was very late — about one o'clock in the morning. I was telling him I was happy about the way the script was coming along. But he seemed troubled and glum. I finally asked him what it was that was troubling him; his answer made me feel glum, too. The dialogue that followed is burned in my brain; it went something like this:

SAM   Abe, I don't think I'm right for this show.

ME   Aw, c'mon, Sam. It's going to be great and you're going to be great. Why are you worried?

SAM   I can't sing.

ME   [*Chuckling*] Ah, come on. You don't have to be a great singer. Look at me. I can't sing but I work nightclubs.

SAM   Abe, I *really can't sing*.

ME   Now wait a minute. Is there any song you *can* sing?

SAM   [*Thoughtfully*] Well, I know "Pony Boy."

ME   [*A bit stunned*] "Pony Boy"??? Well, go ahead. Sing "Pony Boy" for me.

SAM   Now?

ME   Just sing the opening line.

Sam looked around him. There weren't many people in the restaurant so he softly and reluctantly started to sing "Pony Boy" for me. Now just try to imagine "Pony Boy, pony boy, won't you be my only boy" sung on one note and that note a very flat one.

ME   [*After a long silence*] Sam, you *really* can't sing.

SAM   I told you, Abe.

ME   [*Thoughtfully*] Hmmm.

And then I said something like "We'll work it out." However, though Sam was a non-singer in a show full of songs, most of us connected with the show decided that Sam's acting would still make him perfect for the part. And poor Frank Loesser, who had written four songs that Sam was supposed to sing, alone or as part of a group, sadly agreed that Sam was still the perfect Nathan Detroit. The part was written for him and no one has ever topped his performance. Of course, we eventually had to make some musical changes and give some of Sam's songs to other actors.

By opening night in New York Sam wound up with just one song, "Sue Me," which he did beautifully. When he sang to Vivian Blaine, "Sue me, sue me, what can you do me, I love you," he did it with such passion that he stopped the show. The audience didn't seem to notice or didn't care that the notes he sang were flat — as a matter of fact most of them weren't even notes. But his acting plus strong accompaniment from the orchestra made it a great musical moment.

Of course, Sam was never very happy about losing his other songs; but he gave them up with middling good grace. Then came that old unkindest cut. In the show were many group numbers, which consisted of most of the cast singing in harmony. The musical arrangements were difficult and Loesser told Sam that when he was onstage as part of this group, he was *not to sing,* he was just to mouth the words, because if he sang, it would ruin the harmony. This really bugged Sam. And one day during a break in rehearsal, he told us that he felt he was not entirely tone deaf. If he had help, it was possible for him to learn to sing in tune. It was just a matter of hard work and practice. He decided on a test. There was a piano on the stage and Sam asked our rehearsal pianist to help him in this test. Then he asked Cy and Frank and me to sit out front and listen. The

154

piano player was to hit a note, and Sam was to sing that note, and we three were to tell him whether the two matched. The great test began. The piano player hit an A, Sam sang his idea of the A. It was wildly off-key. He looked out at us hopefully and the three of us just shook our heads. This happened about six times. Sam doggedly kept on, singing wrong A's. Each time he tried that A, we shook our heads. Finally, a miracle! Along about the eighth time, Sam got it right. Somehow or other, what came out of his mouth was a true A. We three applauded and said things like "You got it, Sam." Sam stood there and beamed.

Then Frank Loesser said the fatal words "Do it again." The pianist played an A and Sam sang and missed it by a mile. He insisted on doing it again. He kept going and missed the note every time. He wasn't just singing wrong notes. Most of them were no notes. Suddenly, as we were shaking our heads for about the fifteenth time, Sam walked down to the foot of the stage and shouted at us, "I know what you three are doing! It's a lousy trick! You guys have agreed every single time. It ain't possible that you always agree on what's the right note. It was a trick." Poor Sam! He couldn't believe that three people could always agree on what was a true A.

To this day every actor who gets to play the part of Nathan Detroit wonders why he has only one song to sing. He has to be told the sad saga of Sam Levene's singing. But I can't bear to think of what *Guys and Dolls* would have been like without Sam.

In addition to his talent, Sam gave us another plus. A big plus. *Guys and Dolls* had four fine leads, but he was the only one of the four who had had any previous Broadway experience. The other three — Robert Alda, Vivian Blaine and Isabel Bigley — had never worked on the Broadway stage. Alda had made his reputation in a picture called *Rhapsody in Blue,* in which he played George Gershwin. Nevertheless, he quickly made himself at home on the stage. He was a perfect Sky Masterson and was a very pleasant man to work with.

Vivian Blaine was a star at Twentieth-Century Fox. She was

one of the beautiful blondes that Darryl Zanuck originally hired as a potential threat to Betty Grable. Grable was a superstar and like all superstars occasionally balked at doing a picture she didn't like. To protect itself the studio had on hand people like Vivian Blaine and June Haver, beautiful blondes who were never quite superstars but were very good actresses. As a matter of fact, Marilyn Monroe was originally hired because she was a good-looking blonde who might be a threat to Grable. Anyway, whatever it was that kept Vivian Blaine from being another Betty Grable was a great break for *Guys and Dolls*. She played the part of Adelaide, Nathan Detroit's fiancée. When Vivian auditioned for us, she walked out on that stage as though she owned it. She glittered, and when she sang one of Frank's songs she bowled us over.

Isabel Bigley was another beautiful actress who was new to the stage. She was hired about three days before we went into rehearsal. We had auditioned what seemed like hundreds of people for the part of Miss Sarah, the Mission Doll. She had to be young, a soprano — Frank Loesser had sprinkled her songs with high notes — and she had to be beautiful.

The week before rehearsal George Kaufman and I were going over the script at his place in Bucks County. Ernie and Cy were frantically auditioning beautiful girls in New York. One day Ernie phoned us and said he thought he had found *the* girl. She was pretty, a good soprano, and Frank Loesser had auditioned her and approved of her singing. Ernie said he was anxious to sign her quickly and if it was all right with Kaufman, he wanted to drive her down to Bucks County that evening and have her read for Kaufman and me. It was all right with Kaufman.

In those days there was no turnpike to that part of Pennsylvania. One needed a map; Ernie didn't have a map and he got lost. He and Isabel were due around nine o'clock. We all sat around waiting. Carin and I and George and his wife, the actress Leueen McGrath. By eleven o'clock George was getting tired and cross. Ernie and Isabel Bigley finally arrived at around midnight. Poor Isabel. This was her first meeting with the great

George S. Kaufman. She is late; she is tired, bedraggled and, of course, frightened to death. But she did look pretty. As soon as they saw her, Carin and Leueen both looked at us with that approving nod which usually means "not bad." Kaufman, of course, tired though he was, was very kind to her. He was always kind to girls, especially pretty ones. However, he was really bushed and wanted to get this audition over with quickly. We gave Isabel a scene to read. I read the part of the dashing Sky Masterson and she read Miss Sarah, the beautiful Missionary. It was a very tough spot for Bigley, sitting in the dining room of a country house at about one o'clock in the morning and trying to act and play a romantic scene opposite, of all people, me.

Suddenly, as we were struggling through the scene, we got relief. Kaufman raised his hand wearily to stop us and mumbled something like "That's fine, that's fine." And it was very plain that he was ready for bed. Ernie was smart enough not to stick around and discuss things. He said a quick good night to all of us, got Bigley out of the house, into his car and back to New York. That's how Isabel Bigley got the part; and she was perfect in it.

That week in Bucks County was a tough week for me. I was polishing the script under Kaufman's supervision and he was a tough boss. It was late summer, Kaufman's house was beautiful, Leueen was a lovely hostess, the weather was great, the country was gorgeous, but I was there only to work.

I'll always remember one particular beautiful Sunday afternoon. On the patio, Kaufman, Leueen, Carin, Moss Hart and his wife, Kitty Carlisle, and many other interesting guests were drinking, chattering, and having a great time; but I wasn't with them. I was all alone up in Kaufman's study working on the script. I felt like Bob Cratchit. Then I heard one of the servants say, "Lunch is ready," and my wife said, "Where's Abe?" And I heard Kaufman say, "Abe will have lunch in the study. He's working." Just as he said this, a maid walked into the study, carrying a tray for me and I had lunch all by myself.

I wasn't the only one Kaufman treated firmly. I remember one morning that week when I was having breakfast and George came down to join me. As he walked into the room, his three-year-old granddaughter ran to meet him, and threw her arms around his knees. He patted her on the head and said, "Betsy, I'm not in the mood for you this morning." And Betsy, who evidently understood George, quietly walked away.

I think that Betsy, like all other females, understood George. Most women seemed to. I have known many actresses who have worked with him and they all tell me that once they got over their early shakes, they found him to be the kindest director they have ever known. These actresses gradually found out, as I did, that behind his formal — make that formidable — austerity was a lot of pussycat. He would have hated that expression, but I can't think of a better one. All the ladies seemed to spot the pussycat in him.

I got a glimmer of this side of George one night at the end of one of our *This Is Show Business* shows (this was long before we did *Guys and Dolls*). At the end of the show George said to me in a sort of shy way, "Would you like to join me for a bite to eat tonight?" This surprised me because ordinarily George used to disappear right after the show; he never said good night to anyone, he just vanished. I said I'd be happy to join him and then he said in a kind of embarrassed way, "There's a girl I'd like you to meet." He sounded like a seventeen-year-old. He took me to "21," and there we were joined by Leueen McGrath. The "girl" George wanted me to meet was the girl the whole town had been raving about for her performance in *Edward, My Son*. But that night she was George's girl and he was obviously in love. They were married a short time later. That night at "21" I got to see another side of Kaufman. He seemed tender and vulnerable. He was even unusually nice to me. That evening was one of the few times that he softened up around me.

I guess a Johnny-come-lately is always afraid of the guy-who's-been-there. I respected Kaufman's knowledge and talent so much that when he agreed to direct *Guys and Dolls,* I told my wife, "I'm going to do *everything* this man tells me to do." That was a tough decision because I thought of myself as a pretty good comedy writer; but I had to trust the teacher if I were to learn anything.

I had worked hard on the script while George was in France and I had tried to follow his suggestion to "make it funnier." When he came back to New York, I nervously showed him my rought first draft. He started to read it and almost immediately he again rapped me across the knuckles. He pointed to a joke line and said, "Abe, that's too easy." I had known people who criticized a joke by saying understandable things like, "Hey, Abe, that stinks" or "That is lousy," but "too easy" baffled me. I knew instinctively that Kaufman was right. The joke he referred to — which I have since happily forgotten — *was* too easy and I knew it. It was a gag I had written because it was the first line that came to my mind. I hurried to put it down because subconsciously I thought we were going on the air tomorrow. And the joke *was* too easy. I forgot I had plenty of time to think it over and to rewrite it.

The big difference between writing a weekly radio or TV show and writing for the theater is that the theater does not require a new show every week. When you have just a few days to write a program full of funny stuff and you come down to the wire — the awful deadline — you do the best you can. Time governs your thinking, not quality. When you're still writing at three o'clock in the morning and they're waiting for your script, you say to yourself, "What the hell! This may work. I'm going to turn it in and go to bed."

Kaufman would never let me get away with anything. I remember one time when I had a funny joke that I repeated two more times in my script. Kaufman looked at it and said, "Abe, you've done that same joke three times." I answered in a rather patronizing tone, "George, we often do that on radio. We call it a running gag." Kaufman said, "Abe, radio is free. The people coming to see your show have to buy tickets. Give them a new joke." I quickly wrote a new joke.

Kaufman's barbs were painful at times. One of the things that hurt the most was his quiet "Oh, dear." I would bring him a new scene I had written, one I thought was pretty good. Kaufman would look at it and say, "Oh, dear." Sometimes the "Oh, dear" meant it was clumsy or the language was too flowery; but frequently he said it when I wrote a love scene and instead of being funny I was trying for a little tenderness. The only times that I ever resisted doing *"everything* this man tells me to do" were when we disagreed about the subject of tenderness. George wasn't very high on love scenes. He preferred a funny line to a tender moment. Of course, as a director he did many shows that were full of beautiful and tender moments. He directed John Steinbeck's *Of Mice and Men,* a very moving play. Steinbeck once told me that he never could have done the play without George. John wrote the original novel, but he always felt that the play belonged to Kaufman. I think that when it came to comedy, George didn't want any scenes that were even slightly mushy. To this day when I find myself writing an overly purple love scene, I can still remember George's "Oh, dear."

Chapter 10

A big problem Kaufman helped me handle was the playwright's curse, the Exposition. The beginning of a play is very difficult; setting up the plot has always given playwrights trouble. For years the stage was full of what we now call feather dusters. The curtain goes up on the beautiful living room of a home in the suburbs. Onstage there's a maid with a feather duster and she is busily dusting the furniture. The phone rings; she answers it. "Hello. No, Senator Framingham isn't home yet. He's in Washington having a conference with the President of the United States, who is planning to appoint him Secretary of State. What? No, madam isn't here either. She's at the hairdresser getting ready for her daughter's wedding tomorrow. Oh, here comes madam now."

Well, when I started my opening scene of *Guys and Dolls,* I tried to make it funny. Very funny. I avoided the plot as long as I could and when I got to the plot, I desperately buried it in funny stuff. Again, that came from my background in electronic communication. In radio and television you have to bowl over the audience in the first thirty seconds of your show. If there's the smallest hint of dullness, the audience reaches for the dial and switches to another station. The slogan in TV is Grab Them Quick! Once again George reminded me that the theater audience is different. "They've paid good money to see your work and they'll be patient with you at the beginning of the show. They are not going to get up and leave and there are no knobs to turn. So take a deep breath and set up your story." He was right.

He was always right when it came to the construction of a play. That word *construction* is the heart of a playwright's work. Many people, even some drama students, confuse the "wright" part of *playwright* with the word *write*. I even get letters reading, "I would like to be a playwrite." Some of them even say "playwriter." This isn't just dumb spelling; it's the wrong word. A playwright is a man who constructs a play. He is like a wheelwright, or a shipwright, or any other wright who is, as Webster says, "a constructive workman; an artificer; one engaged in a mechanical or manufacturing business." That doesn't sound very glamorous, but it's true of a playwright. He can have a good story and snappy dialogue, but if his construction is faulty his play will be smothered by a jumble of badly placed bricks. Indeed, when I was working on the final draft of *Guys and Dolls,* Kaufman treated me as though I were a member of the Bricklayers' Union.

As a teacher, Kaufman was no kindly Mr. Chips. I would arrive at his apartment and ring the bell. He would open the door. I would say, "Hello, George," or sometimes I would try a cheerful "Hi, George." Kaufman would give me a nod and say something like "Abram." Then he would stand there and wait till I wiped my feet on the doormat before he would let me in. He wasn't very big on hellos and goodbyes. His goodbye generally consisted of a small wave of one finger in the air.

We usually stopped working just before 4 P.M. because at that time George was due for a game at his bridge club. George was a bridge expert. From what I am told by people who played with him, he really had the potential to be a grand master. When he played he was very tough. Kaufman is the man who said that famous line during a bridge game: "I would like a review of the bidding, *with* the original inflections."

On George's bridge days I would walk with him down Madison Avenue toward his club. The first time we took this walk I was chatting away about the show, and suddenly I realized that we had passed the club and Kaufman was gone. He had evidently waved a finger at me and disappeared into the club without my knowing it. He wasn't going to let my chatter delay him.

He was a very punctual man, and he disliked tardiness in other people. Especially me. Actually I, too, was a punctual fellow because of my training in radio and television, which are clock-oriented media. However, when I was working with George I was still stuck with my other TV chores and sometimes I'd be a bit late for our meetings. George would grumble, but as I remember, he grumbled silently. That is, he would glower at me, and when I saw that glowering look, it seemed to me I heard a definite grumble. I once had the temerity to remind George that Oscar Wilde had made a wisecrack about punctuality: "Punctuality is the thief of time." George in a chilly tone said he had read Wilde's remark, and he thought it a witty line but not funny. Punctuality was a passion with George.

There was one time in New York when he really gave me the back of his hand. *Guys and Dolls* was getting close to rehearsal date and I was polishing the final draft. George asked me to meet him at his place on Saturday morning at ten o'clock. That put me on a spot. On this particular Saturday morning I had to go to a bar mitzvah, that solemn confirmation ceremony during which a shaky thirteen-year-old boy is told that he has suddenly become a man. The kid pleases his elders by going along with the idea. He also gets a lot of presents.

This time the boy who was to face this ordeal was George Lyons, the oldest son of the late Leonard Lyons. Lennie and his wife, Sylvia, were dear friends of mine and I wasn't going to miss the bar mitzvah of their firstborn.

When I nervously told Kaufman about this, he didn't take it kindly. George thought that a bar mitzvah was hardly a valid reason for delaying work on a show. He gave me an audible grumble, then he grudgingly agreed that I could come two hours later, at noon. I swore I'd be there on the dot.

My invitation to the bar mitzvah read 10 A.M. but the services at the temple didn't start until ten-thirty. That was bad news for a guy who had a date at noon with George Kaufman. The opening services moved along at a fair pace. When they finally called on George Lyons, he did his part beautifully. He read the prayers, chanted a chapter from the Torah, and made a nice short speech to the congregation without missing a beat. I whispered a "Well done." I was happy for George Lyons and happy that I'd be able to keep my date with that other George who was waiting for me.

However, I hadn't counted on the rabbi's sermon for the Sabbath. This rabbi was handsome, intelligent and a good speaker, but his sermon turned out to be special because the guests at this bar mitzvah were special. Leonard Lyons was a very popular columnist; people liked him because, unlike some of his contemporaries, he was generally kind in his column. So this day the guest list at the bar mitzvah was heavy with celebrities. When the rabbi stood up to speak, he was looking out at an audience that consisted of some pretty important people, with names like Bernard Baruch, Oscar Hammerstein, Mary and Albert Lasker, Richard Rodgers, Leland Hayward, Billy Rose and others, including Ferenc Molnár who — and I was thrilled — was sitting next to me. Some weeks before that, Lennie had introduced me to Molnár. To me it was almost like meeting Shakespeare.

The composition of that audience had a profound effect on the rabbi. He wasn't going to let them off the hook easily and he began what I knew was going to be a very long speech.

He started off by praising George Lyons and his parents. Then he turned his benevolent concentration on us, the audience. He welcomed us, praised us for coming to the synagogue, and then gave us hell for not coming more often. He really chewed us out. As I kept peeking at my watch, he told us lost souls that we only came to worship on special occasions and ignored the Almighty on ordinary days. He went on and on and on. I could feel Molnár fidgeting next to me, and after a while he turned to me and whispered in his lovely Hungarian accent, "Abe, this is a very long rabbi." Then after another half hour he pointed to Lennie's second son, Warren, two years younger than his brother, and he said, "Abe, if this rabbi keeps talking much longer, he could also bar-mitzvah Warren."

Right after the rabbi finished, Albert Lasker came up to me and whispered, "Abe, I left a synagogue thirty-five years ago because of such a rabbi, and I never went back."

By this time, I was an hour late for my date with Kaufman. I stayed for a moment to congratulate George Lyons and his parents and have a quick drink with them. Then I rushed over to Kaufman's place, an hour and a half late. As I rang the bell I was practicing my apologies. When he opened the door and saw me, George didn't greet me with his usual friendly grunt. He just looked at me with angry distaste. He was livid and he made me feel like a worm.

I tried to explain that I couldn't walk out of a synagogue while a rabbi was talking, and I was sure that the rabbi was watching me like a hawk. Kaufman obviously didn't give a damn. He said to me, "You're an amateur! You're wasting your strength on a lot of nonsense." I really thought he was going to ask me to "assume the angle" and paddle me. He finally relaxed — as much as Kaufman could relax — and said, "Let's get on with this damn thing." "This damn thing" was what he affectionately called my script. I was never late again. Well, hardly ever.

Later on, when *Guys and Dolls* was in production and George called a rehearsal, the actors quickly learned that they had to arrive exactly on time. Kaufman himself never arrived a moment late and he left on the dot. One of the odd things I remember is the miracle he performed in the matter of timing. For instance, he would announce that the rehearsal would be from 2 to 4 P.M. He would arrive about two minutes before two and then at four o'clock he would vanish. I mean vanish! He wouldn't say, "Goodbye," or "So long," or "See you later." He *just went*. But nobody saw him go. It was magic. We used to say to each other, "Did you see him go?" Nope. Nobody saw him leave. I finally figured out how Kaufman did it. Nobody was paying attention to the time. That is, nobody but Kaufman. He'd keep his eye on his watch. At five minutes to four, he would begin to drift to the back of the theater. All the rest of us innocents would be watching the stage. The actors were absorbed in their rehearsal and the rest of us were absorbed in looking at them. When Kaufman's watch said four o'clock, he just slipped out through the front lobby and was gone. Gone home or gone to his bridge club — but gone. And no one had a chance to delay him. I learned a lot from Kaufman, but I never learned how to do this trick.

A couple of years later, when I started directing, I found it impossible to leave quickly at the end of a rehearsal. Before I could go, the stage manager would trap me with some question, or an actor would stop me and say, "Abe, could I have just a minute?" Then I would have to listen for twenty minutes while he asked if his part couldn't be made a bit longer or a bit funnier.

I guess that was the kind of thing Kaufman was avoiding when he did his Great Vanishing Act. As I think of it now, it reminds me of some professors at college. At a certain moment, these veteran teachers start slowly toward the door and when the bell rings, they are gone and no student has a chance to ask them stupid questions.

As a matter of fact, George was rather like a professor. He looked scholarly and he dressed casually. When he was directing the actors he was a businesslike professor in his speech and manner. He showed it on the first day of rehearsal.

I had looked forward to that day; I was very excited. No matter how many shows I have been involved with, the first day of rehearsal has always been exciting, but this day was special. It was the first day of rehearsal of the first show I had ever written. I sat there while the actors gathered around. Everyone was introduced to everyone else and then they all sat at a long table with the scripts in front of them. I had heard that directors started out by analyzing the play and talking about the characters, and about acting and other important stuff like that. Kaufman simply opened his script and said, "Act One, Scene One." That's all he said and the actors began to read their lines. They went through the whole play without being interrupted by Kaufman — and certainly not by me.

I've always been a first-name guy, but Kaufman kept a fairly cool distance between himself and the cast. It was *Mister* Levene, *Miss* Blaine, *Mister* Alda, *Miss* Bigley, and the few times he addressed me, I was always *Mister* Burrows. Outside the theater, I became "Abe" again, but while we were in rehearsal I was *Mister* Burrows, a freshman author who had better not get in his way. And of course to everyone connected with the show, *he* was *Mister* Kaufman.

The one person who seemed annoyed with all this formality was Sam Levene. Sam rarely called George *Mister* Kaufman. He used to call him "Sir." That may sound respectful, but Sam always said that "Sir" rather loudly, and with a kind of mock humility. It was obvious that he was kidding the formality of the atmosphere. I'm sure George knew what Sam was doing, but he didn't show it. There were many times when George was sitting out front and watching the rehearsal and Sam wanted to ask a question about a scene. He would go down to the edge of the stage and call out a loud and humble "Sir?" George would answer quietly, "Yes, Mister Levene?" George's quiet response was always very effective.

Kaufman was also strict with the audience, even in the matter of sight lines. Many times when there are several actors onstage, they stand in front of each other in a way that prevents the poor souls on the side aisles from seeing everything.

During rehearsals I would often run around the theater checking the sight lines. Once when I was watching from the side, it seemed to me that several seats were really prevented from seeing some important stuff. I ran up to George and said, "George, in those seats on the left, the people sitting there won't be able to see her while she's singing." George looked at me for a moment and said, "Well, they shouldn't be sitting there."

Eventually, I finally learned what he meant. In order to make a scene look right and have *everyone* in the whole theater see *everyone* on the stage, the actors would have to stand in a long, uninteresting, straight line. So people who buy tickets and find themselves way over on one side should be prepared for looking at some very attractive backs. Usually, it will only be for a brief moment or two.

George was a rather calm director; no wild ranting and raving, no tantrums of the kind you see in movie portrayals of stage directors. I'll always remember how Warner Baxter screamed at all the actors in *Forty-second Street,* and his passionate speech to Ruby Keeler when he shook her and said, "You're going out there as an understudy, but you'll come back a star!"

Kaufman worked quietly and easily. When he had to reprove an actor for something he did it in his own easy way. There was the time when Tom Pedi, a very funny actor who played Harry the Horse, was taking a lot of liberty with the script — ad-libbing little additions here and there. I was annoyed but kept quiet; I assumed that Kaufman would handle it eventually. One day Pedi added a whole new sentence on the way to a joke. I sat in the back row fuming while Pedi's new words were ruining a good laugh line. At that moment Kaufman stopped the rehearsal, walked over to Pedi, and put his hand on his shoulder. Then he called out into the dark theater, "Is Mr. Burrows out there?" I answered, "I'm back here, Mr. Kaufman." He then said in a very pleasant voice, "Mr. Burrows, I've been listening to Mr. Pedi. Would you consider giving him credit as co-author?" I answered in the same pleasant tone, "I'll think about it." The whole company laughed and Pedi never ad-libbed again.

The actors were in awe of Kaufman, sometimes too much so. When the cast was rehearsing in Philadelphia just before our first opening night anywhere, Vivian Blaine came to me with a problem. There was a certain line of dialogue that bothered her and she asked me how I thought she should handle the speech and the little bit of business connected with it. I was shocked. I didn't *dare* give anyone a direction when George Kaufman was the director, and I said to her, "Why don't you ask Mr. Kaufman?" And she looked at me with horror and said, "I wouldn't ask *him*."

Vivian eventually went timidly to George and he helped her. She had no reason to fear him but as a newcomer she did fear the theater itself. Vivian was a movie star who was about to go onstage in her first Broadway show. She turned out to be marvelous in her part. The audience loved her, but she didn't believe they would until she heard them cheer. After that, she was less fearful around George. But to her he was always Mister Kaufman. They were never buddies.

Directing actors in a musical is quite different from directing them in a straight play. One big difference between straight plays and musicals is that actors hired for a musical must be able to both sing and act, preferably in that order. And usually, unless they were born singers, they have worked harder on their singing than on their acting. This troubled Kaufman. He felt very strongly that before actors came to work with him, they should be professionals. He once said to me, "Abe, I don't run an acting school."

There are many Pygmalion-type directors, who like to discover new people (even amateurs) and mold them into actors. Kaufman wanted to be able to concentrate on the flow of the dramatic action, on guiding the actors in their movements and their understanding of their roles — not on teaching them how to say their lines. To work under Kaufman, an actor needed talent, training and experience, and if he had them, Kaufman knew how to use them.

I'm afraid the cast of *Guys and Dolls* didn't quite measure up to Kaufman's standards. Long before Kaufman and I were involved with the show, Feuer and Martin had spent at least two years planning and working on the casting. They were searching for unusual people. Actors who were special. Feuer used to say, "We want people with bumps." By bumps he meant characteristics that made a performer stand out. When Michael Kidd, our choreographer, was auditioning dancers, he of course looked for good dancers, but he also favored dancers with bumps.

Often someone would show up who didn't exactly fit the original concept of the part, but was so talented and had such good bumps that we tailored the script to fit him. For instance, there was Stubby Kaye, who played the part of Nicely-Nicely Johnson. (Runyon called him Nicely-Nicely because when people said to him, "How are you?" he always answered, "Nicely nicely thank you.") This character was famous for being a prodigious eater. In one of Runyon's stories, Nicely-Nicely won a big eating contest at Lindy's restaurant. Runyon described him as a very very thin man, which was kind of odd for a big eater. However, Stubby Kaye was and is fat — well, let's just say rotund — but when he came in to audition for the part, he turned out to have an endearing comic quality and a glorious, ringing tenor voice. He bowled us over. Frank had written an exciting song called Sit Down, You're "Rockin' the Boat" and we decided that a character who ate a lot could also be a fat man. That's how we got chubby Stubby Kaye. Ever since then, wherever *Guys and Dolls* plays, Nicely-Nicely is played by a fat man. If it happens to be a high school or college student, they stuff him with pillows.

We found another oddball who really fitted. One day in the midst of auditions a comic named Gene Bayliss came over to see if there was anything in the show that he could do. He happened to be accompanied by a friend of his named B. S. Pully. Well, the part that Bayliss might have been right for — a character named Benny Southstreet — had already been assigned to Johnny Silver, a good little actor whom I always thought of as Short John Silver. I told that to Bayliss, but when I was introduced to Pully and I heard his low, gravelly voice, I got very excited. There was one part we had not cast: that of Big Jule, the villain in the show. I walked Pully over to Feuer and Martin, who immediately rushed him over to George Kaufman. When George heard Pully's voice, his eyes lit up. As enthusiastic as we all were, there was one little problem. Pully was pretty well known on the nightclub circuit, mainly because his act was very blue. Believe me, Pully's act was much dirtier than blue. Even his initials, B.S., were dirty. He worked with a partner called H. S. Gump. The H.S. initials were relatives of the B.S.

But we hired Pully, and it turned out that this big, rough-voiced man was one of the most disciplined performers in our show. He learned his lines, stuck to them, was never late, and never missed a cue. The only thing he ever did on his own was to get overly creative with his makeup. When we were trying out the show in Philadelphia he kept increasing the amount of eye shadow, lipstick and rouge. After a while he began to look as if he were out for Trick or Treat on Halloween.

We all kept complaining to Kaufman about it but George just said, "I'll take care of it." He did take care of it. On the day the show opened in New York, he called the actors in for a short rehearsal. A lot of people don't rehearse on opening day, but Kaufman said a short rehearsal is much better than letting the actors sit around in hotel rooms or in their homes being nervous. So he held this little rehearsal: a few lines, a few moves. After it was over, he wished the company good luck and then he said, "I know you'll all be fine tonight and if I don't come backstage to see you, it's because I don't like crowds." And as the actors began to leave the stage he stopped Pully and quietly said to him, "Mr. Pully, you're doing very well, but if I were you, I would leave off all that makeup." Pully just nodded and murmured a confused "Yes, Mr. Kaufman" and left the stage. That night he came on without a hint of wild makeup. And he was beautiful in the show. One of the funniest villains of all time. Kaufman told me later that he knew Pully's makeup was bothering us, but he said, "If I'd've told him to leave it off last week, he would have had it all back by tonight."

I think the strangest piece of casting that Feuer and Martin came up with was Pat Rooney, Sr. Pat was in his seventies, a song-and-dance man from vaudeville who turned out to be just right for us. I'm sure the people who are reading this have

171

parents and grandparents who saw Pat Rooney dance the waltz clog. Pat had never played in the legitimate theater but we signed him to play the part of the Mission Doll's grandfather, who was the head of the Save-a-Soul Mission. In his uniform, this little gray-haired man was perfect as a missionary. However, we ran into one big problem.

We had naturally planned to have Pat do his well-remembered dance in our show. Frank Loesser wrote a lovely little waltz version of one of the other songs. It seemed to fit Pat's clog beautifully and Pat worked very hard rehearsing it. But when we saw the number on the stage we were all shocked. It just didn't work! The music was pretty. Pat Rooney was as good as he'd ever been, but when he did the number for the audience, he only got a mildly sympathetic hand. The number was out of key with the rest of the show. *Guys and Dolls* was a comedy, and in a good comedy everyone in the cast must take his role very seriously. And this gentle gray-haired missionary suddenly breaking into a waltz clog was a jarring note.

When Rooney was told that we would have to cut that dance, he was hurt. It was a painful moment for all of us. The song 'n' dance had always been Pat's signature and he thought that if we cut that number he would be contributing nothing to the show. He felt he wasn't needed. But after a few performances, he found out that the audience loved him whatever he was doing. And he scored without doing his dance. Loesser had written another song for him, a lovely ballad that the missionary sang to his granddaughter, called "More I Cannot Wish You." And I remember that Wolcott Gibbs, the hard-to-please critic of *The New Yorker*, said that "More I Cannot Wish You" was "possibly the most charming moment in the show."

The period during which *Guys and Dolls* was rehearsing in New York was a crazy time for me. I was still involved in those three TV shows. I think CBS was beginning to get tired of *The Stork Club* show, and they said I could leave it when I went to Philadelphia for the tryout run of *Guys and Dolls*.

And I think I should mention one more interesting happening. On October 2, 1950, during the first week of rehearsals, Carin and I were married. My first wife, Ruth, and I had been divorced the previous year.

In 1950 most people thought that Carin and I had been married for quite a while. That made "getting married" a bit tricky because we didn't want a lot of publicity on the subject. Because of TV, most people knew my face and if we walked into the marriage-license bureau, it would certainly hit the newspapers. "Abe Burrows marries his wife." That would certainly puzzle a good many people. These days, our attitude would receive a lot of laughs.

Leonard Lyons came to our rescue. Through political connections he arranged for us to get the license quietly. We were told to go to a certain clerk at the license bureau late on a Friday afternoon. It seems that during the late hours on Friday there are seldom any reporters hanging around City Hall. They go home for the weekend. We followed instructions and got our license quickly and quietly.

Now we had to find someone who would perform the marriage ceremony without spilling it to the press. Once again, Lennie Lyons helped. He called on another friend of his, Judge Samuel Liebowitz, the famed Sam Liebowitz who as a young attorney had defended the Scottsboro Boys in Alabama.

Judge Liebowitz, who was then presiding at a court in Brooklyn, agreed to take part in this comic-opera conspiracy. Carin and I went to his office in Brooklyn with our two safe witnesses, my brother and sister. The judge, who was known as a tough judge, turned out to be a very sentimental man on the subject of marriage. He made a short but very graceful speech, and even though this was a clandestine marriage taking place in an office, he managed to give it a ceremonial feeling. And although Sam Liebowitz was a famous judge and a man who enjoyed his fame, there was not one word about our marriage in the newspapers.

After the ceremony Carin went home to our apartment; I kissed her and went off to rehearsal. That wasn't very romantic but it was necessary. I had been missing many of the rehearsals because of my extratheatrical schedule. Ernie Martin used to phone me and bawl me out; he wanted me to see all of them. In his opinion, they weren't going too well. Though I felt that there was no need for me to worry — not when George Kaufman was the director — I did my best to show up oftener.

Yip Harburg, the E. Y. Harburg who wrote *Finian's Rainbow* and a lot of other wonderful things, once said, "Musicals are not written, they're fixed." That's true of just about every musical ever done. Someone writes the songs, someone else writes the libretto, and a choreographer plans the dances. Each of these parts of the show may seem fine but when all of them are put together on the stage, they almost always need fixing. That big joke you thought would make a great curtain line when you put it on paper doesn't always work when a living, breathing actor speaks it. Sometimes it's the actor's fault, but often enough the line doesn't belong in that scene. A song which sounded great when you heard it played in a living room often doesn't sound as good when it's sung on a big stage. That dance you thought was wonderful seems wrong when it follows a certain scene. You have to do a lot of "fixing." And after you fix something you have to fix what you just fixed.

I remember a lovely young dancer in one of my companies who, after she watched me change some dialogue, said to me, "Mr. Burrows, my boyfriend is a playwright. He just wrote his first play." I told her I wished him luck. And she said "I'm very proud of him. He swore to me that he would *never, ever,* make any changes." I don't know what finally happened to that young playwright, but whatever it was, it must have been rough.

I believe that it's this business of fixing and adjusting that troubles many novelists when they try the theater. Henry James wrote some plays but never could really bring one off. My friend Edwin O'Connor, who wrote *The Last Hurrah,* had problems when it came to drama. He did a couple of plays, but they were never as successful as his books.

Balzac was also fascinated by the theater, though the only

works of his we know today are his novels. He once decided that the reason his plays flopped was the fault of the producers. He said that the people they invited to the opening night of his shows were a stupid audience. And he decided that he was going to personally take that job away from them. Balzac insisted that all the opening-night tickets be turned over to him for distribution. Came the opening night of the play, the theater was absolutely empty. He had forgotten to distribute the tickets.

I think the fundamental difference between the novelist and the playwright is that the novelist writes alone. He has an editor, but the novel is basically his product. In the theater the writer has to deal with a director, a producer, and most important of all, the actors. Once the play is on the stage, it really belongs to the actors. Their acting style, their speech and their physical mannerisms affect the whole play. I remember once sitting at rehearsal of *Guys and Dolls* when Tom Pedi gave a line a reading that was wildly different from what I had heard in my ear when I wrote it. When I heard his reading I was shocked, and I started to jump out of my seat. Kaufman was sitting next to me and he put his hand out and pushed me back in my seat and said, "Let him alone. His reading is better than yours." Kaufman was right. When Pedi finally said that line in front of an audience, he got a tremendous laugh and I got the credit for a great line.

Chapter 11

As we kept working away on the fixes and changes, the rehearsals became a bit hectic. We had to spend a good deal of time on the music and that began to irritate Kaufman. The long, complicated music rehearsals interfered with the rehearsals of the book. But there was something else. It turned out that George Kaufman, world-famous director and playwright and my respected teacher, thought that the musical numbers were just entertainment — mild divertissements that interrupted the story at all-too-frequent intervals. To the rest of us — Feuer, Martin, Loesser and me — the music was a fundamental part of the show.

Later on, when the show was playing in the theater, most of the songs became George's "lobby numbers." When a show is going on — especially during an out-of-town tryout and the previews in New York — you can see the people who put the show together standing nervously in the back of the theater watching the proceedings. The director and an assistant, the choreographer and an assistant, the author, the songwriters, the producers and a few of their backers, the set designer, the costume designer, and a lot of other people are all there, pacing up and down. If you're one of the standees, they will bump into you from time to time. You'll know who they are because they seldom apologize.

Every so often, one of these characters will suddenly rush into the lobby for a smoke or a drink, but mostly it's to get away from what is happening onstage. The choreographer's lobby number is usually any scene that has no dancing in it; the composer's is any scene devoted solely to acting. Kaufman used to flee the minute *any* music started. One day when he was sprinting for the lobby during a performance of *Guys and Dolls,* he said to me, "Good God, do we have to do *every* number this son-of-a-bitch ever wrote?" I followed him and tried to explain that I considered Frank Loesser a musical dramatist. His songs were as much a part of the story as the dialogue. George looked at me as though I had gone crazy and without a word he disappeared into the lobby.

And yet in spite of his seeming hostility toward musical numbers, George had been involved with many fine musicals: *Of Thee I Sing, Let 'Em Eat Cake,* and *I'd Rather Be Right,* which brought George M. Cohan back to Broadway.

Of Thee I Sing was a landmark. It was the first musical comedy to receive the Pulitzer Prize in drama. Kaufman and Morrie Ryskind wrote the libretto and the music and lyrics were by George and Ira Gershwin. I saw the show in the thirties and was dazzled by it. As I remembered, it had a great many musical numbers, I think even more than Frank Loesser composed for *Guys and Dolls.* The only explanation I can come up with is that George Kaufman deferred to George Gershwin's status as a musician. However, Kaufman never really changed his attitude to the music. I had this confirmed later on in 1952, when *Of Thee I Sing* was being revived.

George asked me to come down to Philadelphia and take a look at the tryout. He said the revival wasn't going too well. He was always frank about these things, and he said he'd welcome any suggestions from me. When I saw the show, I knew it was in real trouble, the kind of trouble that cannot be licked. That once lovely show was the victim of Time. The original version had opened in New York in 1931, when the Depression had set in and the government in Washington was wide open to satire.

177

But in 1952 the satire just didn't seem very funny anymore.

The next morning I met with George and Morrie Ryskind. Morrie was a well-known screenwriter and he later did several other shows with George. Nobody from the music department was at this meeting. Ira Gershwin was in Beverly Hills, and George had died a long time ago.

Kaufman and Ryskind seemed interested in hearing my reactions and my suggestions, but frankly I crawfished. It's very painful to give suggestions when you know a show is in deep trouble and you really can't help. I mumbled things like "I had a pleasant time" and "The audience seemed to like it." I just couldn't bear to hit George over the head with the fact that the show was dated, so I took the cowardly route and concentrated on the musical stuff. Actually, the musical numbers were pretty good.

George, of course, wasn't too happy with what I was saying but he listened. Finally, I said they had made one very bad move when they cut a certain song. It was a good song and important. They told me that the number hadn't worked and it hadn't been performed well. And since it seemed to hold up the action, they had decided to take it out. I dropped my kindly approach and said, "You may have to give it to someone else to sing, but the show definitely *needs* that song." George thought this over for a moment. Then he turned to Ryskind and said, "Morrie, I think Abe has a point. The audience always does seem to perk up when the band starts playing." I guess George always thought of music as a noisy thing that keeps the audience from going to sleep.

The revival of *Of Thee I Sing* ran very briefly in New York. The critics all said it was dated, and no "perking" from the "band" could help it.

Kaufman's relationship with songwriters was an interesting one. Many of them were his close friends. He often spoke with admiration of the Gershwins, Howard Dietz, Arthur Schwartz, and many others. But when it came to doing shows with them, the honeymoon was over. Aside from the fact that the music would "get in the way of the story," there was another tiny annoyance.

Every so often he would grumble about the extra benefits the songwriters would get from a hit show. When a song hit emerges from a show — a song like "Oh, What a Beautiful Mornin'," or "Some Enchanted Evening," or "I Got Rhythm" — the songwriters do very well from record sales, sheet music and ASCAP royalties. ASCAP is the American Society of Composers, Authors and Publishers, but "Authors" means lyric writers. The librettists are not included. When a record album is made by the cast, the librettists do not share in the royalties.

George felt that this was unfair. Since many of the songs were born because of scenes the librettists had written, they deserved a cut of some of the goodies. He used to talk to me about it, and I'm told that he once brought the matter up at a meeting of the Council of the Dramatists Guild. He couldn't win that argument, but he was always mildly resentful and he enjoyed making slightly bitter jokes about "rich" songwriters.

Cy Feuer once told me that during the tryout of *Silk Stockings* in 1955, he walked into Kaufman's hotel room and found him sitting in a chair looking very glum. "Cy," he said, "I hear Irving Berlin just picked up four hundred thousand dollars from MGM. He sold them half a song." Cy, startled, said, "Half a song?" Kaufman nodded. "Berlin just sold the word 'All' from his hit song 'All Alone.' " It was a funny line, but it was one of George's funny lines that carried deep feeling.

The rehearsal of a musical runs four weeks plus one. That extra one is for the dancers; they start rehearsing a week before the other performers. Some people think that four weeks is a long time. Some think it's too short. "After all," they say, "in summer stock we put the show together in a week." But in summer stock they don't have to make any changes.

To me that four weeks seemed long and tough. As the rehearsal of *Guys and Dolls* went on — I could say dragged on — we all began to get a bit tired. All those funny jokes — even though they were my own jokes — didn't seem so funny after I heard them over and over. The actors began to look weary; the gorgeous dancing girls, bedraggled and sweaty. The excitement of working in the theater began to fade, and the rehearsals became a form of glamorous drudgery. When I'd come home after a day of making changes and worrying about scenes, I found myself exhausted.

At these times Carin and I communicate our feelings by quoting punch lines of certain jokes. We call them Jokes to Live By. One of our favorites is a joke that Howard Lindsay once told me. Lindsay said that an old-time vaudville comedian used to walk out onto the stage with his clothes all torn. He looked as though he'd been in an accident. He would say with a country twang, "Folks, I just had me a terrible experience. I was walking down the road when I saw a pussycat stranded high up in a tree. Well, I felt sorry for him and decided to climb that tree and help the poor little pussycat get down. Well folks, when I finally reached that little pussycat, it turned out that it was no little pussycat. He was a big, mean bobcat. Folks, let me tell you I never got so tired of one animal in my life!"

That punch line can be very useful. When I'm working on a show and I'm tired of it, and I've had a long, hard day and come home looking bushed, my wife will say, "How did the show go today?" I answer, "I never got so tired of one animal in my life." That's all I need to say. She understands.

Of course the reason that the *Guys and Dolls* rehearsals seemed less than enchanting to me was that I was still a raw, green freshman. I should have been wearing a beanie. It takes a while to learn that it's almost impossible to judge a musical by the bits and pieces you see during rehearsal.

When you're doing a straight play, the whole company rehearses together onstage and you watch the play beginning to jell. When you're rehearsing a musical, the cast is scattered all over the place. As soon as the company finishes the first reading of the script, it divides into various departments. The dancers usually do their early work in some nearby dance studio that has the mirrors and the barres that dancers need for rehearsal. Singers are put somewhere else — the lobby, if it's large enough; sometimes they wind up in the basement. The composer is given the use of a small dressing room in which he rehearses and sometimes berates the leading actors while they try to learn their songs.

Of course these days the theater suffers from a housing shortage and many shows don't get to rehearse in a theater at all until they are ready to open. Another show is usually playing in the theater that will eventually be yours, but in the meantime you may have to rehearse in a studio. There are many of these rehearsal studios in New York, and with their large air-conditioned rooms, they are physically more comfortable than the theater. (Theater owners are not too generous about turning on the air conditioning during rehearsals.) However, it's very difficult to judge a show in a rehearsal room. It's never "real theater" until the audience is seated and the actors are on the stage.

Another drawback is working without an orchestra, whether you are rehearsing in a theater or in a rehearsal hall. The orchestra does not join the show until the tryout; therefore, when you're rehearsing you never get to hear the accompaniment that makes any song sound better.

The reason is financial. It's too expensive to have musicians wait around during rehearsals while the performers are learning their songs. The only musicians we use during rehearsals are two pianists. One of them works with the singers and the other with the dancers.

In 1950 the theaters were not as heavily booked as they are today, and *Guys and Dolls* was able to rehearse and eventually to open in the Forty-sixth Street Theatre. There, during the last week of rehearsals, about four days before we left for our tryout in Philadelphia, something magical seemed to happen to the show, and to me as well. I found myself enjoying, actually loving, the rehearsals. All the scattered pieces began to become

181

one beautiful unit. The actors, the singers and the dancers finally got working together. Suddenly, what I had seen as a loosely fragmented project became a show, a real show.

Kaufman's work was fantastic. The actors moved around that stage as though they owned it. The musical numbers, Michael Kidd's dances and the book scenes blended as though the show had been running for months. There was one especially fine example of Kaufman's brilliant staging. In the second act all our muggs were involved in a crap game which, to avoid the cops, took place in a sewer, an interesting subterranean set that was designed by Jo Mielziner. The scene started out with one of Michael Kidd's finest ballets, featuring a group of Runyon's Guys pantomiming a crap game to music. In the program it was just called "The Crap Game Dance." When I first saw it, it took place on a bare stage, but it was stunning. As the dance ended, the scene turned into an actual crap game, a big one involving about twenty crap shooters, some of them rolling the dice, others engaged in arguments, and Kaufman put the whole thing together like a master jeweler assembling a watch.

I watched these rehearsals in a state of euphoria. Maybe it was partly because it was my first show, but I felt that the company was superb. I'm sure that better actors than some of ours could be found, and probably better singers and dancers, but our people blended in such a way that to me the show seemed perfect. I felt that nothing more could be done to make it better.

It took me a while to learn that there has never been a show that didn't need some fixing. We kept on fixing *Guys and Dolls* even after we opened in New York and it had become a tremendous hit. About six weeks after the opening, Kaufman phoned me to say he was calling a rehearsal for the whole company; the performers were getting a bit sloppy. This didn't surprise me. Even I knew that all good shows require periodic brushup rehearsals. A play is not a film. Live actors can't help changing their performances from time to time. I told George I'd be there. Then he *did* surprise me. He told me that I would have to do some work, too. He pointed out six spots in the show that weren't funny enough. I must write some new and funny lines to replace them. Now, I was shaken. "George," I said, "I thought we were finished with the script." His answer: "We're rehearsing on Thursday at two o'clock."

I temporarily stopped taking bows for having a hit; I sat down and wrote six new jokes.

I realize now that my wildly enthusiastic reaction to those final rehearsals before we went out of town was a common theatrical disease called Pre-Philadelphia Hallucination, a virulent form of self-delusion. I didn't think we had a single problem and I didn't know that we were in for some nerve-racking weeks, weeks in which I often asked myself, "Abe, do you really think there is no business like show business?"

I once wrote a pessimistic parody of Irving Berlin's song about show business. My version was only two lines long:

> *Yesterday they told you you would not go far.*
> *Last night you opened and they were right.*

Philadelphia has always been a good tryout town. It was originally chosen because it had a bright, cosmopolitan audience, and it was far enough from New York so that it discouraged the Broadway crowd from coming down to enjoy your troubles. But these days a turnpike makes the trip a quick one, and now many of your show-business friends rush down to see your show, tell you it's fine, and then rush back to New York to rap it. Then you read in the columns that you're "in trouble."

Originally, the most popular tryout place was Atlantic City. Ring Lardner was down there in 1929 to try out *June Moon,* a play he had written with George Kaufman, who was also the director. It was in three acts, and Kaufman, who was famous for his cutting ability, had Lardner cutting scene after scene. One day a friend spotted Lardner on the boardwalk and asked him, "What are you doing down here, Ring?" Lardner sighed and said, "I'm down here with an act."

When I first arrived in Philadelphia with *Guys and Dolls,* I felt uneasy. I was about to spend four weeks working in a strange town. At least it was strange to me. To a born New Yorker, every other city is "out of town" (I lived in Hollywood for ten years and I always felt "out of town").

But the Philadelphians soon made me feel at home. It turned out that Kaufman and I were celebrities there. The reason was our television show, *This Is Show Business*. When Kaufman and I first walked down Broad Street together, we created a mini-sensation. The people we passed stared at us and many of them stepped up and greeted us. There was an interesting difference between the way they greeted me and the way they greeted Kaufman. They would shout, "Hello, Abe" or "Hiya, Abe." Then they would turn to Kaufman and respectfully say, "Hello, Mr. Kaufman." I was enough of a ham to enjoy the popularity. But Kaufman didn't like being accosted (his word) by strangers in the street. He hadn't come to Philadelphia as a vaudeville actor, but as a director. Whenever he and I stood in the back of the theater, he hated to have people staring at us. He once said to me, "What are we supposed to be, goldfish in a bowl?" I smirked and said, "George, you were the one who chose to go on TV. These are your fans. They adore you. Why don't you just relax and enjoy it?" He answered me with a contemptuous grunt and walked away.

He never got used to public adulation. There have been many stories about the ladies in Philadelphia ruffling Kaufman's hair. Well, that crime actually happened only once and I was there to see it. Kaufman and I were sitting at a table in a restaurant (Lou Tendler's old place, which has now disappeared), when a lady who was passing by stopped as she recognized George, and suddenly said, "I can't help myself," and she ruffled his hair with both hands. Then she fled. George sat there looking as though someone had just electrocuted him.

Since the tryout of *Guys and Dolls*, I have taken many shows on tryout trips to Philadelphia and other towns. Wherever you go, the drill is always the same. You arrive at the town. You check into your hotel. You call up various people to find out

1947. This was a trick picture before I ever appeared on television. At that time we all thought that television would disappear.

A rehearsal of The Abe Burrows Radio Show. *That fellow with the accordion is Milton De Lugg.*

This Is Show Business, *1950. With George Kaufman, Clifton Fadiman and a guest star, Faye Emerson.*

A typical happening before we went on the air. Kaufman was always baffled by bow ties.

1946. A party at Nunnally Johnson's. Seated: Nunnally Johnson, me and Danny Kaye. Standing (left to right): Robert Benchley, Marc Connelly, Norman Corwin, Ira Gershwin, Groucho Marx.

A party at our home in New York. Carin with Cy Feuer.

Me with Ernie Martin.

1965. A newspaper photographer grabbed this picture of Lauren Bacall grabbing me. This was a few minutes after the curtain came down on opening night of Cactus Flower.

Moss Hart and me in the fifties.

1953, with Bing Crosby on the Liberté, *entertaining at the ship's gala.*

*With Marilyn Monroe and Tex McCrary.
I like the fondly puzzled look on my face.*

*Forty Carats, 1969. I loved working with
Julie Harris, as you can see.*

*1964. President John-
son and Duke Elling-
ton. This was at the
White House Corres-
pondents' Dinner.
ASCAP put on the show
and I was the master of
ceremonies.*

Frank and me after receiving the Pulitzer Prize. We look rather happy.

what's going on. Things are not yet coordinated and for a while no one is sure about rehearsals or about anything else. So you unpack your bags and relax. At that moment you get a call and are told that everyone is at the orchestra rehearsal.

The orchestra is working in some rehearsal hall or other, or perhaps in the ballroom of one of the hotels. You go over to listen. The cast is there and feeling very happy as they finally get to sing their songs with the backing of all those fiddles, brasses and drums. You listen for a while but you don't say much. This rehearsal is run by the conductor and the composer. The only things you might say are "Great" or "Wow."

After a while, you leave and stroll over to the theater where your show will be playing (when I did *Guys and Dolls,* I'm sure I dashed over to look at the theater before I checked into my hotel). It's always a good feeling. You stand there enjoying the sign on the marquee. You look at a big poster in the lobby and you spend a pleasant minute reading your name among the credits (if it's your first show, you may spend a pleasant hour).

You walk into the theater. It's very dusty, full of rubbish — paper cups and other stuff left over from the previous show — that won't be cleaned up until opening night. On the stage the stagehands are setting up the scenery. They all look weary because they haven't had much sleep. You stroll onto the stage and try to avoid being decapitated by banks of lights and chunks of scenery. The tired stagehands are very polite, but they make it clear that you're in the way. You seek out the stage manager (on *Guys and Dolls,* it was Henri Caubisens) who also has had no sleep. You ask him when the stage will be ready for the rehearsal. (He will be asked that dozens of times by dozens of people.) His answer always is "I hope by tomorrow afternoon." More likely it will be tomorrow night or the morning after that. But you will not get to rehearse on that stage until the stage manager tells you it's ready.

From now on until the show opens, he's in charge of everything that has to do with the physcial production. At this time a good stage manager is invaluable. He may not have written the

185

songs or any of the jokes, but he's the key to getting your show onto that stage. When you want anything done, you must follow protocol. You must tell him what you want and he will see to it. The heads of the various departments all work under him. There's a master carpenter who's in charge of the scenery, a master electrician who's in charge of the lighting, and a master of properties who looks after the props.

Props — short for "properties of the producer" — are everything on the stage but the actual scenery: furniture, pictures, flowers, vases, guns (if it's that kind of show), cigars — anything else that's used in the show. The actors cannot take any of them home, or to put it bluntly, no one is allowed to swipe a prop.

On *Guys and Dolls* we had a property man named Meyer Ecker. Meyer was very skillful but he had one problem: he was bald. During some scene changes, you don't draw the curtain; you black out the stage and in the dark the propman and his assistants dash out wearing black clothes to make themselves invisible, and run around the stage resetting furniture and other props. But because Meyer was bald the audience could see his shiny head moving around the stage. We finally solved it by making him wear a black skullcap, actually a yarmulke borrowed from a local synagogue.

When the show is running, the stage manager is the right arm of the director. He, with his assistants, makes sure that the actors arrive in the theater on time and see to it that the actors get onstage when their cues come up. The law of the theater is that an actor must arrive at the theater a half hour before curtain time. It's part of the rules of Actors' Equity. No matter how big a star is, that star must be there at "half hour." If it's an eight o'clock curtain, he must sign in backstage at seven-thirty. I mean literally sign in. He must put his initials next to his name on a list that is posted on the bulletin board. If an actor is going to be late for some reason, and it better be a very serious reason, he must call the stage manager. This is a matter of life and death for a show. Each actor has an understudy. If the actor is ill and is not going to show up at all, the stage manager must warn the understudy and prepare him to go on. If an actor makes a habit of being late — there are stars who have been known to show up five minutes before the curtain — a good stage manager will bawl him out. If the actor resents this and turns nasty, the stage manager has a very big weapon: he is a member of the same union the actor belongs to — Actors' Equity. This means that if an actor behaves badly, the stage manager, as a brother member, can bring him up on charges. Believe it or not, sometimes the mere threat to start proceedings is much more powerful than a reprimand by the director or a reproof from the producer.

George Kaufman once said that the worst crime an actor can commit in the theater, even worse than being late for "half hour," is being late for an entrance. Missing a cue. Picture yourself as an actor playing on a stage. There's a knock on the door, and your line is "Oh, that must be Harry." You go to the door, open it, and no one is there. You're left in the worst position an actor can be in. Later on, Harry may say to you and the stage manager, "I tore my coat in the dressing room," or "My zipper stuck." What he's done is unforgivable. The only acceptable excuse would be that he had died, and even then he would have to prove it.

One day early in October of 1950, the cast of *Guys and Dolls* officially got to rehearse on the stage of the Shubert Theater in Philadelphia. They began to work within actual sets, amid scenery and furniture they had never seen before. For a little while it was bedlam.

Pre-tryout rehearsals in New York are on a naked stage, which has some taped markings on the floor to indicate where the scenery is eventually going to be. These rehearsals are really just playacting. But when actors start to work for the first time with real scenery and real furniture and real doors, they often go into real shock. They blow their lines and forget their songs. They are busy trying to open doors that stick and they stumble over furniture: "I didn't know that goddamn table was going to be *there*." In this rehearsal you go through all the sets one by one. When a show is finally running on Broadway, the sets are changed in just a few seconds, but when you are rehearsing for the first time, the stagehands have still not practiced the scene changes. This is a rehearsal for them as well. These first scenery changes out of town take hours. Getting through the whole show often takes a day or even two.

This rehearsal was very painful for me. My brilliant dialogue and hilarious jokes sounded dreadful. The actors stumbled over their lines and even if they occasionally did say a funny speech properly, the only audience was us, the weary "us" who knew all the punch lines and who had been listening to them for weeks and weeks. However, our next rehearsal cheered us all up because for the first time the orchestra was in the pit. In addition to playing the music, which makes the whole thing sound more like a show, the musicians make one big additional contribution. They laugh at the jokes. Laughter is the electricity that makes a comedy writer's blood start pumping. The musicians are the only people in the theater who have never heard the jokes before, and they laugh and it makes us — and the actors — feel a lot better.

The next day we had another session, a combination of a rehearsal and a dress parade. This was the first time that the actors worked in costume. I always enjoy this particular rehearsal because it gives me something new to look at. But it can be rough. There are many complaints from the cast. And a good deal of groaning. The first complaint you hear usually comes from the dancers, a complaint I have heard during every musical show I have ever done: "My shoes are too tight." We swear we will fix the shoes. The actors are unhappy with their costumes: "Am I going to have to wear this thing?" "Are you trying to make me look ugly?" We tell him or her that he or she looks beautiful; sometimes they even believe us.

I remember one girl dancer who was embarrassed by her scanty costume. She walked to the front of the stage and said to us, "I can't go on the stage like this. I look almost naked." And one of the producers yelled back from the seats, "That's the whole idea."

This session of *Guys and Dolls* turned into a sort of hostile fashion show. It finally ended with the producers swearing to the company that all the shoes would be fixed, and all the costumes would be fine. And everyone pretended to be happy. The next crisis in Philadelphia came the day before we actually opened the show and faced our first audience.

This is the day that you have your most important rehearsal of all — your final dress rehearsal. In all the previous rehearsals, you start and stop. If something goes wrong — an actor forgets a line or an entrance, the lighting is wrong, a piece of scenery gets stuck — the director stops and corrects it. But in the final dress rehearsal the cast goes right through the whole show without stopping, just as if it were being done in front of an audience.

Chapter 12

There's an old saying in the theater, "A bad dress rehearsal means you'll have a good show." People have lost a lot of money believing sayings like that. It's like saying, "After the rain, comes the rainbow." My response to that is "Not necessarily." Sometimes after the rain comes a flood.

While we were still rehearsing in New York, one of the actors didn't seem to know what he was doing. As we watched him, I worried. Kaufman consoled me by leaning over and announcing, "Abe, I just made up a new old saying. Sometimes an actor may look very bad in rehearsal, but when he finally gets on the stage, he could be terrible."

For *Guys and Dolls* we staged two final rehearsals. We might have had a third final one, but we ran out of time. This all happened because our first final rehearsal didn't go well at all.

In the beginning of the first act the story didn't get off the ground soon enough. As the show went along, the pace improved. As a matter of fact, the second act was pretty good, but our glum feeling about the early stuff spoiled the rest of the show for us. We all sat there morosely for a moment and then panic struck.

In the opinion of the producers and the music department, the book needed a lot of cutting, deep cutting, in the first scene of the show. I resisted this at first, but I wasn't at all sure of my position. Kaufman, who had been through many bad rehearsals, felt that we had some problems, but we ought to let an audience see the show before we made any major changes. A big discussion took place. We were all involved: Feuer and Martin, Michael Kidd, Frank Loesser, Kaufman and I. We stood in the rear of the theater and argued, our voices getting louder. Some of the actors could hear us — they had been told to wait around after rehearsal to get some comments about their performances — and they were getting nervous. Finally, somebody had the stage manager tell the actors that another rehearsal would be held that night, and they were to be there an hour ahead in case we had any changes. This didn't seem to cheer them up and they walked out of the theater grumbling. We all continued our argument. Argument? It was a battle.

I took most of the beating because it was the libretto that seemed to need cutting. As I listened to everybody yammering away, it occurred to me that this was the time when people working on other shows used to ask Kaufman for his advice. George was a famous play doctor. Whenever a show was having trouble out of town, the producers' first thought was "Call Kaufman."

However, George couldn't be the doctor on *Guys and Dolls*. He was too closely related to the patient. Besides, he felt that our show did not need desperate surgery at this time. The rest of us were not thinking very clearly because we were pressed for time.

I began to feel as though I were back in the world of radio, where we made quick changes with our panicky eyes on the clock. At last, I nervously blurted out, "George, maybe we can go back to the hotel and find a few cuts in the opening stuff." Kaufman, who hated arguments, shrugged, looked at all of us, and said, "You're all a bunch of amateurs." And he walked out with me hurrying after him. We went to his hotel room and performed some radical surgery on the opening section of the show.

I was embarrassed and unhappy because I knew that I was willfully making deep cuts in a key area — the Exposition. I remembered when George had lectured me on this subject and told me I should take my time, lay the story out clearly, and the audience would hold still for it. But we did make the cuts and we did give them to the actors. They were unhappy, but as working actors they accepted them.

After dinner, we sat down in the theater to watch our second final rehearsal. For this particular rehearsal, we had a small audience — a few people we had invited to come in: some friends, several of the agents who represented our actors and, of course, all our wives.

The curtain went up, the rehearsal started, and it was an absolute disaster. Compared to it, the first rehearsal seemed like a dazzling hit.

After Michael Kidd's exciting opening ballet — which never failed — nothing else worked. We had taken out the so-called dull spots in the opening scene and the rest of the show just rolled over and died. There were practically no laughs, no excitement. Just nothing.

Once upon a time there was a man who had an odd anatomical problem. He had been born with a screw in his navel. A small metal screw. He had lived with it all his life and every doctor he spoke to looked at it and said, "Just leave it alone." One day he found a new doctor, who looked at the screw and said, "I can remove that for you." He took an ordinary screwdriver and quickly removed the screw and the man's ass fell off.

When the final curtain came down on that dreadful second dress rehearsal in Philadelphia, we all knew that we had committed theatrical malpractice. We asked the weary actors not to leave the theater because we would have to make some changes. The rest of us — the producers, Kaufman and I — had a panicky meeting. All this was taking place at about eleven-thirty on the night before our world première in Philadelphia.

Everyone agreed that we had to restore all the stuff that we had taken out. But Kaufman, who hadn't been happy about making the cuts in the first place, was still furious. He said, "Abe, if you want to put those cuts back, you go ahead and do it. I'm going to bed." And he left.

The actors had to stay in the theater until one in the morning while we reinstated all the lines we had taken out. The people who did the actual work were my wife and myself. Carin had worked with me many times when I was in radio and she was a big help that night. Together we went backstage and gave the new changes to the actors in their dressing rooms. They were all unhappy, but they were too tired to argue with us.

I think Sam Levene was the angriest. He was justified in disliking our yo-yo vacillation. He had worked hard to learn lines that he liked. They had been taken away from him, and now they were back and he was upset all over again. When we were all through working and he was leaving his dressing room to go to his hotel, he said something to me that I will always remember. Pointing his finger accusingly at me, he spoke in Shakespearean tones: "Abe, it's very important for this show that I should be happy. And I'm miserable!" And he stalked out. I stood there and suddenly I laughed — the first laugh I had had all that day. I was enjoying a bit of moderate hysteria.

When we left the theater and wearily walked to our hotel, Carin was very cheerful. She hadn't liked the cuts and was delighted that we had restored them. Carin always loved everything about *Guys and Dolls*.

As for my feelings, I felt nothing. I didn't feel down or up; I was just numb. All the tinkering we had done that day had shortcircuited my brain. My mind was overloaded with the lines we had nervously thrown out and then more nervously restored. I also couldn't shake the feeling that we might have been wrong.

The next day seemed unbearably long. In the afternoon I hung around the theater; Kaufman had called a brief rehearsal. He wanted the cast to run through their lines, especially the ones that had been cut and then restored. The company was fairly grumpy and I couldn't blame them. Sam Levene was still unhappy about all the lines we had made him learn and unlearn and relearn. Robert Alda, who had been very cheerful during rehearsals, took me aside and hit me with a different sort of complaint: his role was dull, unfunny. He said, "Everyone else in the show is getting laughs and I'm a straight man." The laughs that he said "everyone else was getting" were the chuckles that came from the rehearsal-watchers and members of the orchestra. This hunger for laughs affects many actors. When they are doing serious plays or films, they don't miss the laughs; but put them in a comedy, and they become laugh-junkies. I told Alda he was great when he played George Gershwin in *Rhapsody in Blue* and he didn't get laughs in that picture. I reminded Alda that he was the leading man. The hero. The handsome hero. My wife and all the women who watched rehearsals thought he was beautiful. Then I pointed out that he had many lines which he didn't think were laugh lines, but which would get big laughs when we had a real audience. He reluctantly muttered that he would do his part as it was written, but he hoped that after we opened, I would write him some funny stuff.

I got other little beefs. Some of them were kind of touching. One of the male singers came over to me and said, "Mr. Burrows, could I please have a name?" I was puzzled and then I realized what he was getting at. The first song in the show after the opening was a trio sung by Stubby Kaye, Johnny Silver and this fellow. In the program it was listed as "Fugue for Tin Horns" — sung by Nicely-Nicely Johnson, Bennie Southstreet and a horseplayer. This singer, who was listed as "a horseplayer," didn't have any dialogue in the book but he still wanted his character to have a name. I told him I would dig up a name for him and that next week's program would list it. I eventually found a Runyon name for him, Rusty Charlie. That made him happy. Later on through the years, when this fellow took out an ad in *Variety*, he listed himself as having played the part of Rusty Charlie in *Guys and Dolls*.

I took care of several other complaints. I didn't mind them

194

because they took my mind off my own opening-night stage fright.

Actors are not the only people who suffer from stage fright. Authors, directors, producers and the people who back the show all suffer from a similar ailment. You can call it "off-stage fright." Its symptoms are sickening waves of helpless terror.

Actors are understandably nervous on opening night, but their fright is different from the fright that grabs those of us who only stand and wait — and suffer. Actors have a definite job to do, and after some early nervousness, they do it. They get into their roles and their fright usually fades away. But the rest of us remain frightened throughout an entire performance.

I've since done many shows, but on every opening night I still feel that same tension. It causes me to stand in the back of the theater and use Body English. That's my way of helping an actor on the stage. You can't talk to him during the performance, so when his cue comes up and he has to say a line, you silently try to help him by thrusting your shoulder toward the stage as though you are willing him — almost ordering him — to say the line with the proper timing.

If the orchestra's tempo is a bit slow, the composer tries to help out by moving his shoulders faster. I've been at some opening nights where the stuff going on in the back of the theater is more interesting than what's on the stage. Body English is not something that can be taught. It's an instinctive reaction to helplessness.

Finally, the moment came when the Philadelphia critics arrived. They were pointed out to me, which didn't help me to relax. Friends came down from New York — some of them really close friends who came to root for me. They were as nervous as I was, so that didn't relax me either.

At last, all the people were in their seats and the houselights began to dim. I felt like the bull in a bullfight at the Moment of Truth.

For George Kaufman, it was just one of many, many opening

nights. For Feuer and Martin and Frank Loesser, it was their second out-of-town opening night (their first was *Where's Charley?*). But for me it was a very first First. Scary. During the months I had spent working on the show, I had begun to feel like a professional. But now I reverted to feeling like a green kid. As a matter of fact, Carin told me that my face actually *was* green.

We sat in the very last row on the aisle. She and I have sat in those seats in every show I have done since. We held hands tightly as the theater darkened. The overture sounded fine and was applauded. The curtain went up and Jo Mielziner's first set, a scene on Times Square, got a very nice hand. Then Michael Kidd's opening Broadway ballet started and went beautifully. That was no surprise; it was a wonderful ballet and would have been a smash even if it had been done outside our show.

None of this kept me from worrying. I was wondering if the audience would accept our muggs and our Broadway story. There were some New Yorkers in the audience but the majority of the people were Philadelphians. The audience in Philly is always very astute and very generous. But when a Broadway-bound show plays out of town, the magic words are "Show me."

Then came the moment that showed them. Three characters strolled onto the stage — the horseplayers. They were carrying racing forms, and as they came to a stop center stage, a solo trumpet in the orchestra played First Call. It's that trumpet call you hear before a big race. When the audience heard that trumpet, a roar of laughter shook the house, the laughter of instant recognition. It meant that the audience had accepted the basic premise of the show. They weren't laughing at a joke line, they were laughing at the whole show. They had accepted our characters and their milieu. I turned to Carin, kissed her on the cheek, and said, "We're home."

Then I got up and stood in the back of the orchestra. George Kaufman was there, pacing up and down. Feuer and Martin were pacing. Frank Loesser was pacing. So I also began pacing — with one difference. I was pacing on air. I sure was high.

The audience seemed to be laughing at every line and cheering every number. During the intermission all our friends congratulated us hysterically, and George and I were mobbed by the television fans in the audience. (I shook hands with them while George fled.)

I went backstage to see the actors. They were all pretty happy about that first act. Bob Alda, in addition to being happy, was astonished. He had received many, many laughs and all his complaints about being a straight man were forgotten. When he saw me, he ran over and said, "Hey, Abe, did you hear those big boffos I got?" I smugly said, "I told you, didn't I?"

Before intermission ended, Carin and I took our seats and wondered if the second act could possibly go as well as the first. Second acts can be tricky. Many musicals use up most of their ammunition in the first act, and the second act is a fairly short wrap-up. In *Guys and Dolls,* we had a comparatively long second act, but five minutes after it started, I knew, from the audience response, that it was going to go even better than the first. I kissed Carin on the cheek once again and got up and resumed my pacing. As I paced, I started congratulating myself. I was full of self-admiration. I kept thinking, "Why haven't I been doing this sort of thing all my life? This Broadway stuff is a cinch." I was sure we had a big hit. I was sure there was very little work to do on the show. I was sure happy and sure proud. And I was sure dumb. Dumb and wrong.

The reviews in the newspapers were raves. The good news traveled quickly to New York and I got many congratulatory phone calls. Max Gordon, who had been at our opening, sent me his standard "hit" telegram: "Dear Abe. Bend down and pick up the money."

That morning I walked over to the theater and enjoyed looking at the long line of people waiting to buy tickets. That's a thrill you never get when you work in television. The shows on TV come to the audience free. But that line outside a theater is made up of people who actually want to pay money to see something you've worked on.

There were many TV fans in that line who congratulated me on the good notices. One of them called out, "Hey, Abe, is the show as good as they say it is?" And I answered modestly, "Better."

The theater was full of happy actors. No real rehearsal was planned but the cast was called in for a brief meeting. A chance for everyone to hug everyone else. There was joyful buzzing about the beautiful first night and the critical raves. We were all looking forward to dazzling Philadelphia for the rest of the run and having a great time doing it.

Then came the second night.

I have since learned that second nights — out of town or in New York — are frequently traumatic, especially when the first night has been unbelievably successful. In the case of a serious drama, the difference on second night is not too noticeable. But when you're dealing with comedy — especially musical comedy — and the laughter and applause are not as big as they were the night before, it's shocking. Shocking not only to the authors and the director and the producers, but even more to the performers. They become unnerved. When an actor walks out on the stage and gets a mild snicker, or no response at all, to a line that had convulsed the audience the night before, he is badly shaken. This leads to a domino reaction. He starts to press; he gets anxious and loses other laughs. Anxiety is death on comedy. There's a phrase they use about nightclub comedians when they get anxious: "flop sweat." Our actors didn't get to the point of flop sweat on the second night, but they were pressing, and the more they pressed, the less funny their lines seemed.

Bob Alda had a fairly rough time. He lost the big laughs he had received opening night, his funny lines "got nuthin'." When I went back to see him after the first act, he said to me, "Abe, what the hell happened? Every one of my jokes died." I could have soothed him by saying it was the fault of a lousy audience. But I've learned that if a good joke dies, it's not necessarily the fault of the audience. The actor may have committed a cardinal sin. He may have unconsciously let the audience know that a joke was coming. We call it telegraphing a joke. A joke has to surprise the audience; but many actors on their way to a funny line tip it off before they say it. Their eyes will gleam. They almost seem to be licking their lips, and the audience is ready for the joke. No surprise, little laughter.

This is fairly common in comedy. An actor once told me that when he was doing a show directed by George Abbott, he was having a good deal of trouble with a punch line, one of his biggest laughs. Suddenly after a few weeks, the audience stopped laughing at it. He tried different ways of handling the line without success, and finally he went to George Abbott, one of the greatest comedy directors, and said, "Mr. Abbott, I've tried saying that line a million ways and it isn't working at all. What should I do with it?" Abbott looked at him and answered quietly, "Just say it."

"Just saying" a line can be very difficult. Most actors who have a comical style feel they must use that style to help a joke get a laugh. But very often a line — to be funny — has to be said simply. This does not always sit well. I have since worked with actors who've said to me, "If that's the way you want it, why do you need me?" But saying a line without doing something to embellish it sometimes requires more skill than "being funny."

The actor I am talking about followed George Abbott's suggestion. On his next performance he went out and "just said it" without trying to help the line, and he got his laugh back.

When I was talking to Alda about his no-laugh problem, I hadn't yet heard that George Abbott story. Besides, I wasn't the director of the show, so I talked to Bob as a friend. I suggested that maybe he should just do the lines in character and forget that they were jokes. Let the audience find that out for itself. In the second act he got more laughs.

But for me that problem was fairly simple compared to others that suddenly popped out at me: weak spots I hadn't seen before. Or perhaps I was one of those "none so blind as those who don't want to see the problems of a musical."

A shaky second night may be very painful, but it can also be helpful. Very valuable to the people who have put the show together. When there's no gala opening-night uproar; when you have an ordinary, typical audience, you're able to study the show calmly and carefully. As I sat there and watched with a clinical eye, I saw several big holes.

Once when I was a kid, my father gave me a comical definition of a hole: a hole is nothing with something around it. That's actually what a hole in a show is. It's a "nothing" spot which is a nasty abyss into which the audience's interest momentarily disappears and it takes an unbearable couple of minutes for that interest to climb out; sometimes it stays in the hole. This calamity can be caused by a bad joke or a long, unnecessary speech or a dull song. Then there are good numbers done by the wrong people. Or good numbers done by the right people in the wrong spots. And one of the most common problems is a good number that belongs in another show. Not yours.

Chapter 13

On that second night in Philly, Kaufman, Loesser, Feuer and Martin and I all saw the holes. We had a serious meeting after the show, during which each of us attacked his favorite one. The sole thing we agreed on was that we needed to do a helluva lot of work.

I had to change my mind about my silly dream of four carefree weeks in Philadelphia. Eventually we stayed there for five weeks and we needed every minute of that time.

Larry Gelbart once said the definitive line about the painful side of bringing in a musical comedy. At this time he was out of town with the tryout of his first show, *A Funny Thing Happened on the Way to the Forum*, for which he had written the libretto. Larry's tryout was taking place at the same time that Adolf Eichmann, the Nazi war criminal, was on trial in Israel. There was a great deal of talk about how Eichmann should be punished. Hanging? Firing squad? Prison? Larry Gelbart said, "I know what they should do with Eichmann. They should send him on the road with the tryout of a musical."

That line is not just a wisecrack. Like most good jokes it states a bitter truth, one that hits home to those of us who have been in the trenches in Philadelphia, New Haven, Boston and all other towns in which we stick out our nervous necks. Quite often some serious dramatist or a director of classics will irritate me by saying, "Hey, Abe, one of these days I'm going to take a crack at a musical. They must be fun." What he means is they must be easy.

Guys and Dolls was tough to do but it had one great blessing: our tryout run had no financial problems. Many shows run into big money troubles out of town. Empty seats and big losses prevent producers from taking the time to do what is necessary to fix a show. Many of them have to cut their out-of-town tryouts short and take the show into New York before it is ready. A desperate gamble with a hope for a miracle.

Guys and Dolls happily did big business during the entire run in Philly. The audiences were very appreciative. Everyone seemed to like the show; they even tolerated the spots that we were fixing.

We worked day and night, but a live show with real live actors that goes on eight times a week — six nights and two matinees — is quite unpredictable. Every so often a scene we thought was absolutely perfect and needed no work would suddenly, for no reason at all, die on the stage. One evening during our third tryout week one of our most powerful comedy scenes didn't get any laughs. No laughs at all. This was our hilarious crap game scene in the second act. It had never failed before; it had been very funny in all the rehearsals and every night since we had been in Philadelphia. But that one night it just lay there like a big beached whale. The rest of the show suffered from the hole that the failure of the crap game had created.

When the curtain came down, Ernie Martin and I walked back to our hotel together. We were both very quiet and thoughtful. Suddenly Ernie said to me, "The crap game didn't work!" I answered, "I know." Ernie stared at me. "Did the actors do something wrong?" I answered, "No, they sounded fine." Ernie raised his voice. "But they didn't get one single laugh." I sighed: "That's right." We kept walking. And suddenly Ernie stopped, turned to me, and called out in despair, "What the hell kind of a business is this?" Ernie wasn't talking to me, he was talking to the Gods. But neither the Gods nor I had an answer for him. I've always been happy that I never tinkered with that scene.

But we did have to tinker with some other spots. We carefully avoided unscrewing the show's navel, but there were numbers we had to cut. The most painful to make was Pat Rooney's dance.

Frank was having other problems with the score. He had written a song called "Travelin' Light," which was to be done by Robert Alda and Sam Levene. When Frank originally wrote it, he was under the impression that the part of Sky Masterson was going to be played by a dancer. And though that number was very good, it called for singing and dancing. However, Bob Alda could sing but he couldn't dance, and as for Sam Levene, well, someone once said, "He may not be able to sing, but he sure can't dance." Frank had to throw that song out of the show.

Yet another song gave Frank trouble. It was in the first act and was to be sung by a lot of gamblers who were looking for a crap game. Opening night he had a song called "Action" in that spot. It didn't work and a few other ideas he tried out didn't work, either. He was getting desperate. One day, Frank and I were sitting in his hotel room worrying together about this problem and I said, "You know, in the dialogue I have Sam introducing himself as Nathan Detroit, sole owner and proprietor of the oldest established permanent floating crap game in New York. So maybe the guys could . . ." As I spoke, Frank's eyes lit up. And together we spoke that line slowly: "The oldest established permanent floating crap game in New York." We looked at each other; we both had the same thought. The line scanned. I quickly cut it out of the libretto and just as quickly Frank set it to a tune; it turned out to be one of the best songs in the show.

The song "If I Were a Bell" was another troublemaker. It was to be sung by the Mission Doll when she finally falls for the gambler. Isabel Bigley was a good singer, but somehow or other in Philadelphia the number fell flat. For a while we tried taking it away from Bigley and giving it to Vivian Blaine. It didn't belong to Vivian's character and we gave it back to Isabel, who kept struggling with it. Then one day someone, I think it was Cy Feuer, found a way for her to do it. The magic word was "tipsy." In the story, Sky Masterson has made a bet that he can date the young and beautiful missionary. He tricks her into the date and then tricks her into drinking a couple of Bacardi cocktails — which, he says, contain hardly any alcohol, "just enough to act as a preservative." These drinks, of course, changed her ways and that was the key. She sang the song as though she were sweetly and gently tipsy. And it worked beautifully.

One of our biggest problems was the title song, "Guys and Dolls." Frank had written it as a big choral number and it was treated like an argument between the Guys and the Dolls. It didn't work right and we had dropped it from the show. The lyrics and the music were wonderful, but we had to find some way of getting the number into the plot. When you can't find a place for your title song, there is usually something wrong with the book.

Feuer and Martin were getting very nervous. There we were, making a lot of changes, finding new holes, and this was the beginning of our fourth and last week in Philadelphia. Kaufman suggested that perhaps we should take an extra week in Philly before we came into New York. This would mean postponing our New York opening. We all had a rather rancorous meeting in George Kaufman's suite. Ernie and Cy were against postponing. They felt it was no use wasting another week unless we could do something drastic to pull the show together. They finally said they would leave George and me alone to work it out while they went off and did some private talking themselves.

Kaufman and I, left alone, sat there just staring at each other. Suddenly I had a notion. Strangely enough, it had something to do with that pesky title song, "Guys and Dolls." I thought it should be sung by Nicely-Nicely Johnson and Benny Southstreet.

The song starts out:

204

When you see a guy reach for stars in the sky
You can bet that he's doing it for some doll.

They would be singing it as a comment on Sky Masterson's attitude toward the Mission Doll. I needed to write a new scene for
this, and if I could pull it off the whole story would fall into
place. Kaufman immediately phoned Feuer and Martin and
asked them to come up to his suite because "Abe has an idea
that might work." They arrived, heard the idea, and liked it.
They told us that they had just about decided to close in Philadelphia and go to New York immediately. But now they would
postpone the New York opening and take another week in Philadelphia. We had to move to another theater, the Erlanger. It
was an expensive move, an expensive postponement, and a lot
of trouble, but it was worth it.

Frank Loesser had one more big chore to do. We still needed
a new song to open the second act. Frank dug up a song he
used to sing at parties called "Take Back Your Mink." It was
perfect for this spot but we had only one week to get it on. That
is a ridiculously short time to put on a musical number. It
required singing and dancing by the girls (we called them our
"Dollies"). Michael Kidd had to choreograph the whole number,
Alvin Colt had to whip up the costumes. The song had to be
orchestrated and then rehearsed by the orchestra. But we finally
got it on. Just under the wire. It was performed on our very last
night in Philadelphia. It knocked them for a loop. They loved
the "Dollies," and we went to New York feeling very happy.

Chapter 14

Before our official opening night we played two previews in New York. And, naturally, the first preview was a disaster. It was a benefit for some charitable organization which had bought out the house for their members. A benefit audience can be lovely but sometimes they pose a problem: They can be made up of all the "same" people. They come from the same place and they generally think the same way. They all know each other. An ordinary audience consists of a bunch of strangers, people who come from all over. When the curtain goes up and you have a good show, some of the people like it immediately. Some of them take longer to get with it. But pretty soon the enthusiasm of the first group becomes contagious and in a little while the whole audience is enjoying the show.

But when it comes to some benefit audiences, if one person doesn't like it, they all don't like it.

The next night went slightly better. Only part of the audience was a benefit group. We had a lot of people who thought for themselves and the show went pretty well. Twenty-four hours later came our opening night.

For the people who put a show together (and for their friends and relatives) opening nights in New York are exquisite torture. Howard Lindsay, a veteran who wrote many shows with Russel

Crouse, never attended any of his own openings. Instead, he would go down to his club, the Players, and calm his nerves by shooting pool. Crouse could and did attend the opening and after each act, he would rush to a phone to call Lindsay and tell him how the show was going.

If a veteran like Lindsay found New York openings too painful, one can imagine how I, a rookie, felt at my first.

The Philadelphia opening had been frightening enough. But on November 24, 1950, when I stood in the back of the Forty-sixth Street Theatre, I felt like . . . well, actually I had no feelings at all. I was numb. My numbness started at home when I put on my tuxedo. In those days opening nights called for tuxedos for everyone; even the critics wore them. I still dress for any opening. To me it's a symbol.

When Carin and I got to the theater, I went backstage and said some things to the actors, which I don't remember. Then I stood in the rear of the theater meeting friends and watching the critics arrive: Richard Watts, John Chapman, Howard Barnes, Wolcott Gibbs, Brooks Atkinson, and many others. I knew some of them, but tonight they were all critics. One didn't dash up and shake their hands. A defendant doesn't shake hands with the judge before a trial.

The arrival of the critics is the signal for a show to start. As the houselights began to dim, I sat down next to Carin in our regular seats in the last row and held her hand. Or rather, she held my hand. I wasn't capable of very much action. The curtain went up and in minutes I knew that our show could do no wrong.

The performance that night was the best performance of *Guys and Dolls* that I have ever seen. It ran for several years, was on the road for several years and has played in stock, but no performance has ever been quite as exciting as that one on opening night. Many big hit shows, including some of mine, have suffered a touch of opening-night nerves. Actors have been a bit shaky at the beginning, music cues have been late, scenery has stuttered and stuck; but critics always allow for such things. However, the opening night of *Guys and Dolls* was truly perfect.

After five minutes in my seat, I kissed Carin on the cheek, stood up, walked to the rear of the house, and held hands with Frank and Cy and Ernie.

We were enjoying the performance with our eyes popping when suddenly a woman got up from her seat and started tiptoeing up the aisle toward us. Feuer, in horror, whispered in a very loud whisper, "Where are you going?" The woman whispered back, "I have to make a phone call." And Feuer, sounding like Captain Bligh, loudly whispered, "Get back in your seat." She hurried back to her seat. I found out later that she was one of Cy's guests. She just wanted to call home and check with her baby-sitter. I don't know if Cy ever forgave her.

By the end of the first act, things looked pretty good for us. As the audience got up for the intermission and headed for the lobby, they all seemed happy. I watched the critics as they got up to stretch their legs and have a smoke. Critics usually avoid showing their reactions during intermission. But Richard Watts, then the critic for the New York *Post,* helped make my evening. He walked up the aisle, stopped, put his arm around my shoulders, and whispered, "Abe, I'm having a wonderful time . . . and so is Mr. Atkinson." Then he continued up the aisle. I stood there transfixed. In one golden moment we had received a favorable review from Dick Watts and Brooks Atkinson.

But I'm one of those fellows who have a strong need to worry. So that night I worried vigorously. "Would the second act make Dick Watts change his mind?" "Did Atkinson *really* like it?" And what about the other critics? I've seen critics laugh their heads off and then dismiss the show as nonsense. Some of them who think of the theater as a holy shrine are not too friendly toward musicals or comedy. So I had a good comfortable set of worries to work on.

In those days there were seven major newspapers in New York, and each of them had its own theater critic. Those seven critics plus the critics from the Associated Press, the United

208

Press and the magazines, including *Women's Wear,* could all become cheerleaders for your show or turn into a lynch mob. Sometimes you could get an uneven response, called "mixed notices," which means that some of the critics love the show, some of them hate it, and some of them are friendly, with reservations.

Theater people have suffered from "friendly reservations" for centuries. I'm sure that critics have always come out with verdicts like this: "David Garrick was, as always, his dynamic self, although he didn't seem quite at home in the last act." Or, "*King Lear* is a fairly powerful drama, but we missed Mr. Shakespeare's usual wit and charm. As we watched the tragic downfall of the King, we just couldn't get *As You Like It* out of our minds."

The New York *Times* critics have always been the most powerful because the majority of theatergoers believe what the *Times* says about the show. But all theater critics have power; certainly they have more power than movie critics — probably a matter of economics. If you want to see a show, your ticket will cost you about five times the price of a seat at a movie. And these days theater-ticket prices are so high that the critics have actually become Shopping Guides.

Certain stars have always been able to fill those theater seats in spite of bad notices. Ethel Merman is one. So are Mary Martin and Lauren Bacall and a couple of others who have since devoted themselves entirely to motion pictures. *Guys and Dolls,* needless to say, had no such stars. We had a company of talented actors who were not yet theatrical superstars. So even though Dick Watts tried to comfort me, and even though the second act of *Guys and Dolls* went better than the first, and even though at the final curtain everyone was hugging and kissing me and saying we had a big hit, my comment was a nervous "I hope so."

While we were on our way to the opening-night party — another first for me — Carin kept assuring me that everything was fine, but I was more comfortable when I worried.

209

The guests at opening-night parties are not all rooters. Some of them are friends with hit shows of their own who may be unthrilled if another guy has a hit. La Rochefoucauld, a French nobleman who was also that rare thing, a notable wit, once remarked, "It is not enough to have a success; your best friend must have a failure."

Happily, the *Guys and Dolls* opening-night party was crowded with truly friendly rooters. They were so generous with their congratulations that they almost stopped me from worrying. The party took place at "21." One of the Kreindlers who owned "21" — a restaurant that is not ashamed of its high prices — said to me, "Abe, with a show like this, you can now afford to eat here."

The critics' notices finally came in and they sounded as though we had written them ourselves. They were all raves. I grudgingly stopped worrying. I began to accept the fact of our success, but I couldn't forget how tough it had been. We had gone through a lot of trouble to make it happen. I was still very new in the theater.

Chapter 15

I had learned a lot, but the most important thing I learned was that I had a lot to learn. The other people in show business didn't think that way about me. Now that my name was on one of the biggest hits in years, I was automatically "hot." I had become an expert overnight and very soon after *Guys and Dolls* opened, believe it or not (and I still don't believe it), I was back in Philadelphia being paid a large sum to doctor a musical that was in trouble. When the producers asked me to come and save their show, I suddenly remembered the way my mother reacted when I removed that cinder from my grandmother's eye: I was to become a doctor.

The name of the show I was asked to save was *Make a Wish*. It starred Nanette Fabray, an actress who can do anything — singing, dancing, comedy. The songs were by Hugh Martin, the choreographer was Gower Champion, and the show was directed by John C. Wilson. The producers were Jule Styne, Harry Rigby and Alexander H. Cohen. Jule Styne is a friend of mine and he's one of the most respected composers of musicals, but occasionally he's taken a fling at producing shows. *Make a Wish* was based on a play by Ferenc Molnár called *The Good Fairy*. The libretto was written by Preston Sturges, who was then a brilliant screenwriter and director. He had made an excellent movie of *The Good Fairy*, starring Margaret Sullavan.

Make a Wish was graced with a lot of talent, but in spite of it the show was dying. Sturges, after a big argument with the directors and the producers, had abandoned the show and gone back to Hollywood.

Before I agreed to go ahead, I went down to Philadelphia to take a look at it. It wasn't too bad. It had some very good songs and a good deal of charm. The dances were exciting. It was Gower Champion's first shot at Broadway and I was impressed by his work, especially two marvelous comic ballets. But I was bothered by something at the very beginning of the first act. Immediately after the overture, a group of attractive young people came out on the stage to sing their opening song. Before they started, the singer who was to lead the group yawned. It wasn't an accident. He had been directed to do that. He stood in the center of the stage, stretched his arms, and presented the audience with a big yawn and a groan of weariness. A yawn is very contagious, and if you start a show with it you'll put your whole audience to sleep.

After the final curtain, I told the producers that whether or not I worked with them, they must get rid of that yawn, and I told them my reasons. They were puzzled that I had picked on such a small thing, but that was the only specific criticism I gave them. I told them I wanted to get back to New York and think about the show before making my decision. The next day they called to say that I had performed a small miracle. They had followed my suggestion and cut the yawn; and it perked up the opening of the show. Now they had proof that I was an expert. A genius. And they were more eager than ever to have me go to work for them.

Carin had come with me to see the show and she, too, found it pleasant. After I talked over the producers' proposition with her and with my agents, I agreed to take on the project, with one stipulation: I must work on the show without any publicity for myself. I wasn't being modest, just careful. The producers may have thought of me as an expert, but *I* didn't think

212

so. Frankly, I didn't want to stick my neck out. In any event, I insisted on secrecy.

I went back to Philadelphia, holed up in the old Ritz-Carlton Hotel, and began to rewrite the show. Every day I would send over new pages and the producers told me that the actors liked the material and they were dying to know who was "writing this new stuff?"

One Sunday, after about ten days of working under cover, I picked up the Sunday edition of the New York *Times* and there in the drama section was a big article with a big headline that read "MR. FIXIT." Show business has more leaks than Washington, D.C., and there are no plumbers to plug them up. That story started my permanent and unshakable reputation as a show doctor.

I have since performed surgery on a few shows, but not as many as I'm given credit for. I've been involved in nineteen theatrical productions, plus their road company offshoots. Only a few of these have been surgical patients. And I don't usually talk about them. I feel that a fellow who doctors a show should have the same ethical approach that a plastic surgeon has. It wouldn't be very nice if a plastic surgeon were walking down the street with you, and a beautiful girl approached. And you say, "What a beautiful girl." And the plastic surgeon says, "She was a patient of mine. You should have seen her before I fixed her nose."

Doctoring seldom cures a show. The sickness usually starts at the moment the author puts the first sheet of paper in his typewriter. All the redirecting and recasting can never help much if the basic story is wrong. Max Gordon once said a thing about shows that I've always kept in my mind: "You can't fix this show; it has a sandy bottom." Fortunately *Make a Wish* had a sound story going for it. Ferenc Molnár seldom built on a sandy bottom.

The first thing I did as the doctor was to read Molnár's original play. It became immediately obvious that Preston Sturges

213

had paid little attention to it. Much of the patient's illness, I decided, could be cured by changing the libretto to include many of Molnár's ideas.

At this time, in 1951, Molnár was in his seventies. Most of his plays were still well known: *The Guardsman, The Play's the Thing, Liliom,* a great play on which Rodgers and Hammerstein based their lovely, and I think their best, musical, *Carousel.* But most people didn't know he was alive and living in New York.

I had met him briefly at Leonard Lyons' home and had enjoyed his comment about "the very long rabbi" at the bar mitzvah, but it didn't occur to me to consult him — I still thought of him as a legend. Then one day a woman phoned me and said, "Mr. Burrows, this is Mrs. Molnár." I knew the name of only one Mrs. Molnár, Lili Darvas, the actress, so I said, "Oh, is this Lili?" And she said, "No. I was before Lili." Molnár had had several wives and all of them remained his friends. One of their most important jobs was to help him with the telephone; Molnár detested talking on the phone. This Mrs. Molnár told me that Molnár would like to meet me and would I have lunch with him at Mercurio's Restaurant not far from his hotel, the Plaza.

Like many Hungarian playwrights, Molnár wrote a number of his plays at his favorite coffeehouse in Budapest. Mercurio's was an Italian restaurant but Molnár liked it because it was near the Plaza, and he hated crossing New York streets.

When I walked in, I saw him sitting at a table which was covered with a red-and-white checked tablecloth; at hand were a pad and pencils. Here, evidently, was his office. He had turned an Italian restaurant into a Hungarian coffeehouse. The lady who ran the place welcomed me at the door and led me to Molnár's table as if she were his secretary. Women seemed to love to wait on him.

Molnár greeted me very warmly. I think he was euphoric because it seems that I was the first person connected with the musical who had ever bothered to talk to him about it, and he did have a lot to contribute. As he began to discuss the show eagerly, he startled me by saying, "Abe, I have some wonderful

214

gags for you." Though he pronounced it "gogs," I was delighted to hear Ferenc Molnár use the word. Anyone who writes comedy and is honest will admit that the jewel of the comedy form is the joke, or as Molnár said, the "gog."

Many comedy writers — TV or theater — get an attack of stuffy dignity when they hear the word "gag" or "joke." In interviews and in solemn discussions one can hear them saying, "I hate jokes. I'm only interested in funny situations." The fact is that every good joke consists of a funny situation and a funny punch line. Take that oldest of old war-horses:

FIRST MAN   Who was that lady I saw you with last night?
SECOND MAN   That was no lady, that was my wife.

That's a good joke. Tired, worn-out, but good. And it's based on a funny situation. Now let's work on that same joke and change one word in the punch line:

FIRST MAN   Who was that lady I saw you with last night?
SECOND MAN   That was no lady, that was your wife.

Now that situation could be the basis for an entire play. Very funny or very serious.

Molnár's suggestions and gogs were a great help to me. In the original Hungarian play were situations with funny punch lines that had been left out of the libretto of *Make a Wish*. Or they hadn't been properly translated. Molnár also told me about certain bits of physical comedy in the original that were also missing. Some pretty funny stuff.

As I made use of the ideas Molnár gave me, the show kept getting better. I would like to say that it turned into a hit; but it didn't. However, I did fix things so that it was no longer a terrible flop. When *Make a Wish* opened in New York, no one got hit with sticks or tomatoes.

Some of the backers were very important people in business and in politics and they were grateful that they weren't embarrassed. We got mild notices from the New York critics. They admired Gower Champion's work. They praised Nanette Fabray, and Helen Gallagher, who had the second lead. And we did get one big rave. It was from Otis Guernsey, who was then the New York *Herald Tribune* critic. He liked it, and with his help the show ran about five months. The backers lost their money, but at least they didn't feel stupid about having invested in the show.

As for me, I had enjoyed myself and it led to another big first for me: my first crack at directing. In our last week in Philadelphia, John Wilson, the director, became ill. I still had more material to put into the show, including a whole new final scene. The producers asked me to jump in and stage my new stuff. By this time I had become pretty close to the actors and directing them was no problem. Actually, they helped me more than I helped them. The producers seemed to like what I did, and a couple of months after *Make a Wish* closed, Jule Styne called me to say that he was working on a new show, a revue called *Two on the Aisle*. Jule was composing the music, Betty Comden and Adolph Green were writing the lyrics and sketches, and Bert Lahr was to be the star. I told Jule it all sounded wonderful. Then he asked me if I would like to direct it. That's how I became a director. Simple.

Nowadays, when I talk to a group of aspiring directors, I find that the main thing they want to know is "How does one get to be a director?" My answer is pretty discouraging: "Someone has to let you direct." Some producer who is putting on a show that may cost hundreds of thousands of dollars has to be willing to entrust the whole project to you. You may be very talented but what have you directed?

If you're a new, untried playwright, the producer will have a chance to read your play. If you're an inexperienced actor, the producer can at least audition you. But if you have never directed a show, there is no way to check your credentials.

Most theater directors come from the other theatrical professions. They have started out as actors or playwrights. Stage

216

managers often become good directors, too: they get to rehearse the understudies of a show, and very often when a show goes on tour the stage manager gets to direct the road company.

I believe that way back in theatrical history, the director was one of the actors. It probably started with an acting company in ancient Greece. One day during a rehearsal, an actor probably turned to one of the other actors and said, "Hey, Demosthenes, you're not in this scene. Why don't you go out front and see how this thing looks." So Demosthenes walks out into the theater itself, and after a few moments he begins saying things like "Hey, Telly, speak up, I can't hear you." "Ari, you're standing in front of Telly. I can't see him." Or, "Hey, Phineas, if you're gonna play Apollo, you have to walk like a god. You're stumbling around like a stupid mortal." This is a free translation from the Greek, but I assume that, even then, actors used the same kind of insults we use today.

Some of today's best directors — Elia Kazan, Garson Kanin, Josh Logan, Otto Preminger — were all actors. Moss Hart, a fine director and playwright, started out as an actor. George Kaufman was one of the actors in *Once in a Lifetime,* as well as the co-author with Moss Hart.

As for me, the fact that I've been a performer has helped me as a director. I wasn't a great comedian. I got by because my stuff was funny. But I have had enough experience in front of an audience to be in sympathy with the actors, to identify with an acting company. My ability to rewrite my own or someone else's script hasn't hurt me as a director, either.

Most of the actors who have become directors were fairly good actors but not matinee idols. As a matter of fact, great actors frequently have trouble as directors. To them acting has become second nature and they are impatient with actors who lack their talent and skill. "Why can't you do that? It's really so easy." The director may not actually say a thing like that, but he thinks it. And when he thinks it, his face shows it. And an actor can read a director's face. The same is true in sports. The great baseball superstars have seldom made good managers. They get very impatient with the players they are managing. "Now why couldn't you hit that pitch? It's so easy." This makes the young players very tense. I think Joe DiMaggio sensed this when he turned down dozens of offers to manage ball clubs. Ted Williams was talked into managing for a while, and he was not very happy. Most of the best baseball managers are fellows with medium talent who have had to study the game and learn their craft the hard way. They are sympathetic when a man strikes out or makes an error. They don't like his blooper but they can understand his problem and they can help him. They know all the moves even though they may not be able to make them.

The general public really has only a vague idea of what a director does. He is often thought of as some sort of general who moves live puppets around the stage. There are directors who think of themselves that way. To these directors the actors are simply tools and the play is just a blueprint. But I believe that the main part of a director's job is to dig out and carry out the playwright's intent.

Sometimes you read a critic's notice that says, "Brilliantly directed but the play is weak." That brilliant direction may have hidden some of the play's weaknesses, but frequently it may have distorted the author's work, even hidden its strengths. When they watch a play, most people and many critics cannot always tell what was the director's work and what was the writer's. The critics will often praise a director for a lot of funny physical things in a show when the author may have specified those pieces of business in his original script. And frequently a hilarious bit that an actor does has been created by the actor himself.

I believe that in a good show one should not notice the direction at all. Ideally, the actors should sound as if they are making up the lines as they go along. If they do, or come close to it, you can give the director credit for his skill in putting together a good script with good actors.

I've written or been involved in the writing of most of the

218

shows I've directed; so if my direction doesn't work, what I feel is self-hatred.

One of the most painful duties (emotionally painful) a director has is firing an actor before a show opens. Of course, in the theater world people are never "fired." You'll read in the press that they are leaving because "they disagreed with the author's approach" or "the director's approach."

Whatever chocolate-coated phrase is used, the director, the author and the producer all think that the particular actor is wrong for the part, and the director is the one who usually has to do the unpleasant job of letting him go. Sometimes a tough producer will do it (there are a couple of producers who seem to enjoy it) but basically they chicken out.

It's a bit less difficult when you're dealing with actors who have the smaller parts. Vladimir Nemirovich-Danchenko, who with Stanislavsky ran the Moscow Art Theatre, once thundered, "There are no small parts; there are only small actors." Well, the fact is that on Broadway there *are* small parts and those actors get small salaries. Under Actors' Equity rules the producer is allowed a brief tryout period for the minor actors (it used to be five days; now it's two weeks). At the end of this period the actors will either be fired or signed up for the show. If he (the producer) decides on firing, the company manager customarily leaves a dismissal notice in the actor's mailbox. During the last day of the trial period, the actors keep looking in their mailboxes and fearing the worst.

There's an old and terrible story they tell about an uneasy actor who on his fifth day saw an envelope in his box. He pulled it out with trembling hands. He opened it, looked at it, and suddenly burst into hysterical laughter. One of his fellow actors said, "Hey Max, what are you so happy about?" Max waved the letter with a joyous grin and said, "My mother died!"

When it comes to a leading actor, the director usually does the firing personally. And it's tough. Of course, this actor usually has a contract and he will get some kind of cash settlement, so you're not throwing him out on the street to starve. But telling him he's out is still embarrassing and painful.

If this were the corporate world of big business, the boss could say, "Jenkins, I'll trouble you for your key to the washroom." Or he can just put a pink slip in the guy's envelope, but in the theater it's different. You cannot just fire an actor. You have to explain why. (Incidentally, when I say "actor" I mean male or female. I don't much like the word "actress." The word "actor" means one who acts. You've never heard the word "doctress.") Now this actor you're about to fire is someone you have auditioned, or at least you have seen his work in another play. You may even have been friendly with him for a long time. And now you must tell him that he is not right for the part he was hired for.

You can handle it in cowardly fashion. You can say, "Charlie, you're too nice a person for this part. This character is a villain and no one would believe you are a villain." Or, "Charlie, you're wasted in this part. It isn't big enough for a man with your talent." Or, "Sally, this part calls for an older, rather unattractive woman. You're too young and sexy for that."

The most frustrating thing that can happen to a director is working with an actor who is not at all interested in anything the director has to say. In Hollywood they tell a joke that may be based on an actual happening: On the first day of work on a film, the cast was running through a scene and the director walked over to one of the actors and made a small suggestion. The actor stared at the director for a moment and then said, "Look, I don't tell you how to direct; don't tell me how to act."

Sometime ago I agreed to do a show with an actor who was a star on TV, in nightclubs and in movies. I insist on forgetting his name. Before we went into rehearsal we became good friends. He said he was thrilled that I was going to direct the show. He showered me with gifts and we had a lot of laughs together. I was very happy and looked forward to rehearsing with this nice man.

220

Several people warned me that things wouldn't be quite as rosy as I thought. One day I ran into an agent friend of mine, and when I told him I was going to direct this particular performer, he gave me a long look; and then he patted me on the shoulder, sighed, and said, "Well, Abe, maybe you'll be the one."

Well, I wasn't the one. I still feel pretty sad when I think of those rehearsals with this fellow. It turned out that the only person who was going to direct him was Himself. He also directed everyone else in the company.

I never had an argument with him. No harsh words. Everything was quiet, pleasant and useless. After a few days of rehearsal the producer and I had a talk and we agreed on a very good piece of strategy: I simply went home and stayed there. The show went out of town and died. It never opened in New York or anywhere else.

Director's Stage Fright is my name for an occupational disease. I was hit by it in May of 1951, on the day of the first rehearsal of *Two on the Aisle,* my first rehearsal as a director. It was Bert Lahr who helped me through the opening minutes. He got me to relax by kidding me. As I stood up to speak to the company, he said something like "Hey, Burrows, if you're gonna direct the show, we're already in trouble." Everybody laughed and I joined them; and my stage fright vanished. In certain situations a funny jab is much more valuable than a compliment. Since Bert was the theater's most famous worrier, I'm sure he was worried about working with a green director. So although that joke made me feel better, it also helped him to cover his own anxiety.

Lahr was surrounded by a fine cast. His costar was Dolores Gray, a marvelous singer who had just had a big success in London when she starred in *Annie Get Your Gun.* There was Stanley Prager, a very funny man and a good friend who had worked with me in radio, and another talented comedian named Elliott Reid, who almost stole our show with a solo sketch he had written himself: a satirical version of the televised Kefauver hearings on organized crime. Elliott did all the voices and it was hilarious.

One of our strongest performers was the French ballerina Colette Marchand. She had been brought to New York by our producer, Arthur Lesser, an American who had spent most of his life in Paris. Our choreographer was Valerie Bettis. I also had a very good assistant, my wife Carin. She was that rare kind of assistant who really assisted.

I considered myself very lucky when I got to do a revue as my first directing job. I thought a revue would be much easier than a musical with a libretto. I was wrong. A show with a story has a definite structure. You have a beginning, a middle and an end, and it goes in that order. But in a revue, which is a series of unrelated sketches, dances and songs, you have no real form. Everyone connected with the show has a different opinion about what should go where.

The trouble starts after the various parts have been fully rehearsed and you start running through the whole show. During those days the stage manager posts a big sign backstage headed "Running Order," that lists the sequence in which the sketches and songs and dances will appear. The director changes the running order from day to day.

This was pretty annoying in rehearsal, but it got to be serious on the day we were about to open the show in New Haven, our first time before an audience.

That afternoon we were about do do a final run-through in the theater before the performance. Then came the big crisis. Our running order called for the show to open with a number by the whole chorus. That's standard procedure. Then the number two spot was Dolores Gray doing a song. And then the third spot featured our top star, Bert Lahr, doing a sketch. This is the orthodox form of a revue. (Beatrice Lillie, the great English revue star, always insisted on an interesting clause in her contract: "Miss Lillie will not appear onstage before 8:50.")

Well, Miss Gray didn't like my running order. She had just returned from a great success in London and she felt she was Bert Lahr's equal. She insisted on appearing in the number three spot. Bert Lahr, of course, wouldn't accept that. Comden and Green, Jule Styne and I all agreed with Bert.

After a lot of bickering, I said, "I don't know what the hell to do. Somebody has to open the show. Maybe I ought to drag a piano onstage and open the show myself." And I stamped out of the theater and went up to my room in the Taft Hotel, next door to the Shubert Theater.

Carin went with me. She was as upset as I was. I kept saying, "We're in trouble. Nobody wants to open the show. I think I'm going to quit." But I didn't want to quit. Then I got a strange idea. I got out of my slacks and sport shirt and put on my blue suit, plus a white shirt and a tie.

When I walked back into the theater, the actors were startled to see that I didn't look like my casual, sloppy self. First they started kidding me: "Why are you all dressed up? You going to a party?" I answered quietly, "I'm going back to New York." Suddenly there was a hush, and then Anthony Farrell walked in.

Farrell was the biggest backer of the show and he owned the Mark Hellinger Theatre, which was the house we were going to play in in New York. Farrell looked at me in my blue suit and said, "Abe, where are you going?" I said, "I'm going to New York, Tony. Nobody wants to start the show. Dolores doesn't want the number two spot. Bert is set to do the number three spot. Somebody has to do the number two spot or we have no show." Tony gave me a long look. Then he turned to the cast and said, "If Abe goes back to New York, I'm going to close the show." And he walked out. And I followed him. A few minutes later I got word that Dolores Gray didn't want to hurt the show; she'd be willing to take the number two spot.

Ever since then, when I hit an impasse in a show, I have said to Carin, "If we can't straighten out this mess, I'm going to put on my blue suit."

Dolores Gray was a big hit. She had a very exciting entrance. She came riding out on a treadmill, a moving platform that rolls

223

across the stage. It can bring on actors, pieces of furniture, scenery, whatever. When I first heard that the producer had bought a treadmill, I wasn't sure I liked the idea. I phoned George Kaufman, who didn't think much of revues, and wasn't too sympathetic about my doing one. "George, the producer has rented a treadmill and insists that I use it. Have you ever used a treadmill?" He grunted a yes. And then I asked, "Is it helpful to a show?" And he answered succinctly, "It depends on what you say on it." That was George. The only thing important to him was the dialogue.

Except for the episode when I "put on my blue suit," I enjoyed directing *Two on the Aisle*. We got very good notices in New Haven and in Philadelphia. But in Philadelphia business was poor because we were there during the end of June and the beginning of July. It was hot and not many Philadelphians were staying in town. The small audiences made the show seem pretty dull in spots.

Arthur Lesser, our producer, began to panic. One day, before a matinee, he walked into the theater accompanied by George Abbott, who was in Philadelphia directing *A Tree Grows in Brooklyn*. Mr. Abbott, who had written and directed dozens of famous plays, shared with George Kaufman the title of World's Greatest Show Doctor. Our producer told me that Abbott was a friend of his and he just wanted him to take a look at the show and give us his opinion. But I had the sickening feeling that maybe I was going to be replaced.

Abbott watched the whole show from the back of the theater. He never sat down. After the final curtain, the producer went over to him to hear his reaction. Abbott's comments were very brief. He said, "I think it's fine." And then he put his hand on my shoulder and said, "Abe has done a very good job."

I thought about kissing him but before I could do or say anything, Abbott said a quick goodbye, wished us luck, and left. His exits were almost as quick as Kaufman's. He left me feeling happy and secure. I'll never forget him for that.

224

For me the high spot of directing *Two on the Aisle* was working with Bert Lahr. He was a fascinating, talented, kind, generous, cantankerous, insecure, wonderful comedian; and I think he was the funniest man who ever worked on the legitimate stage. Many comedians are only as funny as their material. If the jokes are good, the comic gets laughs. If the jokes are weak, he dies. Bert Lahr had only to walk onto a stage and the audience would immediately start to laugh.

There are youngsters today who never got a chance to see Bert in the flesh, but he comes alive for them every year as the Cowardly Lion in *The Wizard of Oz,* a movie I think will be shown on TV forever. It was the only successful movie Bert did.

Many great stars of the legitimate stage have never been superstars in movies. Ethel Merman was one; Mary Martin, Katharine Cornell, Helen Hayes, Julie Harris, and Ruth Gordon were others. There people light up the stage, but the camera doesn't catch whatever intangible quality it was that made them stars in the theater.

Bert had small parts in unimportant pictures. He was big on Broadway, but in Hollywood nobody paid any attention to him. While he was making *The Wizard of Oz,* he lived next door to Billy Grady, an MGM executive. Grady and he rarely exchanged a word. Bert was not important enough. Then one day Grady called to Bert over the fence and said, "Good morning, Gong Gong." (A lot of friends called Bert that because of the funny sound he made on the stage — it sounded like "gong-gong-gong.") At first, Bert didn't understand why this big executive was suddenly being so friendly, but Bert was very canny and he guessed what had happened. MGM had just had a sneak preview of *The Wizard of Oz,* and it must have been a hit because Billy Grady was talking to him. Bert was right.

Lahr started out as a low comic in burlesque and vaudeville, and I think he was the only actor with a background like that who ever became respected in the legitimate theater. His work ranged from musical comedy to a marvelous performance in *Waiting for Godot.*

225

All the theater critics respected him. Most of them were not crazy about low comedy, but they enjoyed Bert. I saw an impressive example of that when *Two on the Aisle* finally opened in New York. It was in July of 1951, a terrible time of year in which to open a show, but our producer was running out of money. Brooks Atkinson of the New York *Times* was out of town on his vacation. We were resigned to being reviewed by the second-string critic, who may have been a pretty good critic but didn't have Atkinson's clout with the public.

When Lahr heard that Atkinson was not going to review the show on opening night, he was very upset because he considered Brooks a fan of his. "Brooks always likes my stuff." Then the day before our opening we got word that Atkinson did not intend to miss a Bert Lahr first night. He was going to take time off from his vacation and make a long trip into New York on a hot night in July, just to review Mr. Bert Lahr.

I ran into Bert's dressing room to tell him the good news. I thought it would make Bert happy. Instead, he got more upset than ever. He said, "Atkinson is a tough critic. What if he doesn't like me tonight?" Bert couldn't bear a situation that was free from worry.

Once he got on that stage, he was at home. Long after *Two on the Aisle* opened, I used to enjoy coming to the theater and standing in the wings to see Bert work. One night I was watching him in "Space Brigade," one of Comden and Green's funniest sketches. Bert played a spaceman wearing a ridiculously large cape and a silly space helmet; and he walked with his funny idea of how a spaceman walked. Just looking at Bert in his zany outfit made me laugh every time I saw him. But that night the audience was not very responsive, and he was annoyed. Right in the middle of the scene he spotted me standing in the wings. Suddenly he walked over to me with his grand spaceman's walk and said, "They're from the Moose country tonight." Then, without losing a beat, he strode back center stage and went on with the scene. With me watching, he was determined to win that tough audience and he soon had them in stitches.

He was very friendly to the other actors but he set down certain rules of behavior. When he was saying a funny line, nobody else onstage was allowed to move. It's a fact that a quick move on the part of another actor can kill a laugh. The audience must be allowed to focus on the actor who is saying the funny line. The other people onstage do not have to be frozen but they should not make any distracting movements. Bert carried this edict too far. When he was doing something funny, he wanted the other actors to stand absolutely still.

A young actor named Bob Gallagher constantly upset Bert. Lahr would call me to his dressing room and say, "Abe, that kid is moving on every one of my laughs." The next night I would watch the show and I'd keep my eye on Gallagher. I couldn't see him do anything wrong. I would go backstage and say to Bert, "I was watching the guy, Bert, and he didn't move at all." Bert said, "You're wrong. Tonight he was moving his facial muscles." Facial muscles? I had to laugh at that, and Bert had the grace to laugh with me.

But as long as the show played on Broadway, Bert kept policing the other actors. After each scene in which an actor had broken Bert's rule, Bert's valet would be sent to the actor's dressing room, open the door, wag his finger, and say, "Mr. Lahr wants to talk to you." And the actor would go to Bert's dressing room and swear he didn't move. When Bert insisted that he did move, the actor would give up and say with a sigh, "Bert, I'll never do it again."

Bert could be very naughty on the stage himself. He had a trick of making his cheek quiver while another actor was talking. This would make the actor break up in the middle of a scene. It's very embarrassing for an actor to get the giggles while he's doing a speech. I asked Bert to stop the quivering. He categorically denied that he ever did it. But the actors went on giggling. Presently I found out why: Bert was quivering only one cheek — the upstage one — which couldn't be seen from the audience. I kept after him and he finally stopped it, but I think it was probably because his cheek got tired.

Bert just didn't enjoy hearing other people getting laughs on the stage when he was on it. To Bert, laughter was the equivalent of oxygen.

I learned a lot from directing Bert, mainly that you didn't actually direct him. You sort of cleared the way for him. When we started out, I didn't know that. Since I was young, eager and green, and I was doing my first show, when we were trying out the show out of town, I tried to be a "brilliant" director and for a while I got into trouble.

Certain things about Bert's performance bothered me. For instance, when he was talking to someone center stage and he had a funny line to say, he would very often walk down to the footlights, say the line to the audience and then rejoin his fellow actor for the rest of the scene. He kept stepping out of character.

I felt that Bert was potentially a great actor besides being a great comic. And I rashly decided that I would be the one to help him become what I thought was a great actor — a man who didn't just go for the laughs. One day Carin told me something that straightened me out. As my assistant, she was working with Bert helping him learn his dialogue. When we made changes, Carin would sit with Bert and go over the new lines with him.

During these sessions, he began to talk to Carin about me and my direction. One day she came to me with a frightened look on her face and said, "Abe, you've got to do something about Bert. I just left him and he's crying. He says you're trying to change him and you're going to destroy him." I was frightened to death. I sat down with Bert and I talked to him about my own problems and my own ignorance. I admitted I was pushing him too hard. He gave this some thought and then said maybe he should have been listening to me more.

I felt a great sense of relief and both of us relaxed. We agreed that Bert should never abandon all those crazy, funny things he did instinctively. But we also agreed that those things could be handled in a disciplined manner. When I used that word "discipline," he sort of winced for a moment, then he said, "I'll give it a shot."

On opening night in New York, he did many of the things he always did, but at the same time he followed many of my suggestions. Brooks Atkinson gave Bert the rave we expected and the other critics were just as kind about his great performance. About a year after this, when the show closed, he called me into his dressing room and said, "Abeleh" — that's the affectionate Jewish diminutive of "Abe" — "I think you helped me a lot. I want to give you a present." I said something like "Oh, forget it, Bert. It was great working with you." He said, "No, I want to buy you something. I want to buy you a suit." That threw me. A suit? And then I remembered that he was talking as an old vaudevillian. In those circles the greatest thing you could do for a guy was to buy him a suit, because when a guy was broke and out of work he needed to wear a good-looking suit when he was job hunting. A suit was a sweet and generous gift. Bert sent me to his tailors, who turned out to be Arco and McNaughton, famous and high-priced people who dressed such clients as Bob Hope and Danny Kaye. I was embarrassed when I went to be fitted, but these tailors were expecting me and were very pleasant people. However, I was ashamed to take just one suit. I ordered two more and ended up with three suits, one of which was the gift from Bert.

Since *Two on the Aisle*, I have been asked to write and direct other revues, but I have always refused. All the others shows I have done — including the flops — have had some life after the Broadway run. They are performed by touring companies; they are played in summer stock, colleges, high schools, little theaters; and many of them have been turned into motion pictures. But revues don't live long.

Chapter 16

The opening night of *Two on the Aisle* gave me a total (with *Guys and Dolls* and *Make a Wish*) of three openings within eight months. Two of these shows were hits and one was a respectable strikeout. So my batting average was approximately 666.66. In addition to my Broadway activities, I was still appearing weekly on television in *This Is Show Business* and *We Take Your Word*.

I spent many evenings keeping an eye on the performances of *Guys and Dolls* and *Two on the Aisle*. Sometimes I watched them with great pride, and sometimes I would be less proud when the actors had a sloppy evening.

Many people think that once a show opens in New York, the work is over. It's true the basic work of writing the show and putting it on is finished, but after it's running, it takes a lot of tender, loving care. In this respect, the theater is different from all other art forms. A show is a living thing. Once a motion picture is shot and on film, it cannot change. Sometimes cuts are made but nothing else changes. No matter how often you run the picture, the actors still give the same performances and read their lines the same way. The same is true of painting. Once a painting is finished, it remains the same for all time; so does a book or a piece of sculpture. But a show is played live by living human beings whose energy and emotions vary from day to day. Their health changes, their hair grows longer, their enthusiasm goes up and down, as do all the other things that make human beings human or sometimes inhuman.

A live show has to be worked on steadily if you want to keep it fresh. You can't just think of opening night and then let everything go to pot. I had my first lesson in this when George Kaufman had me write that new batch of jokes after *Guys and Dolls* had been running for eight weeks.

No matter how successful a show is, someone has to "mind the store" all the time. The stage manager is the chief watchdog, but most producers and writers hop into the theater regularly to see what's going on.

The reason *South Pacific* was one of the biggest hits of all time and ran for years was partly due to the vigilance of Rodgers and Hammerstein and the director, Josh Logan. When I first saw the show, in 1949, it had been running for several months. It seemed absolutely perfect — except for just one tiny slipup. When the male singers were singing "There Is Nothing Like a Dame," one young singer was a fraction of a second late coming in with his line. I had noticed it in passing but it didn't bother me or hurt the number, which received great applause. But someone else had also noticed that small error.

When the first-act curtain came down for the intermission, Carin and I started up the side aisle. Just then a big angry-looking man came down the aisle in a big hurry. When he came close to us, I saw it was Oscar Hammerstein himself and I said, "Hi, Oscar." And he, with a quick, gruff "Hello, Abe," brushed by me and dashed on. He was on his way backstage. I said to Carin, "Oscar's going backstage to chew out the kid who blew that line in the song." Weeks later I mentioned this to Oscar and he said I was right — that singer would never bobble a lyric again.

Going backstage after one of my own shows has been running for a while is always a chancy thing. If the show has gone

231

well, all the actors are glad to see me and I'm glad to see them. But if the show has not gone well, it's a different story.

An actor may greet me with horror and say, "Were you out there tonight?" Sometimes, as far as I could see, he hasn't done anything wrong. But in his heart of hearts, he feels guilty.

Then there is the actor who, as soon as you see him, starts coughing. Really heavy coughing, as if he were overplaying a death scene. The coughing lets me know that if his performance has been weak, it was due to serious illness.

Another actor will start complaining about the audience, the lights, the sound or a fellow actor before I can say a word.

When I used to come backstage to see Bert Lahr, he always greeted me with a complaint. If it wasn't an actor who had moved on a laugh, it was Dolores Gray's behavior when he sang a certain duet with her: "She's stepping on my foot during the song." I used to watch that duet and I never could see Dolores committing that crime. I once came right out and asked her if she ever stepped on Bert's foot. She said that he was just imagining things. Finally, when Bert for about the twentieth time said, "Abe, she's really stepping on my foot," I gave him a solution. I said, "Why don't you step on her foot?" He looked at me as though I were crazy, but he stopped complaining about that particular crime. Then he dug up a new one to take its place.

Frequently, instead of going backstage, I took the cowardly route: written notes. I sent them to the stage manager, who would then distribute them to the actors. A written note works better than a spoken note because when the actor reads it, he cannot argue with you about it — you're not there.

George Kaufman was famous for his notes to actors. They were sharp, witty and often devastating. One night in the early thirties when he was watching a performance of *Of Thee I Sing*, one of the stars, Bill Gaxton, overplayed a scene very badly. George didn't send him an ordinary note; he sent him a telegram. He actually walked out of the theater and sent Gaxton a telegram, which arrived backstage during the performance. The telegram read: I'M WATCHING YOUR PERFORMANCE FROM THE BACK ROW OF THE THEATER. WISH YOU WERE HERE.

Sometimes an entirely different attack is effective. The star of *How To Succeed in Business Without Really Trying,* the talented Robert Morse, could be naughty on occasion. In one of his scenes he was supposed to say a certain big laugh line on cue (that is, instantly, without pause). Once in a while he would wait before delivering it. It was as though he were enjoying the silence in the theater before he said the big joke. This is a ploy many actors use. They do love silence in the theater — long silences, during which they believe the audience is watching them with adoration. Bobby had already received several notes from me about saying this line on cue. The notes hadn't helped.

One night I found the answer. While watching the show from a side aisle, I was making notes with one of those pens that has a flashlight. When Bobby came to the line that bothered me, his silence was longer than it had ever been before. He looked out at the audience and then he looked in my direction. I was in the dark so he didn't see me. At that moment I had an inspiration. As he was looking toward me, I flashed my flashlight quickly several times. He looked startled and said his line immediately; he got his laugh. When I went backstage later, he told me he had guessed that those flashes had come from me. Bobby never took that long silence again. He had received the message.

Some actors like to prolong exits. They are happiest when they are center stage in the spotlight; and subconsciously they feel that when they make an exit, they are really disappearing into nothingness.

I worked with one actor in *Can-Can* who really took his time on an exit. After a certain very funny exit line he was supposed to hurry off indignantly. But this chap just refused to hurry. He'd speak his exit line and then stroll off very slowly. The other actors had to wait until he was gone before they could go on with the scene. I kept sending him notes to get off faster.

One night when I was watching the show, he made another one of his slow exits. Furious, I dashed backstage and nailed

233

him as he came off. I told him that his slow exit was un-bearable. He finally got angry and said, "Good God, Mr. Bur-rows, do you want me to run?" And I, just as angry, shouted back, "If necessary, yes." Some stagehands overhead this and chuckled.

The next night this fellow decided to teach me a lesson. He said his line and sprinted for the exit. And for the first time since the show opened, his exit got applause.

One of my favorite director's notes is credited to Hans Conried. In the forties, he was directing a radio drama, his first directing job. After the final rehearsal, he gathered the actors around him and gave them notes on their performances. When he came to the last actor, he said with a sigh, "Well, sir, as for your performance, all I can say to you is 'Be better.'" Since then I've used this line many times myself. When Hans said "Be bet-ter," he probably was joking, but when I say it, I mean it.

During this period, while I was keeping an eagle eye on my shows, I wasn't writing anything new. Friends and newspaper-men kept asking me, "What are you going to do next?" I used to mumble, "I'm working on something" or "I'm thinking about something," but the awful truth was that I didn't have a single new idea in my skull. Many producers were making suggestions to me about ideas they had for shows. None of these interested me. And of course there were shows in trouble that I was asked to doctor, but to me they were all suffering from terminal ill-ness.

Then, late in the summer, I received a call for help I just couldn't ignore. It came from a good friend, Arthur Lewis, who with his father, Albert Lewis, was producing a show called *Three Wishes for Jamie*. It was based on a novel, *The Three Wishes of Jamie McRuin,* by Charles O'Neal (the father of an eleven-year-old kid named Ryan, who grew up to be the famous Ryan O'Neal, who is the father of another famous O'Neal, Tatum). The show, which was trying out in San Francisco, was in bad trouble and needed doctoring. My instincts told me to turn it down, but I was very fond of Art Lewis and I admired his

234

father. Al Lewis had been a famous producer in his time. Many years before, he had produced the original version of *Rain,* starring Jeanne Eagels.

It was very hard for me not to accept right away, especially when Art told me that if I didn't take on the show, it would never come to New York and they would lose whatever money they had put into it. I asked for a day to think it over. Next morning they called to say that they had told the Shuberts in New York that I was interested; and the Shuberts were interested in my interest.

The Shuberts controlled most of the theaters in New York and on the road. They told Art that if I would agree to rewrite and restage the show, they would agree to help the Lewises financially and they would also make one of their theaters available for the New York run. After hearing that, how could I say no?

Since *This Is Show Business* and *We Take Your Word* were both taking a summer hiatus, Carin and I decided we would make a sort of vacation out of the trip to the Coast. We would first go to Los Angeles to see some friends and then up to San Francisco to see *Three Wishes for Jamie.*

We went to Los Angeles by train. In those days, if you weren't in a hurry, the trip on a good train was the pleasantest way to go. Though the planes, even then, got you out there quicker than the trains, they weren't as fast as they are today. Nor as comfortable. Nonstop flights didn't start until 1959, and that meant you had your knuckles whitened during several landings and takeoffs. Not much fun.

The train trip took three nights and two days. We rode the famous old Twentieth Century Limited from New York to Chicago. It was like traveling in a fine hotel with a good restaurant. We left New York at five in the afternoon on a Monday and arrived in Chicago at nine the next morning. Then, we did what became a routine for us on our later train trips. We headed for the Ambassador East, an elegant hotel where we were treated royally by the owner, Ernie Byfield. He would have a suite ready for us. We could relax, change our clothes, and have lunch in the Pump Room, where we always met a lot of friends. That evening, feeling all rested, we would board the Super Chief on the Santa Fe. It was like traveling in Sardi's Restaurant or the Hollywood Brown Derby. The train was full of show folk on their way back to the coast.

Some of these people turned up as guests at a big welcoming party that the Frank Loessers gave for us when we arrived in Beverly Hills. I had been away for a couple of years and therefore had earned the Prodigal Son treatment.

That party was a real, old-fashioned Hollywood bash. It took place under a big tent with music from a live orchestra. After a while some of the guests replaced the musicians: Sid Caesar on the saxophone, Benny Goodman on the clarinet, Danny Kaye on the drums. Groucho Marx did some of the vocals. It was a pretty high-priced band.

The morning after, I took a walk outside of our hotel. You could tell I was a New Yorker; people generally don't walk much in Beverly Hills; if a guy takes a walk, his Mercedes feels offended. However, this particular morning I needed to walk off the effects of that party.

About five seconds after I started out, a zippy Jaguar came tearing along Sunset Boulevard and suddenly the driver slammed on the brakes and blew his horn. It was Ernie Martin, and with him was Cy Feuer. Ernie, who doesn't often waste time on the amenities, said they had something important to tell me: it was time we did another hit show and they had a great idea for one. Would I write the libretto? They liked my direction of *Two on the Aisle*. So would I also be the director? Then before I could answer they added that they wouldn't take no for an answer. My answer fell between no and yes.

I said I would be happy to write their show and I would love to direct it, but it would be kind of nice if they told me what the hell the show *was*. This is where they slowed down. All they could tell me was that it would take place in Paris in the 1890's, the sets and costumes were to look like Toulouse-Lautrec

236

posters, and the title was to be *Can-Can*. Ernie ended up by saying, "That's it, Abe. It's going to be a great show. All it needs from you is a little paperwork." Ernie Martin usually described the writing of a whole show as "a little paperwork."

A little paperwork? All there was to work with was an era, a "look," and a title. When they told me that title, I didn't realize how important it was to be: one of the most valuable titles ever used for a musical show. When it went up in lights on the marquee, it called up a happy picture of beautiful girls dancing. It also called up a picture of a beautiful line of people at the box office. But the most important thing about that title I found out after we opened on Broadway: *Can-Can* is the only show title I know that doesn't have to be translated into other languages when it plays in foreign countries.

The idea of doing a show with a Parisian setting bothered this born and bred New Yorker. I couldn't see myself writing English dialogue for French characters to speak. But I did like the idea of working with Cy and Ernie again, so I said I wanted to think about it. Then Feuer gave me some of his typical kindly advice: "Burrows, don't think about it. Do it."

I kept stalling. I reminded them that I couldn't start working right then because I had tentatively agreed to help Art Lewis with *Three Wishes for Jamie*. But Ernie said they didn't expect me to start writing anything until I was finished with Art's show. "After that, Abe, you can get right to work on *Can-Can*. Right?"

Before I could answer, Ernie — he's a talker — said that if the French background bothered me, they had already spoken to someone in Paris who would do research on the period we were talking about. If it was all right with me, they would send me to Paris to get familiar with the background. All right with me? It certainly was. I had never been to Paris before. As a matter of fact, I had never been outside the United States. After that the only thing I could think of saying to them was, "Who's going to do the songs?"

Ernie, after a pause, said, "We don't want to spread it around, but we can tell you that Cole Porter is very interested." When I heard the name Cole Porter, my eyes popped and so did my brain. I said, "Why didn't you guys tell me that right away?" Ernie explained: "We were waiting until it was definite. Our appointment this afternoon is a business meeting with Cole at his house in Brentwood." I said, "Do you mean you were going to go away without telling me it was Cole Porter?" They said, "Oh, we were going to tell you, but we were saving it for a clincher in case you were in doubt." And they drove off into the western sunset.

If they had said "Cole Porter" to me earlier in our talk, we all would have saved a lot of time.

Now I found myself committed to two shows. Actually, I wasn't committed to *Jamie* because I hadn't signed anything. I had read the libretto, which seemed to need work, but I hadn't yet seen the show on the stage. When I did, I was pleasantly surprised. It had problems, but there were some attractive pluses. One was a leading man, John Raitt, who a few years later was the star of *Pajama Game*. He has one of the best voices in the musical theater. Other pluses were some exciting dances that Eugene Loring had choreographed. The libretto staggered a bit, but the main story was an attractive one.

The strongest part of the show was a beautiful score written by Ralph Blane. In a musical, you can rewrite the libretto, recast and restage the show, but if you haven't got decent songs you can forget the whole thing. Blane's score was what sold me.

When I got back to New York, I started the rewriting. After the show ended its run in San Francisco, the Lewises closed it down temporarily and joined me in New York, where we began to recast some of the parts. Of course, John Raitt remained the star. To costar with him we were lucky to get Anne Jeffreys, and Bert Wheeler, a very endearing comic who had become famous as part of the team of Wheeler and Woolsey.

When the word got out that I was trying "to cure" the ills of *Three Wishes for Jamie*, that solidified my medical reputation.

One day while I was working on *Jamie*, Al Lewis invited me

238

to drive up with him to New Haven, where Alan Lerner's musical *Paint Your Wagon* was opening. As I walked into the theater, I heard a lady who was standing behind me say to her friend, "Look, the show is just opening and he came here to fix it." Then, in the lobby, I ran into Cheryl Crawford, who was the producer of the show. When she saw me, she looked annoyed and said to me half seriously, "Have you nothing else to do?" I understood how she felt. She thought that if I were seen at this out-of-town opening, everyone in the show would think that she had secretly called me in to help.

Since then I have never gone to anybody else's opening out of town. Besides the "doctor" image, the public knows my face from television and during the performance people peek at me to watch my reaction.

Three Wishes for Jamie had its first out-of-town tryout in the winter of 1952. We played New Haven and Boston with great success; but we did have one bad moment on our opening night in New Haven. I am now convinced that when a show is not going to be a hit, some little thing will go wrong the first time it is played before an audience.

The theater is a constant test of Murphy's Law — the rule of science that says, "If something can go wrong, it will. And at the worst possible time." That law inevitably came down on us.

During the first half hour I thought we had a hit. The audience loved the opening number and the first few scenes. The trouble began with the first love scene between John Raitt and Anne Jeffreys. It was a gentle bit of dialogue which was to lead into one of Ralph Blane's best songs, a ballad called "You're My Heart's Darling." She was sitting on a large rock and he was on the ground looking up at her. They played the scene beautifully and the audience was caught up in the story. And then came the cue for John to go into his song. At that moment the orchestra was supposed to start playing the lead-in to the song — but nothing happened. There was dead silence. The actors were silent and the orchestra was silent.

I was in the back of the house and I saw the orchestra leader sitting on his stool, not moving. I threw my shoulder toward him with my old Body English. It didn't work. Raitt sat there staring at Anne Jeffreys. He was frozen; he didn't know what to do. And then the audience began to stir and there were rustling sounds all over the theater. Finally, after about thirty seconds or more (it felt like an hour), the conductor stood up, lifted his baton, and started the music. John began to sing, but the spell had been broken. From then on, the audience remained restless. We never recovered our momentum.

During the intermission, I dashed backstage and politely asked the conductor, "What the hell happened?" He looked at me with a gentle smile and said, "I don't know, Abe. I guess it's just because I was sitting there enjoying the dialogue." He was an elderly man and too small to hit. Besides I liked him. But he really hurt our show.

For the rest of the run there, *Jamie* went beautifully. And when we went on to Boston, we played to Standing Room Only for four weeks. We kept getting better and better, and we were looking forward to a smash hit in New York. We were wrong.

All of the New York critics didn't murder us. Some of them just cuffed us a bit, and some of them actually liked the show. But not Brooks Atkinson. He didn't like it at all, and when he didn't like a show, the box office had very little work to do.

George Kaufman, after one of his plays opened, sent a wire to a friend which described what had happened: "Brooksie no likee."

Chapter 17

A few days after the opening of *Three Wishes for Jamie,* I came down with the flu. It's a very interesting medical fact that I never got sick after I opened a hit. A mild case of flu is a marvelous illness for a writer. It's not serious enough to cause him much suffering and yet it gives him an acceptable excuse to keep from going to work.

As I was lying there enjoying my flu, Feuer and Martin came to call. They barreled into the room with enough noise and energy to scare the hell out of any virus that might have been around. They were not there as Angels of Mercy. Instead of flowers they brought me a huge bundle of papers, magazines and pictures — research stuff on the *Can-Can* period that had been sent to them by their man in Paris. "Now, Abe, you can get right to work in digging up an idea for the show."

I plucked weakly at my coverlet and said, "I still feel pretty lousy." Their answer was "Read this stuff and you'll feel better." Then Feuer told me some great news: "Michael Kidd's going to do the choreography." Well, that did make me feel better.

When I started to read the material, I was fascinated. The most interesting parts of it were stories from the French newspapers of 1893, including stuff about the cancan itself. For the first time I learned that the cancan was once considered a dirty dance.

I was stunned to find out how much puritanism and censorship there was in Paris in the 1890's. This was the Victorian
period in England and it affected France, too. Many censorship
leagues were formed. One of them was called the League
Against Licentiousness of the Streets. Police raids were common all over Paris and one of the main targets was the cancan,
but the cops couldn't stop it.

At the beginning of the cancan craze, the dance was not done
in nightclubs by professional chorus girls, but in rather seedy
dance halls by working girls, usually laundresses. Tired though
they were from the day's work, when they danced the cancan,
they more than came to life. They went crazy on the dance
floor — leaping around, screaming, and kicking their legs as
high in the air as possible. The cancan wasn't done in unison as
it is performed today. It was every girl for herself. (The dances
in our discos — the Hustle, Bustle, Rustle, or whatever they are
called — are done solo but they are like stately waltzes compared to the cancan.) You've seen those Toulouse-Lautrec
posters. The girls are holding their skirts way up and there's a
great show of pretty, ruffled panties. Well, the fact is that toward the end of the evening those pretty, ruffled panties came
off.

A lot of etymologists have tried to figure out the derivation of
the word *cancan.* One silly explanation you will find in a lot of
dictionaries is that it came from the Latin *quamquam,* a nonsense word which literally means "how-how." This theory
claims that the students in the Latin Quarter called the dance
quamquam, which evolved into cancan.

Whatever the dictionaries say, I have a theory that when everybody shouted "Cawnhcawnh" (the French pronunciation)
during the dance, they were referring to that part of the anat-
omy which the girls were showing when they removed their
panties. In some of the accounts of the period, I read that after
the dancers went home and the dance halls were cleaned up at
night, they used to find girls' panties left in various hiding

242

places. This suggests that some of the girls got rid of their panties before they even started dancing.

I read many accounts of police raids on the dance halls. The girls were arrested and thrown into a patrol wagon, called a *panier à salade* — salad basket.

The president of the League Against Licentiousness of the Streets was a French senator named René Bérenger. He constantly attacked the immorality in Montmartre; to the people of Paris his nickname was Père la Pudeur, which roughly translated means Papa Decency.

He hated the cancan and he hated the Quatz' Arts Balls, which took place at the famous Moulin Rouge. *Quatz' Arts* is Parisian slang for the Four Arts: painting, sculpture, poetry and architecture. The Quatz' Arts Balls were raided regularly by the police.

After the second one, good old ridiculous Père la Pudeur sent a letter to the public prosecutor describing the horrifying proceedings. In part of his letter he wrote:

I have been informed, and the *Courier Français* confirms it, that about ten entirely nude women, covering their secret parts with some very transparent gauze, were admitted to the costumed procession which preceded the ball, and that they mingled with the guests in the dancing afterward.

I have the honor of pointing out to you that I believe this to be so grave that I am absolutely decided — in the event that you do not believe in the possibility of repression — to bring this to the attention of the Senate Tribunal.

There was an actual trial a couple of months later and many of the women who were at that ball were questioned. One of them, who used the name Sarah Brown, was questioned by the presiding judge, one Courot. Much of her testimony got a lot of laughs from the spectators:

243

JUDGE   You are accused of public immorality. You were wearing a very décolleté costume. Bare flesh appeared.
SARAH   But no, I wore a belt, heavy necklaces and also sequins.
JUDGE   Did you wear tights?
SARAH   No, why should I have? I was dressed.
JUDGE   You walked around at the ball with your torso naked?
SARAH   I only participated in the procession, the rest of the ball I was in a loge.
JUDGE   Who gave you the idea for this costume?
SARAH   No one. I'm a model. I posed as Cleopatra for Rochegrosse, and naturally I chose this costume.

The interrogation of another lady named Manon went as follows:

JUDGE   Your costume consisted only of a black shirt?
MANON   Yes, a very heavy one.
JUDGE   You unbuttoned it?
MANON   Hell, it was hot.
JUDGE   So, you had on only a shirt and you found a way to open even that? [*Laughter in the audience*]

This was fascinating material, and after digesting it all, Feuer and Martin, Cole Porter and I agreed that my libretto should be based on the passionate but funny struggle between the two opposing sides — the censors versus the X-rated cancan dance and the Quatz' Arts Ball.

It seems to me that in most good shows the love story deals with two people who are completely different in background, temperament and ethics. Just plain different.

In *Guys and Dolls,* the hero was a famous gambler and the heroine a pious missionary who hated gamblers.

In *South Pacific,* Ezio Pinza played a French planter on a Pacific island, a widower who had been married to a foreign woman and was the father of two children of mixed blood. Mary Martin played an American nurse from Little Rock, Arkansas, in the Deep South. There was tension between them, but their love story was a fascinating and eventually happy one.

244

In *My Fair Lady,* Professor Higgins was an upper-class expert on speech; the heroine, an ignorant Cockney flower girl. In Shaw's original play, *Pygmalion,* there was absolutely no romance between these two, but when Lerner and Loewe did the musical, it wound up as a love story.

It would be very difficult to do a musical about a girl and the boy next door. Romeo and Juliet came from families that despised each other. And don't forget *West Side Story.*

The libretto I began to write for *Can-Can* was about the love between a woman who is involved in the cancan and the Quatz' Arts Balls and a man who is violently opposed to these illegal and sinful activities.

While I was fishing around for the construction of the book, Cole Porter had started to plan some of the songs. He had spent many years in Paris. (In the twenties he actually had joined the French Foreign Legion. He once told me that all you had to do to join was to get yourself weighed.) I had never met Cole up to this time. At least not in person. But the very first Broadway show I ever saw had a score by Cole Porter. This was back in 1932 and the show was *The Gay Divorce* at the Ethel Barrymore Theatre. Fred Astaire was making his first stage appearance without his sister, Adele. My date and I sat in the last row of the balcony. Cut-rate seats, 55 cents a piece. All I could afford.

It may have been because it was my first show, but *The Gay Divorce* seemed to me to be brilliant. And I'll always be grateful that I got to see Fred Astaire performing. And live. It was beautiful to hear and see him singing and dancing to Cole's music, especially to "Night and Day," which is now a classic. I later saw Astaire do it again in the movie version, but it wasn't as exciting for me as it was when I sat in the balcony of the Ethel Barrymore Theatre. (Incidentally, the movie was called *The Gay Divorcee.* The censors thought *The Gay Divorce* an offensive title. Shades of Père la Pudeur.)

Exactly twenty years after *The Gay Divorce,* I found myself actually collaborating with Cole Porter. I had once heard Billy Rose describe Cole Porter as the Last of the Toffs. "Toff"

245

describes Cole only partially. Toffs are not usually talented men.

Cole was living proof of the fact that lack of money is not necessarily the cause of an artist's drive. He came from the Middle West; he was born in Peru, Indiana (he told me it was pronounced "Peeru"). He had inherited a million dollars when he was eighteen and a good deal more money later on. But that never kept him from working hard and steadily.

Money not only enabled Cole to live comfortably; it was a buffer against great pain. During all the years I knew him and worked with him, he never had a painless day. Back in the thirties he had an accident while horseback riding. The horse fell and Cole's leg was badly crushed. The doctors wanted to amputate it but he wouldn't hear of it. Instead, he had a great many operations on that leg. Most people didn't realize that the Cole Porter who wrote those witty light lyrics was constantly suffering. He always managed his cane with a jaunty air.

I remember one time when we were in Philadelphia trying out *Can-Can*. He came to me and said, "Abe, I'm not feeling well. Do you mind if I go into New York and rest over the weekend? If you need me, I won't go, but I'll really be more comfortable there." I insisted that he should leave.

The next morning a Philadelphia columnist had a big gossip item in the paper: "Things are not going well with *Can-Can*. Abe Burrows and Cole Porter have had a big quarrel and Cole has left the show and gone back to New York." Someone in the company must have told the columnist about Cole's departure, and the columnist dreamed up the rest. When Cole came back, he heard about the news story and apologized to me for being the cause.

In Philadelphia we both stayed at the Barclay Hotel. Carin and I thought our room was beautiful but Cole turned his suite into his home. He had sent down his own bed linens, tablecloths, dishes, cutlery, and photographs of his friends, plus a few favorite paintings.

He talked to me about money one day and said in a most in-

246

nocent way, "Abe, I've liked having money. It's been so good for me." A great number of rich people spend their money on things that are just other investments. They buy paintings that grow in value; they buy antique silver, antique furniture, stately homes, all of which are basically investments — marketable stuff. Not Porter. He used his money for comfortable living. For a while he had four homes, which were always ready for him, places to which he could come at any time without a single piece of luggage. He had an apartment in Paris, a suite at the Waldorf Towers in New York, a house in Williamstown, Massachusetts, and a house in Brentwood, California. He finally gave up his place in Paris but he kept the other three.

One time when we were all working on *Can-Can*, Cole had to go to California on business. It turned out that Ernie Martin and I were going there on the same day. Cole suggested we have dinner together that night. He flew out early in the day and Ernie and I followed a couple of hours later. When we arrived we called Cole to arrange to meet him at a restaurant. Cole wouldn't hear of that. He said we were to dine at his home. We drove out to Brentwood and he had dinner waiting for us. The house was always staffed and the staff was prepared for anything.

He was a very thoughtful man. On New Year's Eve of 1953, after *Can-Can* opened, my wife and I were giving a big party at our apartment. Cole got us out of a lot of trouble. About three hundred people were invited, but before the party started we were in a panic. We had moved into the apartment in November. Our decorator was William Pahlmann. We were assured that the apartment would be all finished in a couple of weeks, so we went ahead and made plans for our party.

About four days before New Year's Eve the apartment was still not finished. We were desperate and I got Pahlmann on the phone and read him our guest list. And I said, "Bill, do you want all these people coming to our apartment and seeing that it's been un-decorated by William Pahlmann? Won't you be embarrassed when I tell people like Marlene Dietrich and Cole Porter that Bill Pahlmann . . ." When I said "Cole Porter," that did it. On the morning of the party, Pahlmann and a battalion of assistants arrived with loads of furniture and decorated the apartment. Bill told me he was putting in all this stuff temporarily, and if I didn't want any of it, he would take it back after the party.

The place looked great and as Carin and I were happily enjoying our beautifully appointed apartment, we got a phone call that sent us into another panic. We had hired a group of people who were going to help our cook, a great cook who had been with us for years. He was from the Philippine Islands and he had arranged for a group of four of his friends to come and work with him. They were going to wait on tables and serve drinks. Now they could not come.

So there we were, stuck with a huge wingding, and except for our cook, no one else to help out. Before I could shoot myself, Cole called to find out what time to come. He said I sounded worried. And I told him about these four people who had conked out on us and that we were short of help.

He immediately said, "I'll send Paul." Paul was Cole's butler, valet, and companion, a wonderful man who could do anything. An hour later he showed up. The party was a great success. (Incidentally, we kept every piece of furniture that Pahlmann had put into our apartment.)

In the early 1960's, Cole finally had to have his leg amputated. He became very depressed and didn't leave his hotel suite after that. He had to endure the phantom pain that usually follows an amputation.

Carin and I saw him from time to time. Cole arranged things so that only two people had dinner with him at one time. He had many friends eager to see him, but he spread out their visits over the week and so never had to spend an evening alone. Those evenings were usually a rather sad experience. We enjoyed an elegant dinner but he himself ate very little. He was still in constant pain. We would do most of the talking but he did seem to enjoy the news we would bring him from the outside world. His social style didn't change even when he was in the hospital.

When Carin and I went to visit him there, we were met by a nurse who said, "Mr. Porter would like you to wait in the solarium." We were seated at a table that was evidently reserved for Cole's guests. Suddenly, Cole's valet came to our table with a bottle of champagne and two glasses (they were Cole's own goblets), and said to us, "Mr. Porter is getting ready and he'll be with you in a few minutes." As we sat there drinking champagne, Cole came into the solarium in a wheelchair. He looked very ill but his manner was cheerful and we spent a very pleasant hour with him. That was the last time we saw him. It was in a hospital, but Cole, as usual, had temporarily turned that hospital into one of his own gracious homes.

In my den hangs a painting that always makes me think of Cole. On the opening night of *Can-Can,* I sent Cole a telegram wishing him luck and thanking him. He didn't send me a telegram, he sent me a gift, that painting on my wall. He had commissioned Marcel Vertes to paint it for me. It's a painting of the finale of *Can-Can.* Feuer and Martin had also sent him telegrams, and they, too, had received paintings of other *Can-Can* scenes by Vertes.

I miss him and next year I'm going to miss him more than ever. *Can-Can* is going to be revived but Cole won't be there at the rehearsals and he won't be there at our opening. Cole loved his opening nights. While the rest of us were standing nervously in the rear of the theater, Cole, in impeccable evening dress, made a grand entrance. He would slowly walk down the aisle with his cane; he'd smile to his friends and finally sit in the third or fourth row of the theater. While we were worrying and praying, Cole would be laughing and applauding heartily. That was Cole Porter.

Chapter 18

While I was still struggling to find a good story line for *Can-Can,* Cole had already started to write some songs for the show. They weren't songs for specific situations because I hadn't thought of any. But he knew I would have a pair of lovers in the libretto and therefore he would have to write some love songs. He wrote a pretty ballad called "C'est Magnifique." And then he came up with a beautiful love song called "I Love Paris." I knew I could fit both of these songs into my libretto.

Cy and Ernie joined me in kicking around ideas for the story, and finally we decided we could base a good story on one of the best known of the dancing laundresses, La Goulue (French for "The Glutton"). One of Toulouse-Lautrec's most famous posters showed La Goulue with her skirts in the air. A big girl, who looked as though she could also be very funny.

Cy and Ernie had an exciting notion of who could play La Goulue: Carol Channing. Carol was then touring with *Gentlemen Prefer Blondes.* We drove down to Philadelphia to talk to her. We told her our idea, the title, the background, and what Cole was writing. Carol was interested, but she said she couldn't do the show because *Gentlemen Prefer Blondes* was going to play in London and she was eager to star in it there. As we rode back to New York, we decided to throw out the La Goulue idea; it would be too tough to cast the part.

Then Feuer came up with a suggestion. He had been in Paris a few months earlier and had seen an actress named Lilo, who had a powerful singing voice. She wouldn't fit the part of La Goulue because she wasn't big enough and she wasn't a dancer, but she was so good that it might be worthwhile building something new around her. Ernie had to go to Paris on business and he proposed that I come with him to see her. Since this was the right time for me to make that promised trip to Paris and become familiar with the locale I was going to write about, I thought this a very pleasant suggestion. There was one problem. If we did like Lilo for *Can-Can,* I would have to tell her the plot, and I didn't have any.

We started kicking this around. Cy told us about Lilo's style on the French stage. She was a take-charge woman. Very strong. And as we talked, an idea emerged. Lilo could play a woman who ran a night spot where the cancan ran on most of the time. This would make her an enemy of the censors and the cops.

By the time the car got us back to New York, we had agreed on the basic idea of the show. That trip to Philly was not wasted.

Musicals seldom leap fully grown out of an author's mind. They usually start with a small idea that gets nourishment and fattening from all the people who eventually gather to put it on the stage.

When I arrived in Paris in 1952, I immediately fell in love with it. It was April. It wasn't sunny, it was rather cold, and there were no chestnuts in blossom. But still, to me, it seemed perfect.

I went right out and bought myself a beret. Then I headed for the Café de la Paix in the rue de la Paix, a place I had read about in hundreds of books. In 1952 the Café de la Paix was not as "in" as it had been in the romantic twenties, but to me it looked just as I thought it would. I sat at a sidewalk table and asked for a cognac and water. I ordered it nervously in my

Brooklyn–high school French: *"Fine à l'eau."* When the drink arrived, I was relieved to find out that it really was cognac and water.

I sat there watching the people walk by. It was just before sunset, the Blue Hour in Paris, and I was euphoric; I felt very French sitting there, wearing my beret at a jaunty angle. A typical French family came along. A man and his wife and their little boy. The man and the boy were wearing berets. As they passed me, the man stopped and shouted to his family, "Hey, look! Abe Burrows!" They were New Yorkers who had seen me on American television. They waved at me and I waved back, but my heart wasn't in it. I finished my drink and went back to my hotel.

I was staying at the Hotel George V (to the French, Georges Cinq), a favorite of many American visitors, I suppose because most of the staff spoke English. Art Buchwald, who was writing his column from Paris at the time, told me that there was a joke around town that the operators at the George V were so anglicized, or anglified, that they would answer phone calls by saying "Hello, Georges Cinq the Fifth."

However, whenever I could, I'd use my weak French. One morning I couldn't find my shoes. They were my favorite pair of heavy-soled brogues. I didn't know that the valet usually picked them up at night to shine them, and I asked the chambermaid what had happened to them. I asked in my stuttering French, *"Où sont mes —"* I reached wildly for the word for shoes and came up with *"sabots."* She burst into laughter. As far as she was concerned, I was asking for my wooden shoes. I couldn't think of the word *souliers*. I got to be known in the hotel as a great wit because my shoes were very big and heavy. The chambermaid would chuckle every time she met me in the hallway and looked down at my *sabots*.

Before we actually met Lilo, Ernie and I went to see her on the stage. She was starring in a big musical show called *Le Chanteur de Mexico*. It was playing in a theater called the Chatelet. The theater was inside a building that had been an infamous prison in the seventeenth century. Later on, part of it was turned into one of the biggest theaters I have ever seen. The stage was one hundred meters deep. Over a hundred yards. It looked to me like a football field.

The producer in charge was Maurice Lehmann, who was known for his spectacular productions. He would sometimes put on a show that came from America if he could make it look spectacular enough. He once brought over *Annie Get Your Gun,* which in Paris was called *Annie du Far West.* There were circus scenes to which he added live elephants and other animals. His production added an hour and a half to the length.

The French theatergoers enjoy long shows. The longer the better. They feel cheated if a show is over too quickly. Through the years I have been involved (as writer or director or both) with the American versions of three French plays: *Cactus Flower, Forty Carats,* and *Four on a Garden.* In New York all these plays ran at least one hour shorter than in France.

Lilo's show, *Le Chanteur de Mexico,* ran about three and a half hours. An American audience would have grown very restive, but the audience around us just loved it, and Ernie and I didn't mind the length because it gave us a chance to see every aspect of Lilo's ability.

Before she came onstage, we wondered how any singer could be effective in this giant-sized theater; but Lilo handled it beautifully. Her singing voice seemed to thrill the audience; and she got a lot of big laughs when she played the few comedy scenes. Of course, our French wasn't good enough to follow the jokes or the plot. We could only catch a word here and there. Every time I have been in a theater in Paris I have gone crazy trying to follow the dialogue. It seems to me that on the stage French actors speak much faster than they do in ordinary conversation.

The plot was magnificently ridiculous. A Frenchman who is in Mexico in the nineteenth century is captured by a band of savages who seem to be a combination of Indians, Mexican buccaneers and Barbary pirates who spoke in modern Parisian French intermingled with jungle grunts. One very serious mo-

253

ment I found hilarious. When the savages were about to burn the hero at the stake, he made a short speech to them which broke me up. He spoke in the manner of a brave but foppish French nobleman, saying solemnly, *"Je suis un citoyen français."* The minute the savages realized he was a French citizen, they shuddered with fright and released him. I was embarrassed because I was the only person in an audience of about three thousand people who laughed at that grave speech. I felt I should apologize by saying, *"Je suis un citoyen américain."*

When this long, long show finally ended, Ernie and I were pretty weary, but we perked up when we heard the applause for Lilo. We were really impressed by her final bow. She came on from the rear of the stage, and slowly walked toward the footlights — a hundred-yard dash — and the audience cheered her every step of the way. When she reached the footlights, she spent minutes throwing kisses, smiling happily, and looking as though she owned that audience. I noticed that she had changed her period costume for a beautiful modern evening gown.

(I later found out that in the French musical theater the leading lady wears a completely new dress for her final bow. This custom came to haunt me later on. About a week before we opened *Can-Can* out of town, Lilo came to me and said, "Abe, what am I going to wear for my final bow?" I was startled and said, "Whatever you're wearing when the final curtain comes down." She was horrified, and said that in Paris she had never taken a final bow without changing her costume. It took us a while, but we finally convinced her that she was now in Philadelphia.)

When Ernie and I left the Chatelet Theatre that night in Paris, we felt fine. We were sure that Lilo would be right for *Can-Can*.

The next day we were to meet in her apartment. She was married to Guy de la Passardière, a very bright fellow who had inherited the title of marquis de la Passardière. I had brought along two of Cole Porter's songs, "C'est Magnifique" and "I

Love Paris," and I played them on the piano for Lilo. Cole shuddered when I told him later on that I had actually played and sung his songs. He, Frank Loesser, and all the other composers I have ever worked with have forbidden me, on pain of death, to play their songs with that fake left hand of mine and my gravelly voice. But no matter how badly I played and sang, Lilo and Guy were enthusiastic. By the time we left her apartment, Lilo was eager to do the show and we were happy to have her.

The rest of my time in Paris I did a lot of walking, especially in Montmartre, the part of Paris that would be the setting of our show. I was going to write about the people of Montmartre and I wanted to hear the way they sounded; and since I was going to direct the show, I wanted to see the way they looked and the way they walked.

But no sooner did I start out on my first tour, than a fellow came up to me and pushed a picture postcard in front of my face. It was a very memorable moment, my first French "feelthy" picture. I couldn't think of the French words for "I'm not interested" or "Beat it, bum," so I just kept on walking. He persisted. I finally shook him off but minutes after that another guy accosted me with more of the same pictures (which I would rate PG — Parisian genitalia). This sort of thing happened to me often in Paris.

One night I was having dinner with Lilo and some of her French friends, and I talked about these postcard pushers. Lilo's husband said that no one like that had ever approached him, and the other French fellows said the same thing. They decided that the man who accosted me knew I was an American. So I asked, "How could they tell?" And one man said, "Your shoes." "Mes sabots" had given me away.

Montmartre is the hilly part of Paris and I would trudge up and down the streets, absorbing the atmosphere. I visited the cabarets in the evenings, and since the villain of my show was the French judicial system of the nineties, I sought out the police stations and the courtrooms.

I made a gaffe early on in my walking tour. I referred to a policeman as a gendarme, and I was corrected sharply. The gendarmes are national police — something like our state police — and for centuries Paris has been off limits to them. A Parisian cop is called an *agent de police;* the French slang for a cop is *un flic.*

In roaming through the palaces of criminal justice, I generally greased my way with a highly prized tip, a pack of Lucky Strike cigarettes. Lucky Strike was then the sponsor of *This Is Show Business,* and I arrived in Paris carrying cartons of Luckies. In 1952 a pack of *cigarettes américaines* was still the most beautiful tip you could give most Frenchmen. Smoking may be injurious to the health, but it was sure useful to me in Paris.

The French courtrooms I visited looked exactly as they did in Daumier's drawings. There were three judges wearing robes and caps. As I watched them, I suddenly got the idea for my leading man. One of the judges was a fairly young, good-looking fellow. Like his two colleagues, he was very stern. He looked as though he'd send you to the guillotine for illegal parking.

Later, when I wrote my libretto, I made the leading man a tough, angry and prudish judge who was absolutely paranoid about the cancan. But of course he eventually falls in love with the leading lady, who naturally belongs to the enemy camp.

When I returned from Paris at the end of April, I settled down to work on the libretto. The show was to open in the fall of 1953. That is, I thought it was to open then; but Feuer and Martin hit me with a new deadline. We would have to open in the spring of 1953. We had made a commitment to put on a London production of *Guys and Dolls* in June, and we had to get *Can-Can* out of the way before we all went to England. Besides, Cy and Ernie felt that the spring was now a good time to open a show.

In the past no one would have thought of opening a show in the spring. Everybody rushed to open in September or October. What changed everything was the arrival of air conditioning. In the old days most of the theaters closed in the summertime and reopened in the fall, and by that time the show was no longer an event. Big hits like *The Gay Divorce* and *Anything Goes* ran no longer than a year. Now many shows open in the spring. With air conditioning and the flood of tourists in New York, theaters flourish in the summer.

I think the big turning point that made all producers accept the spring opening was the opening of *South Pacific* in April of 1949.

Feuer and Martin first thought we should open in mid-April, but they finally took pity on me and moved our date to May 7. That meant we would have to do our out-of-town tryout in April and go into rehearsal no later than the last week of February. That gave us little more than nine months to put our show together. We had to hire a cast, and plan and build the scenery; Michael Kidd had to create the dances; Cole had to write the songs; and I had to do my "little bit of paperwork" on the libretto. In addition to this Horror Schedule, I still had a couple of television commitments. By then I had stopped doing *This Is Show Business*, but I was still on *We Take Your Word* weekly, and I was doing another weekly panel show called *The Name's the Same*, with Meredith Willson and Joan Alexander. The MC was Robert Q. Lewis.

(While I was planning how to handle all this, Carin had plans of her own. After having worked with me on all my programs, from radio to theater, she decided to leave show business and go back to school. She enrolled in Columbia University, where she went in for mathematics and then switched to anthropology. Carin is now on the staff of the Anthropology Department of the American Museum of Natural History, and is acting curator of the Tibetan collection. That's a pretty big leap from show business, but when I'm working, I still find Carin my most valuable counsellor. Besides, I have picked up a few scraps of information about anthropology, and through her I have had a chance to meet many people who don't think Broadway is the Center of the Universe!)

By the time I started to collaborate with Frank Loesser on *Guys and Dolls*, he had already written most of the score, and

257

my job was to write a new libretto to fit his songs. But when I worked with Cole Porter, we were both starting from scratch, and I felt that the libretto might furnish ideas for songs. Of course, Cole had already written "C'est Magnifique," which fitted beautifully in the first love scene; and it was easy for me to find a moment for Lilo to sing "I Love Paris."

Before I started working with Cole, I had heard that he didn't welcome other people's ideas for lyrics. I suspected he was including librettists. As time went on, though, he gradually began to accept song ideas from me. There was a moment in *Can-Can* when our hero and our heroine have split up and our hero is feeling very low. He's seated at a café table and a very attractive prostitute comes over and sits down next to him. At first he tries to wave her away, but then in my first draft he says, "I'm sorry, Miss. This is the wrong time and the wrong place but you *are* charming, so [*he shrugs*] I guess it's all right." I thought there was a song here.

Cole gave it some thought and came up with a song that started out, "It's the wrong time and the wrong place. Though your face is charming it's the wrong face. It's not her face but it's a charming face, so it's all right with me."

"It's All Right with Me" is now a standard. After Cole bought that idea of mine, he spoke to me sort of apologetically and tried to explain why he was always resistant to other people's suggestions for songs. When he was writing his famous "Just One of Those Things," he played a rough, incomplete version of it for some friends of his at a party. When he came to the line "A trip to the moon on gossamer wings," he had not yet thought of the word "gossamer," so what he sang was "A trip to the moon on blank-blank-blank wings." One of the men at the party, who was not a writer but just a friend of a friend, spoke up and said, "How about *gossamer* wings?" Cole said, "Oh, that's very good," and put it in the song. For years after that, strangers would come up to him and say, "My cousin is the man who wrote that song with you." Understandably, Cole became leery of outsider's suggestions.

People always ask songwriters which comes first, the words or the music. I know that Frank Loesser usually started with the lyrics and then composed the tune to fit them.

Oscar Hammerstein used to write his lyrics to a sort of dummy tune that he made up himself. Then he would turn the lyrics over to Dick Rodgers, who then would write the music to Oscar's lyrics, ignoring Oscar's tune.

But when Rodgers worked with Larry Hart, he had to do the reverse. Hart used to disappear for days. Rodgers, left by himself, would compose a number of tunes, and when Hart showed up, those brilliant lyrics were written to fit.

Johnny Mercer once told me about the first time he wrote lyrics with Jerome Kern. When he was asked to collaborate with Kern on songs for a new motion picture, he was thrilled and told his friends he was going to bring a new style of lyrics to Kern. What Mercer didn't know at the time was that Kern wrote a new melody every morning of his life, after breakfast. At their first meeting, Johnny began telling Kern some of his ideas. Kern listened for a few moments and then he said, "I'd like you to hear a tune I wrote yesterday." When he played it, Mercer fell in love with it instantly and started to think of lyrics for it. He wound up happily writing lyrics to about nine of Kern's tunes.

Porter put his songs together in an interesting way. I learned about it the few times he did a song based on an idea that I threw him. In 1955, when we were doing *Silk Stockings* in Philadelphia, we needed a song badly for Gretchen Wyler, who played a movie star. It was to be a song called "Stereophonic Sound." Cole phoned me about one o'clock in the morning. "Abe," he said, "here's the way I think it should go: pom pom, pom pom, pom pom, pom pom." I started to hum, and he said to me very sharply, "Don't hum!" So I shut up and he went on with his "pom poms," giving me the rhythm of the song. That's how he did it. He would think up the rhythm. Then he would write the words to fit the rhythm and then he'd write the music to fit the words.

While I was working with Cole and grinding out my libretto, I used to forget that I was also the director of the show. Supposedly "The General." Luckily I had two co-generals: Feuer and Martin. While I was writing, they worked with the costume people and the set designer, who once again was Jo Mielziner. Every so often, I would take a few minutes from the libretto to look at sketches of Jo's sets and make a valuable comment like "Great!" Ernie and Cy did the early casting and handled the long tough hours of auditions, a murderous task. They would look at hundreds of people, and then I would go into an empty theater once a week to look at their best choices. And as he did with *Guys and Dolls,* Cy Feuer spent many helpful hours with me while I was struggling with the writing.

There are many different kinds of producers. Some are brilliant at publicizing a show after it has opened. Some just raise the money and leave everything else in the hands of the directors and the authors, who are referred to (and sometimes really are) "the creative people." Still others have good knowledge of the theater and can give you valuable advice about what you're rehearsing on the stage. But Ernie and Cy were both real "muscles" — that's a word I use to describe people who actually work on a project instead of just looking at it.

They were astute when it came to casting. One day Ernie met a tall, good-looking fellow named Peter Cookson, an actor who had starred in *The Heiress;* but he had never sung in a musical. Ernie found out Peter could sing and brought him up to my apartment where he sang for Cy and me. We had found our leading man.

Michael Kidd, our choreographer, was responsible for one of the best pieces of casting in our show. In my libretto the second female lead had to be a dancer, preferably a talented dancer who looked beautiful and could also act. Ernie and Cy were auditioning the dancers one day when they got a telegram from Kidd, who was out in California at the time. His wire said something like "Stop looking. Have found the greatest dancer in America. Gwen Verdon." None of us knew much about Gwen at the time, but we took Kidd's advice. Gwen immediately flew to

New York and danced and acted for us. She did her own brief version of a flirty cancan dancer. Her dancing was brilliant and so was her acting. We were dazzled, and since *Can-Can* she has dazzled everyone else in shows like *Damn Yankees* and *Sweet Charity*. I'll always be proud that I was connected with the show that introduced Gwen Verdon to Broadway.

In *Can-Can* Gwen played a young laundress named Claudine. To play her lover, we brought in another Californian, a friend and an elegant comedian, Hans Conried. He played a slightly crazy Bulgarian sculptor named Boris Adzinidzinaze. (We enjoyed digging up names for our cast. Lilo's name in the play was La Môme Pistache, which freely translated means "The Pistachio Kid." The French in that period also used many ancient Greek names. One of our characters was called Hercule; another, Théophile; and the name of our leading man was Judge Aristide Forestier.)

Before *Can-Can* opened at the Shubert Theatre in Philadelphia, the box office told us that we were sold out for the entire four weeks. Cole Porter's name was, obviously, the big draw. But I was surprised when the people in the box office told me that my name on the marquee with Cole's made an interesting combination. The name of the *Guys and Dolls* guy from Brooklyn, combined with the name of the elegant and world-famous Cole Porter, made the show sound kind of amusing. In Philly we had the usual tribulations and we made many changes, but when we closed there, we felt pretty confident about the show.

261

Chapter 19

When *Can-Can* opened in New York on May 7, 1953, there was an exciting but not really unexpected happening. Gwen Verdon, playing the second female lead, stole the show. Everyone else did very well — there was much applause for Lilo, Hans Conried, Peter Cookson and the others — but Gwen stopped the show twice. By "stopping the show," I mean that the audience will not let the show go on until the person who did the "stopping" takes a bow or several bows.

One of her stoppers, in the second act, was eye- and ear-boggling. When she finished her Apache dance, the audience went mad and applauded wildly. At last, the next scene started, but the audience went right on applauding, and the actors couldn't go on with their lines. Gwen had already gone to her dressing room to change her costume; to stop the cheering she had to run back on — in a bathrobe — and take several more bows. I have never seen any showstopper quite like that one.

After the final curtain, we were sure we had a hit. The audience loved it. As usual, I was nervous, but suddenly Josh Logan came backstage and gave me a congratulatory hug. He said he thought the show was wonderful. That lifted my spirits.

The next day, although most of the reviews were raves, the

New York *Times* came up with some reservations. "Reservations" usually means that the critic has a vaguely troubled feeling. Although he doesn't actually hate something, he doesn't really like it; but since he isn't sure why he doesn't like it, he has "reservations." When a critic says that Cole Porter "is not up to his usual standard," he is unconsciously complimenting Porter on his past scores, but at the present time he is not quite sure that Cole's stuff is quite as good as the critic quite expected it would be. In writing about *Can-Can*, the *Times* critic said that Cole's score was "not up to his usual standard."

The morning after the show, Carin and I had breakfast with Cole and his wife. Linda Porter was furious with that critical reservation. She came to the breakfast table with a bunch of reviews of some of Cole's previous shows. Many of them said, "We expect more from Porter" or "Not up to his usual standard."

Can-Can actually had a marvelous score: "C'est Magnifique," "Can-Can," "It's All Right with Me," and "I Love Paris," songs which have since become standards. Because Cole's songs were so fresh and different, you had to hear them played more than once to fully appreciate them.

A week after we opened, the national magazines were packed with raves. Gwen Verdon was on the cover of *Look;* she had become an instant star and a great box-office draw.

With the happy feeling (plus some quiet gloating) that we had a hit, Carin and I took off for England to work on the London company of *Guys and Dolls*.

I have been involved in the British versions of three shows: *Guys and Dolls; Cactus Flower;* and *How To Succeed*. Of the three, *Guys and Dolls* was probably the most exciting. Not only was it my first working experience in England, but it turned out that London was eagerly waiting for us. Damon Runyon was as popular there as he was in New York. The British loved his style and all his characters.

Our show was already in work. Feuer and Martin had asked me to direct it, but *Can-Can* had opened a bit later than we had planned, so they got Art Lewis to go over and get the show up on its feet.

We had put together a very good company, a mixture of Americans and English actors. Since the show was full of New York street people, we were anxious to use as many Americans as possible; but the actors' union in England, British Equity, limits the number of foreign actors that can be brought into a legitimate show. They want to save jobs for their own people. In America, the Actors' Equity Association has the same sort of rule.

The producers convinced British Equity that a certain number of parts could be played only by Americans; and they gave us a special dispensation that allowed us to bring in five of the actors from the New York company — Vivian Blaine, Sam Levene, Stubby Kaye, Johnny Silver and Tom Pedi — plus an American actor who was living in England and had a British Equity card, Jerry Wayne. The rest of the cast was British.

A few months before this, Cy Feuer and I had made a quick trip to London to audition British actors who could talk like New York muggs — or thought they could. Many of them said to me "I do American." But most of them spoke with a kind of southern hillbilly accent or an old cowboy drawl. (English actors usually pick up their American accents from television shows like *Gunsmoke*.)

Fortunately, we found quite a few good performers who could give us an acceptable New York sound, and we also hired a couple of Canadians who could sound New Yorkish. One of them was Lou Jacobi, a very funny man who is now well known in New York. He was valuable in the show.

On that trip, Cy and I also found a lovely Miss Sarah, Lizbeth Webb, whose British style of speaking sounded perfectly natural in the role of the Mission Doll.

Our rehearsals took place in temporary quarters: the old Drury Lane Theatre, where Nell Gwyn had once sold oranges. The Coliseum, where the show would eventually run, was unavailable for rehearsals. Curiously enough, while we were rehearsing at the Drury Lane, a big hit from America called *South Pacific* was also playing there.

The Drury Lane is a very big theater with a very deep stage; it seemed a mile deep. It was so deep that we were able to erect the scenery of *Guys and Dolls* behind the big backdrop of *South Pacific*. And for four weeks, except evenings and matinee days when *South Pacific* was playing before an audience, we rehearsed *Guys and Dolls* behind the *South Pacific* sets.

The rehearsals were very pleasant except for one thing; the owners didn't turn on the heat in the theater during the daytime, so the place was frigid. This was May, and the weather outside wasn't too chilly, but inside we were all close to freezing. I decided that the Drury Lane had collected three hundred years of pure chill and kept it there. Carin and I finally got ourselves some old-fashioned long underwear, which kept our teeth from chattering.

Before we opened officially in the Coliseum, we tried out the show for one week in Bristol on the west coast of England. When we got there we were shocked. For the first time we saw the extent of the destruction that had been done to parts of England by the German bombers. In London there were still signs of the bombing in certain places, but in Bristol the scars were frightful, even eight years after the war was over. Block after block lay flattened. I was told that the Germans had been trying to destroy the plants that manufactured the famous Bristol bomber, and they assumed from its name that the plane was being built in Bristol. Actually, the Bristol bombers were built secretly in several other towns.

One day when I was talking to our driver, a Londoner named Vesy, I got an insight into the average British attitude toward the bombings. I told him how impressed I was by the stamina of the people of Bristol — I had heard that Bristol was once bombed for seventy-two consecutive days. He looked at me with a rather supercilious smile and said, "Only seventy-two days? That ain't hardly nothing. In London we had twice that much and we didn't mind it one bit." He was actually bragging about the bombing of London as though it were a football score. Hitler never understood the British.

Guys and Dolls opened for one week at the Hippodrome Theatre in Bristol, another giant-sized theater. I was pretty tense because I wondered how our Broadway muggs would go with the British people in a provincial town. That was provincial, New Yorkish thinking on my part. The people of Bristol loved the show.

It played beautifully opening night and for the rest of the week. Well, except for the Wednesday matinee. At that particular performance the audience — or most of it — consisted of hundreds of ladies from Cardiff in Wales, who had come over by ferry across the Bristol Channel. They seemed to be a very happy group, but when the show started, they were very quiet and they remained quiet throughout the afternoon. The ladies from Wales seemed baffled by our characters and their Broadway lingo. There were a few chuckles from a few people, but they were Bristol chuckles.

Much to our surprise, at the end of that matinee the applause was thunderous. Were those nice people from Wales just being polite, or were they showing us that enjoyed the love story even though they didn't get the comedy?

Our opening night in London was an exciting success, but it was marred by one unpleasant incident at the end.

A small group of rowdies sitting high up in the gallery were, I was later told, strongly anti-American. When the English actress Lizbeth Webb took her bow, they cheered wildly. But when Vivian Blaine came on for her final bow, they booed her. Nasty boos. It was an ugly sound. Many people in the rest of the theater shouted back at those booers and applauded Vivian. The whole theater was in an uproar, and poor Vivian stood there bravely trying to ignore the boos and react to the cheers.

After the final curtain came down, Kenneth Tynan, a writer I admire (he was then one of the top critics in London), dashed backstage to Vivian's dressing room and apologized for what had happened. Later on, other reporters wrote apologetically about the incident. Nothing like that ever happened again during the rest of our run in London.

The show got excellent reviews from all the critics except one. His reservation struck me as funny. He liked most of the show, but he was bothered by something he found salacious. (*Guys and Dolls* is one of the cleanest shows ever produced.) He was angry because we "took a young Missionary girl to the edge of fornication." A London reporter who was interviewing me said that the line was one of the silliest things he'd ever read and asked me how I felt about it. I said, "The fact is that the *edge* of fornication is a very safe place if you remain there."

We stayed in England for a while after the show opened. We met new people and we went to a lot of parties, and, as usual, I found myself at the piano a good deal of the time. It seems that many Londoners — including Ken Tynan — knew most of my songs.

I remember a negative review that Tynan wrote about a play by Christopher Fry, who used some serious verse in his play. Tynan said, "Mr. Fry's verse reminded me very much of Abe Burrows' songs." It was strange compliment. But I liked it.

Carin and I made the rounds of the London theaters. We saw Noel Coward in George Bernard Shaw's *The Apple Cart*. He played the king of an imaginary country and he was really enjoying himself. He wore beautiful costumes while the rest of the characters in the show wore black suits, except for the leading lady, Margaret Leighton, whose costumes were as elaborate as Noel's.

When we went backstage to see him he told us, with a wicked glint in his eye, that the business of the different costumes was intentional: "The idea was for all of them to look dusty while I look gorgeous."

He also talked about his makeup: "Abe, it's special. It makes me look like an old Chinese character actress."

We left London a few days before the Coronation of Queen Elizabeth. The city was filling up with thousands of tourists.

The hotels were even arranging for guests to sleep in the halls. We were interested in seeing the Coronation but we had not been invited to Westminster Abbey — probably through an oversight. So we decided to avoid the crowds by going to Paris and watching the event on French television.

Frank Loesser and his wife had the same idea. On June 2 Carin and I and some other friends gathered around a television set in the Loessers' rooms at the Lancaster Hotel. Believe it or not, one of the people who was the life of the party was Gary Cooper. It was the first time I met him, and he was completely different from the Gary Cooper I had watched on the screen. That Cooper was a very good, but very solemn, serious, rather square actor. When he arrived, he was completely out of breath. Frank's suite was on the fifth floor of the hotel and Cooper had not taken the elevator, but had run up the four flights of stairs at full speed. He walked into the room gasping for air. He was asked how come. He laughed and said, "I didn't want to miss anything." He turned out to be a charming fellow, full of fun.

We thought we were clever in coming to Paris and comfortably watching the Coronation on French television. There was one hitch. The ceremonies in Westminster Abbey were of course broadcast in English, but the French translation was simultaneous. The two languages sort of merged and then fought each other so we could hardly understand anything. My French was still weak, and when the English words went against it, I was baffled.

A few days after that, we decided to go home. We didn't fly. We traveled aboard the good ship *Liberté* and had that wonderful trip with Bing Crosby.

I got to work with Cole on one more musical, his last one, *Silk Stockings,* which was also produced by Cy and Ernie. I didn't join the show until the tryout in Philadelphia and I joined it with a good deal of reluctance. It was directed by George Kaufman and the book had been written by George and his wife, Leueen McGrath. I didn't really like the idea of trying to doctor the work of a man who was my first teacher and the greatest doctor of them all.

Silk Stockings was based on the famous, satirical Lubitsch film *Ninotchka,* which starred Greta Garbo in her first appearance in a light comedy. (I'll always remember those big ads for the film: "Garbo laughs!") Kaufman's stage version starred Hildegarde Neff and she was very good as the beautiful Russian commissar who falls in love in Paris. Her costar was Don Ameche, who in the movies had helped Alexander Graham Bell become famous. Ameche was an excellent actor, a very good singer, and a very nice man.

Silk Stockings was eventually a long-run success on Broadway, but when it opened in Philadelphia in the winter of 1954, it just didn't work. It was knocked by the local critics and it didn't go well with the audience.

After it had been running for a week or so, Feuer and Martin asked me to go down to Philly and see what I thought of it. I desperately didn't want to do that. But Cy and Ernie thought it would be a great help to them if I just looked at the show and gave them my reaction.

They finally offered me a bribe I couldn't refuse: two tickets to the Army-Navy football game, which was being played that Saturday in Philly. I took Jimmy and we watched Navy win. Then, in the evening, we went to see *Silk Stockings,* which didn't do as well as Navy.

The show just didn't happen. The scenery and costumes were lovely, and Cole's songs were pleasant, but even Jimmy Burrows, who was about fourteen years old then and loved all musicals, didn't like it very much. I didn't have a chance to say anything to the Kaufmans. Having to get Jimmy back to New York gave me a welcome excuse for failing to give them my opinion. Besides, George, as usual, had disappeared right after the show.

I did tell Feuer and Martin how I felt about the show, and they asked me if I had any ideas about how to fix it. I had a few, but when Cy and Ernie asked me if I wanted to get involved, I refused. I just didn't feel right about meddling with a Kaufman show. Feuer and Martin kept after me for weeks. They were desperate and I began to weaken. Basically, it was that terrible Florence Nightingale feeling I have always had for a show in trouble. Somehow that picture of some forty performers struggling on the stage got to me. I finally told Feuer and Martin I would do it, but only if Kaufman asked me to.

A couple of days later Kaufman called me at home to say that he and Leueen were having a tough struggle with the show and a fresh mind wouldn't hurt. He asked me if I would join them in rewriting the book. I said, "If you want me, George, I'll come down." And Kaufman, who wasn't usually given to pretty speeches, said, "Abe, you're a good friend."

Cy Feuer stayed in Philadelphia and looked after the show, while George and Leueen came back to New York and I went to work with them.

I felt rather nostalgic working in that same apartment where we had worked on *Guys and Dolls*. By now I had a few hits under my belt, but George made me feel at home by treating me exactly as he did when I was a newcomer to the theater. He made sure I was punctual, and when he came to the door to let me in, he always gave my shoes that quick check to see that I wouldn't dirty the carpet.

For a few days the work went very slowly. Kaufman wasn't feeling very well and he didn't have his usual energy. Leueen seemed to be happy that I was there to help, and George did like some of my suggestions, although I couldn't help feeling that he would have been just as happy if he and Leueen had been left alone to work on the show by themselves. That was natural. I didn't expect him to leap up and hug a newcomer. Our work sessions were all very polite. Too polite.

The worst thing that can happen when writers are collaborating is excessive politeness. There comes a moment when someone has to say something real, like "That's lousy," or if that's a bit rough, a gentler equivalent: "I don't think that's quite right" or "That's excellent but it could be improved." Collaborators must be honest with each other.

270

The three of us finally stopped doing a graceful minuet around the script and got down to cases. After a week of work, George's theatrical instincts were beginning to tell him that my new suggestions might help the show. Leueen liked my new approach too; and the work started to be fun. Actually, my biggest change in the script was based on the construction of Lubitsch's film and the play, *Ninotchka,* by the Hungarian playwright Melchior Lengyel. That construction had worked beautifully and there was really no reason to have ever changed it. The Kaufmans agreed on that.

While we were working in New York, Cy Feuer was the acting director in Philadelphia and he stayed in charge when the show moved to Boston. George was supposed to join the show there and resume the direction, but for two weeks he didn't feel well enough to make the trip. Instead, I took the new material up to Boston and Cy put it into the show. When the Kaufmans finally arrived, George went immediately to see the matinee, and at the meeting afterward, he told Cy he was calling a rehearsal of the cast the next day because they were getting sloppy. I could see that this worried Cy — Kaufman still didn't seem well and rehearsing a musical is a tough job. But Cy didn't argue with him. Then we all began to discuss the script. I had been doing a lot of work on it on my own in Boston and I had hit on a good idea for an important change in the second act. I told my idea to Kaufman and he said he liked it very much. So I said, "Why don't we meet later and put it together?" And Kaufman said to me, "Abe, I wish you'd let Leueen and me do that by ourselves." I went into small shock — Cy told me later that I turned white — but I didn't argue with George and we ended our meeting.

That night Feuer called Ernie in New York and told him about what was going on. Ernie arrived the next morning and had a meeting with Cy, George and Leueen. I wasn't there. But Ernie and Cy said that they told George it would be bad for him to try to direct the show then. He and Leueen ought to continue working with me and let Cy put the stuff on the stage. Kaufman got very angry and upset at this suggestion, and from the foggy account I heard later, I learned that the conversation got very unpleasant. It ended with George saying something like "Are you asking me to leave?" Cy and Ernie stuck to their suggestion. The next thing I knew, George and Leueen were on their way back to New York. Before they got on the plane, George told the Boston newspapers that he had been "fired from his own show!"

I felt bewildered and very depressed. I began to think that maybe none of this would have happened had I not let myself be involved in the first place. I spent the day moping in my hotel room. But then I made myself get back to work. There was a show on that stage and I couldn't walk away from it now.

Cy and I kept putting new stuff into the show in Boston and it began to look pretty good. But as we approached the end of our Boston run, Ernie decided we weren't quite ready for New York and we moved the show to Detroit. We spent a total of thirteen weeks on the road. The cast used to make jokes about our wandering all over the United States. They referred to the show as the National Company of Silk Stockings. But they all were excited about the new stuff coming in and they worked very hard.

Of course, Cole Porter was also upset by the departure of George and Leueen. But he, too, felt a strong obligation to the show. He kept working on new songs and the show got better every day. Ordinarily, I would have been feeling great by this time, but in the back of my mind the break with George Kaufman remained a painful shadow.

When we eventually got to New York, I had a long talk with Moss Hart. Moss was, of course, very close to George and he wanted to hear my version of what had happened in Boston. I told him the story. The whole story including my sense of guilt. When I had finished with all the gory details, Moss said something that made me feel better. He understood George's bad feelings, but he also felt that I had had no choice but to stay with the show and do my best for it.

On February 24, 1955, after all our troubled weeks in outer space, *Silk Stockings* opened at the Imperial Theatre in New York, and *mirabile dictu,* it got raves from the critics. Brooks Atkinson's notice in the *Times* started out with: "We can all afford to relax now. Everything about 'Silk Stockings,' which opened at the Imperial last evening, represents the best goods in the American musical comedy emporium." And Atkinson also tipped his hat to "Cy Feuer's expert direction."

The critics all loved Cole's score and they said wonderful things about Hildegarde Neff, Don Ameche and Gretchen Wyler. And I didn't mind reading that they gave a lot of credit to George and Leueen and me. That opening night helped heal some of our individual wounds.

The next morning Moss Hart phoned to congratulate me and he added something very interesting: "Abe, I think you'll want to hear this. I was at the Kaufmans' home this morning for breakfast and they were both feeling very merry about those great notices."

I didn't hear from Kaufman directly for a while after that. Carin had been laid up with an attack of phlebitis and when she finally recovered, I had to go out to the Coast and write the screenplay of *The Solid Gold Cadillac.* When I got back to town, I wrote to George and told him I didn't want to feel that we had suddenly become strangers to each other. I described the whole *Silk Stockings* operation as being like a crazy ride on a roller coaster. That letter was very difficult for me to write, but I felt better after I wrote it. George sent me an answer very quickly:

Dear Abe:

Thanks for your friendly letter, and we both hope Carin will be speedily and permanently well.

As for the "crazy ride on a roller coaster," it was more painful for some of us than for others. I would be less than honest if I told you that my own "scar tissue" has completely healed.

Leueen, however, has a feeling that resentments are bad all

273

around and should not be harbored. I am very eager to agree with her.

She too has been painfully ill — when all hands have recovered let's have supper or something — anything but breakfast.

GEORGE

Chapter 20

The business of replacing directors or writers when a show is in trouble has become rather common. These days the cost of producing a show is so high that producers are quick to panic when a show looks shaky. If the show is a musical, the financial loss can be millions. So the producer sends out a fast SOS for a new director or a new writer.

It is not unlike what goes on in baseball and football. When a ball club does not win games, the ticket sales go down. The owner of a losing club doesn't fire the team, he fires the manager. And the manager who has been fired usually gets a new job immediately with another ball club which has fired *its* manager. The club that hires the new manager doesn't worry too much that he was just fired from a losing team; they do know that, good or bad, he has enough experience to handle the magical intricacies of managing.

The same thing happens in the theater. If a show seems to be dying, the prescription is "fresh blood"; and once in a while the fresh blood works. It's an interesting process. You arrive from out of town to take over the direction of a show that's in great trouble. You meet with the authors: the songwriters and the librettists. You've got to establish a relationship. The authors have mixed feelings. They need help but they are unhappy that they need it. Besides, they are very tired and they look it. Now you come in. You're rested, clean-shaven and bursting with annoying vitality. Tired people don't appreciate anyone else's pep. You begin to toss out ideas and they quickly tell you that they have already had those ideas and they didn't work. You finally come up with a couple of notions that interest them, and if you're lucky, you slowly begin to work together. After about a week, you're as tired as the rest of them. But sometimes something good comes out of all this.

When you start rehearsing with the actors, you run into different problems. Some of them welcome you as a sort of savior, but others are wary. They may have been friends of the former director. Teacher's pets. But usually all of them are professionals, and you eventually begin to mesh with them.

I have helped make some shows look more respectable and some of them have had a decent run. One of my most successful patients, a show I doctored and helped to turn into a smash hit in 1964, was *What Makes Sammy Run?* It starred Steve Lawrence and Sally Ann Howes, and my old friend Robert Alda. It was written by Budd Schulberg and his brother Stuart, and the music was by Ervin Drake. The show was based on Budd's famous novel of the same name. I joined it in Philadelphia.

I came in on that one to replace the director, and I had a good time working with Budd, Stu and Ervin. The producer, Joe Cates, previewed the show in New York for six weeks while I worked on it. When it finally had an official opening, Steve Lawrence got raves from the critics and the show ran almost two years. It might have gone on forever, but Lawrence had a commitment in California and when he left the show it closed.

This underground profession, show-doctoring, seems to be fascinating to many people. Whenever I'm interviewed, that old "Mr. Fixit" title comes up. One time an interviewer said, "Well, Abe, I know that nobody ever had to doctor one of *your* shows." I answered, "Oh no?" He laughed and thought I was joking. He might have pursued this subject, but fortunately we were running out of time and they wanted me to stop talking and sing some of my songs, which I did happily. But the fact is that I have felt the pain of leaving, or of being pushed from, a few shows. Three of them. The problems of all of them were the same: a difference of opinion between me and the producers.

After I wrote and directed *Cactus Flower* in 1965, David Merrick, who had produced that play and was very happy with my work, asked me to write the book and direct a show called *Holly Golightly*, which was based on Truman Capote's book *Breakfast at Tiffany's*. The songs were by Robert Merrill (not the opera star but a very talented writer) and the stars were Mary Tyler Moore and Richard Chamberlain.

It was a financial success out of town. The reviews were somewhat mixed but the houses were always full and the people in the audience seemed to enjoy themselves. But Merrick was not happy with it. He felt that the New York critics might kill us. And besides, his idea of the show was different from mine. He thought of it as a beautiful, glamorous story, and I thought of it as a rather bitter story, even though relieved by a lot of comedy.

Finally, after many discussions, David told me he wanted to bring in Edward Albee to rewrite the show. I was to remain as director. I was getting tired of the whole project, and was willing to do anything to solve our problems. I agreed to meet with Albee and listen to his ideas.

I'm a great admirer of Edward Albee's work, but when he told me his plans for *Holly Golightly*, I couldn't agree with his approach. It was completely different from mine. Edward asked me to stay on as the director while he rewrote the show, but I felt I couldn't do it. His ideas called for what was practically a whole new show, and I didn't want to direct it. I went home.

Joseph Anthony, a very good director, took over, but *Holly Golightly* never opened on Broadway. After three previews of the new version in New York, David Merrick closed it.

The second time I ran into trouble was in 1973. It was a show called *Good News,* a revival of the famous musical comedy of the twenties by DeSylva, Brown and Henderson. At first I was unenthusiastic, but the producer hooked me when he mentioned his choice of the star, Alice Faye. The name really made me feel nostalgic. Alice Faye's movies were part of my early life.

I agreed to take on the show and rewrote a lot of it, but I still kept the mood of the original. To costar with Alice Faye we had John Payne; they were a good match-up. Alice is a lovely lady and I grew very fond of her. Her husky voice sounded as warm and attractive as ever, and we had a lot of fun working together.

We toured all over the country for several months before coming to New York, and the audiences flocked to the theater. They were eager to see Alice. The people who remembered her as a movie star, and the people who had never seen her before, all seemed to enjoy what she was doing.

But the producers had different ideas about what the show should be like. I had tried to keep the mood of the original and shamelessly played it for nostalgia. The producers felt there should be more modern excitement in the book and in the songs and dances. They wanted a lot more "pow." Finally, we went our separate ways. They brought in Michael Kidd as director and choreographer. Michael brought in a friend of his to rewrite the show, and I bowed out. When *Good News* finally opened in New York, with a lot of new "pow," it closed in about a week.

One more tough experience was *Hellzapoppin'*, another revival. I collaborated on the book with two very talented men, Hank Beebe and Bill Heyer. (They had written a very bright revue called *Tuscaloosa's Calling Me — But I'm Not Going.*) *Hellzapoppin'* starred Jerry Lewis and Lynn Redgrave, two pretty good stars.

In films, Jerry usually directed himself. I don't know whose fault it was, but we really couldn't work well together. I was through with *Hellzapoppin'* after two weeks of rehearsal. That one went out of town for a few weeks but it never opened in New York.

Those were the shows from which I, let's say, "resigned." I had mixed feelings about those three turkeys. I didn't like to see

278

them flop because I did have a bond with them, a bond that grew fairly strong during the months I spent on them. And I had grown very fond of many of the actors who had worked so hard with me.

But on the other hand I couldn't help having less noble, less charitable and more childish feelings. A little voice in my head grumbled, "Don't mess around with Abe's stuff. If he can't fix 'em, no one can." That of course is just plain silly. If I had remained in charge of those shows, they probably would have died the same death. Maybe.

I have always felt grateful for having had a chance to spend part of my life in the theater at a time when playwrights and directors like George Kaufman were still around. I was younger than most of them and it was a warm experience when I began to be accepted, or at least tolerated, by people who had once been just famous names to me.

I remember my first time, back in the fifties, when I was elected to sit on the Council of the Dramatists Guild. I'll always think of that first meeting of the Council as sort of a dream experience. I sat there, staring at the men around the table: Moss Hart (the chairman), Howard Lindsay, Russel Crouse, Elmer Rice, Sidney Kingsley, Paul Osborn, Richard Rodgers, Oscar Hammerstein, Marc Connelly. A pretty powerful Pantheon.

Feeling the way I did about them, I was dazzled when, in 1956, Lindsay and Crouse asked me to direct a musical called *Happy Hunting*, which they were going to write. They had been responsible for *Life With Father*, *Arsenic and Old Lace*, the Pulitzer Prize–winning *State of the Union;* later, with Rodgers and Hammerstein, they wrote *The Sound of Music*.

Howard Lindsay had done just about everything in the theater. He had started out as an actor. He once told me he had acted in a company headed by Joseph Jefferson, an actor who was famous before the turn of the century. Lindsay and his wife, Dorothy Stickney, had been the brilliant leads of *Life With Father*. Howard was also a good director; he had directed the first show I ever saw, *The Gay Divorce*. Russel Crouse — his friends called him Buck — started to collaborate with Lindsay after a long career as a publicist for the Theatre Guild.

Happy Hunting was the only show I ever did with Ethel Merman, and it all came about in a typically cockeyed way. Ethel had been staying away from Broadway for a few years; everybody tried to get her in a show and she turned them down. One evening she heard and was enchanted by some songs played by two young fellows named Matt Dubey and Harold Karr. Dubey, who wrote the lyrics, had been writing songs without much success. Harold Karr, the composer, was a successful dentist who wrote music in his spare time. Together they had written the songs for a musical about Las Vegas which had never been produced. Nevertheless, they were confident that their songs were good. Ethel not only loved every one of them but she took action immediately.

She asked for a meeting with Lindsay and Crouse (who, with Irving Berlin, had written *Call Me Madam* for her) and said that if they could come up with a new libretto using the Dubey and Karr songs, she would return to the theater.

Howard and Buck leaped at the idea and got Jo Mielziner involved as the producer. Mielziner was the top set designer of his day, but when he heard that the star was to be Ethel Merman, World's Champion Ticket Seller, he decided to make his debut as a producer. Who wouldn't, if he had a star who could guarantee a two-year run with any show?

For example, when Ethel finally did the show, we didn't bother hiring an understudy for her. We knew that if she missed a performance, the entire audience would scream for its money back. But Ethel didn't miss performances, so Mielziner was able to insure her through Lloyd's of London. If she missed a show because of illness or any other problem, they would reimburse the company for the night's proceeds. That was a big compliment to Ethel. I doubt if there are many actors who could get Lloyd's of London to take that kind of risk on them.

Lindsay and Crouse had an interesting idea for the libretto

libretto of *Happy Hunting*. They told me they wanted to write a satirical musical that would take place in Monte Carlo at the same time as Grace Kelly's well-publicized marriage to Prince Rainier. Merman was to play a rich, social-climbing Philadelphia widow who was in Monaco trying to find a royal husband for her daughter. For Merman's love interest, they thought the man should be a handsome Spanish nobleman. Mielziner thought of Fernando Lamas, who was from Argentina. Handsome and a very good singer. Fernando was doing well in motion pictures, but when he heard that Lindsay and Crouse were writing the show, and Ethel Merman was in it, he signed up quickly.

Most of the existing songs were right for the story that Lindsay and Crouse were doing. However, Dubey and Karr did have to write some new numbers to fit the new libretto; they worked very hard and came up with some good songs. They were wildly excited about being involved with a show that was actually going to be produced. But they were young and green. They hadn't ever worked with veteran performers and that eventually caused some problems.

I had met Ethel socially but I had never worked with her. I had heard a lot of conflicting stories about what it was like to direct the Great Merman. Some people told me she was a dream to direct and some said she could be difficult at times. To me Ethel was a legend and legends can be tough to handle. I was prepared for anything.

Many stars treat the first day of rehearsal as they would the opening night. Some of them arrive wearing outfits obviously designed to impress the other actors. I once worked with an actress who arrived looking as though she were going to be presented at court. She was accompanied by her mother, who was also dressed to the teeth, and four large poodles, freshly groomed. And she was late. Many stars make it a point to be late.

When I walked into the rehearsal hall, Ethel Merman was there ahead of me. I think she had arrived before anyone else.

She wore a babushka around her head and looked like an ordinary mortal ready to go to work. She sat down among the rest of the company, pulled out a notebook, and as I started talking to the company, she started writing. I couldn't help watching her as I mumbled my opening remarks, and I realized that her notebook was a steno pad (Ethel used to be a secretary) and she was taking down every word I said in shorthand. That fascinated me and then I suddenly relaxed; when I spoke to the cast, I was mentally dictating a letter to Miss Merman, telling her and the company what the show was all about.

The first few days of rehearsal went beautifully. But it didn't last. One day in that first week Merman and Matt Dubey were in a corner of the rehearsal hall going over one of her numbers with her accompanist while I was talking to Fernando Lamas on the other side of the room. Suddenly Ethel called out to me and beckoned with her finger. When I came over to her, she pointed the same finger at young Matt Dubey, and said, "Abe, he is never to speak to me again." I said something like "Huh?" At first I thought she was joking and so did Dubey. But Ethel didn't joke about songs. She was angry.

It seems that Ethel was singing one of the songs in her style, her own great style; and young Dubey, who had his own ideas about how his songs should be sung, had said to her, "Miss Merman, if I wanted the song sung that way, I'd have written it that way." Ethel had apparently changed the emphasis of a phrase or something like that.

It's not unusual or illegal for a songwriter to quarrel with a singer over interpretation. But here was a young fellow in the first week of rehearsal of his first show, arguing with Ethel Merman, who was actually responsible for his being there. From then on, Ethel never spoke to him again and he wasn't permitted to speak to her. Later on, whenever the boys wrote a new song for the show, I was the one who had to sing the lyrics to her.

Since Ethel was playing a Philadelphian, we all decided that it would be a good idea to do our first tryout in Philly. Most openings out of town take place on a Monday night. However, with *Happy Hunting,* we held a special preview on the Saturday night before we opened. I usually didn't like to do previews before out-of-town openings — you never feel quite ready for that very first performance — but this was a gala affair. It was sponsored by a charity organization headed by Grace Kelly's mother, Margaret Kelly. With the Kellys and the entire Philadelphia social set coming to the preview, we looked forward to some glamorous publicity.

Just after I arrived at my hotel in Philadelphia, an old friend called me, a writer who had formerly been on the editorial staff of *Look* magazine. He was in Philadelphia for a couple of days and asked me to have dinner with him that night.

We had a very pleasant time, reminiscing, and then he started talking about *Happy Hunting.* He talked about Grace Kelly and her husband, Prince Rainier, and how nice things were in Monaco, and then he talked about Grace Kelly's parents and about their having this big preview benefit performance, and he began asking me about the tone of the show and whether it satirized Grace's wedding.

Suddenly I realized that he had asked me to dinner for a special reason. And I said to him, "Hey, this ain't a social date, is it?" And he said, "Well, Abe, I'm very close to the people in Monaco, and also the Kellys are friends of mine, and your show sounds as if you're kind of satirizing Grace's wedding."

Just as suddenly it occurred to me that this was cloak-and-dagger time and that my friend was somehow involved in public relations for Monaco. He didn't admit it or deny it. But he was a charming man, very likable, and I felt no resentment. So I relaxed and told him that Ethel Merman played a Philadelphia lady who was trying to find a royal or at least a noble husband for her daughter. Actually, it was a rather funny plot. The mother manages to find a nobleman — a Spaniard played by Fernando Lamas — and then falls in love with him and winds up marrying him herself. Well, my friend thought that this wouldn't offend anyone in Monaco; but he asked me if I would meet with Grace Kelly's father, Jack Kelly, and put his mind at ease. I said I'd like to meet Mr. Kelly.

The next night I was visited by Jack Kelly, a very impressive man — a tall, very handsome fellow who looked like the athlete he always had been. He had been a sculling champion in his youth, but later he was not allowed to row in the Henley Regatta because he wasn't considered upper-class. He got even afterward when his son became an Olympic sculling champion.

Mr. Kelly came to my hotel room and for privacy we ordered dinner from room service. After some small talk he quietly came to the point: "Abe, Margaret and I are worried about that Saturday night preview of *Happy Hunting*. My wife and I are going to be there. I just want to ask you one thing. Just one thing, Abe. Will Margaret and I be embarrassed?" It was very sweet and completely disarming. I quickly answered, "Jack, I swear you won't be embarrassed." He said, "That's all I want to hear." I went on and told him about the show. He laughed at the things I told him and we had a delightful evening. *Happy Hunting* was a smash the night of the preview and for four weeks in Philadelphia we never had an empty seat in the house.

In his book *Main Street,* Sinclair Lewis wrote in a satirical but affectionate way about the parties in the little fictional town of Sauk Center. The people in this small farm community did stunts to entertain each other. One of the most popular stunts was done by the local grocer, who used to imitate a Norwegian catching a hen. He always got big laughs with the same stuff. The heroine of the book, Carol Kennicott, who had come from the big city to live in Sauk Center, hated these parties because everyone did the same thing every time.

Well, our parties in Hollywood and New York were no different. The guests were more famous and better performers than the Sauk Centerites but they, including me, generally did the old familiar stunts and everyone enjoyed them as much as ever.

One of the unforgettables was Robert Sherwood, the play-

284

wright. The first time I saw him at a party he amazed me. Here was one of America's finest dramatists — *The Petrified Forest, Idiot's Delight, Abe Lincoln in Illinois* and more. He had been Franklin Roosevelt's assistant, confidant and biographer. But when he came to a party, he would, when we insisted, do his stunt. A very tall man — six feet seven — he would pick up a cane and borrow a hat, preferably a top hat, and do a hilarious, high-kicking dance while he sang "When the Red, Red Robin Comes Bob, Bob, Bobbin' Along." I often got to accompany Sherwood at the piano, and I felt as proud as if I were accompanying Nijinsky.

Ray Bolger used to be a big hit at our parties. The first time I saw his party stunt was at Leonard Lyons' home when I was playing the piano. It was a small spinet, and suddenly Ray leaped up onto the top of it and did a marvelous tap dance while I pounded away at the keys.

Celeste Holm was a fine actress on the stage and in films but her stunt at parties had nothing to do with singing or acting. She would lie down on her back on the floor and one of us would put a goblet full of water on her forehead. Then Celeste would slowly rise to her feet without spilling a drop. For that she got bravos.

Howard Lindsay and his wife, Dorothy Stickney, would do very rough and very funny sketches. One of the best had only two lines of dialogue. They played two strangers in an elevator. After a moment, the man says, "Ballroom, please." And the lady says, "Oh, am I crowding you?"

Lindsay had another stunt. He was the only person in the world who knew the second verse of that old song "In the Shade of the Old Apple Tree." It was a very sad verse, about a man coming to visit the grave of his young beloved who apparently had died right after the first chorus. This is that second verse as I remember it:

> *I've traveled here a long way from the city.*
> *And though it isn't far I feel quite brave.*

285

I've brought this bunch of flowers, I think they're pretty.
To lay upon a newly moulded grave.
Oh Father, won't you tell me where she's lying
Or if it's far just point it out to me.
She said to me the day that she was dying,
"Oh bury me beneath the apple tree."

And then Howard would blast into the chorus. For some reason we all broke up.

I once got to do my own stunt for Sinclair Lewis himself. He was at a party given by Bennett Cerf, and the place was loaded with us stunters. After I finished my turn, Lewis took me aside and said, "I enjoyed that but you can't fool me." I was puzzled. He went right on. "You sound like a bum who went to college." A complicated compliment.

At several parties I met a very unusual fellow. He didn't do any stunts. Actually, meeting him was a stunt in itself. He was the Duke of Windsor. I first met him at a party given by Mr. and Mrs. Gardner Cowles. The party was quite formal. The duke may have abdicated, but he was still treated as royalty. In going through the receiving line, the ladies all curtsied and the men did a mild bow and got a mild handshake in return. We had all been briefed on the protocol. One of the things we were told was that no one could leave the party until the duke and duchess left. That made us all feel a bit claustrophobic.

To anyone reading about him in the newspapers, the duke seemed larger than life, a royal personage, a man who had nobly given up his throne for the love of a woman. But when you were near this fellow, you were looking at a short, mild man who was kind of bewildered-looking.

I remember a moment when it was getting very late but the party was still going strong. The duchess, who loved to dance, was whirling around the floor while he was quietly watching. I happened to be sitting next to him in a corner of the room. It has always seemed like a strange situation for me, a Brooklyn kid, with this guy who was once king. It was about three o'clock in the morning and he turned to me and said with a sigh, "I'm very tired." He sure looked tired. I felt sorry for him and I said, "Why don't you go home?" As I remember it, my words in my native dialect sounded like "Whynchoo go home?" He looked across the room at his wife, and said kind of sadly, "*She* doesn't want to." After a pause he sighed and then said, "Mr. Burrows, you're a writer. Don't you find it hard work?" I said I sure did. And he said, "You know, I'm writing now." At the time he was preparing his memoirs with a writer named Charles Murphy. He sighed again and said, "It's very hard work, writing, isn't it?" I nodded. And that was, word for word and nod for nod, the first conversation I had with the former king of England.

On another occasion, a small dinner at the Cowles', I found out that although the duke had been king, he didn't know too much about his country's history. We were in a group of men sitting around the table. An old-fashioned custom was still honored: the women went upstairs and the men sat at the table with their port and cigars. We were talking mostly about war and how it had changed in form. The subject of knighthood and chivalry came up. I mentioned the fact that the idea of ordinary common people being soldiers was a fairly new idea in English history. In King Arthur's day, knights would never fight with their inferiors on the battlefield. And the duke said, "Really? I never knew about that." I guess it was something he had always accepted. Then he chuckled, a small royal chuckle, and said, "That's rather a good thing. Those knights had better not have fought with those common people. The knights would all get killed."

When we talked about the First World War, he referred to the kaiser as "Wilhelm der Zweite." After all, they were cousins. As a matter of fact, he made that war sound like an unpleasant family quarrel.

But as I looked at this quiet man, I couldn't forget that he had been King Edward the Eighth, and the man who had made that famed abdication speech which the whole world had heard. Heads of state don't have to be brilliant to attract attention. They don't have to entertain you with stunts. When they appear at any gathering, the office they hold or have held gives them a special aura.

John F. Kennedy had that aura. A special glow. Those people who were close to him responded to it strongly; his enemies felt it too, but they envied and resented it.

I met him just once. In 1961 he came to see a performance of *How To Succeed in Business Without Really Trying,* his first visit to a theater after his inauguration. For security reasons, his arrival was kept a secret until the last possible moment. I only was told about it an hour before curtain time. When Carin and I got to the theater, we found it surrounded by police and Secret Service men. We stood in the orchestra on the side aisle and waited. Presently, Mr. Kennedy appeared, and as he walked down the aisle I said to Carin, "He looks as though he's carrying his own lights." There really was a glow around that tall, handsome man. The audience stood up and applauded wildly, even the Republicans. JFK smiled, waved to them, and then quickly sat down and gave his full attention to the stage.

The actors had heard he was there and they were naturally excited and pretty nervous throughout the performance. Toward the end of the show, a Secret Service man came to me and said, "Mr. Burrows, he won't be able to go backstage. He has another important appointment." I told him the cast would be very disappointed but he said the President couldn't help it. However, he told Carin and me to wait near the exit because the President wanted to say hello.

When the show ended and Kennedy stood up to go, the audience rose and applauded him again. Before he left the theater, he complimented me on the show and asked me to thank the cast. The audience kept applauding him and remained in the theater quite a while after he had gone. They were glowing too.

President Lyndon Johnson was another impressive head of state with a special aura of his own: he exuded power. I met him in May of 1964 when he was guest of honor at the White House correspondents' annual dinner. Every newsman I had ever read or seen on television was there. I got in on it by serving as master of ceremonies at the invitation of the late Merriman ("Smitty") Smith, who was then dean of Washington correspondents. (Smitty was the man who always ended those TV press conferences by saying, "Thank you, Mr. President.")

ASCAP put together the entertainment for the dinner and called it "Give Me Your Ears." Of course, the title referred to that photograph of Johnson lifting up one of his pet beagles by the ears. But in the program was a small disclaimer:

The foregoing title has nothing whatever to do with beagles, but is a simple, nonpolitical admonition to heed the wonderful music composed by ASCAP for 50 years.

There were some pretty good entertainers on the program. Among them was William Walker, a fine baritone from the Metropolitan Opera and a fellow Texan of LBJ's. Then there were the Smothers Brothers, who were Johnson favorites; the late Godfrey Cambridge, a sharp and satirical comedy actor; and "live onstage," an amazing assembly of America's top songwriters, including Harold Arlen, Duke Ellington, Jerry Herman and Jule Styne.

The President was not a man who enjoyed sitting quietly while other people were holding center stage. He got quickly bored with that sort of thing. Actually, guest of honor or not, he had been reluctant to come to the dinner at all. But Smitty promised him that it wouldn't be a long show, maybe an hour.

The President finally arrived, the show went on, and everyone seemed to enjoy it. But while the people onstage were knocking themselves out, I watched him and I could see that he was bored. He perked up a bit when William Walker sang "Wagon Wheels," one of his favorite songs. Then I momentarily caught his attention when I told a story that Harry Hershfield had once told me.

A male eagle said to a female, "I have just heard of something new in sex. It is called Sex in the Sky," The female said, "I never heard of that. How is it done?" And the male eagle said, "I'll fly up to that mountain peak and you fly up to the other mountain peak. When I give the signal, we will fly and meet in the middle of the sky and there we will have sex." The female eagle was very dubious but said, "I'll try it." She flew up to her peak and he flew up to his. Then they flew swiftly toward each other. They met and had sex in the sky. After they came down to earth, the male eagle said, "Well, what did you think of that?" And the female eagle said, "It's the only way to fly."

That got a big laugh out of the President and he seemed happy for a moment. Unfortunately, the show lasted much longer than we thought it would. In my closing speech I turned on the humility. I apologized to the President, and said, "Mr. President, I know we ran longer than we planned, but everybody was eager to entertain you and we all wanted to show that we love you."

After the show, the President shook hands with all the performers. (His hand was the biggest I ever shook.) He thanked us very graciously and as he left he seemed happy.

But suddenly Merriman Smith dashed up to me looking worried. He said, "I just spoke to Johnson and he's very angry because the show was so long. It ran about two hours." And I said, "But Smitty, he seemed so pleasant a moment ago." Smitty said, "That's an act; he's really sore. I'm going to ride back to the White House with him in his car and try to soothe him."

A little later, Smitty, came back, took me aside, and said with a chuckle, "Abe, I must tell you this. This is really funny. When I got into the car with the President, he was furious. He said, 'Damn it, Smitty, you promised me that was to be a short show. It was too damned long.' I said, 'Mr. President, they all wanted to do a great show for you; you heard Abe say that they loved you. He meant it.' Johnson was silent for a moment and then, in a softer tone, said, 'Well, you could say that.' He was quiet for another few moments and then said, 'Aw, fuck it!' "

An interesting quote from a President.

Chapter 21

I knew other interesting heads of state — a group of them. Actually, they weren't heads of ordinary states; they were kings of small kingdoms. These fellows were the old Movie Moguls who ran the big studios: Louis B. Mayer, the Mayer of Metro-Goldwyn-Mayer; Darryl Zanuck of Twentieth-Century Fox; Jack Warner of Warner Brothers; Harry Cohn of Columbia Pictures; and Sam Goldwyn, who was the original Goldwyn of Metro-Goldwyn-Mayer and finally set up his own private kingdom, Samuel Goldwyn Productions. I knew Mayer, Zanuck and Warner socially but I had business dealings with Cohn and Goldwyn.

I admired Sam Goldwyn and I will always give him credit for good taste because he paid one million dollars for the right to make a movie version of *Guys and Dolls*.

"Legendary" is one of the most misused words in our language, and rather stale besides, but it really fitted Sam Goldwyn. He deserved it because at least half the stories about him were legends made up by press agents and people who claimed to know him and usually didn't. A lot of the fake stories about Sam made him sound silly. He was not silly. He was a bright, tough guy with a great love for films. And he made only films he personally liked. A few of them were ordinary, but most of them were excellent. At any rate, all of them were pictures he personally chose to do, wanted to do, and loved to make. This is now a very rare thing in Hollywood. Those old picturemakers — Goldwyn, Cohn, Zanuck, Mayer and Warner — all had one thing in common: they really liked the movies they made. They went by their own taste and judgment. This often led to ordinary, routine films, but just as often it led to some pretty good ones. Today the picturemakers try to guess what the public will like, and that frequently leads to dull imitations of dull imitations. Sam Goldwyn was special. In a corporate motion-picture world he was a solo performer. If the public didn't agree with his taste, it was their fault.

The press enjoyed writing about him because of his malapropisms. He did phrase things oddly — fascinatingly oddly. One time he came to my home for drinks and said he had to leave early because he was going to the theater to see Mary Martin and Ezio Pinza in Rodgers and Hammerstein's new hit, which Sam called _Southern_ Pacific. That's kind of nice.

When he bought the motion-picture rights to _Guys and Dolls,_ and he talked to me about the hero, Sky Masterson, he called him "Sky Madison." And he never called him anything else. Now that is a lovely combination of Guy Madison and Sky Masterson. Goldwyn had a strange, illogical logic. After he said one of these things, it took you a moment to think it out. He really did call Marilyn Monroe "Marlene Monroe."

The first time I met Sam Goldwyn was really a Goldwynism in itself. For several years he had owned the movie rights to a Broadway show called _Billion Dollar Baby_. It was a funny show written by Comden and Green which Goldwyn had found difficult to turn into a motion picture. One Friday while I was in New York, my agent called me from California in great excitement: "Sam Goldwyn says he thinks you are the man who can lick _Billion Dollar Baby_. He wants you to fly out to the Coast and talk to him about it." Then it emerged that Goldwyn wanted to see me in his office the very next day. Naturally, I would never have turned down a chance to meet Goldwyn. I canceled some dates, packed a bag, and managed to hop an early plane.

Abe Lastfogel met me at the Los Angeles airport with a car. I expected to go to a hotel, get rid of my bags and wash up, but not so: "We have to go right to the studio. Sam is anxiously waiting to talk to you." And off we dashed to the Goldwyn Studios. By the time we got there, I was emotionally winded. We hurried into Goldwyn's office. He greeted me and I greeted him. Then I sat down and he sat down. He looked at me for a moment — a long moment — and then he said to me, "Abe, I want to talk to you about something. Have you got a minute?"

Lastfogel and I looked at each other, stunned, and Lastfogel snapped, "Sam, Abe broke his neck to get here. What do you mean has he got a minute? He came to see you." Sam never knew that there was anything peculiar about what he had said. He quietly proceeded to tell me all about the story of *Billion Dollar Baby*. It had to do with gangsters in the twenties, and he proudly said, "I have never made a gangster picture in my whole career." It seems his wife had bought the play. Sam thought maybe *I* could come up with an idea that would turn this gangster comedy into a comedy without gangsters. I never did the picture and neither did Sam.

When he bought *Guys and Dolls,* Goldwyn visited me in New York several times to talk about the screen treatment and what he was planning to do with the story. He had great charm and my wife was completely won over by him. One day he was having cocktails with us. I had introduced him to a new nosh which he loved, cold aquavit with herring canapés. It made him very mellow and he was talking to my wife and saying, "Carin, I am going to do the picture just the way this boy [pointing to me] wrote it. Sky Madison is going to be just as he was in the play and so is Nathan Detroit." On the stage, Nathan Detroit was played by Sam Levene, and Carin, who loved Sam's performance, said, "That's wonderful, Sam. I hope you'll use Sam Levene." And Goldwyn, snapping out of his sweet talk, said sharply, "No, I don't want him to be Jewish." I would best describe Carin's reaction as puzzled.

Sam's words had nothing to do with Levene's religion, which was the same as Goldwyn's. It was Goldwyn's way of saying he wanted a star to play the part.

I didn't write the screenplay for *Guys and Dolls*. Goldwyn hired Joseph Mankiewicz, a very talented man, to write it, and to direct the movie as well — a common procedure in Hollywood. When Goldwyn was preparing to film *Guys and Dolls*, I was hired to write the screenplay for *The Solid Gold Cadillac* at another studio.

So here was Mankiewicz doing a show of which I was co-author, and I was doing the screenplay of a play written by George Kaufman and Howard Teichmann.

Actually, a change of writing cast often turns out to be a good idea. It can be very tough to adapt a stage play of your own for the screen; sometimes the playwright gets too protective of his original material. I have to admit that I've never been really happy about the screen treatment of the Broadway shows that I have written or directed.

Orson Welles happened to see the screen version of *Guys and Dolls* before I did. I ran into him at a party and asked him what he thought about the picture. Orson, in that marvelous voice of his, wrapped it up in one sentence: "Abe, they put a tiny turd on every one of your lines." Orson, of course, was a master of amusing exaggeration; but it is true that something peculiar happens when comedy that is funny on the live stage is put on film.

I think a good deal of the problem is the casting. When a comedy show becomes a movie, the leads are usually chosen for their popularity, not because they can "think funny." The results are often peculiar.

A few of Sam Goldwyn's choices for *Guys and Dolls* were very good. Jean Simmons was a wonderful Miss Sarah, the Mission Doll. Then Sam wisely hired a couple of people who had played in the original: Vivian Blaine and Stubby Kaye. But Goldwyn had paid a lot of money for the original property of *Guys and Dolls* and naturally he wanted his film to be a great success at the box office. That meant big stars. To play Nathan Detroit, the fumbling, troubled character who ran a floating crap game and was always in trouble with the police and with his fiancée, Goldwyn signed Frank Sinatra. Sinatra, besides being a big box-office draw, is a very talented actor. But I would have chosen him to play the leading man, Sky Masterson, "the greatest gambler of them all." With Frank's style and sex appeal, he would have been a delight in that role. But Sam Goldwyn was planning for a different superstar to play Sky — Marlon Brando.

I heard that Brando was Goldwyn's choice one afternoon when I was in the office of the man who was to be my next head of state: Harry Cohn, the king of Columbia Pictures. A phone call from one of my agents interrupted us. He told me in an excited voice that Sam Goldwyn had made a great coup. He had hired Marlon Brando to play Sky Masterson in *Guys and Dolls*. All I could say was "That sounds very interesting."

When I hung up the phone, I said to Cohn, "Goldwyn has hired Marlon Brando for the lead. What do you think?" And Harry Cohn, who never minced words, said crisply, "Good for Goldwyn, bad for the picture." Brando could never be bad, but he wasn't too comfortable doing a musical comedy.

Some of the best scenes in the show were between Sky Masterson and Nathan Detroit. And Sinatra and Sam Levene would have been wonderful together.

When *Guys and Dolls* was finally finished, Elia Kazan called from the Coast to tell me that he had just been to see the first screening and he knew I would want to know how it went. He wrapped it up in a short sentence: "Abe, I missed Levene."

When I turned *Solid Gold Cadillac* into a screenplay, I had a big advantage. Harry Cohn also wanted to change the cast, but his change helped me do a picture that was as funny as the play. In the Broadway version, the leading lady was Josephine Hull, who was in her seventies. But Harry told me he wanted to star Judy Holliday, who was young and lovely and very funny. That meant the picture could be true to the basic story of the stage play and yet have a funny love story.

Harry Cohn was an interesting and complicated monarch.

Tough, stubborn, but very bright. My first meeting with him we discussed the project while he was ordering loads of corned beef sandwiches for us. I asked him who was going to produce the picture. He leaned back in his chair, pointed to himself, and said quietly, "Me." Actually, I got a call later on from Fred Kohlmar, who said, "Hey, Abe, I'm very happy that I'm going to produce the picture for you." I didn't tell him what Harry had said to me. King Harry Cohn never did the daily work of a producer on a picture; he was forced to hire other people to do all the things that he considered routine stuff. But he controlled every picture that went out of his studio.

Fred Kohlmar, who died a few years ago, was a really good producer. The director was Richard Quine, who had been an actor on the Broadway stage and had great taste when it came to comedy. The three of us worked very closely together. But Harry kept an eye on us.

My first day at Columbia Studio in Hollywood, Cohn gave me a big welcome and did me the honor of personally escorting me to what was to be my office. I had heard that Harry was very tough around the studio, but that day I found him gentle, pleasant and rather jovial. As we walked down the hall, we passed the office doors of other writers and executives; their names were printed on cards that fitted into metal slots. I enjoyed walking along with Cohn and reading the names of some friends and some people I would have liked as friends.

Suddenly he stopped and stared at a name on a door and actually started to growl. The name belonged to a man who had been Cohn's chief executive and who had recently left him to join another studio. For Harry, that was a crime. Nobody had the right to leave Cohn without being fired. He started to pull the card out of the metal slot saying, "How come this damn name is still on the door?" His anger made him fumble and he couldn't get the card out of the slot. Finally, in a rage, he actually tore the entire metal slot off the door, leaving a big scar. Then he put the card in his pocket and walked me down to my office as if nothing had happened.

Once I got angry with him. I had turned in part of my script for *Solid Gold Cadillac* and two days later Cohn sent me a long sheet of notes — suggestions that I cut certain things that would be offensive on the screen, and comments that some scenes were too long. But one note really annoyed me. Following a good line I had written for Judy Holliday, the note read, "Delete. Not funny."

I asked Harry's secretary for an appointment, and when I went in I told him that I understood most of his comments, but that "Not funny" thing upset me. I said "Harry, you hired me because I write funny stuff and if I think something is funny, it's funny." He said softly, "Withdrawn."

Because I was angry I paid no attention and went right on spouting a lot of dumb things — "Comedy is my department" and stuff like that. Then Harry cut in sharply: "I said, 'Withdrawn!'" I suddenly came to and felt foolish. His Majesty had given me a pardon and I had missed it. I left the office feeling vindicated but slightly embarrassed. Later on, I learned from other people that Harry had been testing me. He wanted to see if I had real confidence in that joke.

He always surprised me. Late one Friday afternoon I was in his office going over the script with him and suddenly he looked at me and said in a grave voice, "Abe, what we're doing is all wrong. We're working the wrong way." Since I had most of my script done, his statement upset me. I asked him what he meant. He repeated, "We're not working the right way." Then he added "We have got to work the right way! Tomorrow at my home around the swimming pool."

I'll never know if he was being funny. But the next day was Saturday and I did work with him beside his swimming pool.

Cohn prided himself on his ability to cast important roles; he was pretty good at it. His choice of Judy Holliday for *Solid Gold Cadillac* was perfect. But when it came to the man who was to play opposite her, Fred Kohlmar, Dick Quine and I found ourselves differing with Cohn. No one ever enjoyed differing with Cohn — on casting or anything else.

The man's part was that of a millionaire, the head of a big corporation. The story is basically about him and a small stockholder who badgers him continually. Eventually he falls in love with her. Judy played the small stockholder and for the chairman of the board we wanted Paul Douglas, who played the tough Harry Brock when he starred with Judy in Garson Kanin's play *Born Yesterday*. For some reason Harry Cohn was violently opposed to hiring Douglas and he kept suggesting other actors to us.

One afternoon Kohlmar, Quine and I were in Harry's office. We were determined to get the problem of the leading man settled. There we sat, the three of us, while Harry, stretched out in his own barber chair, was being shaved by his private barber. As the barber wielded his razor, Harry argued with us through the lather. He said he had finally decided who should play the part — Tom Tully. Tully was a good actor, but we didn't feel he was right for the part, and I kept bucking for Paul Douglas. Finally Harry lost his temper. While the razor was still scraping his chin, he roared out, "Oh shit, Burrows, who's going to believe that a rough, coarse son-of-a-bitch could be head of a million-dollar company?"

There was silence in the office as Quine and Kohlmar and I stared at this rough head of Columbia Pictures. Since Harry was lying back in the barber chair, he couldn't see us; he was looking at the ceiling. I remember having a small smile on my face. I took a deep breath and leaned forward as though I were going to say something. Dick and Fred both paled and gave me warning looks. A lot of appropriate lines raced through my head, but this wasn't the time to say them. We all remained silent for at least thirty seconds.

Harry was a very sensitive man. And I think he knew what we were thinking. He suddenly said, "Look. You guys beat it. I'll talk to you later." That afternoon he hired Paul Douglas. Paul and Judy were an excellent combination in the picture.

I never learned why Harry was so opposed to Douglas, who for years had been a famous and skillful radio announcer. A literate, well-spoken gentleman. Maybe sometime, somewhere, Douglas had made a wisecrack about Cohn — he wouldn't be alone in that. Or maybe he had not had a good relationship with Judy when they did *Born Yesterday* on the stage (when Cohn made the movie of *Born Yesterday*, he gave Douglas's part to Broderick Crawford). However Cohn felt about him, Paul Douglas was perfect for *Solid Gold Cadillac*. Harry Cohn always tried to do what was "good for the picture."

Chapter 22

My first straight play, *Reclining Figure* — no singing, no dancing — opened in 1954. Since then I have been involved — as director or writer or both — with five other straight plays: *Cactus Flower; Forty Carats; Say, Darling; Four on a Garden;* and *No Hard Feelings.*

Reclining Figure was a play about art collectors, art dealers and art forgeries — all juicy subjects for satire. It was written by the late Harry Kurnitz and directed by me. Kurnitz was a great wit who had written many films, including some of the *Thin Man* movies for William Powell and Myrna Loy. He had also written some very clever mystery novels under the pseudonym of Marco Page.

The man who hired me to direct the play was Martin Gabel, one of the producers and also one of the stars. He played the part of an elegant, devious and very funny Hungarian art dealer. Martin and his wife, Arlene Francis, have always been close friends of mine, and I've always respected Marty's talent. I was flattered when he actually asked me to direct him. In the theater, friendship doesn't count when you choose a director.

I really enjoyed doing that play. I got to direct a cast of ten people, all of whom were good actors; they were not required to be singers, dancers or acrobats. I didn't have to worry about dance rehearsals, singing rehearsals or orchestra rehearsals. I was there to put on a play in which people just talked.

Our leading man was Mike Wallace, now the tough sharp Mike Wallace who is watched by the whole country on the television program *Sixty Minutes*. *Reclining Figure* was the first and only time Mike ever appeared in a legitimate play. He had had some amateur acting experience back in Chicago. In 1954 he was basically known for doing radio and television talk shows and interviews, but we talked him into playing the lead in our play.

He was excellent in the role he played, though during rehearsals he had one problem because of his reportorial background. Every so often he would be very unhappy about speaking some of his dialogue. He would often say to me, "Abe, this speech I have to say is stupid. The guy would never say that." My answer was usually, "Mike, you as Mike Wallace wouldn't say that. But the character you're playing would." Eventually, Mike began to adjust to the part, and when we opened he got very good notices from the critics.

Reclining Figure gave me a crack at my first experience with a serious Method actor, Nehemiah Persoff. Nicky Persoff is now in Hollywood and stars in many television shows. But when I was directing him back in 1954, he was the kind of serious actor who didn't really trust a director who had done only musicals. It seemed to me he was doing too much heavy thinking, which slowed down his performance.

The style of acting called Method acting is a complicated one; and the methods of many Method actors differ. I felt that in certain scenes Nicky was working too slowly. He wasn't picking up his cues. That couple of seconds seemed interminable on the stage. But Nicky didn't like my pushing him by saying, "Nicky, pick up your cues." He knew this was my first straight play and he reacted as though I was a fresh freshman. Another time when I said, "Nicky, please pick up your cues," he answered with a slight touch of contempt, "You mean you want me to talk faster?" And I answered him in the same tone, "If that'll help, yes."

A little while later, Martin Gabel took me aside and told me, in a fatherly way, some of the things one could say to an actor who is deeply immersed in a certain school of acting: "Abe, don't tell him to talk sooner or pick up his cues. The words to say are 'take an earlier adjustment.'" In other words, when an actor is asked a question, he shouldn't stop to think of what the question was and what his answer will be. He should take theatrical license and be prepared to answer the moment he is asked the question, unless the author has written in the direction "a long pause." And any author who writes such a direction is looking for trouble: if the actor takes your "long pause" seriously, it can add a half hour to your play. The next time I had an argument about a pause with Persoff, I said in professorial tones, "Nicky, please take an earlier adjustment." And I was surprised that he laughed. Coming from me, that classical suggestion struck him funny. After that, his style become crisper and we became very good friends.

In *Reclining Figure,* I once ran into that greatest of disasters, an actor going up in his lines. "Going up" means he forgets the words. Every so often an actor will forget a line and sometimes the stage manager will whisper it from the wings, or he can fake it and get by, but in this instance the actor forgot his entire part. It all happened one night when we were trying out in Philadelphia. We had rehearsed that afternoon and there had been a few small changes in the script. The actor — a competent and pleasant man named Ralph Bunker — walked onstage to play his opening scene with Percy Waram, one of our leads. They started to speak their lines and suddenly Bunker went blank; he couldn't remember anything. He didn't have a long scene and with everybody onstage trying to help him, they sort of muddled through.

I figured that in the second act, where there were no changes, he'd be all right. I visited him between acts and saw that he was very upset, but I calmed him down with uneasy statements like "Don't worry, Ralph, you'll be fine from here on." But once again, he forgot all his lines. By then, we were really worried and the whole cast was shaking.

When the third act started, though, we felt safe because Bunker's only scene was a long one with a character who was a French art expert. Bunker's job was to translate into English what the art expert was saying in French. Since Bunker spoke fluent French in real life, we figured he simply couldn't blow this scene. When the scene started, the French art critic said something in French and I waited for Bunker's translation; but he just stood there. Couldn't say a word. One of the other actors jumped in and translated some of the words. It turned into a shambles. It was the most disastrous evening for an actor (and for a director) I have ever seen.

When the curtain finally came down, the audience and the rest of us were stunned; and Bunker was suicidal. Gabel and I decided that the only thing to do was pretend it never happened. We took Bunker out for supper with the whole company, and we all laughed and joked about it, and he sort of relaxed.

The next day was a matinee day. In the morning our stage manager called me to say, "Abe, we have trouble here. Percy Waram is walking around the stage and saying he can't remember his dialogue." It turned out that Bunker's loss of memory was contagious. I dashed over to the theater and I found Percy walking up and down on the empty stage, mumbling to himself. He had gone over the opening scene with the stage manager but he couldn't retain his lines. When he saw me, he said, "Abe, I'm through. I'm in my seventies and I think my memory is gone."

I was shocked and really rattled. Here was an actor who had made his debut in the theater in 1902. Through the years he had starred with Florence Reed, Jane Cowl, Grace Moore, Rex Harrison and Maurice Evans; and now he looked at me helplessly. I was the director and I had to do or say something.

I said quietly, as though talking to a two-year-old, "Percy, when you enter in the first act, what do you do?" He said, "I come down those steps. But I don't know what I say then." I said, "Never mind that. Go on up to the top of the stairs." He did this like an obedient child, and stood there. He said, "I still don't know my opening line." I said, "Walk down the stairs to the living room." He walked down the stairs and he came to the bottom step and said his opening line perfectly. And it all came back to him. The physical action jogged his memory.

Reclining Figure had a pretty good run. I was always very fond of it. About a year before Kurnitz died, he and I talked about reviving it, and we had some ideas for important changes. Some day I may take another whack at it. It's a funny play with good parts for good actors.

With each production I have worked on, my respect for actors has increased. One of the nicest compliments I ever got in the theater happened when I was standing backstage at an audition and happened to overhear two actors talking. One of them was very nervous about the audition. The other actor said to him, "Don't be nervous. Mr. Burrows *likes* actors."

I do like actors. A few people in the theater, some of the producers and some directors, think of actors as their enemies and consider them childish people who have to be kept in check. They talk about temperament, tantrums and other such nonsense. More and more I have come to realize how truly difficult acting is. I can't separate actors into good actors and bad actors. To me there are actors and nonactors. The people I call actors are those who can transform themselves into the character an author has dreamed up. And an actor who knows his craft can not only play the character as written, but add to it in a way that will give an author goose pimples.

The nonactors who call themselves actors are people who can only play themselves. If the part the nonactor is playing is a duplicate of his own style — the way he speaks, the way he walks, the way he thinks — he can get away with it. If the part calls for something else, he's in trouble.

A beautiful girl with an ordinary voice can play a part that calls for a beautiful girl with an ordinary voice. If she can learn

304

her lines and not trip over the scenery, she can get by. But she creates nothing of her own.

A man with a villainous-looking face can get away with playing a villain. He can just stand there and look mean and the audience will accept him as a villain.

But I remember Helen Hayes when I saw her play *Mary, Queen of Scots*. Helen is a tiny lady, but when she walked out there to play Mary, who was six feet tall, she made me believe it. That's acting.

An actor can be an enormous help to a director if he is allowed to use his ability. One director I knew of, a rather famous one, used to come to the first day of rehearsal with a thick book full of charts that tracked every move every actor was going to make in every scene. Right away he found that the actors didn't move at the pace he had planned on. And if they followed the charts, they would bump into each other. After three days the director used to throw his book away.

I have found that in staging the show physically, it is very valuable to use the actor's natural movement and instinctive reaction to his role. When I directed *Reclining Figure*, I was nervous when I first started to plot the actors' moves. One day I was fumbling while telling Martin Gabel, who is a fine actor, where to move on the stage. And I found myself trying to tell him how to get there. Suddenly he walked down to the footlights and said to me, "Abe, just tell me where you want me to be." I told him. Then we started the scene, and in some magic way, without bumping into anyone or jumping over anyone, there was Gabel standing on the right spot.

At auditions you get a mixture of actors and nonactors. There is a third group I am now used to: people who want to audition but really don't want to act. I remember one time I saw a woman at an audition who showed a bit of talent, and I said to her, "Would you wait, we'd like to talk to you a little more." Immediately she became upset. I told her, "Just relax and wait backstage for a few minutes." A little while later, when I asked the stage manager to bring her to me, he said she had gone.

I'm sure that this lady went home and told her husband or her mother or her father that she had had a big day. She had auditioned for me, for George Abbott, for Harold Clurman, and for others, and felt she had done a good day's work. Though she didn't want to act, she auditioned for everything.

Acting is a tough way to make a living. Once George Kaufman said to me, "Things in the theater are so bad these days that an actor is lucky to be miscast." Only a small percentage of the people who are members of Actors' Equity get steady work. But actors handle their troubles with jokes about the acting profession:

Two struggling actors meet each other on the street.

FIRST ACTOR   Harry, I've had a terrible day. Three auditions and I got turned down on all of them. I haven't had a part in six months. How are *you* doing?

SECOND ACTOR   [*Glowing*] I'm doing great! I just got a part.

FIRST ACTOR   [*A bit shocked*] Really? That's great. Is it a good part?

SECOND ACTOR   Fantastic. It's a marvelous play and I have a nice part. And the best thing about it is that in the second act I get to eat a sandwich.

Again, two actors meet.

FIRST ACTOR   [*Excited and happy*] Bill, I just got a part in the new show the Shuberts are putting on.

SECOND ACTOR   [*Very impressed*] What are they paying you?

FIRST ACTOR   [*Very proudly*] I'm getting the minimum!

Some actors have agents who do the running around for them and some of the agents are as hungry as the actors.

Richard Rodgers once told me about an experience with an actor's eager agent. The leading lady of one of his shows, *By Jupiter,* was leaving and Rodgers was looking for a good replacement. One day as he was crossing Forty-fourth Street, a smalltime agent grabbled his arm and said, "Dick, have I got a great replacement for you! A marvelous girl." And he mentioned the girl's name.

Rodgers said, "I know her, but she's very tall for this part. The leading man would be shorter than she is. She's just too tall." And he started to walk away. The agent grabbed him by the arm again, and said, "Dick, have you seen her lately?"

I include *Say, Darling* among my straight plays, even though it had a few songs in it. It opened in 1958. I was the director and co-author with the late Richard Bissell and his wife, Marian. The songs were written by Betty Comden, Adolph Green and Jule Styne. Jule and Lester Osterman were the producers. There was no orchestra, just a couple of pianists onstage who were part of the plot. In the program we described the show as "A Play About a Musical." The play had a very peculiar history:

In 1952 Richard Bissell wrote a best-selling novel called 7½ *Cents*.

In 1954 7½ *Cents* was turned into a famous musical called *The Pajama Game,* which had a libretto written by Bissell and George Abbott.

In 1957 Bissell wrote another novel, a roman à clef based on his wild experiences as a fledgling librettist doing *The Pajama Game*. He called this book *Say, Darling*.

Then in 1958 Jule Styne persuaded Bissell, Bissell's wife and me to work together and turn this book into a play that would include a few songs by Jule, Betty and Adolph. The show was *Say, Darling*. That's what I call "getting a lot of mileage out of one book."

Our leads were David Wayne, Vivian Blaine, Johnny Desmond and Bobby Morse. We had a few singers and dancers — good ones — who did bit parts. Among the singers was Elliott Gould, whom Hollywood discovered very quickly. Bobby Morse played a small part, but he was marvelous in it.

When he first auditioned for me, I almost turned him down.

He walked onstage and I didn't like his appearance. The part he was auditioning for was that of a slick young Broadway producer; but Bobby, although he sounded pretty good, looked slovenly. His competitors all dressed neatly, doing their best to look the part. Bobby came in wearing sloppy slacks and an oversized Norwegian sweater and his hair was rumpled — not the right image.

When Jule Styne saw my head beginning to shake negatively, he whispered to me, "I saw the kid in *The Matchmaker*. He's really great." Betty and Adolph whispered agreement. I had not seen *The Matchmaker*, but I knew it had been directed by Tyrone Guthrie, so I took another long look at this kid.

There was something special about his eyes, the way he looked out at the empty theater as though he owned it, that interested me, and, of course, everyone else at the audition was whispering raves about his work. Besides, the other young actors who had auditioned may have looked sartorially neat, but they were kind of dull. At least Morse didn't look dull. I decided to give him a second look.

I spoke to his agent, and told him about my reservations. I suggested that he have Bobby come to my apartment the next morning looking neat and very Ivy League-ish — clothes, hair and everything else.

Bobby did so. When he walked through my door, he was completely transformed — the perfect image of the crisp, rich, young Broadway producer. I asked him, "Why didn't you dress like that at the audition?" He answered, "I figured all the other guys would dress like this." He was right, of course. All the other actors did look alike but Bobby's Norwegian sweater made me notice him. I didn't like the way he looked, but I did look. His ploy worked. And a few years later he played the master of the ploy as Finch in *How To Succeed*.

In *Say, Darling*, Morse eventually stole the show. At first, none of the actors paid much attention to him. Once in a while I would suggest some outrageous bit for him to do. For instance, in a scene where he was listening to a pianist playing a number, I had Bobby lope across the room and float up onto the baby grand piano, something he did with ease. A few of the actors said to me, "Are you going to let him do that?" I just nodded.

Generally, they concentrated on their own parts, but none of them was always happy in what he was doing. Many actors worry about their status in a show, but they are too polite to talk about it. Actors won't directly say to you, "I'd like my part to be bigger." They usually use roundabout phrases like "Abe, you really don't need me in this scene." I've had ladies say to me in a sweet tone, "Abe, I feel there's so much more I can give."

I remember one or two actors who've said, "Abe, I have nothing to do in this scene; I feel as though I'm standing there with egg on my face." An actor said that "egg on my face" thing to me once too often. One day when he said it in the middle of a rehearsal, I answered, "Egg on the face is better than no food at all." That quieted him down. Since then I've heard that "egg" complaint many times and I always use the same response. It gets a laugh and it works effectively.

Although actors usually don't complain openly, they do have agents who complain for them. Many times the agent will complain even though the actor feels very satisfied. In *Say, Darling* David Wayne was easy to work with. Seldom a beef. But his agent was always after me, claiming that I was favoring Johnny Desmond, a popular singer doing his first legitimate show. Johnny Desmond was also complaining to me. He said that I was throwing the whole show to David Wayne. But Wayne's agent kept insisting I was doing my best to make Johnny Desmond the star of the show. Every time I gave Desmond a new line, Wayne's agent complained to me.

Came opening night of *Say, Darling*. In the second scene of the play, Bobby Morse made his first appearance. The scene was in an office and Bobby was alone onstage shaving himself with an electric razor. He suddenly twitched his shoulder, the most eloquent twitch that's ever been seen. And there was a tremendous laugh from the audience. Then Bobby did another twitch and there was another roar of laughter. I turned to David's agent and said, "You've been watching the wrong fellow."

Say, Darling had a pretty good run on Broadway, but when the curtain went up on that big opening night, we ran into what I considered at the time a full-fledged disaster: The curtain went up before Brooks Atkinson was seated. I still wince when I think about it. It was the fault of the company manager, the man who signals the stage manager when the curtain should go up on opening night. Part of his job is to be sure that all the critics are seated before the show starts. This particular night our company manager blew it. For some reason he thought that Brooks Atkinson had been seated and he let the show begin. But as the lights came up on the stage, there to my horror was Atkinson, wandering in front of the stage looking for a seat. Evidently there had been another mistake. The seats Atkinson usually sat in were now being occupied by Mr. and Mrs. Walter Kerr, and this night Mr. Atkinson's aisle seats were on the other aisle.

All my friends who saw the powerful New York *Times* critic wandering around in the spotlight after the play had started were horrified. Sam Spiegel, the motion picture producer, couldn't bear it. He leaped up and the whole audience could hear him whisper, "Mr. Atkinson, take my seat." All this was happening while our star, David Wayne, was speaking his opening lines. Atkinson finally found his seats and sat down. But I was in shock.

In his review the next day, Mr. Atkinson didn't like *Say, Darling* very much. I don't think he was the kind of man who would let a mistake affect his review of a show, but I do think that the incident may have spoiled the evening for him.

A year after *Say, Darling,* I directed *Golden Fleecing,* a comedy by Lorenzo Semple, Jr. It starred Tom Poston and Suzanne Pleshette. After it opened, Brooks Atkinson actually spoke to me during an intermission. He said, "I think this should have a nice run." "A nice run" didn't mean it would set the world on fire, but it did fairly well.

Of my straight plays, probably the most successful was *Cactus Flower,* which opened in 1965. It was based on a French smash hit, *Fleur de Cactus,* written by two brilliant French playwrights, Pierre Barillet and Jean-Pierre Gredy. It was produced by David Merrick (My first play with David.) Curiously enough I actually had to be talked into writing and directing this hit.

Cactus Flower was first brought to me by Lee Stevens, who was then a young member of the William Morris Agency. He sent me a literal translation of the play which didn't enchant me, but Stevens was, and happily still is, a very stubborn man, and as we argued about whether or not I should do the play, I gradually began to see possibilities in an American version of the story and finally I gave in and went to work.

On our opening night in New York, the play took off like a rocket. The critics liked it as much as the audience did. And the play was also a personal triumph for Lauren Bacall.

The play was a comedy about a dentist and his nurse. The phrase "cactus flower" was symbolic of the nurse herself. The prickly cactus does blossom and it blooms at odd times. Sometimes there is no flower for years and then suddenly it blooms. That late-blooming nurse was played by Bacall. I had always admired Bacall in her films. We had met a couple of times: once in Philadelphia at dinner with the Kaufmans and Humphrey Bogart, and the other time at Art Buchwald's apartment in Paris.

She was as dynamic in a living room as she was on the screen and stage. She had a great effect on almost every man who met her. One time when we were in Washington trying out *Cactus Flower,* Art Buchwald gave a party for us. A portly, middle-aged British diplomat came over to me and said, "Sir, I just learned that you direct Miss Bacall in your play." I nodded yes. "You mean you're with her all the time?" I said, "Well, we do a lot of work together." He said, "Isn't that wonderful? It must be so exciting. I just stood next to her and I could barely breathe." He grabbed his throat as he said this. Betty often did that to men.

However, when I started writing *Cactus Flower,* I had no idea that she was going to play in it. One day while I was still working on the first scene, David Merrick called me and said, "Abe, for the nurse, how about Lauren Bacall?" My answer was rather positive. I shouted, "Wow, David, would she do it?" She did it.

David had sent her a literal translation of the French play, but she hadn't seen any part of my version. Nevertheless, she seemed to trust me. Having a picture of her in my mind, Bacall as a starchy nurse, was a tremendous help in my writing the play.

I was also the director, so I had to take part in the casting during the time I was writing.

Bacall's costar in the part of the dentist was Barry Nelson, but we didn't hire Barry during our casting period. He joined the show when we were in Washington. Barry was a powerful addition to the play. He really understood comedy and his speech and movements were special. A few years later, when I was directing a second company of *Cactus Flower*, I had to invent a lot of new staging of the part of the dentist because although the other actor was very good, he couldn't move the way Barry did. A remarkably skillful actor.

The rest of the cast was excellent. Robert Moore played the very funny part of the dentist's friend. We got him by accident. He was an understudy in a long-running Broadway show and was getting tired of it. Someone heard him say that and sent him over to Merrick and me for an audition. He was perfect. These days Moore is a famous director in the theater and in films. I like to take an occasional bow as one of his teachers. Another one of my *Cactus Flower* graduates was Burt Brinckerhoff, a good actor who became a good television director.

We found our second leading lady, Brenda Vaccaro, on a Friday evening, two days before we went into rehearsal. We had been auditioning actresses for that part for weeks and had not yet found one we thought was right. We were desperate that Friday, but at the end of the day, at six o'clock, Brenda Vaccaro showed up. She had been in a couple of plays but no big hits. She told me later that she hadn't wanted to come to our audi-

Guys and Dolls, 1950. *The Dollies in the Hot Box.*

Guys and Dolls, *1950. The crap
game in the sewer.*

Guys and Dolls, 1950. *Vivian Blaine playing Miss Adelaide.*

Hans Conried, Gwen Verdon and Lilo in Can-Can.

This was Gwen Verdon's big show-stopper, the Apache Dance.

Three Wishes for Jamie, *1953. A serious director at work.*

Happy Hunting, *1955. With Jo Mielziner, Howard Lindsay and Russel Crouse.*

How To Succeed, *1961. The actors are going through the script for the very first time. During this reading I never stop the actors for corrections. Cy Feuer, Frank Loesser and I are listening and suffering.*

Rehearsing How To Succeed.

Rehearsing How To Succeed

How To Succeed, *1961.*
Bobby Morse, Rudy
Vallee, Lanier Davis
and Paul Reed.

FINAL

DAILY NEWS
NEW YORK'S PICTURE NEWSPAPER®

5¢

Vol. 43. No. 180   Copr. 1962 News Syndicate Co. Inc.   New York 17, N.Y., Saturday, January 20, 1962★   WEATHER: Partly cloudy, early snow.

JFK LEARNS:
HOW TO SUCCEED

DAILY NEWS PHOTO BY ALAN AARONSON

He Needs a Lesson? A double cordon of Secret Servicemen and police hold back enthusiastic wellwishers as a coatless President Kennedy leaves limousine to enter 46th St. Theatre to see "How To Succeed." The theatre capped bu y day in which JFK met with UN's acting Secretary General U Thant and Mayor Wagner.   . —*Story on page 2*

(NEWS foto by Alan Aaronson)

*Provincetown in the sixties.
Carin and I on the dunes. This
was a full-page picture in the old
Holiday magazine.*

*On the beach at Wellfleet in the
sixties. From left to right:
Carin, Anne (Mrs. Alfred)
Kazin, the late Edwin O'Connor,
Ed's wife, the late Veniette
O'Connor, Alfred Kazin.*

tion — she hated auditions — but her husband had talked her into it. She walked out onto the stage and started to speak in that husky voice of hers. I said, "Miss Vaccaro, do you have a cold?" And in that same husky voice she answered with a touch of irritation, "No, this is the way I talk." Then she finally, with a bit of reluctance, read a scene for us. After about a minute of listening to her, Merrick and I shook hands and said, "We've now got our whole cast."

Before we worked together, Betty Bacall had starred in just one other legitimate play. A few years before *Cactus Flower,* she had appeared in a comedy called *Goodbye Charlie.* The play was written and directed by George Axelrod, who had written *The Seven-Year Itch.* It was produced by Leland Hayward and it co-starred Sidney Chaplin.

In spite of all that firepower plus the glamour of Bacall, the play was not a hit. During eight weeks on the road it drew thousands of Bacall's fans, but it also drew bad reviews, and when the play finally came to New York, it had a very short life.

Even though the critics had been kind to her personally, that experience made Betty very wary about doing another play. When she agreed to do *Cactus Flower,* David Merrick and I were flattered that she trusted us and the play.

From the first day of rehearsal, she seemed completely at home. She worked as hard as everyone else. She concentrated on her part and there was no "I'm a glamour girl" stuff. Actually, I have found that the biggest stars are the hardest workers when it comes to plying their trade.

Cactus Flower had its first tryout at the National Theatre in Washington, D.C. From the opening scene between Brenda Vaccaro and Burt Brinckerhoff, who were both marvelous, the show seemed to be a winner. And when Bacall made her first entrance in the second scene, she got an ovation. From then on, we could do no wrong. The next morning the notices were beautiful. We were sold out for the run and broke the house record.

I really enjoyed our National Capital. I had been to Washington on short trips before this, but now we were there for two weeks, the show was doing well, and I had time to look around. Bacall was a big plus. I'm not one of your passionate sightseers but she saw to it that I ingested enough sights to last me forever. Her favorite was the Lincoln Memorial. She had been a close friend of Adlai Stevenson's — he had died a few months before — and Stevenson had been a fervent admirer of Lincoln. At least three times Betty had me join her in climbing what seemed like a thousand steps to see Lincoln's statue. But each time when I arrived, gasping for breath, I would relax when I saw that wonderful sculpture: Lincoln sitting thoughtfully and looking right at me.

One day Bacall had me take her, or rather she took me, to the grave of another one of her heroes, John F. Kennedy. We stood there for almost half an hour and when we left we couldn't say anything to each other for quite a while.

She also got me into the White House for a special visit. One of her friends was Jack Valenti, now a big power in the motion picture industry, but then one of Lyndon Johnson's close aides. Valenti invited Betty and me to have lunch in the White House mess, where many White House employees eat. After lunch he gave us a personal tour of the White House itself. The President and his family were out of town at the time and we got to see every part of the place.

My first reaction was one of surprise. All my life I had thought of the White House as a sort of palace, a grand, impersonal palace, but it wasn't anything like that. In spite of the beautiful furniture, memorable paintings and historical mementos, I felt as though I were visiting someone's lovely home. Somewhat palatial but not a palace.

One modern touch fascinated me. In every room in which President Johnson spent any time, including his office and his bedroom, there were three television sets. I learned that whenever the news programs were on the air, Johnson could keep his eye on all three networks simultaneously and was therefore able to get furious with all of them at once.

In *Cactus Flower*'s second week in Washington, Joseph Campanella left the show and Barry Nelson took his place. It's always a painful thing to have to replace an actor, painful for the actor and painful for the cast and for me. Joe was a very good actor and a very nice man but he just wasn't happy in a farce. At least he didn't suffer any financial loss because he had a contract and David Merrick honored it. Joe is now in Hollywood and doing very well.

The first night Barry Nelson went into the show, I had to admire his cool courage; his was a very gutsy performance. Barry had had only about four days to learn the part but you would never have known it. He may have forgotten a word or two and a move or two, but he did everything, including his mistakes, with such bravura that if he was at all nervous the audience was never aware of it. The rest of the cast was rooting for him and they concentrated on helping him; I joined them mentally from the back of the theater. In a few days Barry was playing the part as through he had been doing it for years, and he seemed to induce sparks from everyone else's performance.

Cactus Flower had its next tryout at the Forrest Theatre in Philadelphia. It's a beautiful theater which has one odd and interesting feature. When it was built, years ago, the architects made a slight mistake: they forgot to put in dressing rooms for the actors. This "slight mistake" was not discovered until the day of the grand opening. There were speeches from the governor, the mayor and other big shots; and then, when all the luminaries started to inspect the building, someone noticed that dressing rooms were missing. That's how they felt about actors in those days.

After much confusion they found a way to handle the gigantic boo-boo. The theater owners bought the building next door, which was separated from the theater by an alley, and the dressing rooms were built in this "annex." The actors reach it by hiking through a tunnel connecting the basements of the two buildings. An elevator takes them to the dressing-room

315

floor. In the summertime, most of the actors just dash back and forth across the alley.

Because it's very large, the Forrest is usually reserved for musicals. With Bacall's name on the marquee, we filled every seat for the entire run.

When we opened in New York in December of 1965, the show bowled over the audience and the critics, and the next morning there was that lovely line outside of the Royale Theatre. Overnight, Lauren Bacall had become a top leading lady on Broadway.

In 1967 the late Hugh Beaumont asked me to come to London to put on *Cactus Flower*. Beaumont, who was known throughout the English theater as "Binkie," was the most famous producer in London, and David Merrick and I were happy to be associated with him. Another plus was Margaret Leighton's interest in playing the part that Lauren Bacall had played in New York.

When I left for London, I took Jimmy with me as my assistant. It was his first trip overseas. In London the show played in the Lyric Theatre on Shaftesbury Avenue. It was a lovely and intimate theater and Jimmy and I liked working there.

Across the street from the stage door was a funny little place where we used to buy snacks. It was a London version of a New York delicatessen and it was called the Nosh Bar. *Nosh* is a Jewish word for snack, usually a delicacy that can lead to heartburn. Harry was very proud of his corned beef (he called it "cawn beef"). He said it was just as good or better than New York corned beef. Actually, it was a nosh that most Londoners called salt beef — a cousin of our own corned beef, a very distant cousin. Harry got me to taste it and I pretended to like it, but after that I avoided it and told him that working in the theater gave me a nervous stomach.

Since it was decided that the locale of the play should be London, we did have to make changes in the script. Arthur Blossom, a friend of Binkie's, helped me translate some of my Amer-English into Anglo-English. One peculiar change had to be

316

made. Our dentist, Dr. Julian Winston, had to be called *Mr. Julian Winston,* according to the old British custom. We also had to change the names of streets, suburbs, and other places; and we had to change some of the slang. For instance, in one scene a character was complaining because she had spoiled something. In New York she said, "I fizzled it!" In London she said, "I ballsed it up!" A little strange to my American ear.

Costarring with Maggie Leighton was Tony Britton, and they played together beautifully. Margaret Leighton was a delight to work with. She was best known as a serious actress but she was very good at comedy. She was married to Michael Wilding then and I got very fond of both of them.

I used to rehearse wearing a sweater because I found out that even in April, London was cold. After rehearsals I would always leave my sweater in Maggie's dressing room. She called my sweater my "woolie." When the show finally opened and I went back to New York, Maggie asked me to leave my woolie in her dressing room. That way she would feel that I was still around.

A year or so later, when she left the show, she mailed my woolie to me in New York. I still have it and I still miss Maggie. She died in 1976. I wish she were still around.

In 1969 I directed another straight play in New York. This was *Forty Carats,* which was also adapted from a French play written by my French friends Barillet and Gredy, who had done the original *Cactus Flower.* This time the English adaptation was written by Jay Presson Allen. Before this she had written *The Prime of Miss Jean Brodie,* which was adapted from the book by Muriel Spark. Jay was great to work with and I enjoyed the whole project.

The star of the play was a lady I will always love, Julie Harris. She is not a big lady, but every inch of her is an actress, and when she wants to, she can look ten feet tall. Her speaking voice is generally soft, but when it is necessary, her voice can shatter every ear in the biggest theater in the world.

She had two leading men. One was Murray Hamilton, the kind of expert actor whom a director never has to push or lec-

317

ture. The other was a young fellow named Marco St. John, who had attracted a lot of attention around the theater world. *Forty Carats* was his first big hit. A very good young actress named Gretchen Corbett played Julie's daughter, and for another important part we were lucky to get Glenda Farrell. She used to play gorgeous show girls in the movies, but in our show she had the part of Julie's lovely mother.

Julie Harris won a Tony Award for her performance as a forty-year-old woman in the real estate business who is divorced and very independent. Then on a trip to Greece she meets a twenty-two-year-old American and falls in love with him. For the rest of the play she fights off the disapproval of her mother, her daughter, the young man's parents and her ex-husband. It was a funny show.

The opening night in New York was hilarious, and the critics agreed with us — all except one, Clive Barnes of the all-powerful New York *Times*.

Barnes has since left the *Times* and is now the critic for the New York *Post*. But on that Friday night, December 27, 1968, he reviewed *Forty Carats* and he didn't like it. He wasn't enchanted by Julie Harris; and he wasn't mad about my work. He didn't exactly hate us, but his notice was not the kind that would create a rush to the box office. All the other critics were full of praise for the show, but when Barnes's review came out, we were all pretty blue. A knock in the New York *Times* is hard to surmount.

When David Merrick read it, he said to me, "Abe, if this was a big musical, I might put up a fight, but in this case . . ." He sighed and then went on: "It looks as though this show is going to have a dignified death."

The next day was Saturday and Merrick was right; we had a very small audience at the matinee and a smaller one in the evening. I was sure we would have to close the following Saturday night. But during that weekend I learned that Walter Kerr, who was the Sunday critic for the *Times,* had turned in a glorious rave, which was to appear the following Sunday.

318

I immediately passed the word to Merrick and he decided that Kerr's review might save us. David was a wizard when it came to publicizing a show, and he put my information to good use. Walter Kerr's review appeared on Sunday, January 6. David had somehow got hold of an advance copy, and on Monday a huge advertisement appeared in the *Times* which reprinted Kerr's notice word for word. A few days later *Forty Carats* in the Morosco Theatre was galloping along with Standing Room Only.

The play ran for several years on Broadway and on the road, where Barbara Rush was very successful in it. Julie Harris played it in New York for almost two years. She was followed by June Allyson, and after June left, Merrick, always a great showman, brought in Zsa Zsa Gabor, who in spite of her glamorous image, turned out to be a very hard-working actor; and she attracted a whole new audience.

I had one more reason for enjoying *Forty Carats*. My stage manager was Jimmy Burrows, a fine stage manager and a great help to his father.

I was mixed up in two more straight plays. "Mixed up" is the appropriate phrase. One was *Four on a Garden,* with Carol Channing and Sid Caesar, which opened in 1970. I had adapted the play from the French version written by my old friends Barillet and Gredy. It consisted of four one-act plays which took place in the same apartment. Even though our leads were both powerful and celebrated performers, the show never worked. It was successful on the road but in New York, it closed rather quickly. This was one time I couldn't help a French play to travel.

Show business is full of pitfalls and the worst of these pitfalls is falling into the pit. The orchestra pit. I took that painful and embarrassing fall in 1973.

I was directing a straight play at the Martin Beck Theatre, and during a rehearsal I fell into the pit, one of the deepest in New York — over twelve feet deep — and broke an assortment of bones. The newspapers, including the London *Express,* carried the story as a very funny item because the play was called *No*

Hard Feelings. It was written by Sam Boberick and Ron Clark and starred Eddie Albert and Nanette Fabray along with Larry Haines and Stockard Channing. I was onstage working on a scene with the actors. This was not a musical, so the orchestra pit was covered up with what I thought was a strong piece of canvas. I suggested a piece of business to Nanette, then backed up a couple of steps to watch her do it. As I stepped back, my foot caught in the covering, which ripped, and I went right through to the floor of the pit. As I fell I heard Nanette's voice screaming "Abe!" When I hit the floor, I felt nothing. I guess I blacked out for a moment. The rehearsal stopped. There's an old rule that says when a director falls in a pit, rehearsal stops for a while.

Everybody told me, "Abe, don't move." I couldn't move. Somebody phoned Carin and she came dashing over. The house doctor — every theater has a house doctor — arrived. He looked at me, poked me a bit — which hurt a lot — and said to my wife, "There's nothing broken." He wrote a prescription for some Valium and told her to take me home and put me to bed. "He'll be all right," he said. Carin didn't believe him. She called up our family doctor and he sent an ambulance to take me to the hospital. There they found broken bones in my shoulder, my pelvis and other places. I spent two weeks in the hospital.

My son, Jimmy, flew in from California and kept the rehearsals going. On the day before the company went to Boston, an ambulance brought me to the theater on a stretcher and I got to see the final run-through of the play. My son had done a very good job and I was grateful. Then he took the show to Boston and I went back to the hospital. A week later, I went to Boston and I worked on the show in a wheelchair. I would love to say that after all this pain and suffering, the show turned out to be a big hit. Not so.

Because of my accident, and a lot of other problems, the show had a very rough opening night in New York. The audience reaction was good, but the critics all said, "No!" The next day the rehearsal I had called was interrupted by one of the producers, who told us that even though the show might have a slight chance to build, they couldn't afford to go with it because they had run out of money. So we closed.

It was a sad moment for all of us, but it eventually turned out to be a rather good break for the authors, Sam Boberick and Ron Clark. The rule in the theater is that if a producer doesn't keep a show running for twenty-one performances, he loses all subsidiary rights. A few months after *No Hard Feelings* closed, it was having successful tours with stars like Paul Lynde, Robert Cummings and others, and it has made a good deal of money for the authors. That's the only flop that I've ever heard of that had a sort of semi-happy ending. The producers lucked out, but the authors got a break.

In show business, the difference between success and failure often seems to be a matter of pure unadulterated luck. Except for gamblers, show people are the most superstitious people in the world. Unsuccessful actors often speak of "not getting a break." They feel that most of the big stars are ordinary actors who happened to get lucky. And deep down many of the stars feel that they did "get lucky" and they keep "knocking on wood." When a play fails, it is much more comforting to say "We're just unlucky" rather than "The play was lousy."

For show people, many things are certain to bring bad luck. Whistling in a dressing room is one. I don't know how this superstition came about. But offhand I'd say that if you whistle in a dressing room while the show is on, the audience would hear it and be disturbed.

Walking under a ladder is very bad luck on the stage. A stagehand may drop a piece of scenery on your head.

Another peculiar superstition is the theory that it's very bad luck to put a hat on a bed. I know actors who will kill you if you walk into their dressing room and throw your hat on the bed. I'm not sure why a hat on the bed is very bad luck. A simple explanation is that if you throw your hat on the bed, and someone sits on it, that is definitely bad luck for the hat. (Incidentally, you have to be loaded with luck to have an actual bed in your dressing room.)

There's another, fairly new superstition: that the words "good luck" can bring bad luck. American actors who have been saying good luck to each other for years have now been influenced by the Europeans. The Germans say the equivalent of "break a leg." This seems to be based on the idea of placating the Gods who didn't like mortals going around wishing people luck because good fortune was the Gods' racket. (However a recent play with the title *Break a Leg* closed on opening night.)

The French have an interesting phrase for wishing you well. They say, "Merde." Opening-night wires now often say "Merde." The Western Union people have never seemed to realize that they are typing a word which in a French dictionary is defined as excrement. I'm always slightly startled when I get a wire which reads "Merde" or "Trois fois merde," which means three times you-know-what. None of these things really bring you good luck if the critics say that the show is just a lot of merde.

I ran into a strange superstition when I was directing *How To Succeed* in London. In one of the scenes the young hero gets to meet the big boss's secretary. She's a very tough dragon, whom the boy eventually wins over. The first time she comes onstage one of the secretaries says, "Oh-oh, here comes Judith Anderson." The British actors were puzzled by this. They all said they'd never heard of Judith Anderson. I told them that she was famous for playing wicked ladies in the movies. I was sure the audience would know who she was, but they begged me to change the name.

Finally I said, "How about changing the line to "Oh-oh, here comes Lady Macbeth?" Everyone looked at me in shock as though I had said something awful. I asked, "What's the matter with that?" And everyone seemed reluctant to answer. Finally, one of the actors took me aside and said in a nervous tone, "Mr. Burrows, we thought you knew about this. In the English theater for years it has been considered very bad luck to use the name Lady Macbeth except when you're acting in Shakespeare's *Macbeth*." I said, "How did that come about?" And he said very gravely, "I don't know why, Mr. Burrows, but it surely is bad luck." I finally changed the line to "Here comes the Dragon Lady." I checked out the Lady Macbeth superstition with other English actors and they all agreed that if you use that name you're heading for trouble.

One time in New Haven, my friend Harry Kurnitz and I were interviewed by a TV reporter before we opened *Reclining Figure*. The reporter asked Harry if he was a superstitious man, and Harry answered, "Yes, I have one superstition. When an actor says one of my best jokes and nobody laughs, I consider that bad luck."

"The show must go on." Now there's a phrase that has taken on a truly mystical meaning. The words imply that no matter what happens — injury, illness, hurricanes, snowstorms, earthquakes, pestilence — the show has to go on. These words have become one of the superstitions. In addition, they are supposed to embody the greatness of heart of most show people. Actually, there's a simple explanation. If the show doesn't go on, you have to give back the money to the customers.

As for me, I'm a realist. I know that every hit show I've been involved in has been the result of good casting, good organization and a lot of hard work. As for my flops, well, I guess I just ran out of luck.

Chapter 23

In the afternoon of May 7, 1962, I was busy taking a nap. I had been working on a vague idea for a new show, but it was going very slowly. Frankly, I was stuck. Most writers know that when one is stuck, there is nothing as inspiring as a good long nap. I wasn't under any pressure to start a new project because *How To Succeed in Business Without Really Trying* had opened a few months before and it was doing very nicely, so I told my secretary to hold all my calls and I hit the sack.

Just as I fell asleep, my secretary buzzed me on the intercom. Before I could be rude to her, she said excitedly, "I don't think you'll mind waking up for this call. It's the Associated Press."

I was puzzled but I picked up the outside line and muttered a drowsy "Hello." A cheerful voice said to me, "Abe, this is the Associated Press. We want to congratulate you. You and Frank Loesser have just won the Pulitzer Prize for *How To Succeed.*"

It was one of those moments when a fellow feels he should say something memorable like "I did it all for the good of mankind." Instead, I remember saying in a weak, shaky voice, "No kidding?" He laughed and said, "Honest, Abe. No kidding." Then he went on: "How do you feel about it?" I pulled myself together and answered gravely, "Wow! It's great."

By this time I was wide awake and I began to call up everybody: my wife, my brother, my sister, Cy, Ernie and Frank, who had just finished talking to the same reporter. Frank was as excited as I was and our telephone conversation consisted almost entirely of memorable words like "Hey, Frankie!" "Hey, Abe!"

A little while later I heard something that made me even happier. My friend Edwin O'Connor had also received the Pulitzer Prize, for his novel *The Edge of Sadness*. Ed called me from Boston and after we finished congratulating each other, he told me about the strange way he had found out about the prize.

He was driving from Boston to Wellfleet and happened to hear on his car radio that they were about to broadcast the Pulitzer Prize awards. Ed slowed down, pulled over to the side of the road, and listened. Suddenly he heard my name as one of the winners. He nodded his head and said quietly, "Good for Abe." Then they came to the novels, and he heard his name, "Edwin O'Connor." He nodded his head again and said, "Good for me." And he started his car and went on his way.

I was very happy for Ed. I had always felt he should have received the Pulitzer for his most famous book, *The Last Hurrah*. But now I was delighted that my dear friend and I had won the prize on the same day.

One more thing delighted me. The Pulitzer Prize for drama had been given to a comedy.

Very rarely has a comedy ever received a Pulitzer, and even more rarely has a musical comedy received one. The Pulitzer Prize in drama was first awarded in 1918, and since then only five musicals have been honored: *Of Thee I Sing* in 1932; *South Pacific* in 1950; *Fiorello* in 1960; *How To Succeed* in 1962; and *A Chorus Line* in 1976.

How To Succeed in Business Without Really Trying. What a crazy title! My associates and their friends thought it was a terrible title. "It's too damn long." "The word 'business' is deadly for a musical." "That title won't fit on a marquee." Well, it turned out to be a pretty good title. I didn't think it up; I was just one of its most stubborn defenders.

325

The man who originally invented the title was Shepherd Mead. In 1952 he wrote a book called *How To Succeed in Business Without Really Trying*, which was subtitled *A Dastard's Guide to Fame and Fortune*. It was a very funny satirical guide for the young man who wants to rise in the tough world of Big Business.

Shepherd Mead (we call him Ed) used to work in an advertising agency, but he really wanted to write — not ad copy but books. He finally figured out a way to do both. He wrote most of his book while working at an advertising agency, but being an honest fellow, he did it on his own time. He would come into the agency office about seven-thirty every morning while the rest of the admen were still in bed, and he'd spend two hours working on his book, the book that was going to get him off Madison Avenue.

Then a curious thing happened. One of the bosses of the agency also used to come in early. He began to notice Ed Mead hard at work (or what seemed to be work) and he was impressed by this eager young man who was at his desk typing away long before anybody else showed up. It wasn't too long before Ed Mead was promoted and he finally was made a vice-president of the agency! This piece of bad luck caused him to be stuck in the advertising business a little longer than he had planned; but the book he wrote and the ones that followed finally did free him. Today he lives and works happily in England. The only copy he writes now is an occasional plug for his books.

I didn't get to read *How To Succeed* until about 1956, when it appeared in paperback. An agent sent me a copy and said he thought it would make a great musical. After I read it, I told him he was crazy. I enjoyed the book, but who the hell would want to see a show about Big Business? And who would want to write a musical about Big Business? Besides, even though the book was funny, there was no plot, no story to build on. So I passed it up.

A couple of years later two writers, Jack Weinstock and Willie

Gilbert, wrote a straight play based on Mead's book. It didn't work as a play and a lot of producers turned it down.

One day in 1959 the play was sent to Feuer and Martin. They didn't like the play either, but somehow or other the basic idea of the original book tickled their fancy, and when Cy and Ernie had their fancy tickled, they did something about it. They came to me and said there was something in the idea and maybe I could do it as a musical. They asked me to write a libretto and direct it.

To paraphrase a certain TV commercial, "When Feuer and Martin talk, I listen." So I listened. But it still sounded strange to me. A musical comedy about Big Business? "I dunno." However . . .

That word *however* seems to be a permanent fixture in my life in the theater. I'm always fairly reluctant and pretty cautious about taking on a new theatrical project. I have learned to be wary of other people's enthusiasm. It's contagious, and sometimes fatal. However . . . This time when Feuer and Martin came to me with an idea of a show that would rib Big Business, they hit me at the right moment.

I had just finished directing a big musical television series for the Revlon Company. Revlon was and is Big Business; and it was run by a really Big Businessman, a tough, brilliant guy, the late Charles Revson. As the director of the TV show, I had to attend a lot of high-level meetings at the Revlon Company. These meetings usually took place at lunch, which was served in Mr. Revson's office. Always very rare, very lean steak. No fats, no cholesterol. Cholesterol was considered an enemy worse than the competition.

These meetings were fairly interesting at times, but usually full of tension. They were attended by various executives of the company, and I had the feeling that everybody's job was on the line all the time. At my first lunch meeting I sat next to a fellow who, I was told, was the new head of the Advertising Department. He was a pleasant man who seemed bright, and I enjoyed talking to him. Two weeks later, when I went to another lunch meeting in Mr. Revson's office, I was introduced to another nice, bright fellow who, I was told, was the *new* head of the Advertising Department. Puzzled, I turned to the man next to me and started to whisper, "What happened to that guy I met last . . ?" He shut me up with a quiet, nervous shake of his head.

The poor formerly new advertising manager had held the job for only one week. This must have been very rough on him, but to me it seemed funny. I think that if a guy has worked in a place for twenty years and is then fired, that's sad. But one week? That's funny.

Later on, when I was writing *How To Succeed,* I put in a scene based on this silly incident. My version was somewhat sillier. I wrote a scene in which J. B. Biggley, the Big Boss of the Company, hires a new advertising manager. Biggley introduces him to the staff with loads of praise and admiration; and then within five minutes Biggley fires him. It turns out that the poor fellow, as a young man, had made the mistake of going to the wrong college, a school that was the archrival of Biggley's beloved Old Ivy.

When *How To Succeed* eventually opened on Broadway, *Time* printed a squib about the libretto: "Instead of throwing vitriol on Big Business, Burrows painted a moustache on it." That pleased me because I knew that I hadn't written the show out of hatred. If you really hate something, it's difficult to satirize it. Max Beerbohm, the English critic who was also a devastating satirist, once said, "Satire should be based on a *qualified* love for the original."

I've always had that qualified love for Big Business. I enjoyed the excitement of my days on Wall Street, I liked my involvement with the big radio and television networks and big companies like Revlon. But I did see a lot of funny things happen in those corporate giants. If I had hated them, I wouldn't have thought the funny things that happened were very funny. And when I started thinking about the show, I remembered many funny things.

Once in 1938 I was in a bar with Ed Gardner and Sylvester

(Pat) Weaver, who was one of the top executives at NBC. Ed began kidding Pat about the stuffiness of all big corporations; and suddenly he said, "Pat, I'll bet you five bucks that at the National Biscuit Company they have a vice-president in charge of Fig Newtons." Weaver laughed and said, "You've got a bet." Gardner said, "I'm gonna check it personally." He went right to a phone, called the National Biscuit Company, and said, "I'd like to speak to the vice-president in charge of Fig Newtons." And the operator answered very crisply, "Do you want the vice-president in charge of sales or the vice-president in charge of production?" There were actually two vice-presidents in charge of Fig Newtons.

During our discussions about the show — when I still needed some urging — Feuer and Martin came up with the clincher. They had a great idea for the actor to play the hero, a character in Ed Mead's book called Finch. Finch was the prototype of the young man who is being instructed in "ways to rise in a big Corporation." To play this role, Cy and Ernie had a perfect choice: Robert Morse. I jumped at the idea. After *Say, Darling* I knew what Bobby Morse could do.

In our show I eventually presented Finch as a charming character who, in a gentle, disarming manner, clawed his way upward, cut down anyone who stood in his path, and yet remained loved by the audience. The moment Bobby Morse's name was mentioned, I felt that nobody else could play the part. And I'll always be grateful to Bobby for trusting me enough to sign a contract before any of the play was written.

A little while later, my old friend Rudy Vallee made me happy by agreeing to play the Big Boss, J. B. Biggley. I knew how Rudy worked, having written his radio show for a couple of years. So in Bobby and Rudy I had two actors I had previously written for. As always, I found it easier to write a show when I knew who the leads were going to be.

I had the same lucky break with Sam Levene in *Guys and Dolls* and Lauren Bacall in *Cactus Flower*. Each of them was signed while I was starting to work on the script. When I was writing, I had the sound of their voices in my head. I knew the rhythm of their speech and it helped make the dialogue sound sharper and more real.

I think most playwrights have (or maybe should have) some particular actor in mind when they are building a character in a play. But that isn't as good as actually knowing who your star will be. When you're writing a show, you always have a picture in mind of what the characters look like and who would be perfect to play them. If it's your first play, you will probably be dreaming about Laurence Olivier or Jason Robards playing your hero. Then if your play gets produced, you may be a bit put off by the actor who finally plays the part. The actor you get may be a very good actor, but he's never *exactly* what you originally had in mind. Eventually, you may grow to love him, but you still may have to do a lot of rewriting to make your dialogue suit his personality and his voice.

Now, Feuer and Martin and I had to face one more big casting problem. Not an actor, but a composer. The show was to be a musical, and musicals have to have music. Getting a good composer to write the songs for this show was going to be a tough problem. We had been so busy figuring out how to make a funny show about Big Business that we hadn't given much thought to the problem of Big Businessmen singing. I certainly couldn't imagine an executive leaping up from his desk and singing a love song.

The person writing the songs would have to be someone who could see the funny side of Big Business and write funny lyrics about it. That would have to be Frank Loesser.

Frank and I had been spending a lot of time together socially, but he and I hadn't written a show together since *Guys and Dolls* in 1950, almost ten years before. We always used to talk about collaborating on another show, but we couldn't come up with the right idea. Meanwhile, I had worked with a lot of other songwriters, but I still thought about doing another show with Frank. He had written a tremendous musical in 1956 called

The Most Happy Fella. He had written the whole show — the songs and the libretto.

When I told Frank about *How To Succeed,* he thought we were crazy. "How the hell can you do a musical without a love story?" I told him we could have a sort of love story in the plot. He said he didn't want "a sort of love story." He turned me down.

By now I was getting a little nervous about this music thing. We talked to other composers. Some of them weren't good enough, and the rare ones who were good enough weren't interested in the subject matter.

My mind kept going back to Frank Loesser and it suddenly hit me that Frank, besides being a songwriter, was also a businessman. He had his own music company; he was famous for the deals he used to make for his songs and other properties.

I remember one time when he made a really tough deal with Metro-Goldwyn-Mayer. The fellow who was negotiating with Frank was one of the vice-presidents, a man named Benny Thau, and he didn't get anywhere with Frank. Finally, Frank had a meeting with L. B. Mayer himself. They negotiated for about two hours. Frank got everything he wanted. As he was leaving, Mayer said to him, "If you ever get tired of writing songs, come to me and I'll give you Benny Thau's job."

As I thought about all this, I realized I had found one of Frank's soft spots. He, too, had a "qualified" love for the Big Business I wanted to satirize. After all, by this time he was president of his own music company, called Frank Music. I went to see him and began prodding him again. I spoke about my funny experiences in the business world, and he loosened up and spoke about some of his experiences, and he began to laugh with me. Finally he agreed, grudgingly, that it could be a very funny show, but could it be a musical? What kind of songs would there be? What kind of dancing? How the hell could people sing and dance in a business office? We would have to figure this out before I could even start writing the libretto.

331

You can describe the libretto as the spine of a show. Some of us call the libretto the Banana Stalk, and the songs are the bananas. But before creating the stalk, the librettist and the composer have to agree on what kind of bananas must grow on it. It's a tricky collaboration. It requires two fairly generous minds working toward one goal: what's best for the show.

I have seen shows in which the librettist has written a long love scene and then the composer has ended it with a love song that repeats exactly what has just been said in words. This is sure to produce yawns in the audience. The situation calls for compromise. If that song is really good, the librettist will have to shorten the scene. A great love song will always have a bigger impact than a great love scene.

I think the best love scene I have ever written was in *Guys and Dolls* and it consisted of three short lines. Frank had written a beautiful song called "I've Never Been in Love Before." It was sung by the gambler, Sky Masterson, who suddenly realizes he is in love with Miss Sarah, the Mission Doll. I had tried several versions of a romantic scene that would help a man with his background express his feelings; and then I finally reduced it to three lines:

SKY MASTERSON [*Quietly*] Obediah.
MISS SARAH Obediah? What's that?
SKY MASTERSON Obediah Masterson. That's my real name. You're the first person I've ever told it to.

After that, Miss Sarah melted and they went into a clinch, and he sang the song, which turned into a moving duet.

The method Frank and I used in our approach to *How To Succeed* was not unlike the method we had used when we worked together on *Guys and Dolls* in 1950. I had the job of making my banana stalk fit the beautiful bananas he had already created. Since I knew in advance what the numbers were, I was able to write dialogue that led to the song but didn't duplicate it.

332

Frank and I began to have long meetings about the music of *How To Succeed.* At the beginning, he put me through a kind of third degree. I had really talked him into doing this show and now I had to get down to brass tacks. The first thing he asked me was "What about the love story? Where's the romance?"

All songwriters are in love with romance. They are rather sentimental people but besides that, the big song hits are usually love songs or torch songs which moan about lost love. Frank was no different, and he kept saying to me, "What's the love story?" I told Frank tentatively that there was a pretty young secretary who could be stuck on Finch, although he's so busy climbing that he has no time for girls.

Frank thought that that "maybe" might make a sort of romantic relationship. Then he began talking about big sounds. "We've gotta make some noise." He was talking about a group number in which we could use a whole chorus. What would people working in an office sing about and not sound foolish? Well, we kicked this around for days and we finally came up with the idea of a coffee break.

We knew that during a coffee break everyone in the office relaxes. The boys and girls mingle and talk and they feel pretty good. We agreed that was the right time for them to sing. We decided on a morning scene with the secretaries arriving in the office. The girls would enter one by one saying, "Good morning," and as the last girl walks in and says her "Good morning," the coffee machine arrives and everybody relaxes and has coffee.

Then Frank, who was a coffee addict, said, "Hey, how about if somebody goofed and there's no coffee in the machine?" No coffee? In the morning? Then he came up with a brilliant idea for a sad song written in an appropriately Latin rhythm that said something like "If I can't take my coffee break, something within me dies." It was a helluva number and suddenly we saw daylight.

Frank came up with several other ideas. One of them was a satirical musical warning to all executives called "A Secretary Is

Not a Toy." Eventually, Bob Fosse, who staged our musical numbers, turned this into a funny, exciting song-and-dance number by all the secretaries.

By now, we had good satirical numbers but Frank was still unhappy. "Where the hell is a love song?" He finally came up with one called "I Believe in You." Frank wrote it for the leading lady to sing to the young ambitious hero. I went to his office and he sang the song to me. It sounded great. But while Frank and I were talking about where it was going to be used in the show, a sudden thought hit me, a thought I knew Frank wouldn't like. I told it to him very carefully and rather nervously. I said, "Frankie, you're going to kill me for saying this." Frank looked at me with suspicion and said, "Go ahead." I went on: "How would it be if our young, ambitious, climbing hero sang 'I Believe in You' to *himself*?"

Frank's first reaction was irritation, which turned into fury. He had been having trouble enough finding a love song for "the goddamn show." He finally writes one and now Burrows is going to louse it up. I just sat there trying to look humble and apologetic. But I had a feeling I was right and I didn't say anything more. I just sat there and let him think. And he sure was thinking. Hating the idea but thinking. Then gradually he began to get a look on his face. A look that was almost a smile. Then he grumbled, "How the hell could it be done on the stage that way?"

My first thought was to have the kid sing the song to his image in the shiny boardroom table (eventually we wound up with the young hero singing it to himself in the mirror in the executives' washroom while he was shaving with an electric razor. It was a great scene.)

That afternoon Frank finally bought my idea, but as I was leaving his office, he worked himself into one more tiny tantrum. As I stood in the doorway, he looked at me as if I were some creature from outer space and he said, "Goddamnit, you're pretty talented. Why can't you ever use that talent for romance?" I thought about this profound statement for a moment and then I said, "Frankie, I think romance is funny." He just stared at me, shook his head in despair, and waved me out of his office.

As usual, we started casting the show while writing the book and the songs. By now we had signed Bobby Morse and Rudy Vallee.

Then we cast a young singer named Bonnie Scott, who played Rosemary, the girl who adores but is ignored by Finch (Finch knows that romance and ambition don't mix). Frank wrote an interesting ballad for Rosemary as she dreams about eventually being married to a busy executive. It was a pathetic, masochistic love song called "I'll Be Happy to Keep His Dinner Warm." Bonnie played in the show for several months, and then she had to leave to have a baby, and she was replaced by Michelle Lee, a powerful singer who stayed with us for a long time and then went on to TV and films.

The toughest part to cast was that of a character named Bud Frump, who was President Biggley's nasty nephew and Finch's biggest rival in the company. Frump was aware of Finch's great ambitions and since he hoped to rise in the firm himself, he was out to do Finch in.

In trying to cast this part, we were looking for a dancer who was about Finch's size. Bobby Morse was of medium height but on the stage he looked small and appealing, and we felt that his rival should be exactly the same height. So we auditioned dozens of actors who could dance, but we couldn't find the right person.

One day Bobby Morse told us of a friend of his who was an understudy for Paul Lynde in the cast of *Bye Bye Birdie*, a hit show at the time. This actor's name was Charles Nelson Reilly. Bobby kept telling us he was a wonderful performer, so we finally called Reilly and asked him to come around and audition. When he walked onstage, we were startled: he was over six feet tall, a big gangling fellow. I was about to say he was all wrong, but when he started to speak we all fell out of our seats. He was very, very funny, and suddenly we all decided that Frump could be a tall, silly character.

As I listened to Charley, I began mentally to rewrite the part. We dropped the idea of the character's being a dancer because Charley told us he wasn't a dancer. But later on in the show there was a moment when Bud Frump did his version of a happy triumphal dance — faking all the steps — and the audience was convulsed with laughter. That nondance was one of the high moments of the show.

Another valuable member of the cast was Virginia Martin, who played "the boss's secret girlfriend" named Hedy LaRue. She was a very funny part of the plot and she had a fine singing voice, which helped stop the show in a duet with Rudy Vallee.

How To Succeed was supposed to open in the spring of 1961 but the producers decided to postpone the opening until the fall, for a fairly sound reason. We weren't ready. Neither the script nor the songs were finished.

We finally went into rehearsal in the late summer. It took a lot of guts for me to start the rehearsal at that time because I had a small problem: I hadn't yet written the last two scenes. I had no ending for the show, no wrap-up of the story and no real idea of what that wrap-up should be. There was no possibility of postponing again. Our out-of-town theaters were booked and so was the Forty-sixth Street Theatre, where we were going to open in October.

So we started rehearsing a show without the last two scenes. I had tried many different finishes and none of them seemed right. But the producers and the actors trusted me and I had the hubris to trust myself to come up with something. We all agreed that I had enough material to start rehearsal, and I could write the final two scenes at night after rehearsals were over.

I was really stuck. I had a funny script but I had painted myself into a corner. The situation was this: In the second act Finch sold J. B. Biggley on the idea of a big television show for the company: the company was going to promote a treasure hunt. A good idea. But during the telecast, someone made a mistake and led the public to believe that the treasure was hidden somewhere within the company's own office building. This led to a riot and the building was practically torn to pieces by treasure hunters. The whole place was a mess and the company was cracking up. Finch was being blamed for the whole thing.

I had to solve this strange problem and somehow save our hero's career. Yet someone had to take the blame; someone had to be punished. I went crazy trying to write a funny ending for the whole wild situation. The ending of this comedy had to be a happy one.

During the first days of rehearsal all the actors kept coming over to me and saying, "How's it going to end, Abe?" I wasn't going to tell them I was stuck, so I said, "I've got a great idea and I'm writing it."

Then a real but unfortunate national event gave me the idea I was looking for: the Bay of Pigs. The abortive attempt to invade Cuba. That incident was a disaster and the newspapers and television were buzzing with the story. Everybody was blaming everybody else. John F. Kennedy finally made a strong statement. He said that since he was the President of this country, he must take the blame for whatever happened.

Suddenly I knew how to end my show. Everything fell into place in a moment. I called Feuer and said, "I think I've got it." Then I explained it to him: "Here's a mighty nation caught in a jam and everybody except the President is blaming everybody else. And everybody else is blaming everybody who's blaming them." It didn't make any sense politically, but on the stage the fact that it didn't make sense would be funny. I was going to handle it like carefully organized nonsense. Cy bought it right away. Frank liked it too.

I wrote both scenes that night. I had J. B. Biggley, the president of the company, give an explanation to the chairman of the board, Wally Womper, who had come there to raise hell and fire everybody. Biggley made a heartfelt speech which went like this:

BIGGLEY Now, Wally, let me tell you before we go any further that I realize that I'm the president of this company, the man who is responsible for everything that goes on here. So I'd like to state right now that anything that happened is *not my fault.*

This speech convulsed the audience. There was recognition in their laughter. Then Biggley proceeded to attempt to put the blame on our hero. But Finch quickly made friends with the chairman of the board, got himself off the hook, and wound up with a big promotion. Bud Frump finally took the rap and the audience was happy. Justice had not been done, the matter had not been cleared up, but the audience was satisfied.

One night in Philadelphia during this wild part of the show, I saw a man and woman going up the aisle. She was sort of dragging him because he wasn't anxious to leave. He kept whispering, "I want to see the finish, I want to see the finish." And she said, "We'll miss our bus." When they got to the rear of the theater, they stood right next to me. The man had stopped to take a last look at the stage and saw that Finch was triumphant. In a loud voice the man said, "I knowed he was gonna make it. I knowed it." And he happily went home.

After the show started running in New York, I was talking on the phone to Arthur Schlesinger, Jr., a fine writer and a man who was close to President Kennedy. I told him how that sad Bay of Pigs business had led me into a finish for the play. I believe he passed the story on to President Kennedy.

That may have been the reason why President Kennedy chose *How To Succeed* as the first show he would see after his inauguration. Later on, I heard that the day after he saw the show, he mentioned it at a Cabinet meeting: "Some of you guys ought to see that show. Especially you, Luther." (That was Luther Hodges, who was Secretary of Commerce.)

We had another exciting group of visitors during the New York run. One night all of America's astronauts came to the show, led by John Glenn and Alan Shepherd, the Americans who took that first ride on one of our rockets. Most of them brought their wives. There were about eighteen people in all. They were a wonderful audience and when they came backstage, the cast was thrilled.

Another couple of visitors were especially exciting for me. One day my secretary buzzed me and said, "Why would Y. A. Tittle want to talk to you?" I got on the phone quickly. It really was the New York Giants' quarterback. I had never met him. He apologized for bothering me (Y. A. Tittle *bothering* me?) and said he would like to get two tickets for himself and Del Shofner, who was then the top pass receiver for the Giants. Of course, I arranged the tickets.

After the show, Tittle and Shofner came backstage raving about the show and asking to meet Bobby Morse. I took them to Bobby's dressing room, where Bobby was still catching his breath after his usual strong performance. Tittle and Shofner were really impressed by the physical amount of work in Bobby's acting. Those two strong atheletes said to him with wonder, "Do you do this tough job every single night?" And Bobby answered, still breathing hard, "And two matinees." They sat in that dressing room talking to us for about an hour and on the floor of that room they showed Bobby and me some of the tricks they used for the forward pass. Morse and I were really enchanted. As far as Morse was concerned, I don't think any rave from a drama critic could have excited him as much as the compliments from Y. A. Tittle and Del Shofner.

How To Succeed opened officially on October 14, 1961. The critics were unanimously ecstatic and the show ran for years. There was just one night when the house was empty. That was in November of 1963, the night after John Kennedy's assassination. All the theaters went dark that night.

Chapter 24

In the summer of 1962 when Frank Loesser and I were still stunned by winning the Pulitzer Prize in drama for *How To Succeed*, I got an interesting call from Walter Kerr. Kerr is now the drama critic of the New York *Times,* but back in '62 he was drama critic for the old New York *Herald Tribune.* He asked me to write a guest column for the Sunday edition of his paper. Walter suggested an interesting and funny title: "How Come I Did Not Turn Down the Pulitzer Prize" by Abe Burrows.

It's common practice for drama critics to honor theater people by allowing them to write guest columns while the critics go off on vacation. Vacations are important to critics: they need some time to rest their ears and their eyeballs. Walter had reached me when I, too, was on vacation, at our summer home in Provincetown. And a vacation on Cape Cod when you have a hit running in New York is extraglorious. I really wasn't too thrilled with the notion of getting to a desk and writing a Sunday piece. But I like Walter and admire him. Besides, his title did interest me.

Usually Sunday drama sections feature Sunday pieces like "The Future of the Living Theater" or "Should Off-Broadway Be Moved Further Off?" or "Where Are the New Dramatists Coming From?" or "Where Are the Old Dramatists Going To?" But

340

Walter's sassy title, "How Come I Did Not Turn Down the Pulitzer Prize," was irresistible.

Great awards in the arts *have* been turned down. The Oscar has been turned down twice, once by George C. Scott and once by Marlon Brando. The Pulitzer Prize in literature has been turned down twice, each time by the same author, Sinclair Lewis.

The Pulitzer Prize in drama also has been turned down, but only once. In 1940 William Saroyan startled the whole theater world by turning down the Pulitzer Prize that had been awarded for *The Time of Your Life*. There are those who say Saroyan was tricked into it by a reporter. When the reporter told Saroyan the good news, he added a wisecrack, something like "Hey, Bill, you're gonna turn it down, aren't you?" And Saroyan, who never could resist shocking people, answered, "Of course." Nobody knows the real story, but Saroyan actually did turn down the prize. In spite of that, he is listed as the 1940 winner in the Pulitzer Prize lists.

It could be that the call from the reporter shook Saroyan for a moment. Reporters talk fast on the phone, and it doesn't give one much of a chance to think. It's not the same as the Academy Award. There you're more or less prepared because you have been nominated weeks before the award is given. So when you win, you have a speech, or at least a few words, ready. However, if you're going to turn it down as Marlon Brando and George Scott did, you don't have to show up at all. But that unexpected phone call from the press can rattle you.

One of the best notices I ever received for *Guys and Dolls* came from Walter Kerr. Back then he had not yet become a drama critic. His notice wasn't a written notice; it was something he said to his wife. One day some years later he told me that when he and Jean first saw *Guys and Dolls*, he turned to her in the middle of the first act and said, "Am I wrong or isn't this the greatest musical we've ever seen?" This review never appeared in any newspaper, but it is permanently lodged in my brain.

341

I now am sure that when Walter suggested that title, he was really offering to hold my coat while I took on those people who don't think comedy — especially musical comedy — deserves much in the way of honorable mention. These are the people who think solemn awards like the Pulitzer should be reserved for "Worthwhile Subjects." By "Worthwhile" they usually mean "No Laughs."

The fact is that comedy is actually too serious to be taken seriously. It may be that comedy touches such deep emotions that people feel better if they can just dismiss it as trivial. Just take a big belly laugh. I have watched people laughing, and for a moment they look — and are — absolutely helpless. Vulnerable. You can be assassinated while you are laughing.

A reaction like that must happen because the person who is laughing has been hit deep down where he lives, somewhere in his unconscious mind, by the laughter of recognition.

Those of us who spend our lives writing comedy know that comedy must be based on truth. A slight distortion of the truth but still truth. In my guest column for Walter Kerr, I popped off a lot on this subject. I'll always be grateful to Walter for giving me an amusing chance to talk about comedy writing. Comedy writers and comedians share a tough occupation. It may look like just fun and it may be fun; but it ain't easy.

There's a story that goes back to the days of vaudeville. There were these two hoofers. Rather ordinary tap dancers. After years of playing all over the country they were finally offered a spot at the Palace in New York. Wow! The Palace! They were on their way to stardom. Of course, the spot on the show they were offered was the number two spot. A vaudeville bill usually opened with acrobats or animal acts. The second spot was generally reserved for hoofers. After that came the stars — big-name comics or singers. These two tap dancers didn't mind being in the number two spot. They were sure they were going to be a smash hit and they spent weeks preparing for their big moment. They worked on their Time Steps, their Buck and Wing and their Back Flips. They trained as though they were going into battle.

Came their opening at the Palace. This was the show that always attracted vaudeville critics, big booking agents and theater owners. A powerful audience. The first act was a group of Japanese acrobats who did some routine tricks to mild applause. Then came our dancing heroes. They dashed out onstage with great energy and did all their specialties. They knocked themselves out. They finished with a big flurry of back flips and everything else they could think of and they wound up getting very mild applause. When they came off the stage, they stood in the wings, panting and perspiring. While they were gasping for air, Frank Fay, a famous comedian, walked onto the stage and was greeted with an ovation. Fay was the smoothest comic of his day. Suave, soft-spoken and very funny. Our two hoofers, still breathing hard, watched Fay's act with interest. In a gentle way he told his first joke and the audience roared with laughter. From then on he could do no wrong. He didn't sweat and he never got out of breath. Calmly, with no apparent effort, he kept the audience convulsed with laughter. As the audience applauded and cheered Fay's humor, our two hoofers studied everything that Fay did. Finally, one of them, still gasping for breath, said to his partner, "Hey Charlie, if that's the kind of shit they want, why don't we give it to them?"

There are people who — in more polite terms — think of comedy in the same way. This has been true for centuries.

Recently I read a piece by Hobe Morrison, who is the knowledgeable critic for *Variety*. He's a man who really loves the theater. Morrison has always been annoyed by some of the criticism of the work of Neil Simon. Simon is a comedy genius and enormously successful. It may be that the very fact of his success is what makes some critics throw barbs. Phrases like "gag lines" or "joke machine" or "one-liner."

This obviously bothered Morrison and he dug up a review written by George Bernard Shaw in 1895 of an Oscar Wilde comedy called *An Ideal Husband*. At that time Shaw was the drama critic for the London *Saturday Review*. In his review, Shaw said:

Mr. Oscar Wilde's new play at the Haymarket is a dangerous subject, because he has the property of making his critics dull. They laugh angrily at his epigrams, like a child who is being coaxed into being amused in the very act of setting up a yell of rage and agony. They protest that the trick is obvious, and that such epigrams can be turned out by the score by anyone lightminded enough to condescend to such frivolity.

As far as I can ascertain, I am the only person in London who cannot sit down and write an Oscar Wilde play at will. The fact that his plays, though apparently lucrative, remain unique under these circumstances, says much for the self-denial of our scribes.

I'm happy that Shaw agrees with me and I'm grateful to Hobe for digging up that notice.

I often give talks to college classes and various other groups. Most of my chatter is about comedy. The audience seems to enjoy the talk and they laugh at my jokes. Then when I feel that I've talked long enough (or run out of gas), I ask for questions. Almost every time, the first question is the same. Someone stands up and says, "Mr. Burrows, haven't you ever wanted to write something serious?"

The same question is thrown at me when I'm being interviewed by reporters or TV hosts or the total strangers I run into at parties. My answer is always the same: "Everything I write is serious; it just happens to turn out funny." That's an honest answer. Life *is* serious. The world we live in is serious. I write about this serious world. But I generally see the comical side of it.

I guess Howard Lindsay's "think funny" applies to me. I'm a serious fellow who thinks funny. I can't help it. It may be a curse, but if you don't have that curse, you'd better not try to be funny.

Some writers who have always thought funny have been able

344

to stifle their frivolous natures and tried to "think serious" or "think grim." When Herman Wouk was a good comedy writer on Fred Allen's staff Fred admired him greatly. Wouk finally busted out and switched to novels. Some of his early books were funny, but now he is accepted as a major author of serious fiction — from *The Caine Mutiny* to his recent *War and Remembrance,* a very powerful novel.

In most instances, however, the critics and the audience really don't want a top comedy writer to hit them with anything that isn't funny.

Neil Simon, the fellow who has GBS on his side, is a serious, thoughtful man. All of his comedies have some very touching moments, but whenever he does a play that goes mainly for dramatic effect rather than comedy, Simon gets some strange reactions. He receives pretty good but rather polite reviews. I've had the feeling that the audience and the critics wish he had stuck to what they consider his strong point. "The stuff is good, but it ain't real Simon."

A while ago, Woody Allen, who's as funny as anyone alive, made a serious film called *Interiors*. It was a very moving story and done with great skill. He got some excellent reviews, but there was always an undercurrent of regret that he hadn't stuck to comedy. Since then he has come up with another film, *Manhattan,* which the critics have called Woody's best. Almost everything in it is funny, but strangely enough, everything in it is serious.

I first met Woody Allen in 1956, before the world discovered him. He happens to be a relative of mine. Sort of a distant cousin by marriage. My father's sister, Anne, married my uncle Paul, who had a sister named Nettie, who later became Woody's mother.

I didn't get to meet Woody until he was about twenty. He was working for a press agent then, writing witty one-liners to put in the mouths of unwitty celebrities.

Press agents are very big buyers of jokes. Jokes enable them to get "plugs." What's a plug? If you have ever read a witticism in a column that was attributed to some celebrity — for instance, to Arthur Murray — and this witticism was supposed to have been said by Mr. Murray in a certain nightclub, that witticism was a plug. The anonymous person who wrote it was hired by a press agent who represented Mr. Murray and also the nightclub. Woody had greater ambitions.

One day he phoned me, told me he was Nettie's son, and asked if we could meet. The next day he came to my home. A wispy little fellow, very innocent-looking, but there was an interesting gleam in his eyes. He told me what he had been doing and I listened. A lot of hopeful young writers have come to my place seeking advice, but the good ones are very rare.

Woody asked me if I would like to see some of his work. It can be very painful to read a bunch of jokes by a new, inexperienced comedy writer, but in this case I had no choice. Woody handed me two pages of jokes. I politely started to read them, and wow! His stuff was dazzling.

I excused myself and went back to my wife's room and said to her, "There's a young cousin of mine visiting me. Woody Allen. You don't know him but I want to tell you that I have just read a couple of pages of about thirty jokes, none of which I could ever have thought of." That's generally my egotistical test for comedy writers.

Frequently I hear a good crack somebody makes and I laugh and give him a polite nod. What I'm thinking is that given the same setup, I would have thought of the same punch line. But Woody's jokes seemed to come from a different world.

I remember one of the jokes, his famous line "My wife and I didn't get along because she was very immature. When I was in the bathtub, she'd always come in and sink my boats." Who the hell would think of a line like that? Woody Allen, that's who.

I wrote letters of recommendation to some friends of mine — Sid Caesar, Phil Silvers, Peter Lind Hayes and others. One day I got a letter from Sid Caesar. Part of it went like this:

It was good to have your letter and very kind of you to think of me with respect to your young cousin, Woody Allen. Your sincere recommendation of him warrants very serious consideration. However, I am sure you realize only too well that any show can profitably use only the talent of "just enough" writers, and after many months of thoughtful planning in this department I believe I am in that position. To add any more at this point would, I think, not be conducive to providing the opportunity which a talented person should have. Needless to say, should my situation change, I shall certainly follow up your recommendation.

I doubt if Sid ever got to read Woody's stuff. The letter didn't sound like him. I'm sure it was written by some protective person who made Sid sound like the vice-president in charge of loans at a bank.

Then Woody went to see Peter Lind Hayes who was doing a radio talk show with his wife, Mary. Peter was not in the market for jokes, but when he saw Woody's stuff he too was dazzled and he gave Woody a check for fifty dollars for the rights to use a few of the lines. Peter has since told me that the check was never cashed. Woody framed it.

After a while, Sid Caesar did meet with Woody and put him on his staff of writers. At that time Mel Brooks was on Sid's staff and he admired Woody's work. He showed his admiration with a typical Mel Brooks compliment. He referred to Woody as "that rotten little kid."

Eventually that "rotten little kid" exploded on his own. His kind of talent cannot be held down.

Most ambitious young comedians start out by imitating the successful comedians of their time. They often actually steal their jokes. And many young comedy writers start out the same way. But Woody is inimitable. The comics and the comedy writers who try to copy his stuff never come close because Woody's wit and style are part of Woody himself. He writes like Woody Allen, he acts like Woody Allen, and he looks like Woody Allen. He's a tough act to copy.

347

In 1959 I stepped out of line with a musical called *First Impressions,* an adaptation of Helen Jerome's play which was based on Jane Austen's book *Pride and Prejudice.* I say "stepped out of line" because the public and the critics knew me as the guy who wrote the mugg dialogue of *Duffy's Tavern* and *Guys and Dolls.* Many people had loved the romantic movie version that Aldous Huxley had written and I knew they were thinking, "How could Burrows dare to take on a famous, elegant British classic, and why did he change the title?"

The fact is that the original publisher changed it. *First Impressions* was Miss Austen's first book. And when the publisher read it, he turned it down. A year later, in 1811, she wrote a book called *Sense and Sensibility,* which was such a big success that the publisher took another look at *First Impressions* and published it under the "catchier" title of *Pride and Prejudice.*

I happen to be a devoted fan of Jane Austen's. People who haven't read her think of her as sedate, a typical eighteenth-century woman. But even though her novels were romantic, she was one of the great satirists of all time. It was that satirical touch that interested me and attracted me to the project.

The music and lyrics of *First Impressions* were written by Robert Goldman, Glenn Paxton and George Weiss. We had some strong performers: Hermione Gingold, Farley Granger, Polly Bergen and Phyllis Newman. The show was a big hit in Philadelphia and Boston, but when we came to New York, we were panned. Some of the critics hinted that I had no business tackling this project. One reporter actually said, "Why would a guy who writes the hilarious stuff that Burrows writes take on this tired costume drama?"

As they used to say in my old neighborhood, "Go fight City Hall."

No matter how negative they may be, I never get into arguments with critics. They have a tough job. I know because I was once given a crack at being a theater critic myself. It was back in the fifties when Edward R. Murrow was doing his famous radio show called *Hear It Now.* William Paley, the head of CBS, suggested to Murrow that there should be a section on the theater, and he picked me as the critic. It turned out to be a terrible idea.

I reviewed exactly two shows. The first one was Cole Porter's musical *Out of This World*. At that time I didn't know Cole Porter personally, but I always had respected him. *Out of This World* was obviously a flop, but in my review I waffled. I just said interesting words like "beautiful scenery," "nice tunes" and stuff like that.

The second and last show I reviewed was called *Bless You All*. I really had a tough time because Harold Rome, the author, and Herman Levin, the producer, were very good friends of mine. I didn't know what to say. I put together a cowardly mess of words that didn't add up to anything. My critique could only be described as pure fog.

John Crosby, another friend who was then the radio and television critic for the *Herald Tribune,* wrote a very good review of the *Hear It Now* program. But when he came to discussing my role as a drama critic, he put me in my place. Deservedly. Crosby said:

Abe Burrows, drafted as theater critic, discussed "Bless You All," a show I happened to have seen. Mr. Burrows — you're in my racket now, Abe — talked about the difficulty of writing topical revues and gave a brief lecture about the nature of satire. He skirted "Bless You All" almost entirely, which isn't quite the idea in the review dodge.

The next day I spoke to Ed Murrow and Bill Paley and told them that I didn't think I was cut out to be a critic, and they heartily agreed with me.

I'm sure that most critics don't like the idea of offending people. I remember being at a party given by Arthur Schwartz a few weeks after he had produced a play called *Hilda Crane*, written by Samson Raphaelson. One of his guests was the late Wolcott Gibbs of *The New Yorker,* who had really been rough on the play, but Schwartz and Wolcott were friends and there was no rancor there. I liked Gibbs and I was glad to have a chance to talk to him about the theater, but he seemed rather uneasy. Suddenly, in the middle of our conversation, Wolcott stopped talking and said, "Abe, I have to leave now. I just heard that Sam Raphaelson is coming up and he's very angry with me." And he ducked out quickly.

The violent anger that negative criticism triggers in theater people is a symbol of one of the biggest problems of today's theater: money.

Time was when a bad notice might have offended an author's ego or an actor's vanity. There were always some hard-line critics. Robert Benchley, Alexander Woollcott, and Percy Hammond were tough but witty. When *Abie's Irish Rose* opened, Bob Benchley gave it a negative review in *The New Yorker* and that knock appeared in *The New Yorker*'s theater listings every year for the entire run of the play, 2,327 performances. But no matter what these critics thought of a show, their notices seldom kept the public away because the price of a theater ticket was very low. And if bad notices did hurt a show to the point of closing it down, the financial loss to the producers was a tiny fraction of what it is today.

I'll always remember the fifty-five cents I paid for a seat to see Fred Astaire in *The Gay Divorce*. Today it would have cost me in the neighborhood of twenty bucks. To be fair, I should say that I was sitting in the rear of the balcony, so today that seat would cost only about a measly twelve dollars.

I'm sure that prices like that make people rely more and more on what the critics say. The critics have become a version of *Consumer Reports*. It's true that there are many people who can afford to go to the theater regularly without worrying about the price. But there are millions of people who worry about their budgets, people who love the theater but just can't afford it. And when they read a bad notice in a respectable newspaper, they decide to spend their money on more necessary things. They stay away from the theater.

350

Of course this inflation waltz that we're all dancing to makes for fantastic profits for some hit shows. But there's a catch.

I recently read a headline in *Variety* that said, "*A Chorus Line*'s record profit of $22 million surpasses *My Fair Lady*." *A Chorus Line* was a wonderful show, but breaking *My Fair Lady*'s record was due to the rise in ticket prices. A ticket for *A Chorus Line* costs about three times the price of a ticket for *My Fair Lady*.

Those ads for shows which proudly state "breaking the house record" have become fairly common. I began to learn about this "record-breaking" a few years ago when I was trying out shows in the National Theater in Washington. In that theater I have broken the house record three times with three different shows: *Cactus Flower, Forty Carats* and *Four on a Garden*. One day I suddenly realized that each time I broke the record, the number of seats in the theater hadn't changed, the number of standees was limited by law, and the box office had sold the same number of tickets. The only thing that had changed was the price of the tickets. The next time you read an ad for a play or a movie that says the old stuff about "record-breaking," you can be sure that it's a pretty good show combined with a pretty weak dollar.

I feel a bit glum when I think about what *Guys and Dolls* was grossing back in the fifties. No way near what it would gross today. The top price of a ticket to *Guys and Dolls* was $6.60. Multiply that by four. You can see that *Guys and Dolls* would have been up there among the world's record-breakers. But I'm comforted by the thought that when *Guys and Dolls* was playing on Broadway, I could buy a hamburger for a quarter.

"Show business" is still thought of as a glittering phrase; the fact is that show business is a business. But it's different from all other forms of business. The steel business, the automobile business, the clothing business, and the food business all sell people stuff they can touch, use or eat. Their prices are high but their products are usually necessities. Tangibles. On the other hand, the theater business asks the customers to spend as much as twenty-five dollars for the honor of sitting in a seat and watching a show. In return for this price, they are promising the audience entertainment: laughter, tears, shock, serious ideas, romance. All of these are food for thought but many people are thinking more often about meat and potatoes.

But the high price of a theater ticket is not a form of highway robbery. Today, putting on a musical costs in the neighborhood of one to two million dollars. And the money lost on these musicals is sometimes in that same painful neighborhood. A straight play with no music and very few actors in the cast can get by with a mere half million.

It would seem that this should touch off a vigorous search for quality. But the great financial risk now necessitates finding and producing a surefire hit. And that is a trap. No one can predict what will be a hit. Every playwright would like to have a hit, but most of the great shows have been written because the author became interested in an idea. When most writers sit down to write a show, they don't say to themselves, "Now I'm going to write a big hit." Frequently, the writer may have doubts, but he keeps going because he's in love with the idea.

When you work on a show, it becomes a living thing. Sometimes it seems to have a mind of its own. When you're writing a script, it doesn't always do what you want it to do. It sometimes takes a turn that you hadn't planned, but if you really care for it, you'll pay attention and do some rewriting. You won't stop loving it.

In a great show, everyone else should share the author's feelings. The actors must love it, the director must love it, and the producer who invests the millions of dollars to back it should be crazy about it. But these days people don't always put on shows they love, or love the shows they put on. The longing for big box-office receipts makes them search for that magic thing, "what the public likes." Guessing what the public will like is a crapshoot, and the dice are loaded against you.

Curiously enough, even though the price of movie tickets is

also very high, the movie critics don't have the same power as the theater critics. The movie critics can kick hell out of a picture, but the people will still spend as much as five dollars for a ticket to see it.

When I was a kid and too young to read reviews, I paid a dime to get into a movie house and could see the whole show twice. And that was in the days of double features plus the Pathé News, short subjects, maybe a Tarzan serial, and the part of the show that I really loved: "Coming Attractions."

This was a time when the Movie Kings reigned and the Goldwyns, the Mayers, the Cohns, and the Zanucks all made movies that they personally liked. Somehow or other, their taste was very close to the taste of the mass audience. Today you can't see anything for a dime, so things have changed. The people who make pictures are very bright people, who seem to ignore their own feelings and spend most of their time trying to guess what will "go" with an audience. They generally settle on stuff that has been "going." I recently saw a headline in *Variety:*

FOUR MORE PIX
HANG PLOTS
ON YOUTH GANGS

That means that four different producers are going to copy a very successful picture called *The Warriors,* which the critics have generally knocked but which is doing very good business. Especially among young people. So every studio wants to cash in on the trend.

I think that some of the problems of the theater came about because theatrical producers are following the trend of the movies. And many movie people are now backing shows because they think the show can eventually be made into a movie that will "go."

The ultimate wooer of the mass audience is television. Television critics have very little power or none at all. After all, TV is free. When television first started, the good shows were written by people who loved them. (A few of them are still on the air but I won't name them here because if I talk about their good quality, it might get them canceled.) Today TV goes by the ratings because of the commercials, which demand the largest possible audience. There are some brilliant people writing and directing television, spending their time shooting for high ratings. These are people who in another time would have become the Kaufmans and Harts of the theater.

The people who write for TV have a very tough chore. When you're doing a successful situation comedy, you are really writing the same play for years. The jokes get changed, new characters are brought in, but the basic play is really the same.

Very often some of these writers have said to me, "Abe, one of these days I'm going to take a crack at Broadway." A few writers have actually done it. But "taking a crack at Broadway" necessitates giving up a job that may be earning a writer $10,000 or $15,000 a week. Of course, there are many writers who don't get anywhere near that kind of money, but their dream is eventually getting it.

Writing a Broadway show is working on speculation. It's a gamble. You get an advance of some sort; then it takes months, sometimes years, to finish a play. And it might be a flop.

All I know is that when I finally got out of radio and did my first show, it was a glorious feeling to know that my show was completed, finished, and running on Broadway, and that I had time to think of something new.

That feeling has always stayed with me throughout my life in the theater. I have had some hits and I have had some flops, and I have learned that hits are better.

I haven't done a show in the past year because I didn't have an idea for one, or at least an idea that I liked. I remember George Kaufman once saying to me, "Moss and I haven't got an idea for this season, so we're going to pass it up." I have learned to wait for that idea.

I recently watched Neil Simon being interviewed by Dick Cavett, and he talked about ideas for shows. He mentioned a play he wrote that didn't go well, *The Star-Spangled Girl*. And he said that he probably shouldn't have written it. He quoted Walter Kerr's review, which started off, "Neil Simon didn't have an idea this year, but he wrote a play anyway." Simon said he agreed with Walter's review.

As I waited for that good idea, I found myself in danger. I was asked to doctor several incurable shows. People called me with wild ideas like "Wouldn't Watergate make a funny musical?" I wouldn't have been surprised if someone had said, "Hey Abe, what about doing a musical, sort of an operetta, about the Son of Sam killer. He shot a lot of pretty girls."

I fended off many bad ideas, but after a while I began getting a bit itchy. I began to think kindly about some of the less-awful notions and I thought that I might get caught up in one of them just to keep busy. That worried me. Suddenly, I got an idea of my own.

I closed myself up in my apartment, sat down at my big dining room table, and wrote a book.

Index

"Abbondanza," 147
Abbott, George, 199, 224, 306, 307
Abbott and Costello, 108–109
Abe Burrows Almanac, 126
Abe Burrows Show, 96–98, 107–108, 109
Abe Lincoln in Illinois, 285
Abe's Hope (horse), 80–81
Abie's Irish Rose, 350
Abrahams, Hoffer, 27
Academy Awards, 142, 341
Ace, Goodman, 79
"Action," 203
Actors' Equity, 186, 187, 219, 264, 306
"Adelaide's Lament," 146
Adler, Eileen, 51
Adler, Larry, 18, 51
Albee, Edward, 277
Albert, Eddie, 320
Alda, Robert, 155, 167, 194, 197, 198, 199, 203, 276
Aleichem, Sholem, 22
Alexander, Joan, 257
Algonquin Hotel, 62
"All Alone," 179
Allen, Fred, 82–83, 84–85, 86–89, 90, 137, 345
Allen, Jay Presson, 317
Allen, Mel, 30
Allen, Woody, 345, 346

Ambassador East Hotel (Chicago), 235
Ameche, Don, 269, 273
American Museum of Natural History, 257
Annie Get Your Gun, 221, 253
Anthony, Joseph, 277
Anything Goes, 257
Apple Cart, The, 267
Aquacade, 148
Arlen, Harold, 289
Arnstein, Nicky, 29
Arsenic and Old Lace, 279
Arthur, Jean, 95
ASCAP (American Society of Composers, Authors and Publishers), 179, 289
Associated Press, 208, 324
Astaire, Adele, 245
Astaire, Fred, 6, 245, 350
Atkinson, Brooks, 150, 207, 208, 226, 229, 240, 273, 310
Atlantic City, 183
Austen, Jane, 348
Axelrod, George, 313

Bacall, Lauren ("Betty"), 209, 311–312, 313, 314, 316, 329
Bailey, Buster, 60
Baker, Kenny, 49

357

Balzac, Honoré de, 174–175
Bankhead, Tallulah, 79–81
Barclay Hotel, 246
Barillet, Pierre, 311, 317, 319
Barnes, Clive, 318
Barnes, Howard, 207
Barrett, Sheila, 36
Barrymore, Ethel, 57–58
Barrymore, John, 45, 53–55, 56–57, 58
Barrymore, Maurice, 55
Baruch, Bernard, 164
Baxter, Warner, 168
Bay of Pigs, 337, 338
Bayliss, Gene, 170
Beatles, the, 59
Beaumont, Hugh ("Binkie"), 316
Beebe, Hank, 278
Beerbohm, Max, 328
Beloin, Ed, 85
Benchley, Robert, 51–52, 62–63, 64–65, 81–82, 111, 124, 350
Benny, Jack, 85–86
Benoff, Mac, 49, 62, 78
Bérenger, René ("Père la Pudeur"), 243, 245
Bergen, Edgar (and Charlie McCarthy), 49
Bergen, Polly, 348
Bergman, Ingrid, 61
Bergman, Teddy (Alan Reed), 60–61
Berle, Milton, 32, 99, 108
Berle, Mrs. (Milton Berle's mother), 99–100
Berlin, Irving, 179, 183, 280
Berson, Joe, 26, 27
Bettis, Valerie, 222
Beverly Hillbillies, 53
Beverly Hills, Calif., 236
Beverly Hills Hotel, 103
"Big D," 147
Bigley, Isabel, 155, 156–157, 167, 203–204
Billingsley, Sherman, 126, 136, 137, 138, 139–142, 147
Billion Dollar Baby, 292, 293
Bissell, Marian, 307
Bissell, Richard, 307
Blaine, Vivian, 154, 155–156, 167, 168–169, 203–204, 264, 266, 294, 307

Blair, Janet, 109
Blane, Ralph, 238, 239
Bless You All, 349
Blossom, Arthur, 316
Blue Angel, 125
Boberick, Sam, 320, 321
Bogart, Humphrey, 311
Bolger, Ray, 285
Booth, Shirley, 43, 60, 61, 63
Born Yesterday, 298, 299
Boston, 271–272
Boswell, Connie, 109
Brando, Marlon, 295, 341
Break a Leg, 322
Breakfast at Tiffany's, 277
Breakfast with Burrows, 126
Brecht, Bertolt, 74–76
Brentwood, Calif., 247
Brice, Fanny, 29, 95
Brinckerhoff, Burt, 312, 313
Bristol, Eng., 265–266
British Equity, 264
Britton, Tony, 317
Brooks, Mel, 347
Brown, Joe E., 79
Brown, Sarah, 243–244
Brown Derby (Hollywood), 94, 236
Brynner, Yul, 98, 127, 139, 140
Bryson, Lyman, 16
Buchwald, Art, 252, 311
Bucks County, Pa., 156–157
Bunker, Ralph, 302–303
Burns, George, 104
Burns and Allen, 52
Burrows, Carin (second wife), 70, 91, 92, 112, 113, 115, 117, 119, 138, 142, 145, 156–157, 173, 180, 193, 196, 197, 207, 209, 212, 222, 223, 228, 231, 235, 246, 247, 248–249, 257, 263, 265, 267, 268, 273, 288, 293, 320
Burrows, David (grandfather), 20
Burrows, Jimmy (son), 58, 63, 87, 91, 269, 316, 319, 320
Burrows, Julia Salzberg (mother), 8, 10, 14, 17–18, 21, 23–24, 25, 26–27, 31, 33, 91–92, 99–100
Burrows, Laurie (daughter). See Grad, Laurie
Burrows, Louis (father), 8, 17,

358

20–21, 26, 31, 55, 92, 99, 100, 104–105, 106, 200
Burrows, Ruth Levinson (first wife), 34, 54, 91, 173
Burrows, Selig (brother), 17, 22, 24, 91, 92, 99, 173
Burrows, Shirley (sister), 17, 22, 99, 173
Bushkin, Joey, 80
Butterworth, Charlie, 51–52
By Jupiter, 306
Bye Bye Birdie, 335
Byfield, Ernie, 235

Cactus Flower, 253, 263, 277, 300, 311–316, 329, 351
Caen, Herb, 109
Caesar, Sid, 236, 319, 346, 347
Café Society Uptown, 125
Cagney, James, 79
Caine Mutiny, The, 345
"California, Here I Come," 102
Call Me Madam, 280
Cambridge, Godfrey, 289
Camelot, 78
Campanella, Joseph, 315
Can-Can, 25, 233, 237–238, 241–245, 246, 247, 249, 250, 254, 256, 260, 261, 262, 263
"Can-Can," 263
Cannon, Jimmy, 100
Cantor, Charlie, 60
Cantor, Eddie, 39, 102, 104
Capote, Truman, 277
Carlisle, Kitty (Mrs. Moss Hart), 157
Carousel, 214
Carroll, Earl, 57
Caruso, Enrico, 103
Cassini, Igor (Cholly Knickerbocker), 140, 141
Cates, Joe, 276
Caubisens, Henri, 185
Cavett, Dick, 354
CBS, 40, 41, 46, 60, 91, 96, 99, 101, 108, 126, 136, 138, 141, 147, 172, 349
CCNY, 25–26
Cerf, Bennett, 286
"C'est Magnifique," 250, 254, 258, 263
Chamberlain, Richard, 277

Champion, Gower, 211, 212, 216
Channing, Carol, 250, 319
Channing, Stockard, 320
Chanteur de Mexico, Le, 252, 253–254
Chaplin, Charlie, 67–71, 72–74
Chaplin, Oona, 69–70, 71, 73–74
Chaplin, Sidney, 313
Chapman, John, 150, 207
Charlie Chan, 90
Chatelet Theater (Paris), 252–253
Chicago, 122–123
Chorus Line, A, 325, 351
Ciro's (Los Angeles), 112–113
City College of New York, 25–26
Clark, Ron, 320, 321
Clurman, Harold, 306
Cohan, George M., 177
Cohen, Alexander H., 211
Cohen, Irving, 33–34, 35
Cohen, Milton, 33, 34
Cohn, Harry, 291, 292, 294–299
Colbert, Claudette, 64, 88
Coliseum (London), 264, 265
Colt, Alvin, 147, 205
Columbia Pictures, 291, 295, 296, 298
Columbia University, 257
Comden, Betty, 64, 216, 223, 226, 307, 308
Comden and Green, 292
Compagnons de Chanson, Les, 125
Connelly, Marc, 51, 66, 279
Conried, Hans, 56, 234, 261, 262
Cookson, Peter, 260, 262
Cooper, Gary, 268
"Cooperation Is the Basis of Progress" (high school essay), 12–13
Copacabana (New York), 93
Corbett, Gretchen, 318
Cornell, Katharine, 225
Cornell Latin Scholarship, 15, 16, 17
Corwin, Norman, 88
Council of the Dramatists Guild, 179, 279
Courot (Parisian judge), 243–244
Cox, Wally, 93
Coward, Noel, 50, 80, 152, 267
Cowl, Jane, 303
Cowles, Mr. and Mrs. Gardner, 286, 287

Crosby, Bing, 6, 59, 114–115, 116–117, 118–119, 120, 268
Crosby, John, 95, 349
Crosby, Lindsay ("Linnie"), 115, 116, 117, 118–119
Crouse, Russel ("Buck"), 206–207, 279–281
Cummings, Robert, 321

Damn Yankees, 261
Darvas, Lili, 214
Daumier, 256
Davis, Joan, 94–95, 96, 99, 100
"Dear Bella," 67
Dear Ruth, 70
DeLugg, Milton, 96
Desmond, Johnny, 307, 309
DeSylva, Brown and Henderson, 277
Detroit, 272
Dewey, Thomas E., 123, 125–126
Diener, Joan, 128
Dietrich, Marlene, 6, 55–57, 247
Dietz, Howard, 178
DiMaggio, Joe, 218
Dinah Shore Show, 91, 93
Dolan, Robert Emmett, 91
Doubleday, 80
Douglas, Paul, 298–299
Drake, Ervin, 276
Dramatists Guild, Council of, 179, 279
Draper, Ruth, 117
Drury Lane Theatre (London), 264–265
Dubey, Matt, 280, 282
Dubey and Karr, 281
Duffy's Tavern, 3, 5, 6, 20, 42, 43, 48, 52–53, 60–63, 72–73, 77–79, 81, 82–83, 88, 99, 137, 138, 152, 348
Dunne, Irene, 95
Durante, Jimmy, 37, 66, 108, 122

Eagels, Jeanne, 235
Earl Carroll's Vanities, 57
Ecker, Meyer, 186
Edge of Sadness, 325
Edward, My Son, 158
Eichmann, Adolf, 201
El Rancho Vegas, 113–114, 120, 121
Elizabeth, queen of England, coronation of, 267–268
Ellington, Duke, 289

Emile (Hotel Blackstone maitre d'), 123
Erlanger Theater (Philadelphia), 205
Ethel Barrymore Theatre, 245
Evans, Maurice, 303

Fabray, Nanette, 211, 216, 320
Fadiman, Clifton, 79, 126, 127, 128
Farrell, Anthony, 223
Farrell, Glenda, 318
Fay, Frank, 343
Faye, Alice, 278
Feuer, Cy, 25, 96, 101, 135, 142–156 passim, 169, 170, 171, 176, 179, 191, 196, 201, 204, 205, 208, 236, 237, 241, 244, 249, 250, 256–273 passim, 325, 327, 329, 330, 337
Fiddler on the Roof, 22
Fields, W. C., 71
Finian's Rainbow, 144, 174
Fink, Hymie, 104
Fiorello, 325
First Impressions, 348
Fitzgerald, F. Scott, 51
Flaming Hotel (Las Vegas), 121
Fleishmann's Yeast, 38
Fleur de Cactus, 311
Ford Motor Company, 91
Ford Symphony of the Air, 101
"Forever," 142
Forrest Theatre (Philadelphia), 315–316
Forty Carats, 253, 300, 317–319, 351
Forty-second Street, 168
Forty-sixth Street Theatre, 147, 181, 207, 336
Fosse, Bob, 334
Foster, Phil, 25
Foster, Royal, 49–50
Four on a Garden, 253, 300, 319, 351
Fowler, Keith, 49
Francis, Arlene, 128, 300
Frank, Mel, 53, 58
Frank Music, 331
French Foreign Legion, 245
Fred Allen Show, 82, 83, 84–85, 86
Friars Club, 103, 108
Friend, Ted, 110
Frisco, Joe, 93–94
Fry, Christopher, 267
"Fugue for Tin Horns," 194

Funny Thing Happened on the Way to the Forum, A, 78, 210

Gabel, Martin, 300, 302, 303, 305
Gable, Clark, 64
Gabor, Zsa Zsa, 319
Galen, Frank, 34–42, 46, 47, 48, 49, 52
Gallagher, Bob, 227
Gallagher, Helen, 216
Garbo, Greta, 269
Garden of Allah (Hollywood), 51
Gardner, Ed, 3, 6, 39, 40–45, 46, 51, 52–53, 57, 58, 60–61, 62, 63, 77, 78, 83, 328–329
Gardner, Simone, 43
Garr, Eddie, 37–39, 40, 41
Garson, Greer, 112
Gaxton, Bill, 232
Gay Divorce, 245, 257, 279, 350
Gay Divorcee, 245
Gelbart, Larry, 78, 201
Gentlemen Prefer Blondes, 250
George, Olive and Ed, 57
George Washington Slept Here, 132
Gerrits, Paul, 39
Gershwin, George, 155, 177, 178, 194
Gershwin, Ira, 64, 177, 178
Gibbon, Edward, 46
Gibbs, Wolcott, 172, 207, 349–350
Gielgud, John, 79
Gilbert, Willie, 326–327
Gilbert and Sullivan, 42
Gilford, Jack, 93
Gingold, Hermione, 348
"Girl with the Three Blue Eyes, The," 4, 64, 82
"Give Me Your Ears," 289
Glenn, John, 338
Goetz, William, 65, 66, 67
Going My Way, 7
Golden Fleecing, 310
Goldman, Robert, 348
Goldwyn, Sam, 92–93, 291–294, 295, 296
Goldwyn Studios, 293
Good Fairy, The, 211
Good News, 277–278
Goodbye Charlie, 313
Goodman, Benny, 51, 236
Gordon, Max, 149–150, 197, 213

Gordon, Ruth, 225
Gould, Elliott, 307
Goulue, La ("The Glutton"), 250, 251
Grable, Betty, 156
Grad, Laurie Burrows (daughter), 63, 87–88, 91, 145
Grad, Nicky (grandson), 63, 145
Grad, Peter (son-in-law), 63
Grady, Bill, 225
Graham, Martha, 127
Granger, Farley, 348
Grant, Cary, 79
Grant, Mrs. (Latin teacher), 15–16, 17
Grauer, Ben, 47
Gray, Dolores, 221, 222–223, 232
Gredy, Jean-Pierre, 311, 317, 319
Greeley, Horace, 63
Green, Adolf, 64, 216, 223, 226, 307, 308; *see also* Comden and Green
Green, Eddie, 60
Green, Martyn, 42
Griffith, D. W., 50
Guardsman, The, 214
Guernsey, Otis, 216
Gump, H. S., 171
Gunsmoke, 264
Guthrie, Tyrone, 308
Guys and Dolls, 4, 25, 60, 83, 96, 115, 127, 131, 132, 135, 138, 142–210 *passim*, 211, 230, 231, 244, 256, 257, 260, 263–267, 270, 291–295, 329, 330, 332, 341, 348, 351
"Guys and Dolls," 204–205
Gwyn, Nell, 264

Haines, Larry, 320
Hackett, Buddy, 25
Haley, Flo, 86
Haley, Jack, 86
Hamilton, Murray, 317
Hamlet, 72
Hammerstein, Oscar, 148, 164, 231, 259, 279
Hammond, Percy, 350
Happy Hunting, 279–284
Harburg, E. Y. ("Yip"), 174
Harlow, Jean, 48
Harris, Julie, 225, 317, 318, 319
Harris, Tommy, 109, 111
Harrison, Rex, 303

361

Hart, Larry, 254
Hart, Moss, 132–133, 134, 157, 217, 272, 273, 279, 354
Haver, June, 156
Having a Wonderful Time, 67
Hayes, Helen, 64, 225, 305
Hayes, Peter Lind, 91, 93, 94, 126, 139, 141, 346, 347
Hayward, Leland, 164, 313
Healy, Mary, 93, 126, 139, 347
Hear It Now, 349
Heflin, Frances, 90
Heiress, The, 260
Hellzapoppin', 278
Henley Regatta, 284
Henning, Paul, 53, 58
Hepburn, Katharine, 43
Herman, Jerry, 289
Hermann, Harry, 42
Herriott, Miss (eighth-grade teacher), 11–12
Hershfield, Harry, 289
Heyer, Bill, 278
Hiken, Nat, 83
Hilda Crane, 349
Hildegarde, 77
Hiller, Miss (Latin teacher), 14
Hippodrome Theatre (Bristol), 266
Hitler, Adolf, 89, 266
Hodges, Luther, 338
Hoffa, Portland, 82, 83, 86, 137
Holiday and Company, 90, 137, 138
Holliday, Judy, 295, 297, 298, 299
Holly Golightly, 277
Hollywood, 48, 49–52, 89, 236
Holm, Celeste, 285
Hooper ratings, 58
Hope, Bob, 115, 117, 229
Horne, Lena, 136–137
Hot Mikado, 60
Hotel Blackstone Mayfair Room (Chicago), 122–123
Hotel Georges Cinq (Paris), 252
Hotel Radisson Flame Room (Minneapolis), 122
Hotel Royalton (New York), 62
House of Harris (San Francisco), 109, 110, 111–112
House of Chan (New York), 85
"How Come I Did Not Turn Down the Pulitzer Prize," 340, 341

How To Succeed in Business Without Really Trying (book), 326
How To Succeed in Business Without Really Trying (musical), 233, 263, 288, 308, 322, 324–339, 340
"How Ya Gonna Keep 'em Down on the Farm After They've Seen the Farm?," 4
Howes, Sally Ann, 276
Hull, Josephine, 133, 295
Huston, Walter, 44
Huxley, Aldous, 348

"I Believe in You," 334
"I Found a Million-Dollar Baby in a Five and Ten Cent Store," 148
"I Got Rhythm," 179
"I Love Paris," 250, 254–255, 258, 263
I'd Rather Be Right, 177
Ideal Husband, An, 344
Idiot's Delight, 285
"Idyll of Miss Sarah Brown," 143–144
"If I Had My Life to Live Over Again, I'd Live It Over a Delicatessen," 82
"If I Were a Bell," 203–204
"I'll Be Happy to Keep His Dinner Warm," 335
"I'm So Miserable Without You That It's Almost Like Having You Around," 4
Imperial Theatre (New York), 273
"In the Shade of the Old Apple Tree," 285–286
Information Please, 128
Interiors, 345
"It Was Only a Paper Moon," 148
"It's All Right with Me," 258, 263
"I've Never Been in Love Before," 332

Jacobi, Lou, 264
Jacoby, Herbert, 125
James, Henry, 174
Jazz Singer, The, 102
Jeffreys, Anne, 238, 239, 240
Joan Davis show, 94, 95, 96, 99, 100
John Kirby Quintet, 60
Johnson, Lyndon B., 288–289, 290, 314
Johnson, Nunnally, 64, 65, 66
Jolson, Al, 37, 101–103, 104, 122
Jolson Story, The, 101

Josefsberg, Milt, 85
Jumbo, 148
June Moon, 183
"Just One of Those Things," 258

Kanin, Garson, 217, 298
Karr, Harold, 280; *see also* Dubey and Karr
Kate Smith Hour, 36
Kaufman, George S., 43, 106, 126–135 *passim*, 149–151, 152, 156–205 *passim*, 217, 224, 231, 232–233, 240, 268–274, 279, 294, 306, 311, 354
Kaye, Danny, 64, 66, 113, 229, 236
Kaye, Stubby, 170, 194, 264, 294
Kaye, Sylvia, 113
Kazan, Elia, 217, 295
Keeler, Ruby, 103, 168
Kefauver hearings, 222
Kelly, Grace, 281, 283, 284
Kelly, Jack, 284
Kelly, Margaret, 283, 284
Kennedy, John F., 288, 314, 337, 338, 339
Kern, Jerome, 259
Kerr, Jean, 310, 341
Kerr, Walter, 113, 310, 318, 319, 340, 341–342, 355
Kidd, Michael, 25, 144, 170, 182, 191, 192, 196, 205, 241, 257, 260, 278
Kind Sir, 70
King and I, The, 139
Kingsley, Sidney, 279
Kirkeby, Mr. (owner of Hotel Blackstone), 122–123
Kismet, 128
Knickerbocker, Cholly (Igor Cassini), 140, 141
KNX, 95–96
Kober, Arthur, 67, 74
Kohlmar, Fred, 296, 297, 298
Krasna, Earle, 70
Krasna, Norman, 70
Kreindler, Mr. (owner of "21"), 210
Kurnitz, Harry, 113, 300, 323
Kyle, Bill, 60

Lady in the Dark, 133
Lahr, Bert, 216, 221, 223, 225–229, 232

Lamas, Fernando, 281, 282, 283
Lambert Pharmaceutical Company, 100
Lambs Club, 62
Lanchester, Elsa, 51
Lancaster Hotel (Paris), 268
Langford, Frances, 49
La Rochefoucauld, François de, 210
Lardner, Ring, 183
Las Vegas, 120–121
Lasker, Albert, 164, 165
Lasker, Mary, 164
Last Hurrah, 105, 174, 325
Lastfogel, Abe, 101, 293
Laugh-In, 78
Laughton, Charles, 51, 54, 74, 76
Lawrence, Steve, 276
Lazar, Irving ("Swifty"), 36
"Leave Us Face It," 77–78
League Against Licentiousness of the Streets (Paris), 242, 243
Le Directoire (New York), 124–126
Lee, Michelle, 335
Lehmann, Maurice, 253
Leighton, Margaret, 267, 316, 317
Lengyel, Melchior, 271
Leonard, Benny, 22
Lerner, Alan Jay, 78, 239
Lerner and Loewe, 245
Lesser, Arthur, 222, 224
Let 'Em Eat Cake, 177
LeVecque, Commodore, 118
Levene, Sam, 147, 153–155, 167, 193–194, 203, 293–294, 295, 329
Levin, Herman, 349
Levy, Parke, 62, 78
Lewis, Albert, 234, 235, 238–239
Lewis, Arthur, 234, 235, 237, 238, 264
Lewis, Jerry, 108, 278
Lewis, Joe E., 108
Lewis, Robert Q., 257
Lewis, Sinclair, 284, 286, 341
Liberté, 115–119, 268
Liebowitz, Samuel, 173
Life of Galileo, 74–76
Life With Father, 279
Liliom, 214
Lillie, Beatrice, 140, 222
Lilo, 251, 252, 253, 254, 255, 258, 262

Lincoln Memorial, 314
Lindsay, Howard, 5, 106, 180, 206–207, 279, 280, 285–286, 344
Lindsay and Crouse, 279–281
Lindy's Restaurant (New York), 106
Listerine Toothpaste, 100, 101, 107–108
Livingston, Mary, 86
Lloyd's of London, 280
Loesser, Frank, 4–5, 64, 77, 78, 82, 86, 88, 135, 142–156 passim, 170, 172, 176, 177, 191, 196, 201, 205, 208, 236, 255, 257, 259, 268, 324, 325, 330–340 passim
Loesser, Jo, 145
Logan, Josh, 217, 231, 262
Lombard, Carole, 95
London, 263–267, 316–317
London Express, 319
London Saturday Review, 344
Look, 103, 263, 283
Loring, Eugene, 238
Lorre, Peter, 74
Loy, Myrna, 300
Lubitsch, Ernst, 269, 271
Lucky Strike, 256
Lumet, Sidney, 127, 139
Lute Song, 139
Lynde, Paul, 321, 335
Lyon, Peter, 149
Lyons, George, 163, 164, 165
Lyons, Leonard, 137, 163, 164, 173, 214, 285
Lyons, Sylvia, 163
Lyons, Warren, 165
Lyric Theatre (London), 316

McCaffery, John K. M., 16
McGrath, Leueen, 156, 157, 158, 268, 270–271, 272, 273–274, 311
Madison Square Garden, 103
Magic Key, 47
Mahagonny, 74
Main Street, 284
Make a Wish, 211–213, 215–216, 230
Man of La Mancha, 128
Man Who Came to Dinner, The, 132
Manhattan, 345
Manhoff, Bill, 78
Mankiewicz, Joseph, 294
Man's Castle, 142

Mansfield, Irving, 127, 128, 139
Marchand, Colette, 222
Mark Hellinger Theatre, 223
Marquis, Don, 87
Martin, Dean, 108
Martin, Dick, 78
Martin, Ernest ("Ernie"), 96, 100–101, 135, 142–157 passim, 169, 170, 171, 174, 176, 191, 196, 201, 202–203, 204, 205, 208, 236–272 passim, 325, 327, 329, 330
Martin, Hugh, 211
Martin, Mary, 139, 209, 244, 292
Martin, Pete, 4, 64
Martin, Tony, 104
Martin, Virginia, 336
Martin Beck Theatre, 319
Marx, Chico, 121
Marx, Groucho, 19, 64, 104, 121, 236
Mary, Queen of Scots, 305
M*A*S*H, 78
Matchmaker, The, 308
Max's Busy Bee, 33
Mayer, Edith, 90
Mayer, Louis B., 65–67, 291, 292, 331
Mayer, Ray, 90
Mead, Shepherd ("Ed"), 326, 327, 329
Meet Millie, 52
Melchior, Lauritz, 77–78
"Memory Lane," 3, 4–5
Mercer, Johnny, 64, 259
Mercurio's Restaurant (New York), 214
Merman, Ethel, 40, 209, 225, 280, 281–282, 283
Merrick, David, 277, 311, 312, 313, 315, 316, 318, 319
Merrill, Robert (opera singer), 25
Merrill, Robert (songwriter), 277
MGM (Metro-Goldwyn-Mayer), 65, 179, 225, 291, 331
Mielziner, Jo, 147, 182, 196, 260, 280, 281
Minneapolis, 121–122
Mitchell, Millard, 61
Mizner, Wilson, 49
Molnár, Ferenc, 164, 165, 211, 213, 214–215
Molnár, Mrs. (Molnár's previous wife), 214
Monroe, Marilyn, 156, 292

Monsieur Verdoux, 70
Moore, Grace, 33
Moore, Mary Tyler, 277
Moore, Robert, 312
"More I Cannot Wish You," 172
Morosco Theatre, 319
Morris High School (Bronx), 25
Morrison, Hobe, 343, 344
Morrow, Bill, 85
Morse, Robert, 233, 307–310, 329, 335, 339
Moscow Art Theatre, 219
Most Happy Fella, The, 147, 331
Mostel, Zero, 93
Mount Sinai Hospital, 145
Murphy, Charles, 287
Murray, Ken, 49, 50, 51
Murrow, Edward R., 348–349
Mussolini, Benito, 89
My Fair Lady, 78, 245, 351
My Sister Eileen, 61

Name's the Same, The, 257
Nathan, George Jean, 62
National Biscuit Company, 329
National Theatre (Washington), 313, 351
NBC, 329
Neff, Hildegarde, 269, 273
Neilsen ratings, 58
Nelson, Barry, 312, 315
Nemirovich-Danchenko, Vladimir, 219
New Haven, 222, 223, 224, 239
New Utrecht High School (Brooklyn), 25, 144
New York Giants, 35, 339
New York *Herald Tribune,* 82, 216, 340, 349
New York *Post,* 208, 318
New York Stock Exchange, 29–31
New York *Times,* 101, 145, 209, 213, 226, 263, 273, 310, 318, 340
New York University, 32
New Yorker, The, 67, 111, 172, 349, 350
Newman, Phyllis, 348
"Night and Day," 245
Ninotchka, 269, 271
Nixon, Richard, 36
No Hard Feelings, 300, 319–321

O'Connor, Edwin, 105–106, 174, 325
Of Mice and Men, 160
Of Thee I Sing, 177–178, 232, 325
"Oh, What a Beautiful Mornin'," 179
Oklahoma!, 124
"Oldest Established Permanent Floating Crap Game in New York, The," 203
Once in a Lifetime, 133, 217
O'Neal, Charles, 234
O'Neal, Ryan, 234
O'Neal, Tatum, 234
Osborn, Paul, 279
Oscars (Academy Awards), 142, 341
Osterman, Lester, 307
Out of This World, 349
Owl and the Pussycat, The, 78

Page, Marco (Harry Kurnitz's pseudonym), 300
Pahlmann, William, 125, 247–248
Paint Your Wagon, 239
Pajama Game, 238, 307
Paley, William, 141–142, 348–349
Panama, Norman, 53, 58
Paramount Pictures, 5–7, 88, 115
Paris, 241–243, 247, 251–256, 268
Park Plaza Hotel (Saint Louis), 124
Parks, Larry, 101
Parsons, Louella, 70
Passardière, Guy de la, 254, 255
Paul (Cole Porter's butler), 248
Paxton, Glenn, 348
Payne, John, 278
Pedi, Tom, 168, 175, 264
Perrin, Sam, 49, 85
Persoff, Nehemiah ("Nicky"), 301–302
Petrified Forest, The, 285
Philadelphia, 183–205, 211–213, 224, 268–269, 282–284, 302–303
Philadelphia Story, The, 43, 61
Philco Dealers, 114
Philip Morris Company, 90
Pickford, Mary, 48
Pinza, Ezio, 244, 292
Players Club (Hollywood), 51
Players Club (New York), 207
Play's the Thing, The, 214
Plaza Hotel (New York), 214
Pleshette, Suzanne, 310
"Pony Boy," 153

Porter, Cole, 124, 238, 244, 245–249, 250, 257, 258, 259, 261, 262, 263, 268, 272, 273, 349
Porter, Linda, 263
Poston, Tom, 310
Powell, William, 48, 300
Prager, Stanley, 93, 221
"Praise the Lord and Pass the Ammunition," 4, 64
Preminger, Otto, 217
Present Indicative, 80
Presley, Elvis, 59
Pride and Prejudice, 348
Prime of Miss Jean Brodie, The, 317
Pulitzer Prize, 132, 177, 279, 324–325, 340, 341
Pully, B. S., 170–171
Pygmalion, 245

Quatz' Arts Balls (Paris), 243–244, 245
Quine, Richard, 296–297, 298

Radio Writers Guild, 45
Rain, 235
Rainier, Prince, 281, 283
Raitt, John, 238, 239, 240
Raphaelson, Samson, 349, 350
Reclining Figure, 300–304, 305, 323
Red (Stork Club headwaiter), 140–141
Redgrave, Lynn, 278
Reed, Alan (Teddy Bergman), 60–61
Reed, Florence, 303
Regency bridge club, 162–163
Reid, Elliott, 221–222
Reilly, Charles Nelson, 335–336
Republic Pictures, 101
Revlon Company, 327–328
Revson, Charles, 327, 328
Rhapsody in Blue, 155, 194
Rice, Elmer, 279
Rigby, Harry, 211
Ritz-Carlton Hotel (Philadelphia), 213
Roaring Dick, 55
Robinson, Bill "Bojangles," 60
Robinson, Hubbell, 147
Robson, Mark, 58
Roche, Jack, 42
"Rock and the Rose, The," 68
Rockefeller, John D., 30–31

Rodgers, Richard, 164, 259, 279, 306–307
Rodgers and Hammerstein, 139, 214, 231, 279, 292
Rome, Harold, 349
Rooney, Pat, Sr., 171–172, 203
Roosevelt, Franklin D., 32, 285
Rose, Billy, 147–148, 164, 245–246
Rosenbloom, "Slapsie" Maxie, 79
Rossmore Arms Hotel (Hollywood), 86
Ross, Bob, 49
Rowan, Dan, 78
Rowan and Martin, 78
Royale Theatre, 316
Rubinstein, Artur, 18–19
Ruby, Harry, 104
Rudy Vallee Show, 38, 53
Rudy Vallee–John Barrymore Show, 45, 53–59, 60
Runyon, Damon, 3, 106, 135, 138, 143–144, 152, 170, 263
Rush, Barbara, 319
Russell, Jane, 109
Ruth, Babe, 31
Ryskind, Morrie, 177, 178

Samuel Goldwyn Productions, 292
San Francisco, 109–111, 234, 238
San Francisco *Chronicle*, 109
San Francisco Civic Auditorium, 109–110
San Francisco–Oakland Newspaper Guild, 109–110
Sante Fe Super Chief, 236
Sardi's Restaurant (New York), 236
Saroyan, William, 341
Savalas, Telly, 98
Say, Darling, 300, 307–310, 329
Schick Injector Razor, 60
Schlesinger, Arthur, Jr., 106, 338
Schulberg, Budd, 276
Schulberg, Stuart, 276
Schwartz, Arthur, 178, 349
Scott, Bonnie, 335
Scott, George C., 341
Scottsboro Boys, 173
Sealtest Company, 53
"Secretary Is Not a Toy, A," 333–334
Seldes, Gilbert, 46
Semple, Lorenzo, Jr., 310
Sense and Sensibility, 348

Sergeant Bilko, 83
7½ Cents, 307
Seven-Year Itch, The, 313
Shakespeare, 72
Shapiro, Miss (piano teacher), 17, 18, 19
Shaver, Buster, 57
Shavers, Charlie, 60
Shaw, George Bernard, 245, 267, 343-344
Shepherd, Alan, 338
Sherwood, Robert, 284-285
Shofner, Del, 339
Shore, Dinah, 91, 93, 102, 104
Shubert Theater (New Haven), 223
Shubert Theater (Philadelphia), 187, 261
Shuberts, the, 235
Silk Stockings, 179, 259, 268-273
Silver, Johnny, 170, 194, 264
Silvers, Phil, 83, 346
Simmons, Jean, 294
Simon, Neil, 343, 345, 354-355
Sinatra, Frank, 59, 66, 295
Sistrom, Joe, 6
"Sit Down, You're Rockin' the Boat," 170
Sixty Minutes, 301
Sly Fox, 78
Small Miracle, 70
Smith, Merriman ("Smitty"), 289, 290
Smothers Brothers, 289
Solid Gold Cadillac, The, 132, 133-134, 273, 294-299
"Some Enchanted Evening," 179
"Songbuster," 4, 64
Sound of Music, The, 279
South Pacific, 143, 231, 244, 257, 265, 292, 325
"Space Brigade," 226
Spark, Muriel, 317
Spencer, O'Neil, 60
Spiegel, Sam, 310
St. Cyr, Lili, 109
St. John, Marco, 318
St. Louis, 124
"Standing on the Corner Watching All the Girls Go By," 147
Stang, Arnold, 90
Stanislavski, Konstantin, 219
Stanton, Frank, 101

Star-Spangled Girl, The, 355
State of the Union, 279
Steinbeck, John, 160
Steiner, Rouse and Strook, 29
"Stereophonic Sound," 259
Stevens, Lee, 311
Stevenson, Adlai, 314
Stickney, Dorothy, 279, 285
Stoopnagle, Colonel (F. Chase Taylor), 46-48
Stoopnagle and Budd, 46
Stork Club Restaurant and TV show, 126-127, 136-142, 147, 172
Sturges, Preston, 211, 212, 213-214
Styne, Jule, 211, 216, 223, 289, 307, 308
"Sue Me," 154
Sullavan, Margaret, 211
Sullivan, Maxine, 60
Sunset Boulevard (Hollywood), 51
Susann, Jacqueline ("Jackie"), 127
Sweet Charity, 261
Swerling, Jo, 142, 143, 144

Taft Hotel (New Haven), 223
"Take Back Your Mink," 205
Taylor, Deems, 40, 46, 61
Taylor, Elizabeth, 104
Taylor, F. Chase (Colonel Stoopnagle), 46-48
Teichmann, Howard, 132, 133, 134, 294
Tendler, Lou, 184
Texaco Star Theater, 48-51, 52
Thau, Benny, 331
"There Is Nothing Like a Dame," 231
"There's No Business Like Show Business," 183
Thin Man, The, 300
This Is Broadway, 126
This Is New York, 40-42, 43, 44, 46, 52
This Is Show Business, 126, 127-130, 132, 136, 149, 158, 184, 230, 235, 256, 257
Thomas, Danny, 104, 109, 110
Thompson, Kay, 125
Threepenny Opera, The, 74
Three Wishes for Jamie, 234-235, 237, 238, 239-240, 241

367

Three Wishes of Jamie McRuin, The, 234
Time of Your Life, The, 341
Tittle, Y. A., 339
Tokyo Rose, 97
Tony Award, 318
Toots Shor Restaurant, 100
Toulouse-Lautrec, 236, 242, 250
Townsend, Leo, 49
"Travelin' Light," 203
Tree Grows in Brooklyn, A, 224
Trotter, John Scott, 114
Truman, Harry S., 123, 125, 126
Tucker, Sophie, 82
Tugend, Harry, 86
Tully, Tom, 298
Tuscaloosa's Calling Me — But I'm Not Going, 278
Twentieth-Century Fox, 291
Twentieth Century Limited, 235
"21" Restaurant, 158, 210
Two on the Aisle, 216, 221–229, 230, 236
Tynan, Kenneth, 266, 267

United Press, 208–209

Vaccaro, Brenda, 312–313
Valenti, Jack, 314
Vallee, Rudy, 53, 55, 58–59, 329, 335, 336
Valley of the Dolls, The, 127
Variety, 30, 81, 110, 126, 153, 194, 343, 351
Vertes, Marcel, 249, 260–261, 262, 263
Victoria, Vesta, 68–69
Virgil's *Aeneid,* 15–16

"Wagon Wheels," 289
"Waiting at the Church," 68–69
Waiting for Godot, 225
Waldorf Towers, 247
Walker, Jimmy, 79
Walker, William, 289
Wall Street, 26–32
Wallace, Henry, 123
Wallace, Mike, 301
Wallington, Jimmy, 49
War and Remembrance, 345
Waram, Perry, 302, 303–304

Warner, Jack, 291, 292
Warner Brothers, 291
Warriors, The, 153
Washington, D.C., 313–315
Watts, Doug, 111
Watts, Richard, 150, 207, 208, 209
Wayne, David, 307, 309, 310
Wayne, Jerry, 264
We Take Your Word, 16–17, 126, 127, 136, 230, 235, 257
Weaver, Sylvester ("Pat"), 328–329
Webb, Lizbeth, 264, 266
Weinstock, Jack, 326
Weisbrod, Sam, 38
Weiss, George, 348
Weissmuller, Johnny, 50–51
Welles, Orson, 79, 294
West, Mae, 50
West Side Story, 245
What Makes Sammy Run?, 276
Wheeler, Bert, 238
Wheeler and Woolsey, 238
"When the Red, Red Robin Comes Bob, Bob, Bobbin' Along," 285
Where's Charley?, 196
White House, the, 314
Whitney, Richard, 30
Wilde, Oscar, 163, 343–344
Wilding, Michael, 317
Wilhelm II, 287
William Morris Agency, 38, 101, 311
Williams, Andy, 125
Williams, Ted, 218
Williams Brothers, 125
Williamstown, Mass., 247
Willson, Meredith, 79, 257
Wilson, Harr Leon, 49
Wilson, John C., 211, 216
Winchell, Walter, 103, 137–138, 143
Windsor, Duke and Duchess of, 286–287
Winters, Roland, 90
"Without a Song," 148
Wizard of Oz, The, 225
Women's Wear, 209
Woods, Johnny, 39
Woollcott, Alexander, 350
World's Fair (New York), 112
Wouk, Herman, 84, 345
Wyler, Gretchen, 259, 273
Wynn, Ed, 37

You Can't Take It with You, 132
"You Put a Piece of Carbon Paper
Under Your Heart and Gave Me
Just a Copy of Your Love," 64
Youngman, Henny, 36

"You're My Heart's Darling," 239

Zanuck, Darryl, 156, 291, 292
Ziegfeld, Flo, 95
Ziegfeld Theatre, 148